the **ESPN cricinfo** guide to

edited by
**steven
lynch**

Note
Whilst every effort has been made to ensure that the content
of this book is as technically accurate and as sound as possible, neither
the author nor the publishers can accept responsibility for any injury
or loss sustained as a result of the use of this material.

First published in the UK in 2009 by
John Wisden & Co
An imprint of A & C Black Publishers Ltd
36 Soho Square, London W1D 3QY
www.wisden.com
www.acblack.com

Copyright © John Wisden & Co 2009

ESPN Cricinfo is the registered trademark of ESPN (EMEA) Ltd

ISBN 978 14081 1997 6

Images supplied by Getty Images.

A CIP catalogue record for this book is available from the British Library.

This book is produced using paper that is made from wood
grown in managed, sustainable forests. It is natural, renewable and
recyclable. The logging and manufacturing processes conform to the
environmental regulations of the country of origin.

Typeset in Mendoza Roman and Frutiger by
Palimpsest Book Production Ltd, Grangemouth, Stirlingshire

Printed and bound in the UK by MPG Books

CONTENTS

ABOUT ESPN-CRICINFO

Cricinfo is, by a distance, the world's No. 1 cricket website, and is now part of ESPN Digital Media. It is also a triumph of passion and entrepreneurship. It started as a lark in 1993, when a group of cricket-besotted expatriates working in the United States created a software application that allowed similarly obsessed fellow fans to submit cricket scores from remote locations. Soon, what started as a form of social networking had turned into a serious business.

Ten years, a few million users, and a dotcom rollercoaster ride later – during which the site sponsored a women's World Cup and the English County Championship – Cricinfo merged with its main rival, Wisden.com, to produce a site of unmatched depth and breadth. Cricinfo not only covers every ball bowled in international cricket, but does so with a distinct and independent voice.

It is a voice now heard by more people around the world than ever before. Cricinfo is accessed by over 12 million users every month. The site's worldwide reach, authority and brand recognition are unrivalled in online cricket – thanks in part to its editorial motto, which is to report not merely on what matters to cricket, but to make sense of it by bringing to bear a unique global perspective that is not the preserve of the traditional media.

The site's database is fully searchable and incorporates the full Wisden archive, dating right back to the first *Almanack* in 1864. There's a comprehensive records section, profiles for every current first-class player, and also **Statsguru**, an interactive query tool that allows users to set their own parameters while searching for statistics relating to every one of the approximately 3000 international and 45,000 first-class cricketers to have played the game.

Live scores and informed ball-by-ball text commentary continue to be the heart of the site, but they are supplemented by in-depth match reports, analysis and comments from a dedicated and talented editorial team across the world, and from some of the most credible voices in world cricket, who also form the backbone of Cricinfo's audio service, which was launched in 2006 and offers match analysis, panel discussions and interviews.

Cricinfo Magazine, bringing together a wide assortment of feature content, from interviews and profiles to columns and stats features, was launched in 2008, and in 2009 the site introduced Page 2, which takes a light-hearted look at the game. The site's roster of popular blogs features players as well as top cricket writers. Cricinfo is also available on the mobile platform.

Cricinfo's acquisition by ESPN has provided access to better technology and given the site the ability to serve sophisticated multimedia content. Cricinfo TV now has a range of video offerings, the latest being a series of documentaries on the legends of the game.

INTRODUCTION

Welcome to the fourth edition of the **ESPN-Cricinfo Guide to International Cricket**, which brings you details – in words and pictures, facts and figures – of 200 leading players, taken from the well-stacked database of ESPN-Cricinfo, the world's largest single-sport website. So you can identify everyone on the field or in the dressing-room, there are also photos and short biographies of the international umpires, coaches and referees. Finally there is a full easy-to-follow records section for all international matches – Tests, one-dayers and Twenty20s – with a country-by-country breakdown too. We have also found new photographs of most of the players.

The main pages feature a photo of each player, with a concise summary of his career, then mix some unusual facts with statistics for Tests, one-day and Twenty20 internationals and first-class matches. There is also a rundown on the players from the other leading non-Test-playing nations – which this year includes Afghanistan for the first time – and a handy guide to the coming year's international fixtures.

We have tried to include every player likely to appear in international cricket in 2010 – but, like all selectors, we will undoubtedly have left out someone who should have been included. Details of anyone who managed to escape our selectorial net can be found on Cricinfo.

Many of the profiles are edited and updated versions from Cricinfo's player pages, for which I should thank the site's current editorial staff, especially Sambit Bal (my successor as the site's global editor), Martin Williamson and Andrew Miller, and several former colleagues and contributors to the Cricinfo and Wisden websites, notably Kamran Abbasi, Tanya Aldred, Lawrence Booth, Tony Cozier, Tim de Lisle, Rabeed Imam, Will Luke, Neil Manthorp, Rob Smyth, Anand Vasu and Telford Vice. Thanks are also due to Christopher Lane of Wisden, Charlotte Atyeo and Kate Turvey at A&C Black, the typesetters Palimpsest, the *Wisden Cricketer's* art director Nigel Davies (who designed the cover), and Cricinfo's technical wizards Robin Abrahams and Travis Basevi. The majority of the photographs are from Getty Images, apart from a few reproduced by kind permission of the International Cricket Council, and some specially shot for Cricinfo.

The statistics have been updated to **September 21, 2009**, the end of the international season in England but before the start of the Champions Trophy in South Africa. The figures have been taken from Cricinfo and include, for the first time in published form, the number of boundaries hit by each batsman in international cricket. The abbreviation "S/R" in the batting tables denotes runs per 100 balls; in the bowling it shows the balls required to take each wicket. A dash (–) in the records usually indicates that full statistics are not available (such as details of fours and sixes, or balls faced, in all domestic matches). Individual figures for players who have appeared for more than one side in official internationals include the additional matches, details of which are given in the player's "Facts" box. These matches are not included in the national records sections, which explains any differences in the figures for the players concerned.

And finally, I couldn't have managed without the support of my wife Karina, who puts up with this annual intervention into our lives with amazing patience, and our son Daniel, who is just starting to work out what all the fuss is about.

Steven Lynch
September 2009

PLAYER INDEX

PLAYER INDEX

ABDUL RAZZAQ

Full name **Abdul Razzaq**
Born **December 2, 1979, Lahore, Punjab**
Teams **Lahore, Zarai Taraqiati Bank**
Style **Right-hand bat, right-arm fast-medium bowler**
Test debut **Pakistan v Australia at Brisbane 1999-2000**
ODI debut **Pakistan v Zimbabwe at Lahore 1996-97**

THE PROFILE Abdul Razzaq was once rapid enough to open the bowling, and remains composed enough to bat anywhere, although the lower order suits him nicely. His bowling is characterised by a galloping approach, accuracy, and reverse-swing, but it is his batting that is more likely to win matches. He is particularly strong driving through cover and mid-off. He has two gears: block or blast. Cut off the big shots and he can get bogged down, although he is very patient, as demonstrated by a match-saving 71 in almost six hours against India at Mohali in March 2005. Just before that he had batted bewilderingly slowly at Melbourne, scoring 4 in 110 minutes – but when the occasion demands he can slog with the best of them. Razzaq suffered a slump, particularly in bowling, between 2002 and 2004, but has rediscovered some of his old guile, if not his nip. And if the pitch is helpful to seam – as Karachi's was for his only Test five-for in 2004, and also against India there in January 2006 – he can still be a danger. Razzaq's allround performance in that win over India was easily his most emphatic: he made 45 and 90 to add to seven wickets. He missed the 2007 World Cup with a knee injury, then joined the unauthorised Indian Cricket League. His international career seemed over when all those involved with the ICL were banned, but after an amnesty he was the first to reappear in official internationals, reinforcing the World Twenty20 squad in England in June 2009, and taking three wickets in the final victory over Sri Lanka at Lord's.

THE FACTS Abdul Razzaq took a hat-trick against Sri Lanka at Galle in June 2000: he is one of only four players to have scored a hundred and taken a hat-trick in Tests (after England's Johnny Briggs, Wasim Akram of Pakistan and the New Zealander James Franklin) ... Razzaq took 7 for 51 – still his best figures – on his first-class debut, for Lahore City v Karachi Whites in the Quaid-e-Azam Trophy final in November 1996 ... He made 203 not out for Middlesex v Glamorgan in 2003 ... His record includes four ODIs for the Asia XI ...

THE FIGURES to 21.9.09   www.cricinfo.com

Batting & Fielding	M	Inns	NO	Runs	HS	Avge	S/R	100	50	4s	6s	Ct	St
Tests	46	77	9	1946	134	28.61	41.04	3	7	230	23	15	0
ODIs	234	201	49	4529	112	29.79	79.62	2	22	336	105	32	0
Twenty20 Ints	7	6	4	84	25*	42.00	118.30	0	0	8	1	2	0
First-class	113	177	27	5159	203*	34.39	–	8	27	–	–	32	0

Bowling	M	Balls	Runs	Wkts	BB	Avge	RpO	S/R	5i	10m
Tests	46	7008	3694	100	5–35	36.94	3.16	70.08	1	0
ODIs	234	9971	7788	250	6–35	31.15	4.68	39.88	3	0
Twenty20 Ints	7	111	132	8	3–20	16.50	7.13	13.87	0	0
First-class	113	18030	10493	328	7–51	31.99	3.49	54.96	11	2

ABDUR RAZZAK

Full name	**Khan Abdur Razzak**
Born	**June 15, 1982, Khulna**
Teams	**Khulna**
Style	**Left-hand bat, slow left-arm orthodox spinner**
Test debut	**Bangladesh v Australia at Chittagong 2005-06**
ODI debut	**Bangladesh v Hong Kong at Colombo 2004**

THE PROFILE Another of Bangladesh's seemingly never-ending supply of left-arm spinners, Abdur Razzak (no relation to the similarly named Pakistan allrounder) first made his mark when he helped unheralded Khulna to their first-ever National Cricket League title in 2001-02. Tall, with a high action, "Raj" played for the A team against Zimbabwe early in 2004, and took the opportunity well with 15 wickets, including a matchwinning 7 for 17 in the third encounter on the batting paradise of Dhaka's old Bangabandhu National Stadium. He has an uncanny ability to pin batsmen down, although his action has often been questioned, most recently late in 2008, when he was suspended by the ICC after tests showed he sometimes flexed his elbow by almost twice the permitted amount. After remedial work, he was cleared to resume playing in March 2009. He was immediately hurried back, playing in the World Twenty20 in England then taking seven wickets in Bangladesh's rare one-day clean sweep against a depleted West Indies side in the Caribbean in July. Razzak took 3 for 17 on his one-day debut against Hong Kong in the Asia Cup in July 2004, but his action was reported for the first time after the next game. He made his Test debut in April 2006, against Australia on a turning track at Chittagong (even the Aussies played three spinners), but failed to take a wicket, and has continued to struggle for penetration in Tests. But he has become an automatic one-day selection, maintaining a miserly economy-rate, and was the only Bangladeshi signed up for the first year of the Indian Premier League in 2008, although he did not return for the second season.

THE FACTS Abdur Razzak took 5 for 33 in an ODI against Zimbabwe at Bogra in December 2006 ... He took 7 for 11 (10 for 62 in the match) for Khulna at Sylhet in 2003-04 ... During 2008 Razzak became the third Bangladeshi, after Mohammad Rafique and Mashrafe Mortaza, to take 100 ODI wickets ...

THE FIGURES to 21.9.09   www.cricinfo.com

Batting & Fielding	M	Inns	NO	Runs	HS	Avge	S/R	100	50	4s	6s	Ct	St
Tests	5	9	3	129	33	21.50	59.17	0	0	21	0	2	0
ODIs	84	56	24	484	33	15.12	70.86	0	0	34	13	21	0
Twenty20 Ints	11	8	4	8	5	2.00	30.76	0	0	0	0	1	0
First-class	43	69	11	1202	83	20.72	57.92	0	6	–	–	16	0

Bowling	M	Balls	Runs	Wkts	BB	Avge	RpO	S/R	5i	10m
Tests	5	1128	561	7	3–93	80.14	2.98	161.14	0	0
ODIs	84	4407	3258	118	5–33	27.61	4.43	37.34	1	0
Twenty20 Ints	11	246	258	19	4–16	13.57	6.29	12.94	0	0
First-class	43	9597	4182	137	7–11	30.52	2.61	70.05	5	1

TIM **AMBROSE**

ENGLAND

Full name	**Timothy Raymond Ambrose**
Born	**December 1, 1982, Newcastle, NSW, Australia**
Teams	**Warwickshire**
Style	**Right-hand bat, wicketkeeper**
Test debut	**England v New Zealand at Hamilton 2007-08**
ODI debut	**England v New Zealand at Chester-le-Street 2008**

THE PROFILE   Tim Ambrose arrived in England at 17, and started by playing club cricket for Eastbourne. Sussex soon came calling, encouraged by the fact that he has an English mother. Small and slight, he was soon enlivening many an innings with his punchy strokeplay, particularly a savage square cut almost indistinguishable from that of his Sussex team-mate Murray Goodwin, a long-established master of the stroke. Ambrose scored well as Sussex took their first County Championship title in 2003, finishing with 931 runs at 40. But there was a big cloud on the horizon – the form of Matt Prior, another wicketkeeper/batsman, who did even better that year (1006 runs at 48). For a while they swapped the keeping gloves, but Prior won that particular battle and Ambrose departed to Edgbaston in 2006. He made a century in his second match for Warwickshire, and pushed on in 2007, clouting a ferocious 251 not out – with 34 fours – at Worcester in May. Meanwhile Prior's form was falling off after his spectacular Test debut, and after he had a poor Sri Lankan tour it was, ironically, Ambrose who replaced him. He started well, making 55 in his first Test and a century in his second in New Zealand in 2008, rescuing England after a poor start at Wellington, but at home later in the year he struggled with the bat, and latterly with the gloves. Eventually he lost his place ... to Prior. Ambrose played one Test in Barbados early in 2009 after Prior's wife gave birth, and scored an unbeaten 76 – but at the end of the year he lost his national contract, suggesting his international future was hardly rosy.

THE FACTS   Ambrose made 102 in only his second Test, against New Zealand at Wellington in March 2008 ... He scored 251 not out for Warwickshire at Worcester in May 2007 ... Ambrose hit 52 on his debut for Sussex, against Warwickshire at Edgbaston in September 2001, when he was 18 ... He played for New South Wales in the Australian under-17 finals in January 2000 ...

THE FIGURES _to 21.9.09_   www.cricinfo.com

Batting & Fielding	M	Inns	NO	Runs	HS	Avge	S/R	100	50	4s	6s	Ct	St
Tests	11	16	1	447	102	29.80	46.41	1	3	55	4	31	0
ODIs	5	5	1	10	6	2.50	29.41	0	0	0	0	3	0
Twenty20 Ints	1	0	–	–	–	–	–	–	–	–	–	1	1
First-class	108	163	15	5208	251*	35.18	51.70	9	29	–	–	245	15

Bowling	M	Balls	Runs	Wkts	BB	Avge	RpO	S/R	5i	10m
Tests	11	0	–	–	–	–	–	–	–	–
ODIs	5	0	–	–	–	–	–	–	–	–
Twenty20 Ints	1	0	–	–	–	–	–	–	–	–
First-class	108	6	1	0	–	–	1.00	–	0	0

HASHIM **AMLA**

Full name **Hashim Mahomed Amla**
Born **March 31, 1983, Durban, Natal**
Teams **Dolphins, Essex**
Style **Right-hand bat, occasional right-arm medium-pacer**
Test debut **South Africa v India at Kolkata 2004-05**
ODI debut **South Africa v Bangladesh at Chittagong 2007-08**

THE PROFILE An elegant, stroke-filled right-hander with a fine temperament, Hashim Amla was the first South African of Indian descent to reach the Test team. His elevation was hardly a surprise after he reeled off four centuries in his first eight innings in 2004-05, after being appointed captain of the Dolphins (formerly Natal) at the tender age of 21. He toured New Zealand with the Under-19s in 2000-01, captained South Africa at the 2002 Under-19 World Cup, and, after starring for the A team in 2004-05 – he made two hundreds against New Zealand A – made his Test debut against India. He was not an instant success, with serious questions emerging about his technique as he mustered only 36 runs in four innings against England later that season, struggling with an ungainly crouched stance and a bat coming down from somewhere in the region of gully. But he made his second chance count, with 149 against New Zealand at Cape Town in April 2006, followed by big hundreds against New Zealand (again) and India in 2007-08, before a fine undefeated 104 helped save the 2008 Lord's Test. Not originally seen as a one-day player, he was given a run in the national side at the end of 2008 and, after slamming 140 against Bangladesh, made 80 not out and 97 in consecutive victories over Australia early the following year. Amla, a devout Muslim whose beard matches Pakistan's Mohammad Yousuf's as the most impressive in the game, remains a candidate to become South Africa's captain eventually.

THE FACTS Amla's highest score is 249, made in nearly 11 hours, for the Dolphins against the Eagles at Bloemfontein in March 2005 ... He averages 104.80 in Tests against New Zealand, but 17.25 v Sri Lanka ... Amla made his first-class debut for KwaZulu/Natal at 16, against Nasser Hussain's 1999-2000 England tourists (and scored 1): in his next match, in February 2002, Amla made his maiden first-class hundred ... His older brother Ahmed also plays for the Dolphins ...

THE FIGURES to 21.9.09   www.cricinfo.com

Batting & Fielding	M	Inns	NO	Runs	HS	Avge	S/R	100	50	4s	6s	Ct	St
Tests	37	65	4	2460	176*	40.32	49.23	6	14	323	2	34	0
ODIs	16	15	3	574	140	47.83	85.79	1	3	60	5	6	0
Twenty20 Ints	2	2	0	52	26	26.00	104.00	0	0	4	1	0	0
First-class	113	187	17	8074	249	47.49	–	24	40	–	–	90	0

Bowling	M	Balls	Runs	Wkts	BB	Avge	RpO	S/R	5i	10m
Tests	37	42	28	0	–	–	4.00	–	0	0
ODIs	16	0	–	–	–	–	–	–	–	–
Twenty20 Ints	2	0	–	–	–	–	–	–	–	–
First-class	113	309	221	1	1–10	221.00	4.29	309.00	0	0

JAMES **ANDERSON**

Full name **James Michael Anderson**
Born **July 30, 1982, Burnley, Lancashire**
Teams **Lancashire**
Style **Left-hand bat, right-arm fast-medium bowler**
Test debut **England v Zimbabwe at Lord's 2003**
ODI debut **England v Australia at Melbourne 2002-03**

ENGLAND

THE PROFILE A strapping fast bowler, and a superb fielder, James Anderson had played only three one-day games for Lancashire when he was hurried into England's one-day squad in Australia in 2002-03 as cover for Andy Caddick. He didn't have a number – or even a name – on his shirt, but a remarkable ten-over stint, costing just 12, in century heat at Adelaide earned him a World Cup spot. There, he produced a matchwinning spell against Pakistan before a sobering last-over disaster against Australia. Five wickets followed in the first innings of his debut Test, against Zimbabwe at home in 2003, then a one-day hat-trick against Pakistan ... but then his fortunes waned. For a couple of years Anderson was a peripheral net bowler – and a shadow of his former self when he did get on the field. Previously silent critics noted that his head pointed downwards at delivery, supposedly leading to a lack of control. A stress fracture kept him out for most of 2006, but he still made the Australian tour and the World Cup. Then, in the absence of the entire Ashes-winning attack in the second half of 2007, Anderson suddenly looked the part of pack leader again. His 5 for 73 helped square the winter series in New Zealand, and three months later against the Kiwis at Trent Bridge his hostile full-pitched late swing brought him 7 for 43, including a perfect outswinger to castle the dangerous Brendon McCullum. In England in 2009 his swing befuddled the West Indians, but in the Ashes he alternated between dangerous and docile, nine of his 12 wickets coming in two sizzling spells at Lord's and Edgbaston.

THE FACTS Anderson was the first man to take an ODI hat-trick for England, against Pakistan at The Oval in 2003: Steve Harmison followed suit in 2004 ... He took the first six wickets to fall on his way to career-best figures of 7 for 43 for England v New Zealand at Nottingham in 2008 ... Anderson went 54 Test innings before being out for a duck at The Oval in 2009, an English record (previously Geraint Jones's 51); only AB de Villiers (78), Aravinda de Silva (75) and Clive Lloyd (58) have started with more duckless innings in Tests ...

THE FIGURES *to 21.9.09*   www.cricinfo.com

Batting & Fielding	M	Inns	NO	Runs	HS	Avge	S/R	100	50	4s	6s	Ct	St
Tests	42	56	27	412	34	14.20	36.91	0	0	48	0	17	0
ODIs	113	46	22	135	15	5.62	39.24	0	0	9	0	30	0
Twenty20 Ints	17	4	3	1	1*	1.00	50.00	0	0	0	0	2	0
First-class	97	112	49	667	37*	10.58	–	0	0	–	–	40	0

Bowling	M	Balls	Runs	Wkts	BB	Avge	RpO	S/R	5i	10m
Tests	42	8453	4883	140	7–43	34.87	3.46	60.37	7	0
ODIs	113	5452	4519	146	4–23	30.95	4.97	37.34	0	0
Twenty20 Ints	17	380	500	17	3–23	29.41	7.89	22.35	0	0
First-class	97	17627	9910	345	7–43	28.72	3.37	51.09	18	2

LIONEL **BAKER**

Full name	**Lionel Sionne Baker**
Born	**September 6, 1984, Montserrat**
Teams	**Leeward Islands**
Style	**Left-hand bat, right-arm fast-medium bowler**
Test debut	**West Indies v New Zealand at Dunedin 2008-09**
ODI debut	**West Indies v Pakistan at Abu Dhabi 2008-09**

THE PROFILE Lionel Baker, an energetic fast-medium bowler, made history when he made his debut for West Indies in November 2008 – he was the first man from the tiny volcano-scarred island of Montserrat to play for the regional side (Jim Allen came close a generation or two before, being one of the signees for Kerry Packer's World Series Cricket). Baker was in the Stanford Superstars squad which beat England late in 2008, although he didn't play in the million-dollar-a-man showpiece game, but his official international debut came shortly afterwards. It scuppered a county stint with Leicestershire as a British passport-holder, although he did get to play in England early in 2009 anyway, as part of the ill-at-ease side which surrendered the Wisden Trophy just a couple of months after winning it at home. Baker, who made his Test debut in a rain-affected game at Dunedin, also played in the final Test against England in the Caribbean, sitting nervously with his pads on as the ninth-wicket pair blocked out time at Port-of-Spain: earlier he had taken four top-order wickets in a match in which England lost only 12 all told. However, in two Tests in England Baker took just one wicket (Ravi Bopara, for 108) for 194 runs, and looked a little short of the pace required for the highest level. He may have more of a future in the shorter game, although Yuvraj Singh got stuck in to him at Kingston in June 2009, when Baker's nine overs cost 62.

THE FACTS Baker took 6 for 84 for the Leeward Islands against the Windwards in February 2009 ... A ball from Baker broke Brian Lara's forearm in a Carib Beer Cup match against Trinidad & Tobago in St Maarten in January 2008, ending Lara's first-class career ... Baker took 6 for 39 against Sri Lanka in the Under-19 World Cup in Bangladesh in 2003-04 ...

THE FIGURES to 21.9.09   www.cricinfo.com

Batting & Fielding	M	Inns	NO	Runs	HS	Avge	S/R	100	50	4s	6s	Ct	St
Tests	4	6	4	23	17	11.50	41.81	0	0	3	0	1	0
ODIs	10	4	2	13	11*	6.50	56.52	0	0	2	0	1	0
Twenty20 Ints	3	0	–	–	–	–	–	–	–	–	–	0	0
First-class	20	27	9	180	26	10.00	–	0	0	–	–	5	0

Bowling	M	Balls	Runs	Wkts	BB	Avge	RpO	S/R	5i	10m
Tests	4	660	395	5	2–39	79.00	3.59	132.00	0	0
ODIs	10	426	355	11	3–47	32.27	5.00	38.72	0	0
Twenty20 Ints	3	48	58	2	1–12	29.00	7.25	24.00	0	0
First-class	20	2678	1655	43	6–84	38.48	3.70	62.27	1	0

ADRIAN **BARATH**

Full name	**Adrian Barath**
Born	**April 14, 1990, Chaguanas, Trinidad**
Teams	**Trinidad & Tobago**
Style	**Right-hand bat, occasional offspinner**
Test debut	**No Tests yet**
ODI debut	**No ODIs yet**

THE PROFILE   Adrian Barath, a diminutive right-hander who usually opens, is one of the brightest young batting talents in the Caribbean. Although he is capable of big hitting, his batting is based on orthodoxy: "As a youngster my dad saw me playing straight which is unusual," Barath told Cricinfo. "Normally players begin by hitting across the line, but I was playing straight without anyone teaching me. Maybe it was because of television. I used to watch a lot and try and emulate what I saw." One of the best examples of those he was watching, Brian Lara, became an early mentor to his fellow Trinidadian – he invited Barath to join him at Lord's for a function honouring Lara's contribution to cricket. Barath might already have joined Lara as a West Indian Test player but for the divisive ongoing disagreement between the board and the players' association – he was originally chosen, at 19, in the squad for the series against Bangladesh in mid-2009, but then joined the other senior players in boycotting the matches in a row over contracts. Earlier in 2009 Barath showed his mettle by making 132 against the England tourists for West Indies A in St Kitts, sharing a partnership of 262 with Lendl Simmons, who went on to 282. Not long after that Barath – who hit centuries in his second and third first-class matches when still a few months short of his 17th birthday – made a career-best 192 for Trinidad & Tobago against the Leeward Islands in St Augustine.

THE FACTS   After making 73 on his first-class debut for Trinidad & Tobago v Guyana in January 2007 when still only 16, Barath hit 131 in his second match (against the Leeward Islands) and 101 in his third (against the Windwards) ... He made 132 for West Indies A against England in St Kitts in January 2009 ...

THE FIGURES *to 21.9.09*   www.cricinfo.com

Batting & Fielding	M	Inns	NO	Runs	HS	Avge	S/R	100	50	4s	6s	Ct	St
Tests	0	0	–	–	–	–	–	–	–	–	–	–	–
ODIs	0	0	–	–	–	–	–	–	–	–	–	–	–
Twenty20 Ints	0	0	–	–	–	–	–	–	–	–	–	–	–
First-class	22	38	3	1612	192	46.05	–	5	7	–	–	13	0

Bowling	M	Balls	Runs	Wkts	BB	Avge	RpO	S/R	5i	10m
Tests	0	0	–	–	–	–	–	–	–	–
ODIs	0	0	–	–	–	–	–	–	–	–
Twenty20 Ints	0	0	–	–	–	–	–	–	–	–
First-class	22	6	0	0	–	–	0.00	–	0	0

IAN **BELL**

Full name	**Ian Ronald Bell**
Born	**April 11, 1982, Walsgrave, Coventry**
Teams	**Warwickshire**
Style	**Right-hand bat, right-arm medium-pace bowler**
Test debut	**England v West Indies at The Oval 2004**
ODI debut	**England v Zimbabwe at Harare 2004-05**

THE PROFILE Ian Bell was earmarked for greatness long before he was drafted into the England squad in New Zealand in 2001-02, aged 19, as cover for the injured Mark Butcher. Tenacious and technically sound, Bell is in the mould of Michael Atherton, who was burdened with similar expectations on his debut a generation earlier and was similarly adept at leaving the ball outside off. Bell had played only 13 first-class matches when called into that England squad, and his form dipped while he was under the spotlight, but by 2004 he was on the up again. He finally made his Test debut against West Indies that August, stroking 70 at The Oval, before returning the following summer to lift his average to an obscene 297 against Bangladesh. Such rich pickings soon ceased: found out by McGrath and Warne, like so many before him, Bell mustered just 171 runs in the 2005 Ashes series. But, like a true class act, he bounced back better for the experience, collecting 313 runs in three Tests in Pakistan, including a classy century at Faisalabad. And when Pakistan toured in 2006, Bell repeated the dose, with elegant hundreds in each of the first three Tests. He improved his record against the Aussies in 2006-07 without going on to the big score, and continued to look good in 2008, hitting 199 against South Africa at Lord's. However, he was dropped after an unproductive winter and missed the start of the 2009 Ashes, returning in mid-series only when Kevin Pietersen was injured. He made 53 at Edgbaston and 72 at The Oval, but still failed entirely to convince.

THE FACTS After three Tests, and innings of 70, 65 not out and 162 not out, Bell's average was 297.00: he raised that to 303.00 before Australia started getting him out – only Lawrence Rowe (336), David Lloyd (308) and "Tip" Foster (306) have ever had better averages in Test history ... Bell was the first Englishman to be out for 199 in a Test, against South Africa at Lord's in 2008 ... None of his eight Test centuries has been the only one of the innings ... Bell made 262 not out for Warwickshire v Sussex at Horsham in May 2004 ...

THE FIGURES to 21.9.09   www.cricinfo.com

Batting & Fielding	M	Inns	NO	Runs	HS	Avge	S/R	100	50	4s	6s	Ct	St
Tests	49	88	9	3144	199	39.79	49.95	8	21	370	13	45	0
ODIs	79	76	6	2483	126*	35.47	72.36	1	15	252	11	23	0
Twenty20 Ints	5	5	1	109	60*	27.25	110.10	0	1	14	1	4	0
First-class	156	265	25	10461	262*	43.58	–	27	56	–	–	111	0

Bowling	M	Balls	Runs	Wkts	BB	Avge	RpO	S/R	5i	10m
Tests	49	108	76	1	1–33	76.00	4.22	108.00	0	0
ODIs	79	88	88	6	3–9	14.66	6.00	14.66	0	0
Twenty20 Ints	5	0	–	–	–	–	–	–	–	–
First-class	156	2809	1564	47	4–4	33.27	3.34	59.76	0	0

SULIEMAN **BENN**

Full name	**Sulieman Jamaal Benn**
Born	**July 22, 1981, Haynesville, St James, Barbados**
Teams	**Barbados**
Style	**Left-hand bat, slow left-arm orthodox spinner**
Test debut	**West Indies v Sri Lanka at Providence 2007-08**
ODI debut	**West Indies v Sri Lanka at Port-of-Spain 2007-08**

THE PROFILE A very tall (6ft 7ins/200cm) left-arm spinner, a handy lower-order batsman and a menacing presence in the gully, Sulieman Benn was part of the West Indies B team before becoming a regular for Barbados. Cementing a place in the island side was a long slog, especially for a slow bowler in a land where pace is usually king – and he had to contend with four Test fast men to get a bowl. But persistence paid off, and he took 32 wickets in 2000-01, his second season, then 24 more in his third. In 2007-08 his 22 wickets in the Carib Series – more than any other Barbadian – earned him a call-up to the West Indian squad for the home series against Sri Lanka. He played in the first Test, at Providence in Guyana, and kept the batsmen quiet without threatening to run through a side well schooled against spin. Benn was one of the Stanford Superstars who embarrassed England in the $1m-a-man Twenty20 game in November 2008 – he mopped up with 3 for 16 to make sure the visitors didn't reach 100 – and when England returned for official Tests early in 2009 he started well, taking four wickets in each innings in the victory at Kingston, although his figures then tailed off. In the return series he again bowled reasonably tightly, although wickets were always going to be hard to come by on juicy early-May English tracks. His one-day appearances have told a similar story: usually thrifty, seldom dangerous. Benn deserves his success, as he works hard on his bowling – although his occasionally scatterbrained batting still needs some attention.

THE FACTS Benn took 5 for 51 (9 for 87 in the match) for West Indies B v Windward Islands at Kingstown in January 2001 ... His eight wickets against England at Kingston in February 2009 were the most by any West Indian spinner in a Test since Lance Gibbs took nine in 1974-75 ... Benn took 3 for 16 as the Stanford Superstars beat England in a Twenty20 challenge in November 2008 ... Benn's highest score is 79 for Barbados v Windward Islands in Grenada in January 2009 ...

THE FIGURES to 21.9.09   www.cricinfo.com

Batting & Fielding	M	Inns	NO	Runs	HS	Avge	S/R	100	50	4s	6s	Ct	St
Tests	9	14	1	150	35	11.53	53.76	0	0	18	4	4	0
ODIs	11	8	1	70	31	10.00	83.33	0	0	7	1	1	0
Twenty20 Ints	10	4	3	18	13*	18.00	100.00	0	0	3	0	6	0
First-class	53	80	12	1358	79	19.97	–	0	6	–	–	36	0

Bowling	M	Balls	Runs	Wkts	BB	Avge	RpO	S/R	5i	10m
Tests	9	2278	1178	24	4–31	49.08	3.10	94.91	0	0
ODIs	11	534	429	6	2–23	71.50	4.82	89.00	0	0
Twenty20 Ints	10	222	284	8	3–24	35.50	7.67	27.75	0	0
First-class	53	11851	5427	172	5–51	31.55	2.74	68.90	5	0

DAVID **BERNARD**

Full name	**David Eddison Bernard junior**
Born	**July 19, 1981, Kingston, Jamaica**
Teams	**Jamaica**
Style	**Right-hand bat, right-arm medium-pacer**
Test debut	**West Indies v Australia at Port-of-Spain 2002-03**
ODI debut	**West Indies v Australia at Port-of-Spain 2002-03**

THE PROFILE David Bernard junior (Bernard senior is Jamaica's long-serving trainer) is a tall, stylish batsman and a stingy medium-pacer who has had a curious international career. He started with the West Indies B team in domestic cricket, and some consistent performances propelled him into the Jamaica side – then, after his first full season with them brought 551 runs (at 45.91) and 26 wickets, he was called up for the second Test against Australia in Trinidad in April 2003. It wasn't a great success – he scored 7 and 4 and bowled 11 expensive overs – and after doing little in four subsequent ODIs he was sent back to domestic cricket. A good 2004-05 season was followed by three modest ones, but just when he seemed likely to fade away he roared back in 2008-09, allying 657 runs to 32 wickets (two years previously he hadn't managed a wicket at all in the Caribbean). This pushed him back into the selectors' thoughts, and he toured England in 2009 without playing in the Tests or the World Twenty20 which followed. He was soon back in the ODI side though, for the home series against India in June; then, when the senior players pulled out of the series against Bangladesh, he made a Test return after more than six years. Suddenly a senior player among novices, Bernard displayed an impressive temperament, collecting three half-centuries in the two Tests, stiffening the middle order in the one-dayers, and generally showing that he deserved further chances once the dissidents returned.

THE FACTS Bernard made 120 for Jamaica v Windward Islands at Nain (Jamaica) in February 2004 ... He made 69 in the second Test against Bangladesh at St George's in July 2009, the first 61 runs coming on his 28th birthday ... Bernard took 5 for 44 for Jamaica v Barbados at Bridgetown in March 2008 ...

THE FIGURES to 21.9.09   www.cricinfo.com

Batting & Fielding	M	Inns	NO	Runs	HS	Avge	S/R	100	50	4s	6s	Ct	St
Tests	3	6	1	202	69	40.40	53.15	0	3	18	3	0	0
ODIs	11	6	0	87	38	14.50	68.50	0	0	6	0	4	0
Twenty20 Ints	1	1	1	1	1*	–	100.00	0	0	0	0	0	0
First-class	74	126	10	3264	120	28.13	–	3	17	–	–	61	0

Bowling	M	Balls	Runs	Wkts	BB	Avge	RpO	S/R	5i	10m
Tests	3	258	185	4	2–30	46.25	4.30	64.50	0	0
ODIs	11	312	272	7	2–59	38.85	5.23	44.57	0	0
Twenty20 Ints	1	24	17	0	–	–	4.25	–	0	0
First-class	74	7419	33842	128	5–44	30.01	3.10	57.96	2	0

DOUG **BOLLINGER**

AUSTRALIA

Full name	**Douglas Erwin Bollinger**
Born	**July 24, 1981, Baulkham Hills, Sydney**
Teams	**New South Wales**
Style	**Left-hand bat, left-arm fast-medium bowler**
Test debut	**Australia v South Africa at Sydney 2008-09**
ODI debut	**Australia v Pakistan at Dubai 2008-09**

THE PROFILE The 2007-08 summer was one of change for Doug Bollinger. He finished it with his first national contract, his first spot in an Australian touring party, a new wife, and a fresh head of hair, courtesy of the same company that rethatched Shane Warne and Graham Gooch (that also led to a new nickname, "Doug the Rug" replacing the old "Bald Eagle"). Finally, just as he was preparing to depart on his honeymoon, Bollinger heard that he was a late addition to the Test squad to tour the West Indies in May 2008. He was unlucky not to have been named in the first place after topping the Pura Cup wicket-takers with 45 at 15.44, an especially good return considering he missed the last three games of New South Wales's successful campaign with a broken foot. He had been instrumental in getting the Blues to the decider, grabbing 12 wickets in an innings victory over Tasmania and ten in a win against Western Australia. A left-arm fast bowler who mixes sharp pace with a consistent line and length, Bollinger finally won a Test cap at home at the SCG early in 2009, and ended up on the winning side against South Africa – but soon found himself overtaken by the likes of Ben Hilfenhaus and Peter Siddle in the return series. In England in 2009 Hilfenhaus was narrowly preferred at the start of the Ashes series, and bowled so well that Bollinger was a back number by the end of the tour. As a similar type of bowler to Mitchell Johnson, but a year older and less of a batsman, Bollinger may struggle to get back in the mix.

THE FACTS Bollinger took a one-day hat-trick for NSW against South Australia at Canberra in December 2004, dismissing Numbers 3, 4 and 5 in the order for ducks ... He took 5 for 15 for Australia A v Pakistan A at Lahore in September 2007 ... Bollinger took 6 for 68 and 6 for 63 for NSW v Tasmania at Sydney in December 2007 ... For Worcestershire in 2007 he took only 16 wickets at 44.56 in seven first-class matches ...

THE FIGURES *to 21.9.09*   www.cricinfo.com

Batting & Fielding	M	Inns	NO	Runs	HS	Avge	S/R	100	50	4s	6s	Ct	St
Tests	1	1	1	0	0*	–	0.00	0	0	0	0	0	0
ODIs	3	0	–	–	–	–	–	–	–	–	–	0	0
Twenty20 Ints	0	0	–	–	–	–	–	–	–	–	–	–	–
First-class	53	59	27	250	31*	7.81	–	0	0	–	–	18	0

Bowling	M	Balls	Runs	Wkts	BB	Avge	RpO	S/R	5i	10m
Tests	1	264	131	2	2–53	65.50	2.97	132.00	0	0
ODIs	3	154	101	5	5–35	20.20	3.93	30.80	1	0
Twenty20 Ints	0	0	–	–	–	–	–	–	–	–
First-class	53	9425	5195	171	6–47	30.38	3.30	55.11	9	2

SHANE **BOND**

Full name	**Shane Edward Bond**
Born	**June 7, 1975, Christchurch, Canterbury**
Teams	**Canterbury**
Style	**Right-hand bat, right-arm fast bowler**
Test debut	**New Zealand v Australia at Hobart 2001-02**
ODI debut	**New Zealand v Australia at Melbourne 2001-02**

THE PROFILE Shane Bond, probably world cricket's most famous ex-policeman, is one of the fastest and most dangerous fast bowlers around ... when he's fit. Unfortunately for New Zealand, that hasn't been too often since his impressive introduction in 2001-02, when his 21 wickets in the annual tri-series helped keep the Aussies out of the finals for once. Bond has suffered stress fractures in his back (something of an occupational hazard for fast bowlers) and also in his feet (rather less so). His speciality is the fast, inswinging yorker, which he used to great effect against the callow Zimbabweans in 2005, when most of his ten wickets in the Bulawayo Test were lbw or caught in the cordon. He zipped to 50 one-day wickets in only 27 matches, which included 6 for 23 as he unsettled the Aussies again in the 2003 World Cup. But those injuries cost him numerous caps, and planned county stints with Warwickshire in 2003 and Gloucestershire in 2006. Fit again for the World Cup in 2007, he took 13 wickets and was the tournament's most economical bowler. But then he signed for the Indian Cricket League: New Zealand Cricket initially gave him their approval, only to get cold feet when their Indian counterparts flexed their muscles against the unauthorised 20-over competition. Bond honourably fulfilled his ICL contract, which seemed to have ended his international career, before an amnesty was declared in mid-2009. Bond, now 34, returned to New Zealand's one-day side in Sri Lanka that September, needing only to prove his fitness before a Test recall.

THE FACTS Bond was the first super-sub to win the Man of the Match award in an ODI, after taking 6 for 19 (New Zealand's best figures in ODIs) v India at Bulawayo in 2005-06 ... He took a hat-trick against Australia in an ODI at Hobart in January 2007 ... In ODIs Bond has taken 34 wickets against Australia at 13.88 – but in Tests against them he has only three wickets at 96.33 ... He scored 100 for Canterbury v Northern Districts in Christchurch in 2004-05 ...

THE FIGURES *to 21.9.09*   www.cricinfo.com

Batting & Fielding	M	Inns	NO	Runs	HS	Avge	S/R	100	50	4s	6s	Ct	St
Tests	17	18	7	139	41*	12.63	39.71	0	0	18	3	6	0
ODIs	69	30	16	211	31*	15.07	72.50	0	0	14	7	15	0
Twenty20 Ints	11	6	1	19	8*	3.80	100.00	0	0	2	0	2	0
First-class	58	67	20	774	100	16.46	–	1	2	–	–	22	0

Bowling	M	Balls	Runs	Wkts	BB	Avge	RpO	S/R	5i	10m
Tests	17	3079	1769	79	6–51	22.39	3.44	38.97	4	1
ODIs	69	3566	2489	128	6–19	19.44	4.18	27.85	4	0
Twenty20 Ints	11	255	289	15	3–18	19.26	6.80	17.00	0	0
First-class	58	9730	5177	211	7–66	24.53	3.19	46.11	11	1

RAVI **BOPARA**

ENGLAND

Full name	**Ravinder Singh Bopara**
Born	**May 4, 1985, Forest Gate, London**
Teams	**Essex, Kings XI Punjab**
Style	**Right-hand bat, right-arm medium-pace bowler**
Test debut	**England v Sri Lanka at Kandy 2007-08**
ODI debut	**England v Australia at Sydney 2006-07**

THE PROFILE Ravi Bopara has had an up-and-down Test career. Uniquely he followed three successive ducks (against Sri Lanka late in 2007, including an embarrassing first-ball run-out) with three successive centuries against West Indies in 2009, despite being dropped after his maiden hundred in Barbados. His success against West Indies meant he was inked in at No. 3 against Australia for the 2009 Ashes – helping usher Michael Vaughan into retirement – but his wristy technique proved too loose, and he made only 105 runs in seven innings before being dropped for the final Test. His usually excellent fielding wavered too, as he dropped a couple of relative sitters, while his energetic medium-pacers proved toothless. He reacted to the chop by making 201 for Essex against Surrey, and was back for the chastening one-day series against Australia, making several starts without going on to a big score. Bopara has packed a lot in since he signed for Essex at 17 in 2002. A good county season in 2006 won him a place in the Academy squad which was based in Perth during that winter's Ashes whitewash. When Kevin Pietersen broke a rib in the first match of the one-day tournament, Bopara was summoned: not worried about having such big boots to fill, he made his debut in front of the Sydney Hill, and bowled Australia's "finisher", Michael Hussey, as England began the amazing turnaround that eventually won them that series. In the 2007 World Cup Bopara showed impressive resolve in making 52, which almost conjured an unlikely victory against eventual finalists Sri Lanka, and has been consistent in one-dayers ever since.

THE FACTS Bopara made 229 for Essex v Northamptonshire at Chelmsford in June 2007, putting on 320 for the third wicket with Grant Flower ... He made 104 (at Bridgetown), 143 (at Lord's) and 108 (at Chester-le-Street) in successive Test innings, all against West Indies, in 2009; his previous three Test innings had all been ducks ... Bopara took 5 for 75 for Essex v Surrey at Colchester in August 2006 ...

THE FIGURES to 21.9.09 www.cricinfo.com

Batting & Fielding	M	Inns	NO	Runs	HS	Avge	S/R	100	50	4s	6s	Ct	St
Tests	10	15	0	502	143	33.46	53.63	3	0	64	2	5	0
ODIs	48	44	8	1006	60	27.94	70.44	0	4	95	9	16	0
Twenty20 Ints	8	7	0	159	55	22.71	111.18	0	1	16	1	2	0
First-class	89	146	20	5448	229	43.23	53.86	15	20	–	–	60	0

Bowling	M	Balls	Runs	Wkts	BB	Avge	RpO	S/R	5i	10m
Tests	10	296	199	1	1–39	199.00	4.03	296.00	0	0
ODIs	48	331	293	6	2–43	48.83	5.31	55.16	0	0
Twenty20 Ints	8	0	–	–	–	–	–	–	–	–
First-class	89	6189	4094	90	5–75	45.48	3.96	68.76	1	0

JOHAN **BOTHA**

Full name	**Johan Botha**
Born	**May 2, 1982, Johannesburg**
Teams	**Warriors, Rajasthan Royals**
Style	**Right-hand bat, offspinner**
Test debut	**South Africa v Australia at Sydney 2005-06**
ODI debut	**South Africa v India at Hyderabad 2005-06**

THE PROFILE Determined and fiercely competitive, Johan Botha started off as a rather ordinary medium-pacer, but one day Mickey Arthur – now South Africa's coach – spotted something else, and Botha dropped his ambitions for speed. He became an offspinner, and started studying the *doosra*. A year later he was touring Sri Lanka with South Africa A, scoring a few runs as well as taking key wickets. He made a promising Test debut in India late in 2005, gating Irfan Pathan during six tidy overs at Hyderabad, and when the selectors later suspected that the Sydney Test pitch would turn, Botha (who was already due to go to Australia for the one-dayers) was flown in early. He managed a couple of wickets, but delight turned to dismay when his jerky action was reported, and he was banned by the ICC on suspicion of throwing. After remedial work he made a low-key international return in the Afro-Asia Cup in India in June 2007, but remains in the frame – especially in one-dayers and Twenty20 games, where he has the priceless ability to keep it tight. He also proved a canny stand-in captain when Graeme Smith was injured in Australia early in 2009, skippering his side to a 4-1 victory in the one-day series. But his *doosra* was reported again, and after tests showed his right elbow flexed by 26.7 degrees – nearly twice the permitted limit of 15 – Botha was told not to bowl his wrong'un again by the ICC. Even without it, he played a useful role in South Africa's World Twenty20 campaign in England.

THE FACTS Botha's best bowling remains 6 for 42, for Eastern Province v Northerns at Port Elizabeth in March 2004, when still a medium-pacer ... He scored 98 for Warriors v Dolphins at Durban late in 2006 ... Botha made 101 for South Africa in an Under-19 Test v New Zealand (for whom Brendon McCullum made 186) in February 2001 ... He played for Ireland against Yorkshire in England's C&G Trophy in 2005 ... Botha's record includes two ODIs for the Africa XI ...

THE FIGURES *to 21.9.09*   www.cricinfo.com

Batting & Fielding	M	Inns	NO	Runs	HS	Avge	S/R	100	50	4s	6s	Ct	St
Tests	2	2	1	45	25	45.00	32.84	0	0	4	0	1	0
ODIs	45	24	10	275	46	19.64	84.35	0	0	28	1	23	0
Twenty20 Ints	15	9	7	59	28*	29.50	122.91	0	0	5	2	8	0
First-class	56	96	15	2614	98	32.27	–	0	18	–	–	42	0

Bowling	M	Balls	Runs	Wkts	BB	Avge	RpO	S/R	5i	10m
Tests	2	225	178	4	2–57	44.50	4.74	56.25	0	0
ODIs	45	2130	1575	41	4–19	38.41	4.43	51.95	0	0
Twenty20 Ints	15	294	294	13	3–16	22.61	6.00	22.61	0	0
First-class	56	7847	3932	125	6–42	31.45	3.00	62.77	4	1

MARK **BOUCHER**

SOUTH AFRICA

Full name	**Mark Verdon Boucher**
Born	**December 3, 1976, East London, Cape Province**
Teams	**Warriors, Bangalore Royal Challengers**
Style	**Right-hand bat, wicketkeeper**
Test debut	**South Africa v Pakistan at Sheikhupura 1997-98**
ODI debut	**South Africa v New Zealand at Perth 1997-98**

THE PROFILE It is a measure of the rapidity of Mark Boucher's rise that no-one is quite sure exactly how many records he has held ... they tumbled out so quickly that it was difficult to keep up. Now, after more than a decade behind the stumps, he is Test cricket's leading wicketkeeper in terms of dismissals, and second in ODIs, with enviable batting statistics too. But probably his most significant achievement came in only his second Test, against Pakistan at Johannesburg in February 1998, when he and Pat Symcox added 195, a Test ninth-wicket record, from a desperate 166 for 8. Boucher had made his debut a few months previously when still not 21, rushing to Sheikhupura to replace the injured Dave Richardson, who retired after the Australian tour that followed. Boucher was not everyone's first choice – Nic Pothas had also been waiting patiently – but once he got his hands into the gloves he refused to let them go, scrapping successfully to regain his spot when a form dip eventually did cost him his place – to Thami Tsolekile, and then AB de Villiers – late in 2004. He returned just as safe behind the stumps, and adapted his attacking batting to become something of a one-day "finisher" – qualities he has often transferred to the Test arena, notably helping Graeme Smith to anchor a tense series-clincher at Edgbaston in 2008. Still in his early thirties, Boucher is on course to become the first wicketkeeper to make 1,000 dismissals in international cricket.

THE FACTS Boucher has more dismissals than anyone else in Tests, and only Adam Gilchrist (472) currently heads him in ODIs ... His 125 v Zimbabwe at Harare in 1999-2000 was a Test record for a nightwatchman until Jason Gillespie surpassed it in 2006 ... Boucher reached his century against Zimbabwe at Potchefstroom in September 2006 in only 44 balls, the second-fastest in all ODIs ... His 75 consecutive Tests between 1997-98 and 2004-05 is a South African record ... His figures include one Test for the World XI and five ODIs for the Africa XI ...

THE FIGURES *to 21.9.09*   www.cricinfo.com

Batting & Fielding	M	Inns	NO	Runs	HS	Avge	S/R	100	50	4s	6s	Ct	St
Tests	126	178	21	4688	125	29.85	49.27	5	29	564	16	453	22
ODIs	280	207	54	4463	147*	29.16	84.91	1	26	337	80	385	21
Twenty20 Ints	19	16	4	239	36*	19.91	99.17	0	0	21	2	13	1
First-class	188	274	39	7796	134	33.17	–	9	47	–	–	631	36

Bowling	M	Balls	Runs	Wkts	BB	Avge	RpO	S/R	5i	10m
Tests	126	8	6	1	1–6	6.00	4.50	8.00	0	0
ODIs	280	0	–	–	–	–	–	–	–	–
Twenty20 Ints	19	0	–	–	–	–	–	–	–	–
First-class	188	26	26	1	1–6	26.00	6.00	26.00	0	0

AUSTRALIA

NATHAN **BRACKEN**

Full name	**Nathan Wade Bracken**
Born	**September 12, 1977, Penrith, New South Wales**
Teams	**New South Wales**
Style	**Right-hand bat, left-arm fast-medium bowler**
Test debut	**Australia v India at Brisbane 2003-04**
ODI debut	**Australia v West Indies at Melbourne 2000-01**

THE PROFILE   Tall and slim like Bruce Reid, Nathan Bracken bowls a full length, moves the ball both ways in the air and off the seam, and fitted easily into Australia's rampant one-day squad in 2000-01. He has also been instrumental in resuscitating New South Wales's fortunes, including 6 for 27 in their 2004-05 final win over Queensland and an amazing 7 for 4 earlier that season when South Australia collapsed for just 29 at the SCG. A shoulder injury cut short his maiden Ashes tour in 2001 after only two matches, but he returned during the 2003 World Cup after Jason Gillespie dropped out with a heel injury. Bracken's Test debut finally came in 2003-04, but in three matches against the powerful Indian batting line-up he failed to make real inroads. In the spring of 2004 he was omitted from Australia's list of contracted players, but returned to the one-day side against the World XI late the following year. Work in the nets refining his swing was rewarded with two Tests in 2005-06, and he also added another variation by delivering across the seam when he wanted to defend. He elbowed his way past Mitchell Johnson to cement a one-day place the following season, and contributed several telling performances in the defence of the World Cup, finishing with 16 wickets at 16.12, but had to watch as Johnson – pacier, and a much better batsman – nailed down a Test spot in 2007-08. Bracken, though, remained a limited-overs regular, and for a time in 2008 was top of the ICC's ranking list for one-day bowlers, helped by one of the slowest slower balls a fast bowler has perfected.

THE FACTS   Bracken's figures of 7-5-4-7 for New South Wales v South Australia at Sydney in December 2004 were described as "more like a PIN number than a bowling analysis" in the *Sydney Morning Herald*, which also called his yorker-heavy bowling to the South Africans "foot theory" … He is 6ft 5ins (195cm) tall … Seven of his 12 Test wickets have come at Brisbane … Bracken averages 12.20 with the ball in ODIs against Sri Lanka – but 94 against Zimbabwe …

THE FIGURES to 21.9.09   www.cricinfo.com

Batting & Fielding	M	Inns	NO	Runs	HS	Avge	S/R	100	50	4s	6s	Ct	St
Tests	5	6	2	70	37	17.50	62.50	0	0	7	0	2	0
ODIs	116	35	18	199	21*	11.70	70.56	0	0	10	5	26	0
Twenty20 Ints	19	6	3	15	4*	5.00	68.18	0	0	1	0	6	0
First–class	67	88	30	1007	63	17.36	–	0	1	–	–	18	0

Bowling	M	Balls	Runs	Wkts	BB	Avge	RpO	S/R	5i	10m
Tests	5	1110	505	12	4–48	42.08	2.72	92.50	0	0
ODIs	116	5759	4240	174	5–47	24.36	4.41	33.09	2	0
Twenty20 Ints	19	377	438	19	3–11	23.05	6.97	19.84	0	0
First–class	67	13634	5603	215	7–4	26.06	2.46	63.41	9	0

DARREN **BRAVO**

WEST INDIES

Full name	**Darren Michael Bravo**
Born	**February 6, 1989, Santa Cruz, Trinidad**
Teams	**Trinidad & Tobago**
Style	**Left-hand bat, occasional left-arm medium-pacer**
Test debut	**No Tests yet**
ODI debut	**West Indies v India at Kingston 2009**

THE PROFILE Darren Bravo is the younger half-brother of the West Indian allrounder Dwayne, but although he can bowl a bit it is his batting – and quicksilver fielding, like Dwayne's – which aroused the interest of the regional selectors. A left-hander, Bravo junior has a style reminiscent of Brian Lara – not a bad role model – as Chris Gayle, who captained Darren in his first internationals, spotted. "There are some similarities, like the batting technique, and they look alike a bit," said Gayle. "Brian is his idol, and he now has the ability to go from strength to strength. He didn't show any form of nerves in the dressing-room – maybe it was his brother who calmed him down a bit – and he did well in the outfield as well." Bravo himself (who is actually a distant relative of Lara's, on his mother's side, and, like Lara, was born in Santa Cruz in Trinidad) has a mature approach to any lofty comparisons: "I go out there and play my game, the Darren Bravo game, and if in the eyes of the people it looks like Lara, then that is their judgment. At the end of the day it is just my game." Bravo scored 605 runs at 45 in 2008-09, his first full season for Trinidad & Tobago, including centuries against Barbados and the Windward Islands. This pushed him to the fringes of the West Indian side, and he made his debut alongside Dwayne in the short one-day series against India in June, scoring 19 and 21 in the only two innings the weather allowed him.

THE FACTS Darren Bravo made his debut for West Indies, alongside his half-brother Dwayne, in the ODI series against India at home in June 2009 ... He made 105 for Trinidad & Tobago v Windward Islands in January 2009, and 111 against Barbados the following month, when he and Kieron Pollard (174) put on 250 for the fourth wicket ... Bravo played in the Under-19 World Cup in Malaysia in 2008, scoring 59 against Papua New Guinea ...

THE FIGURES to 21.9.09   www.cricinfo.com

Batting & Fielding	M	Inns	NO	Runs	HS	Avge	S/R	100	50	4s	6s	Ct	St
Tests	0	0	–	–	–	–	–	–	–	–	–	–	–
ODIs	4	2	0	40	21	20.00	129.03	0	0	5	0	1	0
Twenty20 Ints	0	0	–	–	–	–	–	–	–	–	–	–	–
First-class	15	22	1	701	111	33.38	–	2	2	–	–	19	0

Bowling	M	Balls	Runs	Wkts	BB	Avge	RpO	S/R	5i	10m
Tests	0	0	–	–	–	–	–	–	–	–
ODIs	4	0	–	–	–	–	–	–	–	–
Twenty20 Ints	0	0	–	–	–	–	–	–	–	–
First-class	15	22	9	1	1–9	9.00	2.45	22.00	0	0

DWAYNE **BRAVO**

Full name	**Dwayne John Bravo**
Born	**October 7, 1983, Santa Cruz, Trinidad**
Teams	**Trinidad & Tobago, Mumbai Indians, Victoria**
Style	**Right-hand bat, right-arm fast-medium bowler**
Test debut	**West Indies v England at Lord's 2004**
ODI debut	**West Indies v England at Georgetown 2003-04**

THE PROFILE   Dwayne Bravo, one of that rare breed (especially in the Caribbean), a genuine allrounder, was born in Santa Cruz, like Brian Lara, and made his one-day debut in April 2004, on the tenth anniversary of Lara's 375. He won his first Test cap at Lord's three months later, and took three wickets in the first innings with his medium-paced swingers. He also showed a cool enough temperament at the crease, displaying a straight bat even though his team was facing a big England total. By the end of the series, West Indies were down and out, but at least they knew they had unearthed a special talent. He hit his maiden century against South Africa in Antigua in April 2005, and played an even better innings the following November, a magnificent 113 at Hobart which forced the rampant Australians to wait till the fifth day to complete victory. He continued to chip in with useful runs, while a selection of slower balls makes him a handful in one-dayers, if less so in Tests. He's also electric in the field. Bravo missed the 2009 home Tests against England with a niggling ankle injury, then was left out for the Tests in England too – despite being fit enough to play in the Indian Premier League – although he played (and lifted the side visibly) in both one-day series. He was one of several senior players who boycotted the mid-2009 series against Bangladesh as an interminable dispute about contracts rumbled on, and the worry is that, financially secure with Twenty20 contracts from Victoria in Australia and Mumbai in India, he might turn his back on regular international cricket.

THE FACTS   Bravo's second Test century – 113 at Hobart late in 2005 – came during a stand of 182 with his fellow-Trinidadian Denesh Ramdin, the day after Trinidad & Tobago qualified for the football World Cup for the first time ... Bravo's best Test batting (40.40) and bowling (31.77) averages are both against Australia ... He played 27 Tests before finally finishing on the winning side, against Sri Lanka at Port-of-Spain in April 2008 ... Bravo's half-brother Darren has also played for West Indies ...

THE FIGURES *to 21.9.09*   www.cricinfo.com

Batting & Fielding	M	Inns	NO	Runs	HS	Avge	S/R	100	50	4s	6s	Ct	St
Tests	31	57	1	1833	113	32.73	48.84	2	11	233	15	30	0
ODIs	99	79	16	1511	112*	23.98	81.19	1	4	127	24	43	0
Twenty20 Ints	15	14	5	236	66*	26.22	138.01	0	2	16	11	3	0
First-class	87	160	7	4786	197	31.28	–	7	27	–	–	71	0

Bowling	M	Balls	Runs	Wkts	BB	Avge	RpO	S/R	5i	10m
Tests	31	5139	2771	70	6–55	39.58	3.23	73.41	2	0
ODIs	99	3832	3382	114	4–19	29.66	5.29	33.61	0	0
Twenty20 Ints	15	224	341	14	4–38	24.35	9.13	16.00	0	0
First-class	87	9268	5036	154	6–11	32.70	3.26	60.18	7	0

TIM **BRESNAN**

ENGLAND

Full name	**Timothy Thomas Bresnan**
Born	**February 28, 1985, Pontefract, Yorkshire**
Teams	**Yorkshire**
Style	**Right-hand bat, right-arm fast-medium bowler**
Test debut	**England v West Indies at Lord's 2009**
ODI debut	**England v Sri Lanka at Lord's 2006**

THE PROFILE The stocky Tim Bresnan was tipped for higher
honours in 2001 after becoming, at 16, the youngest to play for
Yorkshire for 20 years. He quickly progressed to England's youth
team, and played in two Under-19 World Cups. The potential
took a few years to ripen, but in 2005 he was given more responsibility in a transitional
Yorkshire team, and responded with 47 wickets with swinging deliveries which, if a shade
short of being truly fast, travel at a fair rate. He can also bat, making three first-class
centuries in 2007, the highest an undefeated 126 for England A against the Indians, when
he and Stuart Broad put on 129 for the eighth wicket. A good start to the previous season
had resulted in a call-up for a new-look one-day squad against Sri Lanka in June 2006, but
Bresnan fell victim to the flashing blades of Sanath Jayasuriya and friends, and took only
two wickets in four appearances in what became a clean sweep for the tourists. He then
suffered a back injury, and was not in serious consideration for a World Cup spot. He
responded well with the bat in 2007, although his form with the ball dipped a little (34
wickets at 34), before a return to bowling form the following year eventually led to a one-
day recall, although the surprise return of Steve Harmison meant there was no place for
Bresnan in the end as South Africa were swept aside. He did finally make his Test debut
against West Indies in May 2009, but failed to shine and had to make way for Andrew
Flintoff in the Ashes series.

THE FACTS Bresnan made all three of his first-class centuries during 2007, including
126 not out for England A against the Indian tourists at Chelmsford ... Bresnan's best
bowling figures are 5 for 42 for Yorkshire at Worcester in July 2005 ... He made his Yorkshire
first-team debut in a National League match in 2001, when he was just 16 ...

THE FIGURES to 21.9.09   www.cricinfo.com

Batting & Fielding	M	Inns	NO	Runs	HS	Avge	S/R	100	50	4s	6s	Ct	St
Tests	2	1	0	9	9	9.00	56.25	0	0	1	0	2	0
ODIs	14	12	6	166	31*	27.66	91.20	0	0	18	1	2	0
Twenty20 Ints	1	1	1	6	6*	–	100.00	0	0	0	0	0	0
First-class	87	116	21	2563	126*	26.97	48.44	3	11	–	–	38	0

Bowling	M	Balls	Runs	Wkts	BB	Avge	RpO	S/R	5i	10m
Tests	2	186	97	3	3–45	32.33	3.12	62.00	0	0
ODIs	14	599	542	14	2–10	38.71	5.42	42.78	0	0
Twenty20 Ints	1	12	20	0	–	–	10.00	–	0	0
First-class	87	13793	7176	222	5–42	32.32	3.12	62.13	3	0

ENGLAND

STUART **BROAD**

Full name	**Stuart Christopher John Broad**
Born	**June 24, 1986, Nottingham**
Teams	**Nottinghamshire**
Style	**Left-hand bat, right-arm fast-medium bowler**
Test debut	**England v Sri Lanka at Colombo 2007-08**
ODI debut	**England v Pakistan at Cardiff 2006**

THE PROFILE   Stuart Broad was shaping up to be an opening bat just like his dad, Chris, until he suddenly shot up. Already well over six feet, he grew three inches over the winter of 2005. He had already transformed himself into a fast-medium bowler good enough to play for England Under-19s. In 2005 he had taken 30 first-class wickets at 27.69 for Leicestershire, his first county. And it got even better in 2006, as he collected four five-fors before an increasingly inevitable summons to England's full one-day side. Brisk, with a smooth action, he made an impressive start to his international career, keeping a cool head in the mayhem of a Twenty20 match, then claiming an early wicket on his ODI debut. He just missed out on initial selection for the World Cup, but stepped in when Jon Lewis returned home, and nervelessly hit the winning runs in England's last game, against West Indies. Nerves were also notably absent later in 2007 when Broad and Ravi Bopara spirited England to an unlikely one-day win over India at Old Trafford, and he even kept reasonably cool shortly afterwards when being swatted for six sixes in an over by Yuvraj Singh in the World Twenty20. But Broad junior has aspirations to be an allrounder, and showed good form with the bat – especially when driving off the back foot – once he cracked the full Test side, and looks like a genuine No. 8. In the 2009 Ashes he was unimpressive at first, but kept his place despite many pundits calling for his head, and shut them up with a superb spell to set up England's series-winning victory at The Oval.

THE FACTS   Broad took 5 for 23 as South Africa were bowled out for 83 in an ODI at Trent Bridge in August 2008 ... He took 6 for 91 (and scored 61) in the fourth Test against Australia at Headingley in 2009 ... Broad made 91 not out for Leicestershire v Derbyshire at Grace Road in 2007 ... Broad's father, Chris, played 25 Tests for England in the 1980s, scoring 1661 runs with six centuries – he's now a match referee (see page 224) ...

THE FIGURES *to 21.9.09*   www.cricinfo.com

Batting & Fielding	M	Inns	NO	Runs	HS	Avge	S/R	100	50	4s	6s	Ct	St
Tests	22	31	6	767	76	30.68	1228	62.45	0	5	104	4	50
ODIs	52	34	14	327	45*	16.35	441	74.14	0	0	21	4	130
Twenty20 Ints	18	10	4	36	10*	6.00	29	124.13	0	0	3	1	60
First-class	61	77	18	1569	91*	26.59	2912	53.88	0	11	–	–	170

Bowling	M	Balls	Runs	Wkts	BB	Avge	RpO	S/R	5i	10m
Tests	22	4187	2290	64	6–91	35.78	3.28	65.42	3	0
ODIs	52	2564	2185	78	5–23	28.01	5.11	32.87	1	0
Twenty20 Ints	18	390	518	22	3–17	23.54	7.96	17.72	0	0
First-class	61	10534	6005	201	6–91	29.87	3.42	52.40	10	0

SHIVNARINE **CHANDERPAUL**

Full name	**Shivnarine Chanderpaul**
Born	**August 16, 1974, Unity Village, Demerara, Guyana**
Teams	**Guyana, Durham**
Style	**Left-hand bat, occasional legspinner**
Test debut	**West Indies v England at Georgetown 1993-94**
ODI debut	**West Indies v India at Faridabad 1994-95**

THE PROFILE Crouched and crabby at the crease, Shivnarine Chanderpaul proves there is life beyond the coaching handbook. He never seems to play in the V, or off the front foot, but uses soft hands, canny deflections and a whiplash pull to maintain an average nudging 50 over more than 120 Tests. Early on he had a problem converting fifties into hundreds, and also missed a lot of matches, to the point that some thought him a hypochondriac. That was rectified when a large piece of floating bone was removed from his foot in 2000: suitably liberated, he set about rectifying his hundreds problem too, and now has 21 (five each against England and India, and four against Australia and South Africa), including 104 as West Indies successfully chased a world-record 418 to beat the Aussies in Antigua in May 2003. In England in 2004 he put his first bad trot behind him, narrowly missing twin tons in the Lord's Test. The following year he was appointed captain during the first of several acrimonious disputes between the players and the West Indian board, and celebrated with 203 at home in Guyana, although he was too passive in the field to prevent South Africa taking the series. In April 2006 he stood down, after an Australian tour where he struggled with bat and microphone. In England in 2007 he was back to his limpet best, top-scoring in each of his five innings, and going more than 1000 minutes without being out in Tests, for the third time in his career (he did it again in 2008). It's not all defence, though: he can blast with the best when he needs to.

THE FACTS Chanderpaul averages 71.86 in Tests against India, but only 28.77 v Zimbabwe ... He scored 303 not out for Guyana v Jamaica at Kingston in January 1996 ... At Georgetown in April 2003 Chanderpaul reached his century against Australia in only 69 balls – the fourth-fastest in Test history by balls faced ... He averages 57.61 in Tests at home, and 42.52 away ... He once managed to shoot a policeman in the hand in his native Guyana, mistaking him for a mugger ...

THE FIGURES *to 21.9.09*   www.cricinfo.com

Batting & Fielding	M	Inns	NO	Runs	HS	Avge	S/R	100	50	4s	6s	Ct	St
Tests	121	206	32	8576	203*	49.28	42.94	21	52	981	24	50	0
ODIs	252	236	38	8250	150	41.66	71.16	10	55	699	80	69	0
Twenty20 Ints	15	15	4	207	41	18.81	104.02	0	0	22	2	6	0
First-class	244	394	70	17368	303*	53.60	–	50	88	–	–	138	0

Bowling	M	Balls	Runs	Wkts	BB	Avge	RpO	S/R	5i	10m
Tests	121	1680	845	8	1–2	105.62	3.01	210.00	0	0
ODIs	252	740	636	14	3–18	45.42	5.15	52.85	0	0
Twenty20 Ints	15	0	–	–	–	–	–	–	–	–
First-class	244	4634	2453	56	4–48	43.80	3.17	82.75	0	0

PIYUSH **CHAWLA**

Full name **Piyush Pramod Chawla**
Born **December 24, 1988, Aligarh, Uttar Pradesh**
Teams **Uttar Pradesh, Kings XI Punjab, Sussex**
Style **Left-hand bat, legspinner**
Test debut **India v England at Mohali 2005-06**
ODI debut **India v Bangladesh at Dhaka 2006-07**

THE PROFILE   Less than a month after he was one of the stars of the Youth World Cup early in 2006, 17-year-old Piyush Chawla was making his Test debut against England, dismissing Andrew Flintoff for 51 as India glided to a nine-wicket win at Mohali. Chawla had always been a young achiever: he first hit the headlines for Uttar Pradesh's Under-14s, scoring 121 then taking 15 wickets for 69 in the demolition of Rajasthan's juniors. In October 2005 he bamboozled Sachin Tendulkar with a googly in the final of the Challenger Trophy (a trial tournament for India's one-day team), and dismissed MS Dhoni and Yuvraj Singh as well, then he led the wicket-takers at the Under-19 World Cup in Sri Lanka. He took 4 for 8 as the holders Pakistan were shot out for 109 in the final, then surveyed the wreckage with 25 not out as India were demolished for 79 themselves. Although he is no slouch with the bat, it is as a legspinner that Chawla has made his mark: he has a well-disguised googly and a flipper, and is not afraid to give the ball air. In 2007, he was given an extended run in the one-day team, replacing Anil Kumble who retired from the shorter game after the World Cup, and did well against England. He was among the leading wicket-takers in the inaugural IPL season early in 2008 with 17, which helped him regain his one-day place for the Asia Cup in Pakistan at the end of June '08. But apart from taking 4 for 23 against Hong Kong he was disappointing there, and was sent back to domestic cricket to polish his variations. He also had a stint with Sussex in 2009.

THE FACTS   Piyush Chawla was 17 years 75 days old when he made his Test debut in March 2006: the only younger Indian debutant was Sachin Tendulkar ... He took 4 for 12 and 6 for 46 as India A hammered a Zimbabwe Select XI at Bulawayo in July 2007... Chawla scored 102 not out – his maiden first-class century – for Sussex v Worcestershire at New Road in June 2009: later in the match he took 6 for 152 ...

THE FIGURES *to 21.9.09*   www.cricinfo.com

Batting & Fielding	M	Inns	NO	Runs	HS	Avge	S/R	100	50	4s	6s	Ct	St
Tests	2	2	0	5	4	2.50	23.80	0	0	1	0	0	0
ODIs	21	10	5	28	13*	5.60	65.11	0	0	2	0	9	0
Twenty20 Ints	0	0	–	–	–	–	–	–	–	–	–	–	–
First-class	50	71	7	1734	102*	27.09	–	1	12	–	–	22	0

Bowling	M	Balls	Runs	Wkts	BB	Avge	RpO	S/R	5i	10m
Tests	2	205	137	3	2–66	45.66	4.00	68.33	0	0
ODIs	21	1102	911	28	4–23	32.53	4.96	39.35	0	0
Twenty20 Ints	0	0	–	–	–	–	–	–	–	–
First-class	50	10805	5350	198	6–46	27.02	2.97	54.57	13	2

STUART **CLARK**

AUSTRALIA

Full name **Stuart Rupert Clark**
Born **September 28, 1975, Sutherland, Sydney, NSW**
Teams **New South Wales**
Style **Right-hand bat, right-arm fast-medium bowler**
Test debut **Australia v South Africa at Cape Town 2005-06**
ODI debut **Australia v World XI at Melbourne 2005-06**

THE PROFILE Stuart Clark is a tall and lanky opening bowler often described as "in the Glenn McGrath mould". Appropriately, in his opening Test series in South Africa early in 2006, 30-year-old Clark – the son of English-born parents who met in India – replaced the temporarily absent McGrath and experienced a dream entry: 20 wickets at 15.75 made him Player of the Series. A borderline selection for the first Test, he earned victory with 5 for 55 and 4 for 34, the third-best match figures by an Australian debutant after Bob Massie and Clarrie Grimmett. A former real-estate agent but now planning a career in finance, Clark was a late cricket developer, finally emerging at 27 after a battle with body as much as talent. He earned a central contract with 45 wickets in 2001-02, but lost it the following summer after ankle and rib injuries. Hernia surgery was next, quickly followed by a leg problem, but he took 40 wickets in NSW's 2004-05 Pura Cup triumph. Clark, who troubles batsmen with his height (6ft 5½ins/197cm) and seam movement, showed there was room for him and McGrath in the same side by topping the averages (26 wickets at 17.03) in the 2006-07 Ashes whitewash, although after that he was a back number in the World Cup. The following season, with McGrath finally retired, Clark took 21 wickets in six home Tests and 13 more in three in the Caribbean, but – amid whispers that he had lost a yard of pace – was a rather surprising omission from the first three Ashes Tests in 2009 before making his mark in a big victory at Headingley.

THE FACTS During the memorable 2005 Ashes tour, Clark was twice called into the Australian squad from county cricket with Middlesex as cover for injured bowlers, but did not play in a Test ... His nickname is "Sarfraz", after a vague resemblance – in appearance and run-up – to the former Pakistan fast bowler ... Clark's international debut was against the World XI in October 2005, and his first wicket was Kevin Pietersen ... He took 8 for 58 for NSW against Western Australia – a hat-trick reducing them to 2 for 4 – at Perth in Feb 2007 ...

THE FIGURES *to 21.9.09*   www.cricinfo.com

Batting & Fielding	M	Inns	NO	Runs	HS	Avge	S/R	100	50	4s	6s	Ct	St
Tests	24	26	7	248	39	13.05	70.05	0	0	21	6	4	0
ODIs	39	12	7	69	16*	13.80	78.40	0	0	6	1	10	0
Twenty20 Ints	9	0	–	–	–	–	–	–	–	–	–	4	0
First-class	102	130	37	1314	62	14.12	–	0	1	–	–	28	0

Bowling	M	Balls	Runs	Wkts	BB	Avge	RpO	S/R	5i	10m
Tests	24	5146	2243	94	5–32	23.86	2.61	54.74	2	0
ODIs	39	1829	1477	53	4–54	27.86	4.84	34.50	0	0
Twenty20 Ints	9	216	237	13	4–20	18.23	6.58	16.61	0	0
First-class	102	20906	10047	369	8–58	27.22	2.88	56.65	13	1

MICHAEL **CLARKE**

Full name	**Michael John Clarke**
Born	**April 2, 1981, Liverpool, New South Wales**
Teams	**New South Wales**
Style	**Right-hand bat, left-arm orthodox spinner**
Test debut	**Australia v India at Bangalore 2003-04**
ODI debut	**Australia v England at Adelaide 2002-03**

THE PROFILE   Michael Clarke was being touted as Australia's next captain before he'd even played a Test. And when he marked his eventual debut with 151 against India in October 2004, his future looked even brighter than the yellow motorbike he received as Man of the Match. Another thrilling century followed on his home debut, and his first Test season ended with the Allan Border Medal. Then came the fall. Barely a year later he was dropped after 15 century-less Tests. He was told to tighten his technique, especially early on against swing. Clarke remained a one-day fixture, but had to wait until the low-key Bangladesh series early in 2006 to reclaim that Test spot. He cemented his place with two tons in the 2006-07 Ashes whitewash, did well in the World Cup, averaging 87.20, and scored a century in each of Australia's three Test series in 2007-08: he also took charge in a few one-day games. In England in 2009 Clarke was the classiest batsman on show, finishing with two centuries and a near-miss (93). He started as a ravishing shotmaker who did not so much take guard as take off: he radiated a pointy-elbowed elegance reminiscent of the young Greg Chappell or Mark Waugh, who both also waited uncomplainingly for Test openings then started with tons. His bouncy fielding and searing run-outs, usually from square on, add to his value, while his slow left-armers can surprise (they once shocked six Indians in a Test at Mumbai). A cricket nut since he was in nappies, "Pup" honed his technique against the bowling machine at his dad's indoor centre.

THE FACTS   Clarke scored a century on his Test debut, 151 v India at Bangalore in 2004-05, and the following month added another in his first home Test, 141 v New Zealand at Brisbane: only two other batsmen (Harry Graham and Kepler Wessels) have done this for Australia ... Clarke averages 55.80 in Tests against England (and 216 v Sri Lanka), but only 20.75 v Pakistan ... A skin-cancer scare late in 2005 persuaded Clarke to swap a traditional cap for a wide-brimmed sunhat ...

THE FIGURES *to 21.9.09*   www.cricinfo.com

Batting & Fielding	M	Inns	NO	Runs	HS	Avge	S/R	100	50	4s	6s	Ct	St
Tests	52	84	10	3652	151	49.35	53.41	12	15	399	17	47	0
ODIs	163	147	31	4945	130	42.62	77.64	4	38	428	28	64	0
Twenty20 Ints	19	15	4	216	37*	19.63	102.36	0	0	9	6	6	0
First-class	109	185	18	7489	201*	44.84	–	25	30	–	–	104	0

Bowling	M	Balls	Runs	Wkts	BB	Avge	RpO	S/R	5i	10m
Tests	52	1540	755	19	6–9	39.73	2.94	81.05	1	0
ODIs	163	2156	1825	52	5–35	35.09	5.07	41.46	1	0
Twenty20 Ints	19	108	153	5	1–13	30.60	8.50	21.60	0	0
First-class	109	2720	1443	30	6–9	48.10	3.18	90.66	1	0

PAUL **COLLINGWOOD**

Full name	**Paul David Collingwood**
Born	**May 26, 1976, Shotley Bridge, Co. Durham**
Teams	**Durham**
Style	**Right-hand bat, right-arm medium-pace bowler**
Test debut	**England v Sri Lanka at Galle 2003-04**
ODI debut	**England v Pakistan at Birmingham 2001**

THE PROFILE While Paul Collingwood was on the fringe of the England team, it seemed that he was perhaps the first specialist fielder to earn regular selection in a Test squad. He made the one-day side in 2001, but four years and numerous tours later had won only three Test caps, although the third of those was the 2005 Ashes decider at The Oval. He still seemed destined to be the uncomplaining stand-in – but that winter struck 96 and 80 at Lahore, and added a brilliant century against India, as England struggled with injuries. Then a superb 186 against Pakistan at Lord's booked a middle-order place at last, and Collingwood later joined rarefied company with an Ashes double-century at Adelaide. By 2008 his technique looked in need of a 50,000-mile service, although a defiant 135 against South Africa at Edgbaston probably saved his Test career. The following season his 344-minute 74 did much to save the first Ashes Test at Cardiff, but he looked careworn by the end of that series, making only 112 more runs in the remaining four Tests. Collingwood remains a superb fielder, capable of breathtaking moments at backward point or in the slips. He is also a vital one-day performer: a maiden century against Sri Lanka in Australia clinched his spot for the 2003 World Cup; after England's travails in the 2007 tournament, he took over as one-day captain, although he gave it up the following year. His bowling, which verges on the dibbly-dobbly, is negligible in Tests, but given the right conditions he can be irresistible in one-dayers – as at Trent Bridge in 2005, when he followed a century against Bangladesh with 6 for 31.

THE FACTS Collingwood's century and six wickets in the same match – against Bangladesh at Nottingham in 2005 – is unmatched in ODI history: his 6 for 31 that day are also England's best one-day bowling figures ... He made 206 at Adelaide in December 2006, England's first double-century in a Test in Australia since Wally Hammond in 1936-37 ... In September 2006 he became the 11th man to play 100 ODIs for England ...

THE FIGURES to 21.9.09   www.cricinfo.com

Batting & Fielding	M	Inns	NO	Runs	HS	Avge	S/R	100	50	4s	6s	Ct	St
Tests	53	93	9	3565	206	42.44	46.19	9	16	394	16	67	0
ODIs	166	150	32	4083	120*	34.60	76.16	4	22	301	51	96	0
Twenty20 Ints	21	19	0	407	79	21.42	135.21	0	2	30	15	6	0
First-class	177	308	25	10354	206	36.58	–	23	52	–	–	194	0

Bowling	M	Balls	Runs	Wkts	BB	Avge	RpO	S/R	5i	10m
Tests	53	1527	846	15	3–23	56.40	3.32	101.80	0	0
ODIs	166	4292	3594	96	6–31	37.43	5.02	44.70	1	0
Twenty20 Ints	21	192	282	16	4–22	17.62	8.81	12.00	0	0
First-class	177	9431	4818	120	5–52	40.15	3.06	78.59	1	0

ALASTAIR **COOK**

Full name	**Alastair Nathan Cook**
Born	**December 25, 1984, Gloucester**
Teams	**Essex**
Style	**Left-hand bat, occasional offspinner**
Test debut	**England v India at Nagpur 2005-06**
ODI debut	**England v Sri Lanka at Manchester 2006**

THE PROFILE   Those in the know were saying that the tall, dark and handsome Alastair Cook was destined for great things very early on. A correct and stylish left-hander strong on the pull, Cook was thrown in at the deep end by Essex the year after he left Bedford School. He captained England in the Under-19 World Cup early in 2004, making two centuries en route to the semi-finals, then scored his maiden first-class hundred later that year. After a fine 2005, which included a double-century against the Australians, he was called up by England the following spring when injuries struck in India. He had been in the Caribbean with the A team when the SOS came but, unfazed, he cracked 60 at Nagpur then added a magnificent 104 to complete a memorable debut. He succumbed to illness himself before that tour was done, but bounced back with 89 against Sri Lanka at Lord's in May 2006, then made sure his name was on MCC's honours board by scoring 105 against Pakistan two months later. He made another upright century in the next Test, at Manchester, and survived a tough Ashes baptism, scoring 276 runs (with 116 at Perth) in the 2006-07 whitewash. Bowlers began to notice a tendency to play around the front pad, but Cook still did well at home in 2007 – two hundreds against West Indies – and 2008, when he reached 50 five times in Tests without going on to three figures. There were downers ahead, though: he lost his one-day place after a moderate run, and in the 2009 Ashes series 95 at Lord's was his only score above 32 as the Aussies exploited that front-pad problem.

THE FACTS   Cook was the 16th England batsman to make a century on Test debut ... Cook's stand of 127 with Marcus Trescothick v Sri Lanka at Lord's in 2006 was the second-highest in Tests by unrelated players who share a birthday (they were both born on Christmas Day), behind the 163 of Vic Stollmeyer and Kenneth Weekes (both born Jan 24) for West Indies at The Oval in 1939 ... Cook made 195 for Essex at Northampton in 2005 ...

THE FIGURES to 21.9.09   www.cricinfo.com

Batting & Fielding	M	Inns	NO	Runs	HS	Avge	S/R	100	50	4s	6s	Ct	St
Tests	48	87	5	3509	160	42.79	47.17	9	20	417	2	44	0
ODIs	23	23	0	702	102	30.52	68.15	1	3	77	0	7	0
Twenty20 Ints	2	2	0	24	15	12.00	96.00	0	0	4	0	1	0
First-class	112	200	16	8265	195	44.91	53.06	21	47	–	–	110	0

Bowling	M	Balls	Runs	Wkts	BB	Avge	RpO	S/R	5i	10m
Tests	48	6	1	0	–	–	1.00	–	0	0
ODIs	23	0	–	–	–	–	–	–	–	–
Twenty20 Ints	2	0	–	–	–	–	–	–	–	–
First-class	112	180	129	5	3–13	25.80	4.30	36.00	0	0

CRAIG **CUMMING**

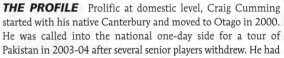

Full name	**Craig Derek Cumming**
Born	**August 31, 1975, Timaru, Canterbury**
Teams	**Otago**
Style	**Right-hand bat, right-arm medium-pacer**
Test debut	**New Zealand v Australia at Christchurch 2004-05**
ODI debut	**New Zealand v Pakistan at Lahore 2003-04**

THE PROFILE Prolific at domestic level, Craig Cumming started with his native Canterbury and moved to Otago in 2000. He was called into the national one-day side for a tour of Pakistan in 2003-04 after several senior players withdrew. He had a mixed time, and in ten matches that season was out five times in single figures. It wasn't enough, and he has played only three ODIs since. He has been a similarly peripheral figure in Tests. After a good start against Australia, when he made 74 to set up a handy total of 433, his performances tailed off and he hasn't passed 50 since. His fine reputation against pace bowling earned him a recall for the South African tour late in 2007, although he might have wished it hadn't: in the second Test he made his way patiently to 48 before trying to hook Dale Steyn, and was smacked on the right cheek through the helmet visor. Cumming needed reconstructive surgery after sustaining multiple fractures. He was back for the less taxing opposition of Bangladesh early in 2008, and although he failed twice in the first Test, 42 in the second settled the nerves a little. Although he bounced back with his best domestic season in 2008-09 – 784 runs at 65 for Otago after working on a tendency to plant his front foot down the wicket, making him an lbw candidate – Cumming missed the home Tests against West Indies and India, but the selectors showed he was still in their thoughts by taking him to Sri Lanka late in 2009, although he did not play in the Tests there.

THE FACTS Cumming scored 187 for Canterbury at Wellington in February 1999 ... He has never taken more than three wickets in a first-class match, but managed 4 for 24 in a Twenty20 game for Otago v Northern Districts in Dunedin in February 2009 ... Cumming's first ten ODIs were all against Pakistan: the other three were against Australia ...

THE FIGURES *to 21.9.09*   www.cricinfo.com

Batting & Fielding	M	Inns	NO	Runs	HS	Avge	S/R	100	50	4s	6s	Ct	St
Tests	11	19	2	441	74	25.94	34.86	0	1	56	2	3	0
ODIs	13	13	1	161	45*	13.41	53.48	0	0	20	0	6	0
Twenty20 Ints	0	0	–	–	–	–	–	–	–	–	–	–	–
First-class	118	210	17	6866	187	35.57	–	15	32	–	–	52	0

Bowling	M	Balls	Runs	Wkts	BB	Avge	RpO	S/R	5i	10m
Tests	11	0	–	–	–	–	–	–	–	–
ODIs	13	18	17	0	–	–	5.66	–	0	0
Twenty20 Ints	0	0	–	–	–	–	–	–	–	–
First-class	118	3485	1592	30	3–31	53.06	2.74	116.16	0	0

DANISH KANERIA

Full name	**Danish Parabha Shanker Kaneria**
Born	**December 16, 1980, Karachi, Sind**
Teams	**Baluchistan, Habib Bank, Essex**
Style	**Right-hand bat, legspinner**
Test debut	**Pakistan v England at Faisalabad 2000-01**
ODI debut	**Pakistan v Zimbabwe at Sharjah 2001-02**

THE PROFILE   A tall, wiry legspinner, Danish Kaneria mastered the dark arts of wrist-spin at an early age. His stock ball drifts in to the right-hander, and he has a googly as cloaked as any. His whirling approach is reminiscent of Abdul Qadir's, and he picked up the baton from Mushtaq Ahmed as Pakistan's premier legspinner. Kaneria was hyped as a secret weapon when England toured in 2000-01, and although his impact in that series was minimal he has certainly made his mark since. Initially he did so against Bangladesh, but then turned it on against South Africa too, when his five-for decided the Lahore Test in October 2003. Since then, Kaneria has confirmed himself as a matchwinner, and has quietly moved past 200 Test wickets. Two tours in 2004-05 – to Australia and India, the graveyard of legspin – were arduous but satisfying stepping stones to the big league. In each series he out-scalped the opposition's leading legspinner – Shane Warne, then Anil Kumble – and although Pakistan still lost to Australia, Kaneria's 19 wickets were crucial to a morale-boosting draw in India. He ended 2005 with two more matchwinning last-day turns against England at home, but proved expensive when the teams reconvened the following summer in England, where he has had a lot of success with Essex. Early in 2009 he took 12 rather expensive wickets in three Tests against Sri Lanka. A back number in one-dayers, he had played only one of Pakistan's previous 27 ODIs before being a surprise inclusion for the 2007 World Cup. He did well enough, but lost his place again in the fallout from that disastrous campaign.

THE FACTS   Danish Kaneria was only the second Hindu to play for Pakistan – the first, 1980s wicketkeeper Anil Dalpat, is his cousin ... He took 12 for 92 in his third Test, against Bangladesh in August 2001 ... Kaneria averages 16.41 v Bangladesh – but 45.14 v England ... He has conceded more than 100 runs in an innings 35 times in 54 Tests ... He took 0 for 208 for Essex v Lancashire at Manchester in 2005, equalling the most expensive wicketless spell in the County Championship, set by Peter Smith, another Essex legspinner, in 1934 ...

THE FIGURES *to 21.9.09*   www.cricinfo.com

Batting & Fielding	M	Inns	NO	Runs	HS	Avge	S/R	100	50	4s	6s	Ct	St
Tests	54	71	31	266	29	6.65	46.34	0	0	35	2	16	0
ODIs	18	10	8	12	6*	6.00	54.54	0	0	1	0	2	0
Twenty20 Ints	0	0	–	–	–	–	–	–	–	–	–	–	–
First-class	162	261	77	1294	65	10.43	–	0	1	–	–	54	0

Bowling	M	Balls	Runs	Wkts	BB	Avge	RpO	S/R	5i	10m
Tests	54	15947	8022	232	7–77	34.57	3.01	68.73	13	2
ODIs	18	854	683	15	3–31	45.53	4.79	56.93	0	0
Twenty20 Ints	0	0	–	–	–	–	–	–	–	–
First-class	162	43440	21007	800	8–59	26.25	2.90	54.30	57	9

AB de VILLIERS

Full name	**Abraham Benjamin de Villiers**
Born	**February 17, 1984, Pretoria**
Teams	**Titans, Delhi Daredevils**
Style	**Right-hand bat, occ. medium-pacer, wicketkeeper**
Test debut	**South Africa v England at Port Elizabeth 2004-05**
ODI debut	**South Africa v England at Bloemfontein 2004-05**

THE PROFILE Few newcomers have been asked to play so many roles so quickly as AB de Villiers, and fewer still have risen to the challenge with such alacrity that, at just 21, he was already being regarded as the future of South African cricket. He is a natural sportsman, gifted at tennis, golf, cricket and rugby. Cricket won out, however, and he made his Titans debut in 2003-04, racking up 438 runs with five half-centuries. He won his first Test cap against England the following season, and, after a composed debut as an opener, was handed the wicketkeeping gloves for the second Test, which he helped save with a maiden half-century from No. 7. By the end of the series he was opening again, and after falling eight short of a deserved century in the first innings at Centurion, made instant amends second time around. His development continued apace in the Caribbean, where he helped seal the series with a wonderful 178 at Bridgetown. Then came the almost inevitable dip in fortunes. In Australia in 2005-06 de Villiers managed just 152 runs at 25.33 – despite playing Shane Warne well – and missed the one-dayers. But he re-established himself in 2006-07, especially impressive in the shorter game, although he had a curious World Cup, collecting four ducks as well as 92 against Australia and a stroke-filled 146 against West Indies. Test centuries followed against West Indies and India (his first double), before a memorable 174 at Headingley in July 2008 gave his side a decisive lead over England. Then in 2008-09 he made three centuries in six Tests against Australia.

THE FACTS de Villiers made 217 not out at Ahmedabad in April 2008, after India had been bowled out for 76 ... He averages 58.28 in five Tests at Durban – but only 20.80 from six at Johannesburg ... He scored 151, his maiden first-class century, for Titans v Western Province Boland in October 2004, sharing a stand of 317 with Martin van Jaarsveld ... de Villiers went a Test-record 78 innings before falling for a duck, against Bangladesh at Centurion in November 2008 ... His record includes five ODIs for the Africa XI ...

THE FIGURES *to 21.9.09*   www.cricinfo.com

Batting & Fielding	M	Inns	NO	Runs	HS	Avge	S/R	100	50	4s	6s	Ct	St
Tests	52	89	8	3558	217*	43.92	53.04	9	17	434	18	75	1
ODIs	85	81	10	2761	146	38.88	85.82	3	18	284	48	52	0
Twenty20 Ints	21	20	4	362	79*	22.62	127.46	0	3	33	10	22	2
First-class	76	132	13	5407	217*	45.43	56.61	12	31	–	–	121	2

Bowling	M	Balls	Runs	Wkts	BB	Avge	RpO	S/R	5i	10m
Tests	52	198	99	2	2–49	49.50	3.00	99.00	0	0
ODIs	85	12	22	0	–	–	11.00	–	0	0
Twenty20 Ints	21	0	–	–	–	–	–	–	–	–
First-class	76	228	133	2	2–49	66.50	3.50	114.00	0	0

JOE **DENLY**

Full name	**Joseph Liam Denly**
Born	**March 16, 1986, Canterbury, Kent**
Teams	**Kent**
Style	**Right-hand bat, occasional legspinner**
Test debut	**No Tests yet**
ODI debut	**England v Ireland at Belfast 2009**

THE PROFILE   Joe Denly has been associated with Kent since he was 13, and made his first-class debut for them against Oxford University in 2004, unluckily bagging a duck in the only two overs that rain allowed during the whole match. He did rather better against Cambridge two years later: two centuries. At first he found opportunities elusive, but when Kent's former captain David Fulton was released (the fear that Denly might go elsewhere may have contributed to that decision) a place became available at the start of 2007. Denly grabbed it eagerly, finishing with 1003 runs at 41.79. A good puller and hooker, he played pace with ease, although he was a little less assured against spin – Paul Coupar wrote in the *Wisden Cricketer* that "in excellent touch otherwise, he handled Danish Kaneria's leg-spin like soap in the bath". But it was Denly's one-day form that really caught the eye. As Kent lifted the Twenty20 Cup in 2007 he made 279 runs, and was even more prolific the following year with 451, although this time Kent lost the final. In 2008 he carried that form over to the longer limited-overs game, making more than 400 runs, including 102 against Durham in the Friends Provident semi-final (again Kent lost the final), and also played for England Lions. When the runs continued to flow in 2009 – there was another FPT hundred, against Warwickshire, to go alongside three first-class ones – the England selectors finally called. Denly started with 67 against Ireland, but his chances against Australia in September weren't helped when he injured his knee in a pre-match game of football, although he returned to make a promising 53 as England finally won, at Chester-le-Street.

THE FACTS   Denly scored 115 and 107 not out for Kent against Cambridge UCCE at Fenner's in May 2006 – then did not play another first-class game for four months ... His highest score of 149 came against Somerset at Tunbridge Wells in May 2008 ... Denly scored five half-centuries in the Twenty20 Cup in 2008, including 91 (from 57 balls) against Essex at Beckenham ...

THE FIGURES *to 21.9.09*   www.cricinfo.com

Batting & Fielding	M	Inns	NO	Runs	HS	Avge	S/R	100	50	4s	6s	Ct	St
Tests	0	0	–	–	–	–	–	–	–	–	–	–	–
ODIs	5	5	0	201	67	40.20	63.40	0	2	21	1	3	0
Twenty20 Ints	1	1	0	0	0	0.00	0.00	0	0	0	0	0	0
First-class	52	88	5	3058	149	36.84	59.91	9	14	–	–	23	0

Bowling	M	Balls	Runs	Wkts	BB	Avge	RpO	S/R	5i	10m
Tests	0	0	–	–	–	–	–	–	–	–
ODIs	5	0	–	–	–	–	–	–	–	–
Twenty20 Ints	1	0	–	–	–	–	–	–	–	–
First-class	52	877	447	10	2–13	44.70	3.05	87.70	0	0

MAHENDRA SINGH **DHONI**

Full name **Mahendra Singh Dhoni**
Born **July 7, 1981, Ranchi, Bihar**
Teams **Jharkhand, Chennai Super Kings**
Style **Right-hand bat, wicketkeeper**
Test debut **India v Sri Lanka at Chennai 2005-06**
ODI debut **India v Bangladesh at Chittagong 2004-05**

INDIA

THE PROFILE The odds against a Virender Sehwag clone emerging from the backwaters of Jharkhand (formerly Bihar) were highly remote – until MS Dhoni arrived (a one-time railway ticket collector, his first love was football). His batting is swashbuckling, and his wicketkeeping secure. It wasn't until 2004 that he became a serious contender: there was a rapid hundred as East Zone clinched the Deodhar Trophy, an audacious 60 in the Duleep Trophy final, and two tons against Pakistan A which established him as a clinical destroyer of bowling attacks. In just his fifth ODI – against Pakistan in April 2005 – Dhoni cracked a dazzling 148, putting even Sehwag in the shade, and followed that with 183 against Sri Lanka in November, beating Adam Gilchrist's highest ODI score by a wicketkeeper. He made an instant impact in Tests, too, pounding 148 at Faisalabad in only his fifth match, when India were struggling to avoid the follow-on. His keeping improved, and he quickly became a key member of a revitalised side. He stepped up to captain the eventual winners in the World Twenty20 in September 2007, then made headlines as the most expensive signing ($1.5million) for the inaugural IPL season. He took over as full-time Test captain when Anil Kumble retired in November 2008, rubber-stamping victory over Australia then defeating England and New Zealand in short series. Some feel he looks more at home as a limited-overs skipper, where the team has been shaped around him, rather than in Tests when he is still seen as junior to the likes of Dravid and Tendulkar, but Dhoni has nonetheless started well, and has a formidable team at his disposal.

THE FACTS Dhoni's unbeaten 183 against Sri Lanka at Jaipur in November 2005 is the highest score in ODIs by a wicketkeeper, and included 120 in boundaries – 10 sixes and 15 fours – a record at the time but later beaten by Herschelle Gibbs ... The only other Indian to score a century in an ODI in which he kept wicket is Rahul Dravid ... Dhoni's record includes three ODIs for the Asia XI ...

THE FIGURES to 21.9.09   www.cricinfo.com

Batting & Fielding	M	Inns	NO	Runs	HS	Avge	S/R	100	50	4s	6s	Ct	St
Tests	37	59	7	1962	148	37.73	61.93	1	16	229	33	92	18
ODIs	142	127	34	4666	183*	50.17	90.25	4	32	353	102	140	46
Twenty20 Ints	18	17	4	301	45	23.15	101.68	0	0	20	5	5	2
First-class	77	124	10	4114	148	36.08	–	4	30	–	–	199	34

Bowling	M	Balls	Runs	Wkts	BB	Avge	RpO	S/R	5i	10m
Tests	37	12	14	0	–	–	7.00	–	0	0
ODIs	141	0	–	–	–	–	–	–	–	–
Twenty20 Ints	18	0	–	–	–	–	–	–	–	–
First-class	77	42	34	0	–	–	4.85	–	0	0

TILLAKARATNE **DILSHAN**

Full name **Tillakaratne Mudiyanselage Dilshan**
Born **October 14, 1976, Kalutara**
Teams **Bloomfield, Basnahira South, Delhi Daredevils**
Style **Right-hand bat, offspinner**
Test debut **Sri Lanka v Zimbabwe at Bulawayo 1999-2000**
ODI debut **Sri Lanka v Zimbabwe at Bulawayo 1999-2000**

THE PROFILE Tillakaratne Mudiyanselage Dilshan, who started life as Tuwan Mohamad Dilshan before converting to Buddhism, is a light-footed right-hander who burst onto the international scene with an unbeaten 163 against Zimbabwe in only his second Test in November 1999. Technically sound, comfortable against fast bowling, possessed of quick feet, strong wrists and natural timing, Dilshan has talent in abundance. But that bright start was followed by a frustrating time when he was shovelled up and down the order, and in and out of the side. After a lean series against England in 2001 he didn't play another Test until England toured again, late in 2003. He came back determined to play his own natural aggressive game. This approach was immediately successful, with several good scores against England and Australia. He has continued to be a steady middle-order influence, and was one of four centurions in an innings victory over India in July 2008. He put a lean trot in ODIs behind him just in time for the 2007 World Cup, where he made some useful runs in Sri Lanka's march to the final. Against Bangladesh at Chittagong in January 2009 he hit 162 and 143 then wrapped up the match with four wickets, and later in the year lit up the World Twenty20 in England with some spectacular batting, including his own trademark cheeky scoop over the shoulder. He was the leading runscorer, with 317, although he made a duck in the final defeat to Pakistan. Dilshan, who started out as a wicketkeeper, is an electric fielder, and once effected four run-outs in an ODI at Adelaide.

THE FACTS Dilshan made 200 not out while captaining North Central Province v Central in Colombo in February 2005 ... His highest Test score of 168 came against Bangladesh in Colombo in September 2005: he put on 280 with Thilan Samaraweera, a Sri Lankan fifth-wicket record in Tests ... Dilshan made his first ODI century in the record total of 443 for 9 against the Netherlands at Amstelveen in July 2006 ... He was the leading runscorer (317) at the World Twenty20 in England in 2009 ...

THE FIGURES *to 21.9.09*   www.cricinfo.com

Batting & Fielding	M	Inns	NO	Runs	HS	Avge	S/R	100	50	4s	6s	Ct	St
Tests	57	90	10	3443	168	43.03	63.87	9	13	424	15	66	0
ODIs	163	140	27	3492	137*	30.90	82.14	2	16	304	16	70	1
Twenty20 Ints	21	20	3	572	96*	33.64	132.10	0	5	68	11	12	2
First-class	192	309	21	11109	200*	38.57	–	28	46	–	–	330	23

Bowling	M	Balls	Runs	Wkts	BB	Avge	RpO	S/R	5i	10m
Tests	57	878	433	13	4–10	33.30	2.95	67.53	0	0
ODIs	163	2623	2067	47	4–29	43.97	4.72	55.80	0	0
Twenty20 Ints	21	84	104	3	2–4	34.66	28.00	0	0	
First-class	192	3490	1684	56	5–49	30.07	2.89	62.32	1	0

BANGLADESH

DOLAR MAHMUD

Full name	**Mohammad Dolar Mahmud**
Born	**December 30, 1988, Narail, Khulna**
Teams	**Khulna**
Style	**Right-hand bat, right-arm fast-medium bowler**
Test debut	**No Tests yet**
ODI debut	**Bangladesh v Pakistan at Mirpur 2008**

THE PROFILE Dolar Mahmud is a handy fast-medium bowler who played in the Under-19 World Cups of 2006 and 2008. He was only 17 at the first one, but failed to shine in either, although his 36 against England in 2008 helped Bangladesh to a narrow 13-run victory in a low-scoring game. Despite these uninspiring returns, the selectors liked the look of his easy action, and gave him plenty of junior representative experience. Shortly after taking a hat-trick for Khulna against Rajshahi in a domestic match – and hitting the winning boundary to end the game – he toured South Africa with the Under-19s at the end of 2007, and took five wickets in the second Test at Potchefstroom. Overall Mahmud did enough to earn promotion to the full squad, and fulfilled a childhood dream by making his full ODI debut in the Kitply Cup at home in Bangladesh in June 2008. Again the returns were modest – he failed to score in either of his innings, but did take a wicket (Kamran Akmal and Virender Sehwag) in each of his two matches. This was enough for him to retain his place for the Asia Cup, where he finally got off the mark with the bat (he hit his second ball for six, after a first-ball single), although this was only against the lowly United Arab Emirates – when they played Sri Lanka he failed to take a wicket. He boosted his stats with 4 for 28 in an ODI against Zimbabwe in August 2009, but battles lie ahead as he has to contend for a place with several bowlers of similar style.

THE FACTS Dolar Mahmud took a hat-trick for Khulna v Rajshahi at Khulna in November 2007: his victims included Test players Junaid Siddique and Mushfiqur Rahim ... Mahmud finished that innings with 7 for 52, his best first-class figures ... He also took 5 for 44 against Barisal in November 2006 ... Mahmud played in the Under-19 World Cups of 2006 and 2008 ... He took 5 for 75 in an Under-19 Test against South Africa in December 2007 ...

THE FIGURES *to 21.9.09*   www.cricinfo.com

Batting & Fielding	M	Inns	NO	Runs	HS	Avge	S/R	100	50	4s	6s	Ct	St
Tests	0	0	–	–	–	–	–	–	–	–	–	–	–
ODIs	5	3	0	20	20	6.66	142.85	0	0	1	1	0	0
Twenty20 Ints	0	0	–	–	–	–	–	–	–	–	–	–	–
First-class	25	45	5	559	65	13.97	60.76	0	2	–	–	9	0

Bowling	M	Balls	Runs	Wkts	BB	Avge	RpO	S/R	5i	10m
Tests	0	0	–	–	–	–	–	–	–	–
ODIs	5	151	193	7	14–28	27.57	7.66	21.57	0	0
Twenty20 Ints	0	0	–	–	–	–	–	–	–	–
First-class	25	3576	1969	73	7–52	26.97	3.30	48.98	2	0

TRAVIS **DOWLIN**

Full name	**Travis Montague Dowlin**
Born	**Feb 24, 1977, Guyhoc Gardens, Georgetown, Guyana**
Teams	**Guyana**
Style	**Right-hand bat, occasional offspinner**
Test debut	**West Indies v Bangladesh at Kingstown 2009**
ODI debut	**West Indies v Bangladesh at Roseau 2009**

THE PROFILE Travis Dowlin, a solidly built right-hander from Guyana, looked set to see his career out in domestic cricket before thrusting himself into the limelight with a matchwinning 80 in the first Stanford 20/20 final in Antigua in August 2006. It won him the match award, and put him into the selectors' thoughts: he was in the preliminary list for the 2007 World Cup but missed out on the final cut, and the following year was part of the Stanford Superstars squad which embarrassed the full England team, although he did not actually play in the $1m-a-man showpiece. Dowlin backed that up by producing his best-ever first-class season in 2008-09, despite turning 32 during it, racking up 580 runs in all, without a century. Still an international call-up looked unlikely, until all the first-choice players declined to play against Bangladesh in July as a long-running and bitter contracts dispute dragged on. Dowlin was one of seven debutants in a second-string side cobbled together at a day's notice for the first Test in St Vincent, but he grabbed his opportunity. Running out of partners, he fell five short of a maiden century in the second Test at St George's, but made sure of three figures in his second ODI a few days later. He played Bangladesh's posse of spinners well, nudging and defending patiently before putting the bad balls away, favouring the sweep and cut. Tony Cozier, the veteran West Indian commentator, felt that Dowlin's temperament marked him out as "the possible No.4 we've been searching for", so he should still be in line for a place when the senior players return.

THE FACTS Dowlin scored 176 not out for Guyana v Windward Islands at Providence in March 2008 ... He made 80 (and was Man of the Match) as Guyana beat Trinidad & Tobago in the inaugural Stanford 20/20 final in August 2006 ... Dowlin's 100 not out against Bangladesh in June 2009 was the first international century at Roseau in Dominica ... His maiden first-class century, against Jamaica at Kingston in January 2000, followed 18 innings in which he had failed to reach 50 and been out in single figures ten times ...

THE FIGURES *to 21.9.09*   www.cricinfo.com

Batting & Fielding	M	Inns	NO	Runs	HS	Avge	S/R	100	50	4s	6s	Ct	St
Tests	2	4	0	185	95	46.25	47.68	0	1	20	1	2	0
ODIs	3	3	1	148	100*	74.00	78.30	1	0	12	1	1	0
Twenty20 Ints	1	1	1	37	37*	–	100.00	0	0	5	0	0	0
First-class	75	124	10	3444	176*	30.21	–	4	20	–	–	66	0

Bowling	M	Balls	Runs	Wkts	BB	Avge	RpO	S/R	5i	10m
Tests	2	0	–	–	–	–	–	–	–	–
ODIs	3	0	–	–	–	–	–	–	–	–
Twenty20 Ints	1	0	–	–	–	–	–	–	–	–
First-class	75	960	399	15	4–59	26.60	2.49	64.00	0	0

RAHUL **DRAVID**

INDIA

Full name **Rahul Sharad Dravid**
Born **January 11, 1973, Indore, Madhya Pradesh**
Teams **Karnataka, Bangalore Royal Challengers**
Style **Right-hand bat, occasional wicketkeeper**
Test debut **India v England at Lord's 1996**
ODI debut **India v Sri Lanka at Singapore 1995-96**

THE PROFILE Rahul Dravid has scored more than 10,000 runs in both Tests and ODIs at imposing averages – but impressive as his stats are, they don't show his importance, or the beauty of his batting. When he started, he was pigeonholed as a blocker (an early nickname was "The Wall"), but he grew in stature, finally reaching maturity under Sourav Ganguly's captaincy. As a New India emerged, so did a new Dravid: first, he became an astute one-day finisher, then produced several superb Test performances. His golden phase really began with a supporting act, at Kolkata early in 2001, when his 180 helped VVS Laxman create history against Australia. But after that Dravid became India's most valuable player: at one point he hit four double-centuries in eight months, finishing with an epic 270 to seal the 2004 tour of Pakistan with a victory. In October 2005 he was appointed as one-day captain, began with a 6-1 hammering of Sri Lanka at home, and soon succeeded Ganguly as Test skipper too. He continued to score well, and bounced back from the crushing disappointment of early exit from the 2007 World Cup by leading India to a rare series victory in England, although his own batting lacked sparkle. He relinquished the captaincy after that, but the runs refused to flow: he lost his one-day place, but just as serious questions were being asked about his Test future, Dravid ground out 136 in nearly eight hours against England at Mohali, to ensure a series victory in December 2008. He then did well in New Zealand, to show that The Wall wasn't ready to be demolished just yet.

THE FACTS Dravid hit centuries in four successive Test innings in 2002, three in England and one against West Indies ... He kept wicket in 73 ODIs ... Unusually, Dravid averages more in away Tests (56.90) than at home in India (47.23) ... He averages 97.90 in Tests against Zimbabwe, but only 36.51 v South Africa ... Dravid's record includes one Test and three ODIs for the World XI, and one ODI for the Asia XI ...

THE FIGURES to 21.9.09   www.cricinfo.com

Batting & Fielding	M	Inns	NO	Runs	HS	Avge	S/R	100	50	4s	6s	Ct	St
Tests	134	233	27	10823	270	52.53	41.73	26	57	1367	15	184	0
ODIs	336	311	40	10685	153	39.42	71.14	12	81	936	42	194	14
Twenty20 Ints	0	0	–	–	–	–	–	–	–	–	–	–	–
First-class	261	433	59	20719	55.39	–	56	108	–	–	317	1	

Bowling	M	Balls	Runs	Wkts	BB	Avge	RpO	S/R	5i	10m
Tests	134	120	39	1	1–18	39.00	1.95	120.00	0	0
ODIs	336	186	170	4	2–43	42.50	5.48	46.50	0	0
Twenty20 Ints	0	0	–	–	–	–	–	–	–	–
First-class	261	617	273	5	2–16	54.60	2.65	123.40	0	0

J-P **DUMINY**

Full name	**Jean-Paul Duminy**
Born	**April 14, 1984, Strandfontein, Cape Town**
Teams	**Cape Cobras, Mumbai Indians**
Style	**Left-hand bat, occasional offspinner**
Test debut	**South Africa v Australia at Perth 2008-09**
ODI debut	**South Africa v Sri Lanka at Colombo 2004-05**

THE PROFILE A slightly built but stylish left-hander, Jean-Paul (better known as "J-P") Duminy had trouble finding a place in South Africa's strong middle order – but when an injury to Ashwell Prince finally let him into the Test side in Australia late in 2008, more than four years after his one-day debut, he certainly made it count. First Duminy stroked a nerveless 50 not out as South Africa made light of a target of 414 to start with victory at Perth, then he set up a series-winning victory at Melbourne with a superb 166, most of it coming during an eye-popping ninth-wicket stand of 180 with Dale Steyn. A four-hour 73 followed in the return series in a defeat at Durban: Duminy had arrived, a fact confirmed by a big-money IPL contract. He had first featured in a one-day series in Sri Lanka in 2004. He struggled in the one-dayers there, scoring only 29 runs in five attempts (22 of them in one innings), and dropped off the national radar for a couple of years. But he continued to make runs at home, and was given an extended run in the one-day side after the 2007 World Cup, showing signs of developing into a late-innings "finisher": he batted into the final over in three successive matches against West Indies, all of which were eventually won. He finished that series with 227 runs at 113.50, although he was less of a hit in England later in 2008. Duminy is also a superb fielder, while his part-time offbreaks occasionally come in handy.

THE FACTS Duminy scored 169 as Cape Cobras followed on against the Eagles at Stellenbosch in February 2007 ... He scored 265 not out for the South African Academy against Pakistan's at Lahore in August 2005 ... Duminy made 116 in an Under-19 Test at Worcester in August 2003, before being caught and bowled by Alastair Cook ... He is not related to the JP Duminy who played three Tests for South Africa in the 1920s ...

THE FIGURES *to 21.9.09*   www.cricinfo.com

Batting & Fielding	M	Inns	NO	Runs	HS	Avge	S/R	100	50	4s	6s	Ct	St
Tests	6	10	2	389	166	48.62	40.56	1	2	46	1	9	0
ODIs	47	40	10	1094	90	36.46	79.33	0	6	78	10	15	0
Twenty20 Ints	16	16	4	364	78	30.33	125.08	0	2	32	9	11	0
First-class	55	92	17	3956	169	52.74	48.86	12	20	–	–	44	0

Bowling	M	Balls	Runs	Wkts	BB	Avge	RpO	S/R	5i	10m
Tests	6	210	125	2	1–14	62.50	3.57	105.00	0	0
ODIs	47	565	454	13	3–31	34.92	4.82	43.46	0	0
Twenty20 Ints	16	36	41	3	1–3	13.66	6.83	12.00	0	0
First-class	55	1863	1101	26	5–108	42.34	3.54	71.65	1	0

FIDEL **EDWARDS**

Full name	**Fidel Henderson Edwards**
Born	**February 6, 1982, Gays, St Peter, Barbados**
Teams	**Barbados, Deccan Chargers**
Style	**Right-hand bat, right-arm fast bowler**
Test debut	**West Indies v Sri Lanka at Kingston 2002-03**
ODI debut	**West Indies v Zimbabwe at Harare 2003-04**

THE PROFILE Fidel Edwards had an extraordinary start in international cricket, the kind that can either haunt or add lustre to a career. He was spotted in the nets by Brian Lara early in 2003 and called up for his Test debut after only one match for Barbados: he promptly took five wickets against Sri Lanka. He added five in his first overseas Test, and six in his first ODI. Edwards has a slingy round-arm action which leaves him vulnerable to back strains. It doesn't often seem to result in him straying down leg, though, and his unusual action has troubled many a distinguished batsman. He is more of a protégé of his neighbour Corey Collymore than of his half-brother Pedro Collins, a left-armer – who replaced him when another injury (a hamstring this time) forced him out of the series against India in 2006. Edwards bowls fast, can swing the ball and reverse it too, but insists that he doesn't go for out-and-out pace – which is just as well, because he has learned that pace without control leads straight to the boundary at international level. He showed his increased maturity with a testing spell in Antigua in June 2006 that had India's Virender Sehwag in all kinds of trouble before a hamstring twanged. And he hurried England's batsmen up in 2007, taking nine wickets in two Tests and ten – including 5 for 45 at Lord's – as West Indies won the one-day series 2-1, then grabbed eight more, including both openers in both innings, in the first Test against Australia at Kingston in May 2008. He's not much of a batsman, yet twice hung on tenaciously to deny England series-leveling victories in the Caribbean early in 2009.

THE FACTS Edwards had played only one first-class match – taking one wicket – before his Test debut against Sri Lanka at Kingston in June 2003, when he took 5 for 36 ... He later took 6 for 22 on his ODI debut, against Zimbabwe at Harare in November 2003 ... Edwards opened the bowling in Tests several times with his half-brother Pedro Collins ... Edwards averages 21.45 with the ball in Tests against Sri Lanka, but 90.36 in eight matches against South Africa ... Unoriginally, his nickname is "Castro" ...

THE FIGURES to 21.9.09   www.cricinfo.com

Batting & Fielding	M	Inns	NO	Runs	HS	Avge	S/R	100	50	4s	6s	Ct	St
Tests	43	69	21	248	21	5.16	25.59	0	0	32	2	7	0
ODIs	50	22	14	73	13	9.12	45.62	0	0	5	0	4	0
Twenty20 Ints	12	2	1	3	2*	3.00	75.00	0	0	0	0	2	0
First-class	63	97	34	394	40	6.25	–	0	0	–	–	11	0

Bowling	M	Balls	Runs	Wkts	BB	Avge	RpO	S/R	5i	10m
Tests	43	7259	4811	122	7–87	39.43	3.97	59.50	8	0
ODIs	50	2138	1812	60	6–22	30.20	5.08	35.63	2	0
Twenty20 Ints	12	219	308	10	3–24	30.80	8.43	21.90	0	0
First-class	63	9992	6634	187	7–87	35.47	3.98	53.43	10	1

GRANT **ELLIOTT**

Full name	**Grant David Elliott**
Born	**March 21, 1979, Johannesburg, South Africa**
Teams	**Wellington, Surrey**
Style	**Right-hand bat, right-arm medium-pacer**
Test debut	**New Zealand v England at Napier 2007-08**
ODI debut	**New Zealand v England at Edgbaston 2008**

THE PROFILE   Grant Elliott left his native South Africa for New Zealand in 2001 looking for new horizons, and found them in March 2008 when he was named in NZ's 13-man squad for the first Test against England less than a year after completing his residency qualification. He missed out then, but won his first cap in the final Test after Jacob Oram was injured. However, Elliott was not a success, with two batting failures and a solitary wicket, although he was included in the squad for the one-dayers in England later in the year. A compact and correct batsman, and a swing bowler of modest pace, albeit from a nice high action, he enjoyed a productive season for Wellington in 2006-07, with 361 runs at 45.12, and backed that up with 565 at 37.66 the following year. In England, he took three wickets in the second ODI, and made 56 in the third, but it was his controversial run-out in the fourth one at the Oval which made all the headlines – after he collided with the bowler while trying a quick single Elliott was lying on the ground clutching his thigh when the bails were removed, and England's captain Paul Collingwood declined to withdraw the appeal. Elliott stomped off, and later the New Zealand dressing-room door was firmly shut in Collingwood's face. Elliott made more of a mark with the bat in Australia in 2008-09, following a matchwinning 61 not out at Melbourne with a superb rearguard 115 at Sydney. Wickets still proved hard to come by, but he looked to have cemented a one-day place for the time being.

THE FACTS   Elliott scored 196 not out for Wellington v Auckland in April 2008 ... He represented South Africa in the Under-19 World Cup in 1997–98, and also played a one-day game for South Africa A against India A in 2001–02 ... Elliott's maiden first-class century came for Griqualand West against Bangladesh at Kimberley in October 2000 ...

THE FIGURES *to 21.9.09*   www.cricinfo.com

Batting & Fielding	M	Inns	NO	Runs	HS	Avge	S/R	100	50	4s	6s	Ct	St
Tests	3	5	1	27	9	6.75	23.47	0	0	2	0	2	0
ODIs	23	15	5	484	115	48.40	77.07	1	2	29	3	4	0
Twenty20 Ints	1	1	1	23	23*	–	76.66	0	0	1	0	0	0
First-class	49	76	4	2193	196*	30.45	–	5	12	–	–	31	0

Bowling	M	Balls	Runs	Wkts	BB	Avge	RpO	S/R	5i	10m
Tests	3	240	129	2	1–15	64.50	3.22	120.00	0	0
ODIs	23	386	327	13	3–14	25.15	5.08	29.69	0	0
Twenty20 Ints	1	6	11	1	1–11	11.00	11.00	6.00	0	0
First-class	49	5265	2393	63	4–56	37.98	2.72	83.57	0	0

BANGLADESH

ENAMUL HAQUE

Full name **Enamul Haque**
Born **December 5, 1986, Sylhet**
Teams **Sylhet, Maharashtra**
Style **Right-hand bat, slow left-arm orthodox spinner**
Test debut **Bangladesh v England at Dhaka 2003-04**
ODI debut **Bangladesh v Zimbabwe at Chittagong 2004-05**

THE PROFILE Enamul Haque was born in the hill country of Sylhet, on Bangladesh's eastern border, and there was some confusion about his age when he was selected for the Board President's XI in the opening match of England's 2003-04 tour: he was supposedly 16, most people had him pegged as two years older than that, and he bowled like a veteran at England's nonplussed batsmen – at one point four wickets went down for no runs, three of them to Enamul. It propelled him straight into the following week's Test, where he bowled with skill and impressive composure to embarrass England's batsmen again. He gives the ball a big rip from a high, economical action, and took 6 for 45 – and the historic final wicket – to send the country wild with an inaugural Test victory over Zimbabwe in January 2005. He added 7 for 95 (and 12 in the match) in the drawn second Test. He was kept out of the firing line in England later that year, but bounced back as Bangladesh nearly embarrassed Australia in the first Test of their 2006 tour. His form dipped after that, and other spinners were tried. Enamul played for Maharashtra in India's Ranji Trophy late in 2008, and won a national recall shortly after that while Abdur Razzak's bowling action was investigated. Recalled for the second Test in the Caribbean in July 2009, Enamul took three wickets in each innings as Bangladesh completed a 2-0 clean sweep over a depleted West Indies side, then had a rare run in one-dayers when Razzak's injured hamstring kept him out of the five-match series in Zimbabwe.

THE FACTS Enamul took 7 for 95 – and 12 for 200 in the match, a Bangladesh record – against Zimbabwe at Dhaka in 2004-05 ... He also took 7 for 47 in an A-team Test against Zimbabwe at Bulawayo in February 2005 ... The "junior" is added to Enamul's name to distinguish him from an earlier Bangladesh left-arm spinner of the same name (born February 27, 1966, Enamul Haque senior played 10 Tests, and is now an international umpire) ...

THE FIGURES to 21.9.09 — www.cricinfo.com

Batting & Fielding	M	Inns	NO	Runs	HS	Avge	S/R	100	50	4s	6s	Ct	St
Tests	14	24	15	53	13	5.88	20.62	0	0	6	0	3	0
ODIs	7	4	1	12	5	4.00	80.00	0	0	0	0	6	0
Twenty20 Ints	0	0	–	–	–	–	–	–	–	–	–	–	–
First-class	64	102	40	695	42	11.20	–	0	0	–	–	24	0

Bowling	M	Balls	Runs	Wkts	BB	Avge	RpO	S/R	5i	10m
Tests	14	3189	1609	41	7–95	39.24	3.02	77.78	3	1
ODIs	7	414	320	8	2–37	40.00	4.63	51.75	0	0
Twenty20 Ints	0	0	–	–	–	–	–	–	–	–
First-class	64	15416	7201	238	7–47	30.25	2.80	64.77	15	3

FAISAL IQBAL

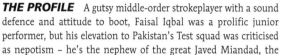

Full name **Faisal Iqbal**
Born **December 30, 1981, Karachi, Sind**
Teams **Karachi, Pakistan International Airlines**
Style **Right-hand bat, occasional right-arm medium-pacer**
Test debut **Pakistan v New Zealand at Auckland 2000-01**
ODI debut **Pakistan v Sri Lanka at Lahore 1999-2000**

PAKISTAN

THE PROFILE   A gutsy middle-order strokeplayer with a sound defence and attitude to boot, Faisal Iqbal was a prolific junior performer, but his elevation to Pakistan's Test squad was criticised as nepotism – he's the nephew of the great Javed Miandad, the coach when Iqbal made his Test debut in New Zealand in 2000-01. But he silenced the critics with three pleasing knocks then, and a counter-attacking 83 off 85 balls against Australia in Colombo in October 2002. He was particularly impressive against Shane Warne, using his feet superbly, and did it all with a swagger reminiscent of his uncle. However, he couldn't repeat his performance in the rest of that series, or in South Africa shortly afterwards. He lost his place, but continued to score heavily in domestic cricket, and won a recall against India at Karachi in January 2006 when Inzamam-ul-Haq was injured. First-innings failure meant the pressure was on in the second, but it didn't seem to affect Iqbal, who made an attractive maiden Test hundred, with some assured back-foot play and composed defence, helping Pakistan to a comfortable series-clinching win. A battling 60 followed against Murali in Colombo. Another good season in 2008-09, which included his second double-century, ensured he retained his place after Pakistan's barren year (for various reasons they played no Tests at all in 2008). He made 57 against Sri Lanka at Karachi in February 2009, but dropped out of the side for the return tour later in the year, although he was in the squad. He stayed in Sri Lanka to captain Pakistan's A team there, so remains firmly on the selectors' radar, although rather surprisingly he isn't seen as a one-day player.

THE FACTS   Faisal Iqbal's maiden Test century, 139 at Karachi in January 2006, helped Pakistan defeat India by a record margin of 341 runs, even though they were 0 for 3 after the first over of the match, and later 39 for 6 ... He made 200 not out for PIA v Sui Southern Gas in Karachi in January 2009, and 200 for Karachi Blues v Sargodha in January 2001 ... His uncle Javed Miandad is Pakistan's leading scorer in Tests, with 8832 runs from 124 matches ...

THE FIGURES *to 21.9.09*   www.cricinfo.com

Batting & Fielding	M	Inns	NO	Runs	HS	Avge	S/R	100	50	4s	6s	Ct	St
Tests	23	38	2	954	139	26.50	45.04	1	7	120	4	17	0
ODIs	18	16	2	314	100*	22.42	60.50	1	0	24	4	3	0
Twenty20 Ints	0	0	–	–	–	–	–	–	–	–	–	–	–
First-class	140	219	22	7884	200*	40.02	–	15	47	–	–	113	0

Bowling	M	Balls	Runs	Wkts	BB	Avge	RpO	S/R	5i	10m
Tests	23	6	7	0	–	–	7.00	–	0	0
ODIs	18	18	33	0	–	–	11.00	–	0	0
Twenty20 Ints	0	0	–	–	–	–	–	–	–	–
First-class	140	162	126	1	1–6	126.00	4.66	162.00	0	0

FAWAD ALAM

Full name	**Fawad Alam**
Born	**October 8, 1985, Karachi, Sind**
Teams	**Karachi, Sind, National Bank**
Style	**Left-hand bat, slow left-arm orthodox spinner**
Test debut	**Pakistan v Sri Lanka at Colombo 2009**
ODI debut	**Pakistan v Sri Lanka at Abu Dhabi 2006-07**

THE PROFILE Critics scoffed when left-hander Fawad Alam, who had never opened before, went in first in his debut Test, in Colombo in July 2009, after Salman Butt was dropped. Fawad's pronounced shuffle across the crease seemed to open him up to Sri Lanka's swing bowlers, and he duly made an unconvincing 16. But in the second innings he silenced the doubters with a superb 168, working the ball well off his pads when the bowlers targeted that shuffle. The jury remains out on whether he really is an opener – but he certainly has a future as a Test batsman somewhere in the order. Fawad had long been seen as an international prospect: he made his first-class debut at 17, and was part of the side that won the Under-19 World Cup in Dhaka early in 2004. He made 1027 runs at 53.60 in his first full season (2005-06), and averaged around 50 over the following two years as well, just to show that was no fluke. He is also a handy slow left-armer. He made a low-key start in the one-day side, falling to the only ball he faced on his debut. But the selectors kept faith, and he played in the inaugural World Twenty20 championship in 2007 and most of Pakistan's ODIs at the start of 2008, although he did little beyond 63 not out against the minnows of Hong Kong. A triple-century in a tour match in Kenya was followed by a near-miss in a first-class game at home, then in June 2009 Fawad was part of the side that won the second World Twenty20 in England – and then came that surprising promotion in Sri Lanka.

THE FACTS Fawad Alam made 168 against Sri Lanka in Colombo in July 2009: he was the tenth Pakistani to score a century on Test debut, but the first to do so away from home ... He scored 296 not out for National Bank v Customs in Karachi in January 2009 ... For Pakistan's Academy against Kenya in a non-first-class tour match in Mombasa in September 2008 Fawad scored 302 not out and shared an unbroken stand of 612 with Raheel Majeed (318 not out) ... His father, Tariq Alam, had a long first-class career in Pakistan ...

THE FIGURES to 21.9.09   www.cricinfo.com

Batting & Fielding	M	Inns	NO	Runs	HS	Avge	S/R	100	50	4s	6s	Ct	St
Tests	2	4	0	216	168	54.00	60.50	1	0	19	1	1	0
ODIs	14	12	7	210	63*	42.00	73.68	0	1	13	1	4	0
Twenty20 Ints	13	7	5	64	23*	32.00	164.10	0	0	3	4	2	0
First-class	50	86	18	3848	296*	56.58	–	6	26	–	–	29	0

Bowling	M	Balls	Runs	Wkts	BB	Avge	RpO	S/R	5i	10m
Tests	2	0	–	–	–	–	–	–	–	–
ODIs	14	362	332	4	1–8	83.00	5.50	90.50	0	0
Twenty20 Ints	13	90	95	8	3–7	11.87	6.33	11.25	0	0
First-class	50	1484	718	22	4–27	32.63	2.90	67.45	0	0

CALLUM **FERGUSON**

AUSTRALIA

Full name	**Callum James Ferguson**
Born	**November 21, 1984, North Adelaide, South Australia**
Teams	**South Australia**
Style	**Right-hand bat, right-arm medium-pacer**
Test debut	**No Tests yet**
ODI debut	**Australia v New Zealand at Melbourne 2008-09**

THE PROFILE   After a few stutters, Callum Ferguson came of age in 2008-09 and ended the Australian summer as a regular international performer and the owner of a national contract. An easy-to-watch right-hander, more of an accumulator than a big hitter, he had suffered from giving away regular starts, but came back from a summer of club cricket in England in 2008 more determined to cash in. His 644 first-class runs in the season that followed included two hundreds (his first for nearly four years) and, despite being lightly built, he exhibited some power too, with 401 one-day runs at almost a run a ball and more explosiveness in the Twenty20 competition. It all earned him a call-up for the Chappell-Hadlee one-dayers against New Zealand in February 2009. He made a good impression, especially with a rapid 55 not out in the final rain-affected match, and carried on his good start in South Africa before kicking off the one-day series against England in September with 71 not out at The Oval and 55 at Lord's. All this was a welcome return to form for a player who had shone in his debut season of 2004-05, scoring 733 runs in the Pura Cup – including 93 in his second match and a maiden century in his fourth – while the rest of South Australia's strokemakers struggled. Over the next three seasons Ferguson found it hard to replicate that form, although he scored consistently without going on to a big score, before the retirements of Darren Lehmann and Matthew Elliott thrust more responsibility onto his shoulders in 2008-09 – and he showed he could handle it.

THE FACTS   Ferguson made 132 for South Australia v Queensland at Brisbane in November 2008 ... In January 2002 he scored 258 not out for South Australia Under-19s v Queensland ... Ferguson scored 93 (v Queensland) in his second first-class match in 2004-05, and 103 (v New South Wales) in his fourth, in 2004-05 ...

THE FIGURES *to 21.9.09*   www.cricinfo.com

Batting & Fielding	M	Inns	NO	Runs	HS	Avge	S/R	100	50	4s	6s	Ct	St
Tests	0	0	–	–	–	–	–	–	–	–	–	–	–
ODIs	20	19	8	570	71*	51.81	87.82	0	5	55	0	6	0
Twenty20 Ints	3	3	0	16	8	5.33	84.21	0	0	1	0	1	0
First-class	47	88	7	2842	132	35.08	56.42	4	19	–	–	21	0

Bowling	M	Balls	Runs	Wkts	BB	Avge	RpO	S/R	5i	10m
Tests	0	0	–	–	–	–	–	–	–	–
ODIs	20	0	–	–	–	–	–	–	–	–
Twenty20 Ints	3	0	–	–	–	–	–	–	–	–
First-class	47	42	38	0	–	–	5.42	–	0	0

DILHARA **FERNANDO**

Full name	**Congenige Randhi Dilhara Fernando**
Born	**July 19, 1979, Colombo**
Teams	**Sinhalese SC, Kandurata**
Style	**Right-hand bat, right-arm fast-medium bowler**
Test debut	**Sri Lanka v Pakistan at Colombo 2000**
ODI debut	**Sri Lanka v South Africa at Paarl 2000-01**

THE PROFILE When Dilhara Fernando burst onto the international scene, young and raw, he was seen as the long-term replacement for Chaminda Vaas as the cutting edge of Sri Lanka's attack. He has natural pace – six months after his debut he was clocked at 91.9mph in Durban – hits the pitch hard, and moves the ball off the seam. He rattled India at Galle in 2001, taking five wickets and sending Javagal Srinath to hospital. At first he paid for an inconsistent line and length, but worked hard with the former Test opening bowler Rumesh Ratnayake and became more reliable. He also learnt the art of reverse swing, and developed a well-disguised slower one. But injuries intervened. Fernando was quick during the 2003 World Cup, but bowled a lot of no-balls, a problem he later blamed on a spinal stress fracture. He returned after six months, only for another one to be detected in January 2004. He reclaimed his place in the national squad later that year, and has been there or thereabouts ever since, often going for a few in ODIs but always threatening wickets. Between injuries, he has been a Test regular too, although the no-ball problem resurfaced, and he was omitted after the first Test against Pakistan in March 2006 before returning later that year for the one-day series in England, which Sri Lanka swept 5–0, with Fernando grabbing three quick wickets in the first match at Lord's. He beat off the challenge of Nuwan Zoysa for a place in the 2007 World Cup, where he did well against England but managed only two other wickets – one in the final, when he brought down the curtain on Adam Gilchrist's epic 149.

THE FACTS Fernando averages 19.28 with the ball in Tests against Bangladesh – but 43.63 v India, even though his best figures of 5 for 42 came against them ... He took 6 for 27 against England in Colombo in September 2007: overall he averages 20.05 against England in ODIs, but 70.42 in 14 matches v South Africa ... Fernando's record includes one ODI for the Asia XI ...

THE FIGURES *to 21.9.09*   www.cricinfo.com

Batting & Fielding	M	Inns	NO	Runs	HS	Avge	S/R	100	50	4s	6s	Ct	St
Tests	33	40	13	198	36*	7.33	31.68	0	0	22	1	10	0
ODIs	133	53	30	231	20	10.04	62.60	0	0	19	2	25	0
Twenty20 Ints	13	5	2	24	21	8.00	120.00	0	0	4	0	2	0
First-class	93	97	28	505	42	7.31	–	0	0	–	–	37	0

Bowling	M	Balls	Runs	Wkts	BB	Avge	RpO	S/R	5i	10m
Tests	33	5126	3072	88	5–42	34.90	3.59	58.25	3	0
ODIs	133	5790	5014	167	6–27	30.02	5.19	34.67	1	0
Twenty20 Ints	13	276	337	15	3–19	22.46	7.32	18.40	0	0
First-class	93	12788	7601	263	6–29	28.90	3.56	48.62	6	0

ANDREW **FLINTOFF**

Full name	**Andrew Flintoff**
Born	**December 6, 1977, Preston, Lancashire**
Teams	**Lancashire, Chennai Super Kings**
Style	**Right-hand bat, right-arm fast bowler**
Test debut	**England v South Africa at Nottingham 1998**
ODI debut	**England v Pakistan at Sharjah 1998-99**

THE PROFILE In 2005, "Freddie" Flintoff confirmed himself as England's best allrounder since Ian Botham, reaping 402 runs and 24 wickets in the Ashes series. It propelled him to the superstar status his admirers had long believed was within his grasp. Big, northern and proud of it, he hammers the ball, then uses his colossal frame to reach 90mph – which, coupled with accuracy and reverse-swing, make him among the most intimidating bowlers around. Flintoff's precocious skills led to a Test debut at 20, but then he struggled with weight, motivation and back trouble. But he tonked a maiden Test ton in New Zealand early in 2002, then did well at home. A hernia ruled him out of the 2002-03 Ashes, but he returned as the most economical bowler at the 2003 World Cup, then thumped a therapeutic 95 in the remarkable Oval Test comeback against South Africa after a defiant Lord's century. In the Caribbean in 2004 he finally learned to slip the handbrake and become a genuine attacking option with the ball. Then, when Michael Vaughan was injured, he stepped in as captain, setting him up for the fall: Australia's revenge. Flintoff occasionally looked powerless during the Ashes whitewash, struggling for runs and wickets, and things got worse during the 2007 World Cup, when he was found drunk in charge of a pedalo at 3am. Ankle and knee injuries disrupted the next two years, and he limped through the 2009 Ashes, producing one memorable matchwinning spell at Lord's. After that he gave up Tests, promising to become the world's best limited-overs cricketer: he refused an England contract and went freelance to improve his chances. But they will depend on his recovery from yet another knee operation.

THE FACTS Flintoff won 47 Test caps before he played against Australia ... In 2005 he was the fourth cricketer to be voted BBC Sports Personality of the Year, following Jim Laker (1956), David Steele (1975) and Ian Botham (1981) ... He took 68 Test wickets in 2005, a record for an England bowler ... Flintoff averages 17.36 with the ball in ODIs against Sri Lanka, but 42.52 v Australia ... His record includes one Test and three ODIs for the World XI ...

THE FIGURES to 21.9.09   www.cricinfo.com

Batting & Fielding	M	Inns	NO	Runs	HS	Avge	S/R	100	50	4s	6s	Ct	St
Tests	79	130	9	3845	167	31.77	62.04	5	26	513	82	52	0
ODIs	141	122	16	3394	123	32.01	88.82	3	18	308	93	47	0
Twenty20 Ints	7	7	1	76	31	12.66	126.66	0	0	7	2	5	0
First-class	183	290	23	9027	167	33.80	–	15	53	–	–	185	0

Bowling	M	Balls	Runs	Wkts	BB	Avge	RpO	S/R	5i	10m
Tests	79	14951	7410	226	5–58	32.78	2.97	66.15	3	0
ODIs	141	5624	4121	169	5–19	24.38	4.39	33.27	2	0
Twenty20 Ints	7	150	161	5	2–23	32.20	6.44	30.00	0	0
First-class	183	22799	11059	350	5–24	31.59	2.91	65.14	4	0

DANIEL **FLYNN**

Full name **Daniel Raymond Flynn**
Born **April 16, 1985, Rotorua**
Teams **Northern Districts**
Style **Left-hand bat, occasional left-arm spinner**
Test debut **England v New Zealand at Lord's 2008**
ODI debut **New Zealand v England at Christchurch 2007-08**

THE PROFILE The early days of Daniel Flynn's international career will be remembered for him walking off Old Trafford in May 2008 with a mouthful of blood and two fewer teeth than he started with, after being hit by James Anderson. Such an injury could have severely dented the confidence (as well as the gums) of a young batsman, but Flynn is made of sterner stuff. He made his first-class debut for Northern Districts soon after the 2003-04 Under-19 World Cup, in which he captained New Zealand. A stocky, powerful left-hander, he struck his maiden century in December 2005, but two mixed seasons followed, and it wasn't until 2007-08 that he showed his true colours – particularly in one-dayers – and earned a call-up to the national Twenty20 squad. He didn't get many opportunities in his early games, but was named for the tour of England that followed. He made his Test debut at Lord's, playing a cool defensive knock of 29 not out from 118 balls in the second innings that led his captain Daniel Vettori to declare that "He's got the No. 6 spot basically for as long as he wants it". Flynn then suffered that sickening blow in the mouth in the next game. However, he was fit enough to play in the final Test at Trent Bridge, and generally looked a readymade replacement for the retired Stephen Fleming (an altogether different type of left-hander). In 2008-09 Flynn just missed a maiden Test century, falling for 95 against West Indies at Dunedin, then – after being moved up to No. 3 by new coach Andy Moles – made 67 against India at Hamilton. However, he lost his one-day place after a run of low scores.

THE FACTS Flynn made his maiden first-class hundred for Northern Districts v Otago at Gisborne in December 2005, then didn't make another one for almost two years ... In 2007–08 he hit 143 (from 117 balls) against Wellington and 149 (from 141 balls, with six sixes) against Canterbury in one-day games for ND ...

THE FIGURES *to 21.9.09*   www.cricinfo.com

Batting & Fielding	M	Inns	NO	Runs	HS	Avge	S/R	100	50	4s	6s	Ct	St
Tests	13	24	5	627	95	33.00	40.68	0	4	82	3	6	0
ODIs	16	13	2	167	35	15.18	57.19	0	0	14	1	4	0
Twenty20 Ints	4	4	0	37	23	9.25	115.62	0	0	1	2	2	0
First-class	45	78	10	2262	110	33.26	43.46	5	10	–	–	18	0

Bowling	M	Balls	Runs	Wkts	BB	Avge	RpO	S/R	5i	10m
Tests	13	0	–	–	–	–	–	–	–	–
ODIs	16	6	6	0	–	–	6.00	–	0	0
Twenty20 Ints	4	6	7	0	–	–	7.00	–	0	0
First-class	45	198	87	0	–	–	2.63	–	0	0

JAMES **FOSTER**

Full name	**James Savin Foster**
Born	**April 15, 1980, Whipps Cross, Leytonstone**
Teams	**Essex**
Style	**Right-hand bat, wicketkeeper**
Test debut	**England v India at Mohali 2001-02**
ODI debut	**England v Zimbabwe at Harare 2001-02**

THE PROFILE James Foster was earmarked early on as a possible England wicketkeeper: he was chosen for the A tour of the West Indies early in 2001 after only four first-class games. At that point he was still studying at Durham University, but once he graduated and committed full-time to Essex he was soon being touted as Alec Stewart's probable successor, and he got a chance at the end of 2001, when Stewart opted out of the winter tours. Foster started nervously, missing a huge skyer in Harare and keeping jumpily at Mohali, but gradually got more assured, and also batted tidily, without threatening to make the runs the selectors craved. Foster, who is tall for a keeper at 6ft, was expected to keep his Test place at home in 2002, but broke his arm in the Chelmsford nets and had to watch Stewart stroll back in. Still, Foster made the Ashes tour that winter, stepping in at Melbourne when Stewart injured his arm, but his batting was not perceived as strong enough, and when Stewart did finally retire the selectors tried Chris Read, Matt Prior and then Tim Ambrose. But Foster, who vies with Read as England's best pure keeper, has been steadily improving his batting – he collected his second county double-century during 2007 – and finally got a look-in in 2009, when he was called up for the World Twenty20. He snapped up a couple of lightning stumpings, but had little chance with the bat and was overlooked again later on in the summer when Prior returned for the one-day internationals.

THE FACTS Foster scored 212 for Essex v Nottinghamshire at Chelmsford in July 2007: his opposite number Chris Read made 240, the first time that opposing wicketkeepers had scored double-centuries in the same first-class match ... Foster hit five sixes off five balls from Durham's Scott Borthwick in a Pro40 League match for Essex at Chester-le-Street in September 2009 ... He took eight catches in the match (one short of the Essex record) against Nottinghamshire at Chelmsford in September 2003 ...

THE FIGURES to 21.9.09   www.cricinfo.com

Batting & Fielding	M	Inns	NO	Runs	HS	Avge	S/R	100	50	4s	6s	Ct	St
Tests	7	12	3	226	48	25.11	34.55	0	0	27	1	17	1
ODIs	11	6	3	41	13	13.66	57.74	0	0	0	0	13	7
Twenty20 Ints	5	5	2	37	14*	12.33	115.62	0	0	0	1	3	3
First-class	156	232	29	7314	212	36.02	–	13	37	–	–	435	38

Bowling	M	Balls	Runs	Wkts	BB	Avge	RpO	S/R	5i	10m
Tests	7	0	–	–	–	–	–	–	–	–
ODIs	11	0	–	–	–	–	–	–	–	–
Twenty20 Ints	5	0	–	–	–	–	–	–	–	–
First-class	156	84	128	1	1-122	128.00	9.14	84.00	0	0

JAMES **FRANKLIN**

Full name	**James Edward Charles Franklin**
Born	**November 7, 1980, Wellington**
Teams	**Wellington, Gloucestershire**
Style	**Left-hand bat, left-arm fast-medium bowler**
Test debut	**New Zealand v Pakistan at Auckland 2000-01**
ODI debut	**New Zealand v Zimbabwe at Taupo 2000-01**

THE PROFILE A left-armer who can swing the ball, James Franklin first represented New Zealand in 2000-01, when barely out of his teens, but made little impact. Back in domestic cricket he worked on his batting, which he had neglected, and filled out generally. He returned to the side in England in 2004. He was playing club cricket in Lancashire, but was called up when Shane Bond suffered a back injury. Franklin played in the third Test at Trent Bridge, and although New Zealand lost he claimed six wickets, five of them Test century-makers. He stayed on for the one-dayers, and took 5 for 42 at Chester-le-Street as England were skittled for 101. Then, in Bangladesh, he grabbed a Test hat-trick at Dhaka. Back home he took 6 for 119 against Australia early in 2005, then bowled superbly – finding reverse-swing – against Sri Lanka, although his figures didn't reflect his excellence. In April 2006 Franklin did his allrounder claims no harm with an unbeaten 122 – and a stand of 256 with Stephen Fleming – against South Africa at Cape Town. He bowled capably during the 2007 World Cup, although he was occasionally expensive – as when he took 3 for 74 in eight overs as Australia cut loose in Grenada. A stubborn knee injury, which eventually required surgery, kept him out for most of 2007-08 and the England tour that followed, but he was back for the Tests against India early in 2009, doing more with bat than ball (1 for 290 in 89 overs). Rather surprisingly, since he hadn't played an ODI since the 2007 World Cup, he did take part in the World Twenty20 in England in 2009, which was bookended by a successful season with Gloucestershire.

THE FACTS Franklin was the fourth man to take a hat-trick and score a century in Tests ... The only other New Zealander to take a Test hat-trick was Peter Petherick in 1976-77 ... Franklin made 219 for Wellington at Auckland in November 2008: in the next match (v Northern Districts) he scored 160 ... He made 208 for Wellington v Auckland in 2005-06: in the previous match (v Central Districts) he had taken a career-best 7 for 30 ...

THE FIGURES *to 21.9.09*   www.cricinfo.com

Batting & Fielding	M	Inns	NO	Runs	HS	Avge	S/R	100	50	4s	6s	Ct	St
Tests	26	36	6	644	122*	21.46	38.53	1	2	68	4	11	0
ODIs	65	44	15	508	45*	17.51	74.81	0	0	35	6	19	0
Twenty20 Ints	9	8	3	73	20	14.60	108.95	0	0	3	4	4	0
First-class	112	166	24	4699	219	33.09	–	8	21	–	–	39	0

Bowling	M	Balls	Runs	Wkts	BB	Avge	RpO	S/R	5i	10m
Tests	26	4399	2612	80	6–119	32.65	3.56	54.98	3	0
ODIs	65	2804	2392	64	5–42	37.37	5.11	43.81	1	0
Twenty20 Ints	9	102	117	3	3–23	39.00	6.88	34.00	0	0
First-class	112	18032	9461	353	7–30	26.80	3.14	51.08	11	1

GAUTAM **GAMBHIR**

Full name	**Gautam Gambhir**
Born	**October 14, 1981, Delhi**
Teams	**Delhi, Delhi Daredevils**
Style	**Left-hand bat, occasional legspinner**
Test debut	**India v Australia at Mumbai 2004-05**
ODI debut	**India v Bangladesh at Dhaka 2002-03**

THE PROFILE Gautam Gambhir's attacking left-handed strokeplay has set tongues wagging ever since he was a schoolboy. Compact footwork and high bat-speed often meant defence was replaced by the aerial route over point. He looked certain to make his Test debut early in 2002, after pasting successive double-centuries (one of them against the touring Zimbabweans), but surprisingly missed out. Gambhir soldiered on, doing well in the Caribbean with India A early in 2003, and joined the one-day squad when several seniors took a rest after that year's World Cup. He finally made the Test side late the following year, hitting 96 against South Africa in his second match and 139 against Bangladesh in his fifth. Leaner times followed, punctuated by cheap runs in Zimbabwe, and although he celebrated his one-day return after 30 months on the sidelines with 103 against Sri Lanka in April 2005, he struggled for big scores and soon found himself out again. After the disasters of the 2007 World Cup Gambhir was given another chance, and immediately looked the part. He made two one-day centuries in Australia early in 2008, and carried his good form into the inaugural IPL season. The runs kept coming: he crashed 67, 104 and a superb 206 in successive innings as Australia were beaten in October 2008 then – after a one-match ban for elbowing Shane Watson while running – helped ensure a series victory over England with 179 and 97 in the drawn second Test at Mohali in December. In ODIs he crashed 150 against Sri Lanka in Colombo in February 2009. By September he was top of the ICC's ranking lists for Test batsmen (Sachin Tendulkar – 15th – was the next-highest Indian).

THE FACTS Gambhir made 206 against Australia at Delhi in October 2008: VVS Laxman also scored a double-century, the first time Australia had ever conceded two in the same innings ... Gambhir made 214 (for Delhi v Railways) and 218 (for the Board President's XI v Zimbabwe) in successive innings early in 2002 ... Gambhir was the leading Indian runscorer of the inaugural IPL season in 2008, with 534 at a strike rate of 140.89 ...

THE FIGURES to 21.9.09   www.cricinfo.com

Batting & Fielding	M	Inns	NO	Runs	HS	Avge	S/R	100	50	4s	6s	Ct	St
Tests	25	45	3	2271	206	54.07	52.18	6	10	287	6	23	0
ODIs	78	76	7	2594	150	37.59	83.92	6	15	293	12	24	0
Twenty20 Ints	17	16	0	476	75	29.75	120.81	0	5	54	8	4	0
First-class	107	182	18	9179	233*	55.96	–	29	38	–	–	70	0

Bowling	M	Balls	Runs	Wkts	BB	Avge	RpO	S/R	5i	10m
Tests	25	0	–	–	–	–	–	–	–	–
ODIs	78	6	13	0	–	–	13.00	–	0	0
Twenty20 Ints	17	0	–	–	–	–	–	–	–	–
First-class	107	385	277	7	3–12	39.57	4.31	55.00	0	0

CHRIS **GAYLE**

Full name	**Christopher Henry Gayle**
Born	**September 21, 1979, Kingston, Jamaica**
Teams	**Jamaica, Kolkata Knight Riders, Western Australia**
Style	**Right-hand bat, offspinner**
Test debut	**West Indies v Zimbabwe at Port-of-Spain 1999-2000**
ODI debut	**West Indies v India at Toronto 1999-2000**

THE PROFILE An attacking left-hander, Chris Gayle earned himself a black mark on his first senior tour when the new boys were felt to be insufficiently respectful of their elders. But a lack of respect, for opposition bowlers at least, has served him well since then. Tall and imposing, he loves to carve through the covers off either foot (without moving either of them much), and has the ability to take any opening bowler apart. In a lean era for West Indian cricket in general – and fast bowling in particular – Gayle's pugnacious approach has become an attacking weapon in its own right, in Tests as well as one-dayers. His 79-ball century at Cape Town in January 2004, after South Africa had made 532, was typical of his approach. He came unstuck against England shortly afterwards, when that lack of positive footwork was exposed – but men with little footwork often baffle experts, and in May 2005 he punched 317 against South Africa in Antigua. Gayle also bowls brisk non-turning offspin, which make him a genuine one-day allrounder. He took over the one-day captaincy after a miserable Test series in England in 2007, and electrified the side with unexpected flair. Later that year he inspired a stunning Test victory in South Africa, although the series was eventually lost. But after a chastening time in England in 2009 he suggested he wouldn't be around for much longer in Test cricket, and two months later he and other senior players boycotted the home series against Bangladesh as a divisive contracts dispute rumbled on. Gayle, who has lucrative Twenty20 contracts to play in Australia and India, would be a major loss if he turns his back on West Indian cricket.

THE FACTS Gayle's 317 against South Africa in Antigua in May 2005 has been exceeded for West Indies only by Brian Lara (twice) and Garry Sobers ... Gayle hit the first century in Twenty20 internationals, 117 v South Africa at Johannesburg in September 2007 ... He made 208 for Jamaica v West Indies B in February 2001, sharing an unbroken opening stand of 425 with Leon Garrick ... His record includes three ODIs for the World XI ...

THE FIGURES *to 21.9.09*   www.cricinfo.com

Batting & Fielding	M	Inns	NO	Runs	HS	Avge	S/R	100	50	4s	6s	Ct	St
Tests	82	144	5	5502	317	39.58	57.46	10	31	837	57	79	0
ODIs	205	200	14	7429	153*	39.94	83.07	19	39	871	151	90	0
Twenty20 Ints	12	12	1	454	117	41.27	148.36	1	4	44	24	4	0
First-class	156	277	20	11256	317	43.79	–	26	57	–	–	137	0

Bowling	M	Balls	Runs	Wkts	BB	Avge	RpO	S/R	5i	10m
Tests	82	6707	2929	71	5–34	41.25	2.62	94.46	2	0
ODIs	205	6497	5139	151	5–46	34.03	4.74	43.02	1	0
Twenty20 Ints	12	171	189	7	2–16	27.00	6.63	24.42	0	0
First-class	156	11983	4949	128	5–34	38.66	2.47	93.61	2	0

HERSCHELLE **GIBBS**

Full name	**Herschelle Herman Gibbs**
Born	**February 23, 1974, Green Point, Cape Town**
Teams	**Cape Cobras, Glamorgan, Deccan Chargers**
Style	**Right-hand bat, occasional legspinner**
Test debut	**South Africa v India at Calcutta 1996-97**
ODI debut	**South Africa v Kenya at Nairobi 1996-97**

THE PROFILE Herschelle Gibbs was summoned from the classroom at 16 to make his first-class debut in 1990: his feet moved beautifully at the crease, but struggled to find the ground in real life. Admitting that a Test debut in front of 70,000 at Eden Gardens wasn't as nerve-wracking as his final exams, as well as the fact that he reads little other than magazines and comics, contributed to a reputation for simplicity: his passion for one-liners and verbal jousting hampered his advancement, and his brush with career death in the match-fixing scandal in 2000 added to the impression of one who had failed to grasp the magnitude of his impact on South Africa's youth. But Gibbs can be a warm and generous person, and at the crease no shot is beyond him, while opening did not temper his desire for explosive entertainment. The speed of his hands is hypnotic, frequently allowing him to hook off the front foot and keep out surprise lifters. His trademark is the lofted extra-cover drive, hit inside-out with the certainty of a square cut. He is stunning at backward point, even in his mid-thirties. Gibbs had two double-centuries among his 14 Test tons, and 21 one-day hundreds too – the best of them in March 2006, when his 111-ball 175 powered South Africa past Australia's 434 with a ball to spare in arguably the greatest one-day cracker of them all. He lost his Test place soon after the 2007 World Cup, although he remains a force in the shorter formats.

THE FACTS Gibbs and Graeme Smith are the only opening pair to share three stands of 300 or more in Tests ... He hit six sixes in an over from Holland's Daan van Bunge during the 2007 World Cup, winning a million dollars for charity ... He averages 56.42 in Tests against New Zealand, but only 23.30 v Sri Lanka ... He was bowled in 33 (23%) of his Test innings ...

THE FIGURES *to 21.9.09*   www.cricinfo.com

Batting & Fielding	M	Inns	NO	Runs	HS	Avge	S/R	100	50	4s	6s	Ct	St
Tests	90	154	7	6167	228	41.95	50.26	14	26	887	47	94	0
ODIs	244	237	16	8038	175	36.37	83.32	21	37	923	126	106	0
Twenty20 Ints	20	20	1	359	90*	18.89	129.60	0	3	43	10	3	0
First-class	193	331	13	13425	228	42.21	–	31	60	–	–	176	0

Bowling	M	Balls	Runs	Wkts	BB	Avge	RpO	S/R	5i	10m
Tests	90	6	4	0	–	–	4.00	–	0	0
ODIs	244	0	–	–	–	–	–	–	–	–
Twenty20 Ints	20	0	–	–	–	–	–	–	–	–
First-class	193	138	78	3	2–14	26.00	3.39	46.00	0	0

MARTIN **GUPTILL**

NEW ZEALAND

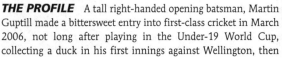

Full name	**Martin James Guptill**
Born	**September 30, 1986, Auckland**
Teams	**Auckland**
Style	**Right-hand bat, occasional offspinner**
Test debut	**New Zealand v India at Hamilton 2008-09**
ODI debut	**New Zealand v West Indies at Auckland 2008-09**

THE PROFILE A tall right-handed opening batsman, Martin Guptill made a bittersweet entry into first-class cricket in March 2006, not long after playing in the Under-19 World Cup, collecting a duck in his first innings against Wellington, then making 99 in the second before tickling a catch behind off his future New Zealand teammate Jesse Ryder. By 2007-08 Guptill was tickling the selectors, too: he topped the State Shield run-lists that season with 596 as Auckland reached the final, which they lost to Otago. Guptill carried his purple patch into an Emerging Players tournament in Australia, finishing as NZ's highest run-scorer there too with 280. His rise continued with an A-team tour of India – Guptill (80) and Aaron Redmond (105) shared an opening stand of 190 in the second representative match at Chennai – and, after a maiden first-class century followed at home, he received the national call for the one-day series against the touring West Indians early in 2009. He lit up his debut in familiar surroundings in Auckland, reaching three figures with a huge six off Chris Gayle and finishing with a superb unbeaten 122 – the second-highest score by anyone in their first ODI, and only the fifth debut century. He was dropped three times before he reached 30, but his running (not one of New Zealand's strengths) was notable. Indeed, Guptill's general speed – between wickets or in the outfield, from a high-stepping run – is particularly remarkable as he has only two toes on his left foot after a forklift accident when he was 13.

THE FACTS Guptill was only the fifth batsman to score a century on ODI debut, following Dennis Amiss, Desmond Haynes, Andy Flower and Saleem Elahi ... Guptill's only first-class century to date was 148 for Auckland against Otago in December 2008 ... On his first-class debut, against Wellington in Auckland in March 2006, Guptill made 0 and 99 ...

THE FIGURES *to 21.9.09*   www.cricinfo.com

Batting & Fielding	M	Inns	NO	Runs	HS	Avge	S/R	100	50	4s	6s	Ct	St
Tests	5	9	0	241	49	26.77	58.21	0	0	34	3	1	0
ODIs	14	13	3	473	122*	47.30	83.12	1	3	39	10	5	0
Twenty20 Ints	10	9	1	214	45*	26.75	123.69	0	0	15	10	3	0
First-class	26	44	1	1210	148	28.13	42.39	1	6	174	11	12	0

Bowling	M	Balls	Runs	Wkts	BB	Avge	RpO	S/R	5i	10m
Tests	5	0	–	–	–	–	–	–	–	–
ODIs	14	12	12	0	–	–	6.00	–	0	0
Twenty20 Ints	10	0	–	–	–	–	–	–	–	–
First-class	26	102	63	1	1–8	63.00	3.70	102.00	0	0

BRAD **HADDIN**

Full name **Bradley James Haddin**
Born **October 23, 1977, Cowra, New South Wales**
Teams **New South Wales**
Style **Right-hand bat, wicketkeeper**
Test debut **Australia v West Indies at Kingston 2007-08**
ODI debut **Australia v Zimbabwe at Hobart 2000-01**

THE PROFILE   For years Brad Haddin held the most nerve-fraying position in Australian cricket – wicketkeeper-in-waiting, entrusted with warming the seat whenever Adam Gilchrist needed a rest. Now Haddin is up there to be shot at himself. He became Australia's 400th Test cricketer in the West Indies early in 2008, and did well enough, playing through the series despite breaking a finger in the first Test, which might explain his comparative lack of runs to start with. But he cemented his place with a blazing – almost Gilchristian – 169 against New Zealand at Adelaide in November, pulling and cutting strongly, and added another century in the first Ashes Test in 2009, then made a valiant 80 in defeat at Lord's. After that, though, his fortunes waned: he broke another finger just before the start of the third Test, returned for the fourth but made little impression with the bat, then had to surrender the gloves to Tim Paine for the one-dayers that followed. He returned home for surgery, and missed the Champions Trophy in South Africa too. Haddin has long been a consistent scorer at domestic level, making 916 runs at 57.25 in 2004-05, leading NSW to a one-wicket Pura Cup final victory over Queensland. He passed 600 runs in each of the next two seasons, and although his output dipped to 489 in 2007-08, that still included three centuries. A former Australia Under-19 captain who grew up in Gundagai, Haddin began his senior domestic career in 1997-98 with the Australian Capital Territory in their debut season in Australia's one-day competition.

THE FACTS   Haddin took up a novel batting position behind the stumps when facing a Shoaib Akhtar "free ball" (after a no-ball) early in 2005: he reasoned that he had more time to sight the ball, and if it hit the stumps it would confuse the fielders (it did hit the stumps, and he managed a bye) ... Haddin was the unwitting "villain" of the 2005 Ashes Test at Edgbaston: he rolled a ball near Glenn McGrath, who stepped on it, badly sprained his ankle, and missed the match, which England eventually won by just two runs – in 2009 Haddin himself missed the Edgbaston Test when he broke a finger minutes before the start ...

THE FIGURES to 21.9.09   www.cricinfo.com

Batting & Fielding	M	Inns	NO	Runs	HS	Avge	S/R	100	50	4s	6s	Ct	St
Tests	19	32	2	1179	169	39.30	56.30	2	3	139	17	70	1
ODIs	53	49	3	1490	109	32.39	83.10	1	9	127	37	59	5
Twenty20 Ints	10	9	3	111	24	18.50	98.23	0	0	6	3	4	0
First-class	112	185	19	6767	169	40.76	–	12	35	–	–	342	26

Bowling	M	Balls	Runs	Wkts	BB	Avge	RpO	S/R	5i	10m
Tests	19	0	–	–	–	–	–	–	–	–
ODIs	53	0	–	–	–	–	–	–	–	–
Twenty20 Ints	10	0	–	–	–	–	–	–	–	–
First-class	112	0	–	–	–	–	–	–	–	–

HARBHAJAN SINGH

Full name **Harbhajan Singh**
Born **July 3, 1980, Jullundur, Punjab**
Teams **Punjab, Surrey, Mumbai Indians**
Style **Right-hand bat, offspinner**
Test debut **India v Australia at Bangalore 1997-98**
ODI debut **India v New Zealand at Sharjah 1997-98**

THE PROFILE Harbhajan Singh represents the spirit of the new Indian cricketer. His arrogance and cockiness translate into self-belief and passion on the field, and he has the talent to match. An offspinner with a windmilling, whiplash action, remodelled after he was suspected of throwing, he exercises great command over the ball, has the ability to vary his length and pace, and bowls a deadly *doosra* too. His main wicket-taking ball, however, is the one that climbs wickedly from a good length. In March 2001 it proved too much for the previously all-conquering Australians, as Harbhajan collected 32 wickets in three Tests while none of his team-mates managed more than three. He has since been bothered by injury, while in Pakistan early in 2006 he went for 0 for 355 in two Tests before bouncing back with five-fors in St Kitts and Jamaica (5 for 13 in only 4.3 overs). He still sailed past 300 Test wickets before he turned 30. Harbhajan's rivalry with the Aussies (against whom he has taken 79 wickets at 28 in 14 Tests) boiled over in Sydney in January 2008 when he was charged with racially abusing Andrew Symonds. He was initially given a three-Test ban before the charge was reduced, on appeal, to abuse and insult not amounting to racism. Then in April Harbhajan slapped his Indian team-mate Sreesanth without any provocation after an IPL game, which cost him an 11-match ban. When he can control his temper – as in New Zealand early in 2009, when he took 16 wickets in the three Tests – Harbhajan remains a world-beater.

THE FACTS Harbhajan's match figures of 15 for 217 against Australia at Chennai in 2000–01 have been bettered for India only by Narendra Hirwani (16 for 136 in 1987–88, also at Chennai) ... Harbhajan took 32 wickets at 17.03 in that three-match series: his haul at Kolkata included India's first-ever Test hat-trick, when he dismissed Ricky Ponting, Adam Gilchrist and Shane Warne ... He has taken 45 wickets at 21.93 in Tests against West Indies, but 25 at 52.04 against Pakistan ... His record includes two ODIs for the Asia XI ...

THE FIGURES to 21.9.09   www.cricinfo.com

Batting & Fielding	M	Inns	NO	Runs	HS	Avge	S/R	100	50	4s	6s	Ct	St
Tests	77	108	20	1497	66	17.01	65.00	0	7	203	20	38	0
ODIs	192	100	27	944	46	12.93	80.27	0	0	75	23	55	0
Twenty20 Ints	17	6	1	57	21	11.40	105.55	0	0	7	1	5	0
First-class	141	189	37	2905	84	19.11	–	0	11	–	–	71	0

Bowling	M	Balls	Runs	Wkts	BB	Avge	RpO	S/R	5i	10m
Tests	77	21471	10040	330	8–84	30.42	2.80	65.06	23	5
ODIs	192	9977	7076	216	5–31	32.75	4.25	46.18	3	0
Twenty20 Ints	17	360	393	16	3–30	24.56	6.55	22.50	0	0
First-class	141	35410	16561	607	8–84	27.28	2.80	58.33	37	7

STEVE **HARMISON**

Full name	**Stephen James Harmison**
Born	**October 23, 1978, Ashington, Northumberland**
Teams	**Durham**
Style	**Right-hand bat, right-arm fast bowler**
Test debut	**England v India at Nottingham 2002**
ODI debut	**England v Sri Lanka at Brisbane 2002-03**

THE PROFILE   With his lofty, loose-limbed action and a painful knack of jamming fingers against bat-handles, Steve Harmison had long been likened, tongue-in-cheek, to Curtly Ambrose, when suddenly he loped in and produced a spell Ambrose himself could hardly have bettered. West Indies were humbled for 47 at Kingston in March 2004, Harmison taking a remarkable 7 for 12. He was initially held back by niggling injuries (including somehow dislocating his shoulder after catching his hand in his trouser pocket while bowling) and a tendency to homesickness, and mixed magical spells with times when the radar went haywire. But in the Caribbean he seemed finally to come of age. A dip followed in South Africa, but after a cathartic five-for against Bangladesh at home in Durham, he tore into Australia at Lord's on the first morning of the 2005 Ashes series. He couldn't secure victory then, but popped up to seal the two-run thriller at Edgbaston. A year later he demolished Pakistan with 6 for 19, but the much-hyped 2006-07 Ashes rematch was the pits, kicked off by Harmison's mega-wide with the first ball of the series. He often looked fed up, retired briefly from ODIs, then picked up a hernia during a hit-and-miss series against West Indies. He lost his Test place after a lacklustre performance in New Zealand early in 2008, but plenty of bowling for Durham relocated the magic, and he returned for the Oval Test against South Africa. Still, though, doubts remained about his commitment, and he was kept on the sidelines until towards the end of the 2009 Ashes. After that he lost his central contract despite professing a desire to be part of England's future.

THE FACTS   Harmison's 7 for 12 in March 2004, as West Indies were shot out for 47, are the best figures in Tests at Kingston ... Harmison took 67 Test wickets in 2004, a record for an England bowler at the time (Andrew Flintoff beat it by one in 2005) ... His brother Ben also plays for Durham: they were born in Ashington, the same Northumberland village as football's Charlton brothers ... His record includes one Test for the World XI ...

THE FIGURES to 21.9.09   www.cricinfo.com

Batting & Fielding	M	Inns	NO	Runs	HS	Avge	S/R	100	50	4s	6s	Ct	St
Tests	63	86	23	743	49*	11.79	57.19	0	0	97	10	7	0
ODIs	58	25	14	91	18*	8.27	64.53	0	0	3	0	10	0
Twenty20 Ints	2	0	–	–	–	–	–	–	–	–	–	1	0
First-class	188	246	68	1776	49*	9.97	–	0	0	–	–	27	0

Bowling	M	Balls	Runs	Wkts	BB	Avge	RpO	S/R	5i	10m
Tests	63	13375	7192	226	7–12	31.82	3.22	59.18	8	1
ODIs	58	2899	2481	76	5–33	32.64	5.13	38.14	1	0
Twenty20 Ints	2	39	42	1	1–13	42.00	6.46	39.00	0	0
First-class	188	36352	18985	678	7–12	28.00	3.13	53.61	26	1

PAUL **HARRIS**

SOUTH AFRICA

Full name	**Paul Lee Harris**
Born	**Nov 2, 1978, Salisbury (now Harare), Zimbabwe**
Teams	**Titans**
Style	**Right-hand bat, slow left-arm orthodox spinner**
Test debut	**South Africa v India at Cape Town 2006-07**
ODI debut	**South Africa v Bangladesh at Chittagong 2007-08**

THE PROFILE   Slow left-armer Paul Harris is the latest man tasked with curing South African cricket's chief ailment – their continued failure to develop matchwinning spinners for the national team. Tall and not unlike the former England bowler Phil Tufnell in appearance and style, Harris was called up for the 2006-07 series against India. He made his debut in the New Year Test at Cape Town, and took four wickets in the first innings, including Sachin Tendulkar and Virender Sehwag. He added the scalp of Rahul Dravid in the second innings: his nagging over-the-wicket line kept the Indians quiet, and helped his side reclaim the initiative. Until then the selectors had ignored Harris, even though he led the 2005-06 SuperSport Series wicket-takers with 49, and it seemed possible that he might be lost to South African cricket altogether after a successful stint for Warwickshire in 2006 as a Kolpak player. But then Nicky Boje retired, finally disenchanted with his country's treatment of spinners, and the call went out to Harris – a departure from South Africa's usual policy of choosing slow bowlers who can also contribute in the field and with the bat (although he can be a useful blocker). Harris was born in Zimbabwe but grew up in Cape Town, where his rise was originally blocked by Paul Adams and Claude Henderson. More of a roller than a big spinner, he is accurate and can get surprising bounce, from an unprepossessing approach, and he silenced some of his critics by taking nine wickets in the victory over Australia at Cape Town in March 2009.

THE FACTS   Harris took 7 for 94 (12 for 180 in the match) for Titans v Eagles at Benoni in 2008-09 ... When he took 6 for 127 against Australia at Cape Town in March 2009 Harris became the first South African spinner to take a five-for in a home Test since off-spinner Harry Bromfield, also at Newlands, against England in 1964-65 ... For Warwickshire v Durham at Chester-le-Street in July 2007 Harris reached his maiden fifty in 34 balls ...

THE FIGURES *to 21.9.09*   www.cricinfo.com

Batting & Fielding	M	Inns	NO	Runs	HS	Avge	S/R	100	50	4s	6s	Ct	St
Tests	24	33	4	304	46	10.48	31.50	0	0	30	1	12	0
ODIs	3	0	–	–	–	–	–	–	–	–	–	2	0
Twenty20 Ints	0	0	–	–	–	–	–	–	–	–	–	–	–
First-class	88	107	15	1306	55	14.19	–	0	3	–	–	35	0

Bowling	M	Balls	Runs	Wkts	BB	Avge	RpO	S/R	5i	10m
Tests	24	5080	2315	71	6–127	32.60	2.73	71.54	2	0
ODIs	3	180	83	3	2–30	27.66	2.76	60.00	0	0
Twenty20 Ints	0	0	–	–	–	–	–	–	–	–
First-class	88	19455	8861	294	7–94	30.13	2.73	66.17	15	1

NATHAN **HAURITZ**

Full name	**Nathan Michael Hauritz**
Born	**October 18, 1981, Wondai, Queensland**
Teams	**New South Wales**
Style	**Right-hand bat, offspinner**
Test debut	**Australia v India at Mumbai 2004-05**
ODI debut	**Australia v South Africa at Johannesburg 2001-02**

THE PROFILE   Nathan Hauritz, a former Australian Under-19 captain, leapfrogged several other spinners to finish the 2008-09 season as the only specialist slow bowler with a national contract. It was a stunning turnaround for a tidy, flighty offspinner who had been largely ignored since his first Test in November 2004. Having watched Beau Casson, Jason Krejza, Cameron White and Bryce McGain take turns following Stuart MacGill's retirement early in 2008, Hauritz was suddenly picked for the second Test against New Zealand at Adelaide in November despite being left out by New South Wales the previous week. He took nine wickets in three home Tests, and also played his first ODI for nearly six years. In South Africa early in 2009 he missed the Tests but played throughout the one-dayers after taking four wickets in the first one, at Durban, and was duly selected for the Ashes tour. Despite being written off in the English media, Hauritz did well enough in the three Tests he played, taking ten wickets at 32, which compared favourably with Graeme Swann's 14 at 40 in five matches for England. Hauritz also kept it quiet – and made regular breakthroughs – in the subsequent one-day series. Before this, Hauritz's five wickets on his surprise Test debut (including Sachin Tendulkar and VVS Laxman) in November 2004 became a distant memory when he struggled back home. He was dropped by Queensland before the end of that season, and moved to NSW after another disappointing summer. He still did little in first-class cricket – the four seasons after his return from India produced only ten wickets – although he was a one-day fixture. He finally returned to first-class favour in 2008-09, before his international rebirth.

THE FACTS   Hauritz has never taken five wickets in an innings: his best first-class figures of 4 for 86 came for New South Wales v Tasmania at Newcastle early in 2009 ... He took 4 for 29 in an ODI for Australia v South Africa at Durban in April 2009 ... Hauritz took a wicket (Anil Kumble) with his third ball in Test cricket, at Mumbai in November 2004 ... He scored 94 for Queensland v Western Australia at Perth in January 2004 ...

THE FIGURES to 21.9.09   www.cricinfo.com

Batting & Fielding	M	Inns	NO	Runs	HS	Avge	S/R	100	50	4s	6s	Ct	St
Tests	7	9	1	117	41	14.62	53.42	0	0	16	0	1	0
ODIs	27	15	8	141	24*	20.14	87.03	0	0	7	4	11	0
Twenty20 Ints	3	2	0	6	4	3.00	60.00	0	0	1	0	1	0
First-class	50	64	14	800	94	16.00	–	0	2	–	–	26	0

Bowling	M	Balls	Runs	Wkts	BB	Avge	RpO	S/R	5i	10m
Tests	7	1628	773	24	3–16	32.20	2.84	67.83	0	0
ODIs	27	1291	988	35	4–29	28.22	4.59	36.88	0	0
Twenty20 Ints	3	44	47	2	1–20	23.50	6.40	22.00	0	0
First-class	50	9265	4587	100	4–86	45.87	2.97	92.65	0	0

RANGANA **HERATH**

Full name	**Herath Mudiyanselage Rangana Keerthi Bandara Herath**
Born	**March 19, 1978, Kurunegala**
Teams	**Moors, Wayamba, Surrey**
Style	**Left-hand bat, left-arm orthodox spinner**
Test debut	**Sri Lanka v Australia at Galle 1999-2000**
ODI debut	**Zimbabwe v Sri Lanka at Harare 2003-04**

THE PROFILE   Slow left-armer Rangana Herath first came to international prominence late in 1999, when his so-called mystery ball – *Wisden* called it "a wonderful delivery, bowled out of the front of his hand, which turned back into right-handers" – befuddled the touring Australians. He took four wickets on Test debut at Galle, including Steve Waugh and Ricky Ponting, but after just two more caps he was unceremoniously dumped as Sri Lanka tried out several other spinners as foils for the peerless Muttiah Muralitharan. Herath's unprepossessing body shape – he's rather short with a hint of excess padding around the midriff – may have counted against him, but he continued to be a regular wicket-taker in domestic cricket. He was back in 2004, taking 17 wickets in four Tests, including seven in a rare Murali-less Sri Lankan victory, over Pakistan at Faisalabad, flighting the ball well and making it grip and turn. However, after five more caps scattered through 2005 he was left out again, seemingly for good. But the wickets still kept coming at home: 45 in 2006-07 and 31 the following season, all at an average under 20, and he eventually won a recall in 2008, although he did little at first and might have returned to anonymity but for a knee injury which forced Murali out of the home series against Pakistan in July 2009. Herath partnered Ajantha Mendis, and did so well – five wickets in each of the three Tests – that when Murali returned against New Zealand it was Mendis who made way, and Herath took eight wickets to Murali's six in the series-clinching victory in Colombo in August. After that Herath hurried off to England for a brief stint with Surrey.

THE FACTS   Herath took 8 for 43 (11 for 72 in the match) for Moors v Police in Colombo in 2002–03 ... In January 2002 he took 8 for 47 (and caught one of the others) for Moors v Galle ... Herath took 72 wickets at 13.59 in Sri Lanka in 2000–01 ... His highest four scores in first-class cricket are 71 not out, 71 not out, 71 and 70 not out ...

THE FIGURES *to 21.9.09*   www.cricinfo.com

Batting & Fielding	M	Inns	NO	Runs	HS	Avge	S/R	100	50	4s	6s	Ct	St
Tests	18	23	4	179	33*	9.42	35.51	0	0	21	0	4	0
ODIs	6	1	1	0	0*	–	0.00	0	0	0	0	3	0
Twenty20 Ints	0	0	–	–	–	–	–	–	–	–	–	–	–
First-class	170	241	56	3026	71*	16.35	–	0	10	–	–	79	0

Bowling	M	Balls	Runs	Wkts	BB	Avge	RpO	S/R	5i	10m
Tests	18	4222	2031	59	5–99	34.42	2.88	71.55	3	0
ODIs	6	234	149	5	3–28	29.80	3.82	46.80	0	0
Twenty20 Ints	0	0	–	–	–	–	–	–	–	–
First-class	170	32827	14647	613	8–43	23.89	2.67	53.55	34	5

BEN **HILFENHAUS**

Full name	**Benjamin William Hilfenhaus**
Born	**March 15, 1983, Ulverstone, Tasmania**
Teams	**Tasmania**
Style	**Right-hand bat, right-arm fast-medium bowler**
Test debut	**Australia v South Africa at Johannesburg 2008-09**
ODI debut	**Australia v New Zealand at Hobart 2006-07**

THE PROFILE A few years ago Ben Hilfenhaus – Ricky Ponting's second cousin – was working on a building site, but now he can safely lay down his trowel after a series of dramatic performances for Tasmania catapulted him to a national contract. "Hilfy" established himself quickly in 2005-06 – Man of the Match against Victoria in only his second game, ten wickets against NSW, then called up for Australia A after 39 wickets at 30.82 in his first season. "It has been a fast ride," he admitted after picking up the prestigious Bradman Young Cricketer of the Year prize in February 2007. A month earlier he played a Twenty20 international and then his first ODI, on his home ground at Hobart, trapping Brendon McCullum in front in his second over. He had to wait until the South African trip early in 2009 to crack the Test side, but settled in fast, keeping the runs down. He was duly selected for the Ashes tour, but was not assured of a place, even when Brett Lee broke down. He finally got the vote for the first Test ahead of Stuart Clark and Doug Bollinger, and immediately looked at home, shaping the ball away and finding swing with the Duke ball more readily even than England's practised performers. Hilfenhaus finished the series with 22 wickets – at least four in each game – and seemed set for a long run as the side's willing workhorse. Hilfenhaus was crucial to Tasmania's maiden Pura Cup victory in 2006-07. He took 60 wickets at 25.38, the third-most in the competition's history, and delivered 509.1 first-class overs, nearly 200 more than any of his domestic fast-bowling counterparts.

THE FACTS Hilfenhaus took 7 for 58 (and 10 for 87 in the match) for Tasmania against New South Wales at Hobart in March 2006: in December 2006 he took 7 for 70 against South Australia at Hobart ... He took 5 for 14 as Queensland were bowled out for 62 at Brisbane in October 2008 ... Hilfenhaus was named Australia's Bradman Young Cricketer of the Year for 2006-07 by a landslide, polling 97 votes to 11 for the next man ...

THE FIGURES to 21.9.09   www.cricinfo.com

Batting & Fielding	M	Inns	NO	Runs	HS	Avge	S/R	100	50	4s	6s	Ct	St
Tests	8	11	5	68	20	11.33	59.13	0	0	10	0	1	0
ODIs	13	6	4	13	5	6.50	25.49	0	0	0	0	4	0
Twenty20 Ints	6	2	1	2	2	2.00	22.22	0	0	0	0	0	0
First-class	45	60	21	376	34	9.64	–	0	0	–	–	12	0

Bowling	M	Balls	Runs	Wkts	BB	Avge	RpO	S/R	5i	10m
Tests	8	1835	970	29	4–60	33.44	3.17	63.27	0	0
ODIs	13	638	562	16	2–42	35.12	5.28	39.87	0	0
Twenty20 Ints	6	138	143	8	2–15	17.87	6.21	17.25	0	0
First-class	45	10377	5456	182	7–58	29.97	3.15	57.01	6	1

JAMES **HOPES**

AUSTRALIA

Full name	**James Redfern Hopes**
Born	**October 24, 1978, Townsville, Queensland**
Teams	**Queensland**
Style	**Right-hand bat, right-arm medium-pacer**
Test debut	**No Tests yet**
ODI debut	**Australia v New Zealand at Wellington 2004-05**

THE PROFILE James Hopes was earmarked for higher honours after some outstanding performances for Australia's youth teams, but he took a few years to settle once he made it to the first-class scene. A brisk medium-pacer whose aggressive batting has been shuffled up and down the Queensland order, Hopes has made three Sheffield Shield centuries (and two for Australia A), and in 2004-05 his average was in the mid-forties. Bowling was his main weapon the following season – 16 first-class wickets and 15 more in the one-day competition – but he was unable to transfer his regular success into the international arena. In nine ODI appearances, he did not manage more than one wicket in a match, although his batting showed some promise, with a top score of 43 against Sri Lanka. He was dropped early in 2006, but when Shane Watson suffered a calf problem in Bangladesh he was replaced by his Queensland team-mate. Despite that, Hopes was briefly cut from the national-contract list and returned to the domestic fray, although he was put on standby when Watson suffered another injury scare during the 2007 World Cup. A regular sweater in the gym, Hopes would love to be a professional golfer, but instead drives powerfully through the covers. He remained a one-day regular, although he was omitted from the second half of the one-day series in England in September 2009. Evenly balanced as an allrounder – both disciplines still need polish if he is to survive in the international game – his bowling has variety, and tight final overs have regularly picked up wickets and saved runs.

THE FACTS Hopes made his highest score of 146 when opening (with Michael Hussey) for Australia A v Pakistan A at Rawalpindi in September 2005 ... He scored 105 (against West Indies), 51 (v India) and 71 (v Pakistan) in successive innings during the 1997-98 Youth World Cup in South Africa ... Hopes took 6 for 70 for Queensland v Tasmania at Hobart in March 2006 ... Hopes took his 118th one-day wicket for Queensland in 2008-09, beating Michael Kasprowicz's previous record of 117 ...

THE FIGURES *to 21.9.09*   www.cricinfo.com

Batting & Fielding	M	Inns	NO	Runs	HS	Avge	S/R	100	50	4s	6s	Ct	St
Tests	0	0	–	–	–	–	–	–	–	–	–	–	–
ODIs	61	44	5	958	63*	24.56	90.12	0	2	84	4	19	0
Twenty20 Ints	11	6	2	75	18	18.75	107.14	0	0	4	1	3	0
First-class	58	96	1	2900	146	30.52	–	5	14	–	–	24	0

Bowling	M	Balls	Runs	Wkts	BB	Avge	RpO	S/R	5i	10m
Tests	0	0	–	–	–	–	–	–	–	–
ODIs	61	2322	1679	52	3–30	32.28	4.33	44.65	0	0
Twenty20 Ints	11	216	275	10	2–26	27.50	7.63	21.60	0	0
First-class	58	8389	3852	119	6–70	32.36	2.75	70.49	2	0

JAMIE HOW

Full name	**Jamie Michael How**
Born	**May 19, 1981, New Plymouth, Taranaki**
Teams	**Central Districts**
Style	**Right-hand bat, right-arm medium-pacer/offspinner**
Test debut	**New Zealand v West Indies at Auckland 2005-06**
ODI debut	**New Zealand v Sri Lanka at Queenstown 2005-06**

THE PROFILE Jamie How first played for the full New Zealand side in 2005 after solid performances for Central Districts – 704, 682 and 592 runs in the three seasons from 2002-03. A well-organised opener, more of an accumulator than a dasher, he has a penchant for big scores: after taking a while to find his first-class feet, he scored 163 not out and 158 in consecutive innings in March 2003, against Northern Districts and Canterbury, and started the following season with 169 against Otago. Picked for his one-day debut against Sri Lanka on New Year's Eve 2005, How ensured his celebrations would go well with a sparky 58, including eight fours and a six, in an easy victory. His first encounter with West Indies resulted in 66 in an opening stand of 136 with Nathan Astle, but his other four one-day innings brought him only 17 runs. After a moderate domestic season in 2006-07 he fell off the one-day radar and missed the World Cup, but in 2007-08, buoyed by a fine 139 in a high-scoring tied ODI with England and a career-best 92 in the first Test against them, he finally looked the part, and was one of the few batsmen to show anything like Test class on the England tour that followed. He started that trip as NZ's captain, keeping the seat warm while Daniel Vettori was away at the Indian Premier League. But after only one half-century in five Tests in 2008-09 he found himself overtaken by the likes of Martin Guptill and Tim McIntosh, and while the Test side was in Sri Lanka late in 2009 How was schlepping around India with the A team.

THE FACTS How scored 190 not out while captaining New Zealand A against the touring England Lions at Queenstown in March 2009 ... He played in the 1999-2000 Under-19 World Cup in Sri Lanka, when his captain was James Franklin and the wicketkeeper was Brendon McCullum ... Six of How's seven highest Test scores have come against England ... He also played soccer for New Zealand's youth sides, but eventually chose cricket ...

THE FIGURES to 21.9.09   www.cricinfo.com

Batting & Fielding	M	Inns	NO	Runs	HS	Avge	S/R	100	50	4s	6s	Ct	St
Tests	19	35	1	772	92	22.70	50.45	0	4	104	2	18	0
ODIs	31	28	1	930	139	34.44	70.08	1	7	105	6	13	0
Twenty20 Ints	5	5	0	56	31	11.20	83.58	0	0	5	1	1	0
First-class	83	144	11	4586	190*	34.48	–	11	24	–	–	87	0

Bowling	M	Balls	Runs	Wkts	BB	Avge	RpO	S/R	5i	10m
Tests	19	12	4	0	–	–	2.00	–	0	0
ODIs	31	0	–	–	–	–	–	–	–	–
Twenty20 Ints	5	0	–	–	–	–	–	–	–	–
First-class	83	1902	1077	20	3–55	53.85	3.39	95.10	0	0

PHILLIP **HUGHES**

AUSTRALIA

Full name **Phillip Joel Hughes**
Born **November 30, 1988, Macksville, New South Wales**
Teams **New South Wales, Middlesex**
Style **Left-hand bat**
Test debut **Australia v South Africa at Johannesburg 2008-09**
ODI debut **No ODIs yet**

THE PROFILE Phillip Hughes made an unconvincing start in Tests – a four-ball duck at the Wanderers after becoming Australia's youngest player since Craig McDermott 25 years previously – but he made 75 in the second innings, and by the end of the next Test had shown he was a highly accomplished if unconventional batsman. At Durban he became the youngest ever to make two centuries in the same Test, bringing up the first one with two sixes. His 415 runs in the series were followed by centuries in each of his three Championship games for Middlesex, which further irritated England supporters angry he had been given the chance to fine-tune before the 2009 Ashes series. As it happened it didn't do him that much good, as he failed to shine in the first two Tests and was replaced by Shane Watson, a change made public on Hughes's Twitter site before the official announcement, which provoked reactions ranging from rage to raucous laughter. His country-baked technique includes compulsive slicing through point and slashing to cover, as well as stepping away to provide room for tennis-style drives down the ground. After a superb first season in 2007-08, when he became the youngest to score a century in a Pura Cup final and toured with Australia A, Hughes piled up 963 more runs in his second summer. His timing was impeccable: a replacement was needed for Matthew Hayden, and a week before the team for South Africa was picked, Hughes hit 151 and 82 not out against Tasmania. His meteoric rise might have suffered a setback in England, but it's still pretty impressive stuff for a young man who grew up on a banana farm in northern New South Wales.

THE FACTS Hughes made 115 and 160 in only his second Test, against South Africa at Durban in March 2009: at 20 years 98 days he was the youngest to hit twin centuries in a Test, beating the record of George Headley (20 years 271 days) for West Indies v England at Georgetown in 1929-30 ... Hughes scored 198 for New South Wales v South Australia at Adelaide in November 2008 ... He hit 195 for Middlesex v Surrey at The Oval in May 2009 ...

THE FIGURES to 21.9.09   www.cricinfo.com

Batting & Fielding	M	Inns	NO	Runs	HS	Avge	S/R	100	50	4s	6s	Ct	St
Tests	5	9	0	472	160	52.44	58.56	2	1	61	6	3	0
ODIs	0	0	–	–	–	–	–	–	–	–	–	–	–
Twenty20 Ints	0	0	–	–	–	–	–	–	–	–	–	–	–
First-class	28	50	5	2786	198	61.91	61.01	10	15	371	17	22	0

Bowling	M	Balls	Runs	Wkts	BB	Avge	RpO	S/R	5i	10m
Tests	5	0	–	–	–	–	–	–	–	–
ODIs	0	0	–	–	–	–	–	–	–	–
Twenty20 Ints	0	0	–	–	–	–	–	–	–	–
First-class	28	18	9	0	–	–	3.00	–	0	0

DAVID **HUSSEY**

AUSTRALIA

Full name	**David John Hussey**
Born	**July 15, 1977, Morley, Western Australia**
Teams	**Victoria, Kolkata Knight Riders**
Style	**Right-hand bat, occasional offspinner**
Test debut	**No Tests yet**
ODI debut	**Australia v West Indies at Basseterre 2007-08**

THE PROFILE David Hussey copied his older brother Michael's talent for ridiculous scoring in the English county competition. And, like Michael, David – a big-hitting right-hander – was forced to pile up mountains of runs in Australia before gaining the confidence of the national selectors. It took his first thousand-run home season before he was finally chosen for a tour, the one-day series in the West Indies early in 2008, and earned his first national contract. Earlier that season he made his Twenty20 debut against India at the MCG. He made his first ODI century in 2009 – but it was against Scotland, and couldn't get him into the side for the series against England that followed. Hussey was one of the big surprises in the inaugural Indian Premier League auction when Kolkata paid $625,000 for him – far more than his brother fetched. Despite his crash-and-bash style, David is desperate not to be pigeonholed as a Twenty20 player. His first-class record suggests it is a fair request: he boasts an average in the mid-fifties, a shade higher than his brother's. But his one-day exploits include a 60-ball century – the second-fastest in Australia's domestic history – and in 2007-08 he was Victoria's Player of the Year in all three formats. He was also a run-machine during his time with Nottinghamshire, finishing with 5417 runs at 66.06 in 4½ seasons. An aggressive batsman with a strong bottom-hand technique, Hussey hit a breathtaking breakthrough 212 not out at nearly a run a ball in 2003-04, his first full season, as Victoria chased a record-breaking 455 for victory against NSW: Steve Waugh, the opposing captain, was impressed.

THE FACTS David Hussey hit 275 (with 27 fours and 14 sixes) for Nottinghamshire v Essex at Nottingham in May 2007 ... He reached 50 in only 19 balls – Australia's second-fastest ODI half-century – against West Indies in St Kitts in July 2008 ... Hussey fetched $625,000 at the inaugural Indian Premier League auction in February 2008, much more than his brother Michael ($350,000) and Australia's captain Ricky Ponting ($400,000) ...

THE FIGURES to 21.9.09   www.cricinfo.com

Batting & Fielding	M	Inns	NO	Runs	HS	Avge	S/R	100	50	4s	6s	Ct	St
Tests	0	0	–	–	–	–	–	–	–	–	–	–	–
ODIs	23	21	0	598	111	28.47	88.46	1	4	41	12	12	0
Twenty20 Ints	11	10	1	236	88*	26.22	140.47	0	1	11	14	4	0
First-class	132	203	21	10048	275	55.20	70.83	35	44	–	–	159	0

Bowling	M	Balls	Runs	Wkts	BB	Avge	RpO	S/R	5i	10m
Tests	0	0	–	–	–	–	–	–	–	–
ODIs	23	257	230	3	1–6	76.66	5.36	85.66	0	0
Twenty20 Ints	11	132	140	7	3–25	20.00	6.36	18.85	0	0
First-class	132	2025	1281	20	4–105	64.05	3.79	101.25	0	0

MICHAEL **HUSSEY**

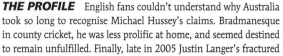

Full name **Michael Edward Killeen Hussey**
Born **May 27, 1975, Morley, Western Australia**
Teams **Western Australia**
Style **Left-hand bat, occasional right-arm medium-pacer**
Test debut **Australia v West Indies at Brisbane 2005-06**
ODI debut **Australia v India at Perth 2003-04**

THE PROFILE English fans couldn't understand why Australia took so long to recognise Michael Hussey's claims. Bradmanesque in county cricket, he was less prolific at home, and seemed destined to remain unfulfilled. Finally, late in 2005 Justin Langer's fractured rib gave Hussey a chance after 15,313 first-class runs, a record for an Australian before wearing baggy green. His first Test was a disappointment, but he relaxed for his second and made an attractive century. A memorable 122 followed against South Africa at the MCG, when he and Glenn McGrath added 107 for the last wicket. The fairytale continued in the 2006-07 Ashes, when he topped the batting averages with 91.60, although his one-day form did finally drop off a little. Like Langer and Graeme Wood, predecessors as left-hand WA openers, Hussey has a tidy, compact style. Skilled off front foot and back, he is attractive to watch once set. Reinventing himself in one-day cricket as an agile fielder and innovative batsman with cool head and loose wrists, once he made the national side Hussey underlined his credentials with more Bradman-like scoring. He supplanted Michael Bevan as the Aussies' one-day "finisher", although he was hardly needed during the 2007 World Cup. His sky-high standards dipped a little in 2008, with a modest time in the West Indies, and a patchy 2009 Ashes series was redeemed slightly by a fighting century (his first for 16 Tests) at The Oval, although that was tinged with regret as he was the last man out as Australia surrendered the urn again. At 34, with youngsters like Callum Ferguson snapping at his heels, the senior Hussey faces an important season in 2009-10.

THE FACTS Hussey scored 229 runs in ODIs before he was dismissed, and had an average of 100.22 after 32 matches ... He took only 166 days to reach 1000 runs in Tests, beating the 228-day record established by England's Andrew Strauss in 2005 ... Hussey's 331 not out against Somerset at Taunton in 2003 is the highest individual score for Northamptonshire ... He has captained Australia in four ODIs, and lost the lot ... Hussey averages 64.79 in Tests in Australia, and 42.29 overseas ...

THE FIGURES *to 21.9.09*　　　　　　　　　www.cricinfo.com

Batting & Fielding	M	Inns	NO	Runs	HS	Avge	S/R	100	50	4s	6s	Ct	St
Tests	42	72	9	3317	182	52.65	48.19	10	16	374	18	37	0
ODIs	115	92	32	3162	109*	52.70	86.36	2	22	228	51	70	0
Twenty20 Ints	18	12	3	226	53*	25.11	134.52	0	1	19	8	10	0
First-class	225	401	40	19242	331*	53.30	–	51	87	–	–	242	0

Bowling	M	Balls	Runs	Wkts	BB	Avge	RpO	S/R	5i	10m
Tests	42	168	100	1	1–22	100.00	3.57	168.00	0	0
ODIs	115	192	167	2	1–22	83.50	5.21	96.00	0	0
Twenty20 Ints	18	6	5	0	–	–	5.00	–	0	0
First-class	225	1608	872	21	3–34	41.52	3.25	76.57	0	0

RAO **IFTIKHAR ANJUM**

Full name **Rao Iftikhar Anjum**
Born **December 1, 1980, Khanewal, Punjab**
Teams **Islamabad, Federal Areas, Zarai Taraqiati Bank**
Style **Right-hand bat, right-arm fast-medium bowler**
Test debut **Pakistan v Sri Lanka at Kandy 2005-06**
ODI debut **Pakistan v Zimbabwe at Multan 2004-05**

THE PROFILE With a high arm action modelled on Glenn McGrath's, Iftikhar Anjum is another addition to Pakistan's seemingly endless production line of pace bowlers. Iftikhar, however, is more Aqib Javed than Waqar Younis, and his outswinger is considered by many to be just as lethal as Aqib's. He can bowl reverse-swing, when the ball gets a bit rougher, and a decent yorker. Iftikhar has performed consistently well on Pakistan's generally lifeless pitches, taking 367 of his 375 first-class wickets at home, including 73 in 2000-01, his first full season. Two years later, he captained the Zarai Taraqiati Bank to victory in the Patron's Trophy final at Karachi, taking 7 for 85 in the first innings and ending with ten in the match. Not surprisingly, he was called into Pakistan's one-day squad for the series against India early in 2004, before making his debut that September. He has since been a handy back-up bowler in one-dayers, although he rarely plays when everyone is fit. A long injury list meant he won his first Test cap in Sri Lanka in April 2006: he was expensive and didn't take a wicket as Pakistan won inside three days. He was one of the few to emerge with much credit from the 2007 World Cup, taking five wickets in the first two games. He wasn't needed with the ball in the final match, against Zimbabwe, but earlier made 32 – from just 16 balls – to boost the total to a massive 349. He remained in the one-day mix, without really threatening to add to that solitary Test cap, and took a career-best 5 for 30 against Sri Lanka in Colombo in August 2009.

THE FACTS Iftikhar Anjum's best bowling figures are 7 for 59, for Zarai Taraqiati Bank v WAPDA at Hyderabad in February 2005 ... Two years previously he took 7 for 85 (10 for 116 in the match) against the same opposition in the Patron's Trophy final at Karachi ... Iftikhar took 7 for 94 – after a career-best innings of 78 – for Zarai Taraqiati Bank v Karachi Port Trust at Peshawar in December 2003 ...

THE FIGURES to 21.9.09   www.cricinfo.com

Batting & Fielding	M	Inns	NO	Runs	HS	Avge	S/R	100	50	4s	6s	Ct	St
Tests	1	1	1	9	9*	–	23.07	0	0	2	0	0	0
ODIs	60	32	19	213	32	16.38	61.56	0	0	13	2	10	0
Twenty20 Ints	2	0	–	–	–	–	–	–	–	–	–	0	0
First-class	92	138	30	1809	78	16.75	–	0	5	–	–	52	0

Bowling	M	Balls	Runs	Wkts	BB	Avge	RpO	S/R	5i	10m
Tests	1	84	62	0	–	–	4.42	–	0	0
ODIs	60	2844	2327	76	5–30	30.61	4.90	37.42	1	0
Twenty20 Ints	2	48	67	1	1–34	67.00	8.37	48.00	0	0
First-class	92	16745	8908	375	7–59	23.75	3.19	44.65	21	3

IMRUL KAYES

Full name	**Imrul Kayes**
Born	**February 2, 1987, Meherpur, Kushtia**
Teams	**Khulna**
Style	**Left-hand bat, occasional offspinner**
Test debut	**Bangladesh v South Africa at Bloemfontein 2008-09**
ODI debut	**Bangladesh v New Zealand at Chittagong 2008-09**

THE PROFILE The elevation of left-hand opener Imrul Kayes to Bangladesh colours was hastened by the mass defections to the unauthorised Indian Cricket League late in 2008. With more than a dozen leading players suddenly unavailable, "Sagar" was called up after a fine home season in 2007-08, when he was the leading scorer for Khulna less than a year after making his first-class debut. His haul included two centuries in separate matches against Sylhet (in between he also hit a hundred against them in a one-day game), and he finished the season with 600 runs. He also scored consistently on the Bangladesh Academy's tour of Sri Lanka in September 2008, and was given a run as Tamim Iqbal's opening partner. Kayes has a solid, compact technique, and likes to hit through the covers off the back foot, but he had the misfortune to make his Test debut against South Africa: he rarely looked settled against their high-quality pacemen, and managed only 25 runs in four attempts in the Tests. On his debut, at Bloemfontein, he was out twice in the space of about three hours on the second day. He fared a little better in two Tests against Sri Lanka, but equalled his Test-best 33 (and added a two-hour 24 in the second innings, in an opening stand of 82 with Tamim) in Bangladesh's victory over a depleted West Indian side in St Vincent in July 2009. He has not yet had much success in ODIs, and may need to polish his technique in domestic cricket before exposing it again to Test-class bowling.

THE FACTS Both Imrul Kayes's first-class hundreds were scored for Khulna against Sylhet late in 2007 (121 at Fatullah and 138 at Khulna): in between he made 121 against them in a one-day game ... He scored 83 in his second first-class match, for Khulna against Barisal in February 2007 ...

THE FIGURES to 21.9.09   www.cricinfo.com

Batting & Fielding	M	Inns	NO	Runs	HS	Avge	S/R	100	50	4s	6s	Ct	St
Tests	6	12	0	161	33	13.41	38.70	0	0	22	0	4	0
ODIs	3	3	0	27	14	9.00	35.06	0	0	1	0	1	0
Twenty20 Ints	0	0	–	–	–	–	–	–	–	–	–	–	–
First-class	25	47	1	1296	138	28.17	–	2	5	–	–	11	0

Bowling	M	Balls	Runs	Wkts	BB	Avge	RpO	S/R	5i	10m
Tests	6	6	7	0	–	–	7.00	–	0	0
ODIs	3	0	–	–	–	–	–	–	–	–
Twenty20 Ints	0	0	–	–	–	–	–	–	–	–
First-class	25	12	11	0	–	–	5.50	–	0	0

RAVINDRA **JADEJA**

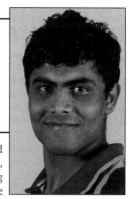

Full name	**Ravindrasinh Anirudhsinh Jadeja**
Born	**December 6, 1988, Navagam-Khed, Saurashtra**
Teams	**Saurashtra, Rajasthan Royals**
Style	**Left-hand bat, left-arm orthodox spinner**
Test debut	**No Tests yet**
ODI debut	**India v Sri Lanka at Colombo 2008-09**

THE PROFILE Left-handed allrounder Ravindra Jadeja elbowed his way into national contention with a stellar 2008–09 season, which followed a good showing in the inaugural IPL season, during which Shane Warne labelled him "a superstar in the making". He extended his maiden first-class hundred for Saurashtra against Orissa at Rajkot in November 2008 to 232 not out, although even that was overshadowed by his batting partner Cheteshwar Pujara's triple-century. The pair shared an unbroken partnership of 520 for the fifth wicket, a record for all first-class cricket, erasing the 464 of the Waugh twins for New South Wales against Western Australia in 1990–91. Jadeja collected his best bowling figures, and another century, the following month, finishing the Ranji Trophy season with 739 runs and 42 wickets. He leapfrogged Pujara into the national side, making his ODI and Twenty20 debuts in Sri Lanka early in 2009. Jadeja started with a rearguard 60 not out in Colombo, and although his batting and bowling returns were modest after that he remained in the mix for the World Twenty20 in England in June 2009, helped by his fine fielding. There, though, he was criticised for using up 35 balls over 25 in the defeat by England (in truth the blame lay with whoever put him in at No. 4, ahead of hitters like Yuvraj Singh and MS Dhoni). Before all that Jadeja enjoyed a glittering youth career. He was part of the Indian side that lost the 2006 Under-19 World Cup final to Pakistan, but was still young enough to take part in the 2008 competition in Malaysia – when his 2 for 25 in the final helped defeat South Africa.

THE FACTS Jadeja scored 232 not out for Saurashtra v Orissa at Rajkot in November 2008: he shared an unbroken world-record fifth-wicket stand of 520 with Cheteshwar Pujara, who made 302 not out ... Jadeja took 7 for 31 (10 for 88 in the match) for Saurashtra v Hyderabad at Rajkot in December 2008 ... Ravindra is not related to the former Indian batsman Ajay Jadeja ...

THE FIGURES to 21.9.09   www.cricinfo.com

Batting & Fielding	M	Inns	NO	Runs	HS	Avge	S/R	100	50	4s	6s	Ct	St
Tests	0	0	–	–	–	–	–	–	–	–	–	–	–
ODIs	3	3	1	67	60*	33.50	74.44	0	1	6	0	1	0
Twenty20 Ints	4	4	1	56	25	18.66	87.50	0	0	2	1	3	0
First-class	22	32	2	1130	232*	37.66	52.82	2	5	136	8	15	0

Bowling	M	Balls	Runs	Wkts	BB	Avge	RpO	S/R	5i	10m
Tests	0	0	–	–	–	–	–	–	–	–
ODIs	3	90	86	0	–	–	5.73	–	0	0
Twenty20 Ints	4	90	85	3	2–26	28.33	5.66	30.00	0	0
First-class	22	4822	1920	65	7–31	29.53	74.18	–	5	1

SANATH **JAYASURIYA**

Full name	**Sanath Teran Jayasuriya**
Born	**June 30, 1969, Matara**
Teams	**Bloomfield, Ruhuna, Mumbai Indians, Dolphins**
Style	**Left-hand bat, left-arm orthodox spinner**
Test debut	**Sri Lanka v New Zealand at Hamilton 1990-91**
ODI debut	**Sri Lanka v Australia at Melbourne 1989-90**

THE PROFILE Sanath Jayasuriya found fame as a pinch-hitter at the 1996 World Cup, then showed he was also capable of massive scoring in Tests, making 340 against India and eventually becoming the first Sri Lankan to win 100 caps. He has now retired (finally) from Test cricket, but remains dangerous in one-dayers, especially on the subcontinent's slower surfaces – in January 2009 he became the oldest batsman to make an ODI century, and played in the World Twenty20 in England when rising 40. Short but muscular, he cuts and pulls with great power; his brutal bat-wielding is at odds with his shy, gentle nature. Streetwise opponents set traps in the gully and third man, but when on song Jayasuriya can be virtually unstoppable, scoring freely on both sides of the wicket. He is also a canny left-arm spinner, mixing his leg-stump darts with clever variations of pace. He had a successful stint as captain after Arjuna Ranatunga was dumped in 1999, but the responsibility took its toll. He stepped down after the 2003 World Cup, but Jayasuriya was far from finished: in 2004 he blazed a hundred against Australia and a marathon double-century against Pakistan. He added twin centuries in the Asia Cup, and sailed past 10,000 one-day runs the following year. He looked rusty at first in England in 2006 when summoned from short-lived Test retirement, but soon showed his old form in pyjamas, with 122 at The Oval then 152 and 157 in successive innings against England and Holland. Then he hit two more tons in the 2007 World Cup before briefly giving Sri Lanka hope in the final with 63. Enjoy him while he lasts.

THE FACTS Jayasuriya made 340 against India in Colombo in August 1997, as Sri Lanka made the highest Test total of 952 for 6: he shared a world-record second-wicket partnership of 576 with Roshan Mahanama ... In the next Test Jayasuriya hit 199 ... He was 39 years 212 days old when he made 107 against India in Jan 2009, to surpass Geoff Boycott as the oldest ODI centurion ... Jayasuriya's record includes four ODIs for the Asia XI ...

THE FIGURES to 21.9.09   www.cricinfo.com

Batting & Fielding	M	Inns	NO	Runs	HS	Avge	S/R	100	50	4s	6s	Ct	St
Tests	110	188	14	6973	340	40.07	–	14	31	910	59	78	0
ODIs	438	426	18	13343	189	32.70	91.26	28	68	1486	270	122	0
Twenty20 Ints	21	21	1	549	88	27.45	136.56	0	4	64	22	3	0
First-class	261	415	33	14742	340	38.59	–	29	70	–	–	162	0

Bowling	M	Balls	Runs	Wkts	BB	Avge	RpO	S/R	5i	10m
Tests	110	8188	3366	98	5–34	34.34	2.46	83.55	2	0
ODIs	438	14694	11668	319	6–29	36.57	4.76	46.06	4	0
Twenty20 Ints	21	281	355	14	3–21	25.35	7.58	20.07	0	0
First-class	261	15113	6719	205	5–34	32.77	2.66	73.72	2	0

MAHELA **JAYAWARDENE**

Full name **Denagamage Proboth Mahela de Silva Jayawardene**
Born **May 27, 1977, Colombo**
Teams **Sinhalese Sports Club, Wayamba, Kings XI Punjab**
Style **Right-hand bat, right-arm medium-pacer**
Test debut **Sri Lanka v India at Colombo 1997-98**
ODI debut **Sri Lanka v Zimbabwe at Colombo 1997-98**

THE PROFILE A fine technician with an excellent temperament, Mahela Jayawardene's exciting arrival in 1997 heralded the start of a new era for Sri Lanka's middle order. Perhaps mindful of his first Test, when he went in against India at 790 for 4, he soon developed an appetite for big scores. His 66 then, in the world-record 952 for 6, was followed by a masterful 167 on a Galle minefield against New Zealand in only his fourth Test, and a marathon 242 against India in his seventh. However, Jayawardene lost form in 2002. His declining one-day productivity was particularly alarming, although that was partly explained by being shuffled up and down the order. He hardly scored a run in the 2003 World Cup, and was dropped. But he soon regained his confidence, and benefited from a settled spot at No. 4 after Aravinda de Silva retired. A good Test series against England was followed by more runs in 2004. He deputised as captain for the injured Marvan Atapattu in England in 2006, producing a stunning double of 61 and 119 to lead the fine rearguard which saved the Lord's Test. Later he put South Africa to the sword in Colombo, hitting a colossal 374 and sharing a world-record stand of 624 with Kumar Sangakkara. In 2007 he inspired his side to the World Cup final with 548 runs at 60, including a century in the semi-final victory over New Zealand, then became Sri Lanka's leading Test runscorer during 2007-08, a period that included three successive centuries, one of them a double against England. He stepped down as captain early in 2009 to concentrate on his batting – not that leadership had affected it much, as he averaged 66.93 in Tests when skipper – and soon added another hundred to his bulging collection.

THE FACTS Jayawardene made 374 against South Africa in Colombo in July 2006 ... He has taken 73 Test catches off Muttiah Muralitharan, a record for a fielder-bowler combination ... Jayawardene has scored 2467 runs at the SSC in Colombo, a record for a single Test ground ... Against New Zealand in Colombo in August 2009 he was only the fifth batsman to be out twice in the nineties in the same Test ... His record includes five ODIs for the Asia XI ...

THE FIGURES *to 21.9.09* www.cricinfo.com

Batting & Fielding	M	Inns	NO	Runs	HS	Avge	S/R	100	50	4s	6s	Ct	St
Tests	107	177	13	8747	374	53.33	52.50	26	35	1048	40	151	0
ODIs	307	288	29	8278	128	31.96	76.45	11	49	697	49	162	0
Twenty20 Ints	21	21	3	420	78	23.33	130.43	0	2	45	8	5	0
First-class	188	298	22	14456	374	52.37	–	43	63	–	–	241	0

Bowling	M	Balls	Runs	Wkts	BB	Avge	RpO	S/R	5i	10m
Tests	107	547	292	6	2–32	48.66	3.20	91.16	0	0
ODIs	307	582	558	7	2–56	79.71	5.75	83.14	0	0
Twenty20 Ints	21	6	8	0	–	–	8.00	–	0	0
First-class	188	2947	1595	52	5–72	30.67	3.24	56.67	1	0

PRASANNA **JAYAWARDENE**

SRI LANKA

Full name	**Hewasandatchige Asiri Prasanna Wishvanath Jayawardene**
Born	**October 9, 1979, Colombo**
Teams	**Sebastianites, Basnahira South**
Style	**Right-hand bat, wicketkeeper**
Test debut	**Sri Lanka v Pakistan at Kandy 2000**
ODI debut	**Sri Lanka v Pakistan at Sharjah 2002–03**

THE PROFILE A neat, unflashy wicketkeeper rated by Sri Lanka's captain Kumar Sangakkara as the best in the world, Prasanna Jayawardene looked set for a long international career after touring England at 19, but he became a back number after Sangakkara's own rocket-fuelled arrival in 2000. Waiting on the sidelines had already been a feature of Jayawardene's career: in his first Test, against Pakistan in June 2000, he was confined to the dressing-room throughout, as rain washed out play on the last two days before Sri Lanka fielded. With the selectors worried about overburdening Sangakkara in Tests, Jayawardene was recalled in April 2004. Sangakkara soon got the gloves back that time, but there was something of a sea-change two years later after the England tour, during which Jayawardene showed that his batting had improved. He was recalled for South Africa's visit in July 2006, and this time the decision to lighten Sangakkara's load paid off spectacularly – he hammered 287, and shared a world-record stand of 642 with Mahela Jayawardene in the first Test in Colombo. Prasanna Jayawardene (no relation to Mahela) contented himself with a couple of catches and a stumping as the South Africans went down by an innings, but finally seemed to have booked in for a long run behind the stumps – at least in Tests, with Sangakkara continuing in one-dayers – and cemented his place in June 2007 with a Test ton of his own, against Bangladesh. A finger injury kept him out of the home series against Pakistan in August 2009, but he was back for the New Zealand Tests which followed.

THE FACTS Prasanna Jayawardene made 120 not out, his first Test century, against Bangladesh in Colombo in June 2007, sharing a record seventh-wicket stand of 223 with Chaminda Vaas ... He has scored five other first-class centuries, the highest 166 not out for Sebastianites v Panadura at Moratuwa in February 2007 ... All Jayawardene's ODIs have been in the United Arab Emirates (Sharjah and Abu Dhabi) ...

THE FIGURES to 21.9.09   www.cricinfo.com

Batting & Fielding	M	Inns	NO	Runs	HS	Avge	S/R	100	50	4s	6s	Ct	St
Tests	27	35	5	747	120*	24.90	45.68	1	2	79	2	59	19
ODIs	6	5	0	27	20	5.40	61.36	0	0	3	0	4	1
Twenty20 Ints	0	0	–	–	–	–	–	–	–	–	–	–	–
First-class	163	251	29	5702	166*	25.68	–	6	27	–	–	390	74

Bowling	M	Balls	Runs	Wkts	BB	Avge	RpO	S/R	5i	10m
Tests	27	0	–	–	–	–	–	–	–	–
ODIs	6	0	–	–	–	–	–	–	–	–
Twenty20 Ints	0	0	–	–	–	–	–	–	–	–
First-class	163	18	9	0	–	–	3.00	–	0	0

76

MITCHELL **JOHNSON**

Full name	**Mitchell Guy Johnson**
Born	**November 2, 1981, Townsville, Queensland**
Teams	**Western Australia**
Style	**Left-hand bat, left-hand fast-medium bowler**
Test debut	**Australia v Sri Lanka at Brisbane 2007-08**
ODI debut	**Australia v New Zealand at Christchurch 2005-06**

THE PROFILE   Mitchell Johnson was Australia's most exciting fast-bowling prospect since Brett Lee first dyed his roots. He's quick, he's tall, he's talented – but most of all, he's a left-armer, and only two others like him (Alan Davidson and Bruce Reid) have taken 100 Test wickets for Australia. Dennis Lillee spotted him at 17, and called him a "once-in-a-generation bowler". Injuries kept intruding, but Johnson played a full season in 2004-05 and toured Pakistan with Australia A. In December 2005 he was supersubbed into the final match of the one-day series in New Zealand, but the following season was a sobering one. Johnson started by reducing India to 35 for 5 in a one-dayer in Kuala Lumpur, but narrowly missed out to the steadier Stuart Clark in the 2006-07 Ashes series, then sat out the World Cup as Shaun Tait and Nathan Bracken bowled consistently well. Test rewards finally came in 2007-08, and he was composed in his first two matches against Sri Lanka, then grabbed 16 wickets against India and 10 in the West Indies. In 2008-09 Johnson was superb against South Africa both home and away, adding a wicked in-ducker to his armoury and claiming 33 wickets in six Tests (and also hammering a maiden century), but then he struggled at first in England, spraying the ball around from an arm seemingly lower than usual. He got it together for the fourth Test, taking 5 for 69 in an innings victory at Headingley, but overall he was a disappointment given the advance hype. But Johnson, who runs up as if carrying a delivery of milk bottles in his left hand, has the height to worry batsmen, and despite his English hiccough looks likely to keep on doing so for many years yet.

THE FACTS   Johnson took 8 for 61 – the best bowling figures in Tests by any left-arm fast bowler – against South Africa at Perth in 2008-09 ... He took 6 for 51 (and 10 for 106 in the match) against Victoria in the Pura Cup final at Brisbane in March 2006: when Queensland batted, they made 900 for 6 ... Johnson reached his maiden Test (and first-class) century against South Africa at Cape Town in March 2009 with a six ...

THE FIGURES to 21.9.09   www.cricinfo.com

Batting & Fielding	M	Inns	NO	Runs	HS	Avge	S/R	100	50	4s	6s	Ct	St
Tests	26	34	8	799	123*	30.73	62.76	1	4	100	15	6	0
ODIs	62	32	10	247	43*	11.22	81.25	0	0	19	5	13	0
Twenty20 Ints	12	6	3	61	28*	20.33	164.86	0	0	6	2	3	0
First-class	54	72	19	1479	123*	27.90	–	1	8	–	–	13	0

Bowling	M	Balls	Runs	Wkts	BB	Avge	RpO	S/R	5i	10m
Tests	26	6285	3284	114	8–61	28.80	3.13	55.13	3	1
ODIs	62	2984	2433	98	5–26	24.82	4.89	30.44	2	0
Twenty20 Ints	12	234	276	14	3–22	19.71	7.07	16.71	0	0
First-class	54	11103	6094	200	8–61	30.47	3.29	55.51	5	2

JUNAID SIDDIQUE

Full name	**Mohammad Junaid Siddique**
Born	**October 30, 1987, Rajshahi**
Teams	**Rajshahi**
Style	**Left-hand bat, occasional offspinner**
Test debut	**Bangladesh v New Zealand at Dunedin 2007-08**
ODI debut	**Bangladesh v New Zealand at Auckland 2007-08**

THE PROFILE   Left-hander Junaid Siddique made a sensational start in Test cricket at 20 when, along with his fellow debutant Tamim Iqbal, he flayed the New Zealand attack in an opening stand of 161 to light up the inaugural Test at Dunedin's University Oval at the start of 2008. *Wisden* said the pair "started the second innings with an entrancing display of classical strokes, their timing perfect as the ball was distributed around the short boundaries". Sadly, their fine start came to nothing: the other batsmen made only 83 between them, and Bangladesh lost yet again. "Imrose" also made a stylish 74 against South Africa at Mirpur – no-one else made more than 24 – and added 71 on his Twenty20 international debut. However, the faster bowlers noticed a compulsion to get onto the front foot – bred on slow, low pitches in Bangladesh – and Junaid began to cop a lot of short stuff. He dropped down the order in Tests, making 78 in victory over a depleted West Indian side in St Vincent in July 2009, while his ODI performances improved: after an anaemic start (62 runs in eight innings), he made 85 against New Zealand in November 2008, then scored consistently against admittedly modest attacks in the West Indies and Zimbabwe. Junaid worked his way up through Bangladesh's age-group sides, reaching the A team against England A in 2006-07. That season he recorded a notable double with 88 and 114 not out (in more than five hours) for Rajshahi against Khulna, and was in the 30-man preliminary squad for the 2007 World Cup without making the final cut.

THE FACTS   Junaid Siddique scored 74 on his Test debut at Dunedin in January 2008, putting on 161 for the first wicket – a new national record – with Tamim Iqbal, who was also winning his first cap: it was the highest opening stand between debutants in Tests since Billy Ibadulla and Abdul Kadir put on 249 for Pakistan v Australia at Karachi in 1964-65 ... Junaid hit 71 off 49 balls in his first Twenty20 international, against Pakistan at Cape Town in September 2007... He captained Bangladesh A in England in 2008 ...

THE FIGURES *to 21.9.09*   www.cricinfo.com

Batting & Fielding	M	Inns	NO	Runs	HS	Avge	S/R	100	50	4s	6s	Ct	St
Tests	12	23	0	526	78	22.86	41.84	0	4	64	1	6	0
ODIs	24	23	0	43	85	18.82	59.23	0	2	46	0	8	0
Twenty20 Ints	5	5	0	134	71	26.80	159.52	0	1	13	6	0	0
First-class	32	60	1	1438	114*	24.37	–	1	8	–	–	22	0

Bowling	M	Balls	Runs	Wkts	BB	Avge	RpO	S/R	5i	10m
Tests	12	12	2	0	–	–	1.00	–	0	0
ODIs	24	12	13	0	–	–	6.50	–	0	0
Twenty20 Ints	5	0	–	–	–	–	–	–	–	–
First-class	32	192	110	1	1–30	110.00	3.43	192.00	0	0

JACQUES **KALLIS**

Full name	**Jacques Henry Kallis**
Born	**October 16, 1975, Pinelands, Cape Town**
Teams	**Cape Cobras, Bangalore Royal Challengers**
Style	**Right-hand bat, right-arm fast-medium bowler**
Test debut	**South Africa v England at Durban 1995-96**
ODI debut	**South Africa v England at Cape Town 1995-96**

THE PROFILE In an era of fast scoring and high-octane entertainment, Jacques Kallis is a throwback – an astonishingly effective one – to a more sedate age, when your wicket was to be guarded with your life, and runs were an accidental by-product of crease-occupation. He blossomed after a quiet start into arguably the world's leading batsman, with the adhesive qualities of a Cape Point limpet. In 2005, he was the ICC's first Test Player of the Year, after a run of performances against West Indies and England that marked him out as the modern game's biggest scalp. His batting is not for the romantic: a Kallis century (of which there have now been 31 in Tests) tends to be a soulless affair, with ruthless efficiency taking precedence over derring-do, and he has never quite dispelled the notion that he is a selfish batsman, something the Aussies played on during the 2007 World Cup. He also had a subdued time in England the following year, amid whispers that he was carrying some extra weight. But he has sailed to the top of South Africa's batting charts, and until Andrew Flintoff's emergence was comfortably the world's leading allrounder, capable of swinging the ball sharply at a surprising pace. Strong, with powerful shoulders and a deep chest, Kallis has the capacity (if not always the inclination) to play a wide array of attacking strokes. He won his 100th Test cap in April 2006, and has a batting average in the mid-fifties to go with more than 500 international wickets all told. He's a fine slip fielder too.

THE FACTS Kallis and Shaun Pollock were the first South Africans to play 100 Tests, reaching the mark, appropriately enough, at Centurion in April 2006 ... Kallis averages 169.75 in Tests against Zimbabwe, and scored 388 runs against them in two Tests in 2001-02 without being dismissed ... Including his next innings he batted for a record 1241 minutes in Tests without getting out ... Kallis scored hundreds in five successive Tests in 2003-04 (only Don Bradman, with six, has done better) ... His record includes one Test and three ODIs for the World XI, and two ODIs for the Africa XI ...

THE FIGURES to 21.9.09   www.cricinfo.com

Batting & Fielding	M	Inns	NO	Runs	HS	Avge	S/R	100	50	4s	6s	Ct	St
Tests	131	221	33	10277	189*	54.66	44.15	31	51	1158	68	147	0
ODIs	291	277	51	10239	139	45.30	71.87	16	73	807	120	105	0
Twenty20 Ints	9	9	1	281	64	35.12	122.17	0	2	32	6	4	0
First-class	221	361	50	16629	200	53.46	–	48	89	–	–	209	0

Bowling	M	Balls	Runs	Wkts	BB	Avge	RpO	S/R	5i	10m
Tests	131	17040	8021	258	6–54	31.08	2.82	66.04	5	0
ODIs	291	9790	7881	247	5–30	31.90	4.83	39.63	2	0
Twenty20 Ints	9	84	120	3	2–20	40.00	8.57	28.00	0	0
First-class	221	25775	11985	393	6–54	30.49	2.78	65.58	8	0

KAMRAN AKMAL

Full name	**Kamran Akmal**
Born	**January 13, 1982, Lahore, Punjab**
Teams	**Lahore, National Bank**
Style	**Right-hand bat, wicketkeeper**
Test debut	**Pakistan v Zimbabwe at Harare 2002-03**
ODI debut	**Pakistan v Zimbabwe at Bulawayo 2002-03**

THE PROFILE Kamran Akmal made his first-class debut at the age of 15 as a useful wicketkeeper and a hard-hitting batsman. Several good performances earned him an A-team spot in 2002, and after doing well he was called up for the Zimbabwe tour ahead of the veteran Moin Khan. He was not expected to play in the Tests, but made his debut – and chipped in with a handy 38 – when Rashid Latif suffered a recurrence of a back injury. By October 2004 Akmal was Pakistan's first-choice keeper. He responded with a magnificent showing with the gloves in Australia, then, in 2005, hit five international centuries. Three of them came while opening in one-dayers, and two in Tests, the first saving the match against India at Mohali, while the second, a blistering 154, came in the emphatic series-sealing win over England at Lahore. However, a nightmare series in England in 2006 set him back again. He retained his place throughout 2006-07 without quite regaining his best touch with bat or gloves: he did make an important 119 against India in the Kolkata Test, but continued fumbles behind the stumps eventually led to Sarfraz Ahmed being given a run. Akmal caned Bangladesh for an 80-ball ODI century at the start of 2008, although that was not enough to earn him a place in the Asia Cup which followed. But he re-established himself in 2009, starting with an unbeaten 158 in a Test against Sri Lanka, then a century against Australia to underline his one-day credentials. Comfortable again, he played his part as Pakistan won the World Twenty20 in England in June.

THE FACTS Six of Kamran Akmal's ten first-class centuries have come in Tests: he scored five international hundreds in December 2005 and January 2006, including 154 in the Lahore Test against England, when he shared a sixth-wicket stand of 269 with Mohammad Yousuf ... Akmal has scored more Test hundreds than any other Pakistan wicketkeeper: Moin Khan made four and Imtiaz Ahmed three ... His brother Umar joined him in the national side in 2009 ...

THE FIGURES to 21.9.09

www.cricinfo.com

Batting & Fielding	M	Inns	NO	Runs	HS	Avge	S/R	100	50	4s	6s	Ct	St
Tests	43	72	5	2226	158*	33.22	63.16	6	9	314	8	142	20
ODIs	104	89	12	2053	124	26.66	84.90	5	3	242	19	108	17
Twenty20 Ints	25	20	3	348	59*	20.47	120.83	0	2	27	14	9	17
First-class	139	215	25	5970	174	31.42	–	10	27	–	–	460	40

Bowling	M	Balls	Runs	Wkts	BB	Avge	RpO	S/R	5i	10m
Tests	43	0	–	–	–	–	–	–	–	–
ODIs	104	0	–	–	–	–	–	–	–	–
Twenty20 Ints	25	0	–	–	–	–	–	–	–	–
First-class	139	0	–	–	–	–	–	–	–	–

SRI LANKA

CHAMARA **KAPUGEDERA**

Full name	**Chamara Kantha Kapugedera**
Born	**February 24, 1987, Kandy**
Teams	**Colombo Cricket Club, Kandurata, Chennai Super Kings**
Style	**Right-hand bat, occasional right-arm medium-pacer**
Test debut	**Sri Lanka v England at Lord's 2006**
ODI debut	**Sri Lanka v Australia at Perth 2005-06**

THE PROFILE   A naturally aggressive right-hander and a fine fielder, Chamara Kapugedera is one of the few genuinely exciting batsmen the Sri Lankan selectors have unearthed recently from the Under-19s. From his first appearances for Dharmaraja College in Kandy when he was 11, "Kapu" has rarely wasted an opportunity. After a prolific 2003-04 season, when he scored over 1000 runs at schoolboy level, he was picked for the following year's Under-19 tour of Pakistan and made two centuries in the representative matches. The selectors eventually fast-tracked him into the national squad after glowing reports from his youth coaches: Kapugedera was picked to go to India in November 2005, but injured his knee. However, he made his ODI debut, still only 18, against Australia at Perth early in 2006. A maiden fifty followed against Pakistan in March. He won his first Test cap at Lord's that May, but was unlucky enough to receive the perfect inswinging yorker first ball from Sajid Mahmood (another debutant). But Kapugedera put that disappointment behind him with a composed 50 in the third Test, which Sri Lanka won to level the series. He had a quiet time in 2006-07, missing the World Cup after going 12 ODIs without a fifty, then the following season stepped up in one-dayers – he hit 95 against West Indies at Port-of-Spain and 75 against India in the Asia Cup in June 2008 – without cracking the Test side. However, modest form in 2009 – apart from a Test-best 96 against Bangladesh and a matchwinning 67 not out in a one-dayer against Pakistan in August – meant Kapugedera faced stiff competition to keep his place.

THE FACTS   Kapugedera scored 70 on his first-class debut, for Sri Lanka A v New Zealand A in Colombo in October 2005 ... He was selected for the 2006 tour of England after playing only three first-class matches, and made his maiden century – 134 not out v Sussex at Hove – the game after collecting a first-ball duck on his Test debut at Lord's ... Kapugedera averages 67.50 in ODIs against West Indies – but 1.00 against England ...

THE FIGURES *to 21.9.09*   www.cricinfo.com

Batting & Fielding	M	Inns	NO	Runs	HS	Avge	S/R	100	50	4s	6s	Ct	St
Tests	8	15	3	418	96	34.83	53.18	0	4	48	7	6	0
ODIs	66	58	4	1207	95	22.35	74.14	0	6	94	23	21	0
Twenty20 Ints	9	8	2	125	27	20.83	104.16	0	0	10	3	3	0
First-class	33	57	10	1739	150*	37.00	59.73	3	11	184	25	24	0

Bowling	M	Balls	Runs	Wkts	BB	Avge	RpO	S/R	5i	10m
Tests	8	12	9	0	–	–	4.50	–	0	0
ODIs	66	228	192	2	1–24	96.00	5.05	114.00	0	0
Twenty20 Ints	9	0	–	–	–	–	–	–	–	–
First-class	33	299	173	3	1–1	57.66	3.47	99.66	0	0

INDIA

DINESH **KARTHIK**

Full name	**Krishnakumar Dinesh Karthik**
Born	**June 1, 1985, Madras (now Chennai)**
Teams	**Tamil Nadu, Delhi Daredevils**
Style	**Right-hand bat, wicketkeeper**
Test debut	**India v Australia at Mumbai 2004-05**
ODI debut	**India v England at Lord's 2004**

THE PROFILE Dinesh Karthik may be shy off the field, but he has shown his ability to attack under pressure and improvise on it. He gave glimpses of batting talent at 17, but his keeping wasn't up to scratch and he was dropped for the later stages of the Ranji Trophy. However, in 2004 an impressive display in the Under-19 World Cup (including a whirlwind 70 in a must-win game against Sri Lanka), two vital hundreds in the Ranji Trophy, and some improved keeping alerted the national selectors. Karthik replaced Parthiv Patel in the one-day squad in England in September 2004, and pulled off a superb stumping to dispose of Michael Vaughan on debut at Lord's. Then he won his first Test cap against Australia but, after just one fifty in ten matches, he was dropped in favour of the flamboyant MS Dhoni, whose instant success meant Karthik had to rethink. He reinvented himself as a specialist batsman. After India's forgettable 2007 World Cup (for which he was selected but didn't play), he made a maiden Test century in Bangladesh, and forged a successful opening partnership with Wasim Jaffer which continued in England, where Karthik was India's leading scorer in the Tests. Leaner times followed – he was dropped after six single-figure scores in his next ten innings – but he kept his name in the frame with a fine domestic season in 2008–09. His 1026 first-class runs included five centuries (one of them a double), and he also did well in the IPL. With Dhoni occasionally suffering from back trouble, meaning a spare keeper is a necessity, Karthik looks likely to remain a valuable squad member.

THE FACTS Karthik made 213 for Tamil Nadu v Uttar Pradesh at Ghaziabad in November 2008 ... He made 153 and 103 for South Zone v Central Zone in the Duleep Trophy at Bangalore in January 2009 ... Karthik averages 49.33 in Tests against South Africa, but only 1.00 in two Tests against Zimbabwe ... He prefers his surname to be spelt with two As ("Kaarthik") as it is more astrologically propitious ...

THE FIGURES to 21.9.09   www.cricinfo.com

Batting & Fielding	M	Inns	NO	Runs	HS	Avge	S/R	100	50	4s	6s	Ct	St
Tests	22	35	1	973	129	28.61	49.76	1	7	128	4	47	5
ODIs	32	25	5	468	67	23.40	74.05	0	3	43	4	23	2
Twenty20 Ints	6	5	1	67	31*	16.75	115.51	0	0	9	1	3	2
First-class	71	113	6	3857	213	36.04	56.77	9	21	–	–	197	16

Bowling	M	Balls	Runs	Wkts	BB	Avge	RpO	S/R	5i	10m
Tests	22	0	–	–	–	–	–	–	–	–
ODIs	32	0	–	–	–	–	–	–	–	–
Twenty20 Ints	6	0	–	–	–	–	–	–	–	–
First-class	71	30	28	0	–	–	5.60	–	0	0

SIMON **KATICH**

Full name	**Simon Mathew Katich**
Born	**August 21, 1975, Middle Swan, Western Australia**
Teams	**New South Wales, Kings XI Punjab**
Style	**Left-hand bat, left-arm unorthodox spinner**
Test debut	**Australia v England at Leeds 2001**
ODI debut	**Australia v Zimbabwe at Melbourne 2000-01**

THE PROFILE Simon Katich resurrected his international career with a stunning season in 2007-08. He broke the record for runs in a Pura Cup season (1506 at 94.12) captained NSW to the title, and regained his Test place. All this must have seemed unlikely when he lost his national contract the preceding winter (he conceded he was struggling at the highest level and deserved to be dropped). His campaign featured five centuries, including 306 against Queensland, of which 184 came in an extended 150-minute post-lunch session. The Australian selectors, notoriously reluctant to go back to a jettisoned player, just could not ignore his runs, and after 30 months out of the Test side Katich made a hundred in Antigua and added 157 at Bridgetown in June 2008. He continued his renaissance with centuries against India, New Zealand and South Africa, but tailed off a little in the 2009 Ashes series, after starting with 122 in the first Test at Cardiff, as the bowlers exploited his exaggerated movement across the stumps. During his break from international cricket Katich simply enjoyed batting without the expectation heaped on a Test player. He had also worked on some technical issues that plagued him during 2005, when he was upset by reverse-swing in the Ashes then bamboozled by Murali in the Super Series. Ever since Katich was included in Western Australia's state squad in 1994-95, he looked destined for bigger things. He made his Test debut in England in 2001, then enjoyed surprising success with his chinamen against Zimbabwe at Sydney, later his home ground, at the end of 2003.

THE FACTS Katich made 306 for New South Wales v Queensland in October 2007, the highest score at the SCG since Don Bradman's 452 not out, also against Queensland, in 1929-30 ... Katich made 1506 runs in 2007-08, a record for a Pura Cup/Sheffield Shield season, beating Michael Bevan's 1464 for Tasmania in 2004-05 ... In 2000-01 Katich's 1282 runs for NSW included a century against every other state ... A third of his Test wickets came in one innings, during his 6 for 65 against Zimbabwe at Sydney in 2003-04 ...

THE FIGURES *to 21.9.09* www.cricinfo.com

Batting & Fielding	M	Inns	NO	Runs	HS	Avge	S/R	100	50	4s	6s	Ct	St
Tests	43	74	5	2990	157	43.33	49.53	8	16	357	6	32	0
ODIs	45	42	5	1324	107*	35.78	68.74	1	9	138	4	13	0
Twenty20 Ints	3	2	0	69	39	34.50	146.80	0	0	8	2	2	0
First-class	207	354	45	16787	306	54.32	–	47	87	–	–	191	0

Bowling	M	Balls	Runs	Wkts	BB	Avge	RpO	S/R	5i	10m
Tests	43	919	560	18	6–65	31.11	3.65	51.05	1	0
ODIs	45	0	–	–	–	–	–	–	–	–
Twenty20 Ints	3	0	–	–	–	–	–	–	–	–
First-class	207	5679	3405	92	7–130	37.01	3.59	61.72	3	0

ZAHEER **KHAN**

INDIA

Full name	**Zaheer Khan**
Born	**October 7, 1978, Shrirampur, Maharashtra**
Teams	**Mumbai, Mumbai Indians**
Style	**Right-hand bat, left-arm fast-medium bowler**
Test debut	**India v Bangladesh at Dhaka 2000-01**
ODI debut	**India v Kenya at Nairobi 2000-01**

THE PROFILE Like Waqar Younis a decade before, left-armer Zaheer Khan yorked his way into the cricket world's consciousness: his performances at the Champions Trophy in Kenya in September 2000 announced the arrival of an all-too-rare star in the Indian fast-bowling firmament. Well-built, quick and unfazed by reputations, Zaheer can move the ball both ways off the pitch and swing the old ball at a decent pace. After initially struggling to establish himself, he came of age in the West Indies in 2002, when he led the attack with great heart. His subsequent displays in England and New Zealand – not to mention some eye-catching moments at the 2003 World Cup – established him at the forefront of the new pace generation, but a hamstring injury saw him relegated to bit-part performer as India enjoyed some of their finest moments away in Australia and Pakistan. In a bid to jump the queue of left-arm hopefuls, Zaheer put in the hard yards for Worcestershire in 2006, bowling a lot of overs and, against Essex, taking the first nine wickets to fall before Darren Gough's flailing bat – and a dropped catch – spoilt his figures and his chances of a rare all-ten. It worked: Zaheer reclaimed his Test place, survived the fallout from the World Cup, and led the way in England in 2007, where his nine wickets at Trent Bridge gave India the match and the series: *Wisden* named him one of their Cricketers of the Year. An ankle injury restricted him in 2007-08, but he was back in form the following season, sailing past 200 Test wickets in New Zealand early in 2009.

THE FACTS Zaheer Khan's 75 against Bangladesh at Dhaka in December 2004 is the highest score by a No. 11 in Tests: he dominated a last-wicket stand of 133 with Sachin Tendulkar ... He took 9 for 138 (including a spell of 9 for 28) for Worcestershire v Essex at Chelmsford in June 2006, but a last-wicket stand of 97 cost him the chance of taking all ten wickets ... Khan averages 17.46 with the ball in ODIs against Zimbabwe, but 48.52 v Australia ... His record includes six ODIs for the Asia XI ...

THE FIGURES to 21.9.09   www.cricinfo.com

Batting & Fielding	M	Inns	NO	Runs	HS	Avge	S/R	100	50	4s	6s	Ct	St
Tests	65	86	22	883	75	13.79	52.62	0	3	98	17	18	0
ODIs	162	88	35	701	34*	13.22	75.62	0	0	58	23	35	0
Twenty20 Ints	9	2	1	4	4	4.00	133.33	0	0	0	0	1	0
First-class	127	167	37	1900	75	14.61	–	0	4	–	–	42	0

Bowling	M	Balls	Runs	Wkts	BB	Avge	RpO	S/R	5i	10m
Tests	65	12962	7107	210	5–29	33.84	3.28	61.72	7	0
ODIs	162	8097	6566	225	5–42	29.18	4.86	35.98	1	0
Twenty20 Ints	9	184	222	11	4–19	20.18	7.23	16.72	0	0
First-class	127	26046	14377	519	9–138	27.70	3.31	50.18	29	7

KHURRAM MANZOOR

Full name	**Khurram Manzoor**
Born	**June 10, 1986, Karachi, Sind**
Teams	**Karachi, Pakistan International Airlines**
Style	**Right-hand bat, occasional offspinner**
Test debut	**Pakistan v Sri Lanka at Karachi 2008-09**
ODI debut	**Pakistan v Zimbabwe at Sheikhupura 2007-08**

THE PROFILE Khurram Manzoor is a solid but aggressive opener with a distinctive stance not unlike that of the former Pakistan batsman Ijaz Ahmed – backside jutting out and legs planted wide apart. It served him well on his first-class debut, at the tender age of 16, when he made 73 for Karachi Blues in December 2002 – but he faded away for a couple of seasons after that before making two centuries, and nearly 500 runs, in 2004-05. The selectors started to take an interest during a stellar 2007-08 season, which eventually produced 1283 first-class runs with four centuries (one of them a double). After playing against Australia A, Manzoor made his full ODI debut against Zimbabwe early in 2008, marking it with an impressive half-century, and added another in his next match, against West Indies in Abu Dhabi the following November. Pakistan's seemingly perennial struggle to find a settled Test opening pair led to Manzoor being given a run alongside Salman Butt in 2009, and he responded with 59 at Lahore in his second Test (he was the not-out batsman when the match was abandoned after the terrorist attack on the Sri Lankans), and adding a confident 93 in Colombo later in the year, by which time his opening partner was Fawad Alam as Butt had been jettisoned. In that innings Manzoor played well off the back foot, and showed good judgment of which deliveries to play, until nerves got the better of him in the nineties and he poked at one that left him from the wily Chaminda Vaas (it was Vaas's 355th and last Test wicket).

THE FACTS Khurram Manzoor made 201 not out (in 708 minutes) for Sind v Punjab at Lahore in November 2008 ... He scored 200 for Karachi Urban v Mumbai in the Mohammad Nissar Trophy match at Karachi in September 2007 ... Manzoor made 73 on his first-class debut, for Karachi Blues at Peshawar in December 2002 ... He made 50 (v Zimbabwe) and 63 (v West Indies) in his first two ODIs in 2007-08 ...

THE FIGURES *to 21.9.09*   www.cricinfo.com

Batting & Fielding	M	Inns	NO	Runs	HS	Avge	S/R	100	50	4s	6s	Ct	St
Tests	5	8	1	239	93	34.14	44.09	0	2	28	0	3	0
ODIs	7	7	0	236	83	33.71	62.93	0	3	21	0	3	0
Twenty20 Ints	0	0	–	–	–	–	–	–	–	–	–	–	–
First-class	54	92	6	3512	201*	40.83	–	9	14	–	–	40	0

Bowling	M	Balls	Runs	Wkts	BB	Avge	RpO	S/R	5i	10m
Tests	5	0	–	–	–	–	–	–	–	–
ODIs	7	0	–	–	–	–	–	–	–	–
Twenty20 Ints	0	0	–	–	–	–	–	–	–	–
First-class	54	156	62	1	1–14	62.00	2.38	156.00	0	0

NUWAN **KULASEKARA**

Full name	**Kulasekara Mudiyanselage Dinesh Nuwan Kulasekara**
Born	**July 22, 1982, Nittambuwa**
Teams	**Colts, Basnahira North**
Style	**Right-hand bat, right-arm fast-medium bowler**
Test debut	**Sri Lanka v New Zealand at Napier 2004-05**
ODI debut	**Sri Lanka v England at Dambulla 2003-04**

THE PROFILE From a bustling run-up and a whippy open-chested action, Nuwan Kulasekara generates a lively pace, and moves the ball off the seam at upwards of 80mph. He can also maintain a tight line and length, and, after adding a yard or two of pace, suddenly emerged as a formidable bowler, especially in one-day internationals. He did so well in 2008 (33 wickets at 20.87 in 21 matches) that by March 2009 he was proudly sitting on top of the ICC's world one-day rankings. He maintained that form and at last showed signs of emerging as a force in Tests too, grabbing four wickets in each innings as Pakistan went down in the second Test in Colombo in August, and finishing the series with 17 victims. Prior to that, his biggest mark on Test cricket had been with the bat: at Lord's in May 2006 Kulasekara hung on for more than three hours for 64 – his maiden Test fifty – helping Chaminda Vaas to ensure that Sri Lanka clung on for a draw after England made them follow on 359 behind. It was his second adhesive performance of the match, following 29 as he and Vaas pushed the first-innings total from 131 for 8 to a more respectable 192. Before all that Kulasekara had made an instant impression in his first one-dayer, taking 2 for 19 in nine overs as England subsided for 88 at Dambulla in November 2003. That came soon after a fine first season, in which he took 61 wickets at 21.06 for Colts. He started as a softball enthusiast before shifting his focus to cricket, first with Negegoda CC and then with Galle.

THE FACTS Playing for North Central Province at Dambulla in March 2005, Kulasekara dismissed all of Central Province's top six, finishing with 6 for 71 ... He took 7 for 27 for Colts against Bloomfield in January 2008 ... In March 2009 Kulasekara went to the top of the ICC world rankings for ODI bowlers ... He made 95 for Galle against Nondescripts in Colombo in October 2003: he and Primal Buddika doubled the score from 174 for 6 ...

THE FIGURES to 21.9.09   www.cricinfo.com

Batting & Fielding	M	Inns	NO	Runs	HS	Avge	S/R	100	50	4s	6s	Ct	St
Tests	10	14	1	214	64	16.46	46.72	0	1	27	4	2	0
ODIs	59	39	19	306	39*	15.30	63.22	0	0	18	3	15	0
Twenty20 Ints	7	7	1	36	19*	6.00	120.00	0	0	0	2	4	0
First-class	70	93	21	1320	95	18.33	–	0	3	–	–	24	0

Bowling	M	Balls	Runs	Wkts	BB	Avge	RpO	S/R	5i	10m
Tests	10	1492	757	24	4–21	31.54	3.04	62.16	0	0
ODIs	59	2674	1973	74	4–40	26.66	4.42	36.13	0	0
Twenty20 Ints	7	167	234	5	1–21	46.80	8.40	33.40	0	0
First-class	70	9762	5267	240	7–27	21.94	3.23	40.67	9	1

PRAVEEN **KUMAR**

Full name	**Praveenkumar Sakat Singh**
Born	**October 2, 1986, Meerut, Uttar Pradesh**
Teams	**Uttar Pradesh, Bangalore Royal Challengers**
Style	**Right-hand bat, right-arm fast-medium bowler**
Test debut	**No Tests yet**
ODI debut	**India v Pakistan at Jaipur 2007-08**

THE PROFILE   Praveen Kumar is a man of many parts: a fast bowler with the ability to toil away on unresponsive Indian wickets, he can also double up as a carefree hitter down the order and even, sometimes, as a surprise opener. He shone on his debut in November 2005, collecting nine wickets against Haryana, and was a key performer – 41 wickets and 368 runs – as Uttar Pradesh won the Ranji Trophy in 2005-06, his first season. He followed that with 49 wickets the following term, which earned him an A-team place for a one-day tri-series in Kenya in August 2007. He excelled with both bat and ball, winning the Man of the Series award. He continued his fine run in the Challenger Trophy (trial games for the full national team), and was called up for the one-dayers against Pakistan, although he failed to strike in his only outing. But another strong Ranji season – including 8 for 68 in vain in the final against Delhi – earned him a trip to Australia for the one-day series early in 2008. He returned with reputation enhanced after claiming ten wickets in his four games, including a matchwinning 4 for 46 in the second (and conclusive) final at Brisbane – he dismissed Adam Gilchrist and Ricky Ponting for single figures in both finals. After that Kumar toiled manfully in the IPL's inaugural season, then produced another matchwinning four-wicket effort against Pakistan in a one-dayer in Bangladesh. His progress stalled a little in 2008-09 – only 18 first-class wickets – and other pacemen muscled past him, but Kumar remains very much in the mix, in one-dayers at least.

THE FACTS   Kumar took 8 for 68 for Uttar Pradesh v Delhi in the Ranji Trophy final at Mumbai in January 2008 ... He took 5 for 93 (and 4 for 55 in the second innings) on his first-class debut for UP v Haryana at Kanpur in November 2005 ... Kumar scored 78 and 57, and also took 5 for 73 and 5 for 87, for UP v Andhra at Anantapur in January 2006 ...

THE FIGURES to 21.9.09   www.cricinfo.com

Batting & Fielding	M	Inns	NO	Runs	HS	Avge	S/R	100	50	4s	6s	Ct	St
Tests	0	0	–	–	–	–	–	–	–	–	–	–	–
ODIs	24	11	3	63	15	7.87	69.23	0	0	4	0	6	0
Twenty20 Ints	1	1	0	6	6	6.00	60.00	0	0	0	0	0	0
First-class	32	51	2	1150	98	23.46	73.95	0	7	124	36	6	0

Bowling	M	Balls	Runs	Wkts	BB	Avge	RpO	S/R	5i	10m
Tests	0	0	–	–	–	–	–	–	–	–
ODIs	24	1134	941	30	4–31	31.36	4.97	37.80	0	0
Twenty20 Ints	1	12	15	1	1–15	15.00	7.50	12.00	0	0
First-class	32	7240	3377	144	8–68	23.45	2.79	50.27	10	1

VVS **LAXMAN**

INDIA

Full name	**Vangipurappu Venkata Sai Laxman**
Born	**November 1, 1974, Hyderabad, Andhra Pradesh**
Teams	**Hyderabad, Lancashire, Deccan Chargers**
Style	**Right-hand bat, occasional offspinner**
Test debut	**India v South Africa at Ahmedabad 1996-97**
ODI debut	**India v Zimbabwe at Cuttack 1997-98**

THE PROFILE At his best, VVS Laxman is a sight for the gods. Wristy and willowy, he can match – sometimes even better – Tendulkar for strokeplay. His on-side game is comparable to his idol Azharuddin's, yet he is decidedly more assured on the off side, and has the rare gift of being able to hit the same ball to either side. The Australians, who have suffered more than most, paid him the highest compliment after India's 2003-04 tour by admitting they did not know where to bowl to him. Laxman, a one-time medical student, graduated after a five-year international apprenticeship in March 2001, when he tormented Steve Waugh's thought-to-be-invincible Aussies with a majestic 281 to stand the Kolkata Test on its head. His form dipped after that, until an uncharacteristic grinding century in Antigua in May 2002 marked his second coming: he has been a picture of consistency since, often dazzling, but less prone to collaborating in his own dismissal. Laxman was left out of the 2003 World Cup, but made an emphatic one-day return with a string of hundreds in Australia, followed by a matchwinning 107 in the deciding ODI of India's ice-breaking tour of Pakistan in March 2004. Eventually he was confined to Tests, and reached 6000 runs in August 2008, at the end of a series in which he scored well but was consistently dismissed by Sri Lanka's latest spin sensation Ajantha Mendis. Earlier in the year Laxman had scored his third Test century at Sydney. The Aussies conceded another double-century at Delhi in 2008-09, followed by 64 in the next Test – Laxman's 100th – as the series was won.

THE FACTS Laxman's 281 against Australia at Kolkata in March 2001 was India's highest Test score at the time (since passed by Virender Sehwag), and included a national-record fifth-wicket stand of 376 with Rahul Dravid ... He averages 55.10 against Australia, and his highest four scores (281, 200 not out, 178, 167) have all come against them ... Laxman has scored two first-class triple-centuries for Hyderabad – 353 v Karnataka at Bangalore in April 2000, and 301 not out v Bihar at Jamshedpur in February 1998 ...

THE FIGURES *to 21.9.09*   www.cricinfo.com

Batting & Fielding	M	Inns	NO	Runs	HS	Avge	S/R	100	50	4s	6s	Ct	St
Tests	105	174	25	6741	281	45.24	49.07	14	39	913	4	111	0
ODIs	86	83	7	2338	131	30.76	71.23	6	10	222	4	39	0
Twenty20 Ints	0	0	–	–	–	–	–	–	–	–	–	–	–
First-class	232	377	45	17271	353	52.02	–	50	79	–	–	247	1

Bowling	M	Balls	Runs	Wkts	BB	Avge	RpO	S/R	5i	10m
Tests	105	324	126	2	1–2	63.00	2.33	162.00	0	0
ODIs	86	42	40	0	–	–	5.71	–	0	0
Twenty20 Ints	0	0	–	–	–	–	–	–	–	–
First-class	232	1829	754	22	3–11	34.27	2.47	83.13	0	0

BRETT **LEE**

Full name **Brett Lee**
Born **November 8, 1976, Wollongong, New South Wales**
Teams **New South Wales, Kings XI Punjab**
Style **Right-hand bat, right-arm fast bowler**
Test debut **Australia v India at Melbourne 1999-2000**
ODI debut **Australia v Pakistan at Brisbane 1999-2000**

THE PROFILE Brett Lee is determined that age and injury shall not weary him. Always positive and flashing a smile from a toothpaste ad, he insists his body "still feels really young", but after years as Australia's youthful pin-up he has entered fatherhood and his thirties. At first there was pace, but then came injuries and long layoffs. It is a recurring theme in Lee's career. His speed thrills, but after overcoming another serious ankle problem in 2009, there is no guarantee he will be able to continue slamming his foot down. When he began he struggled with injury and accusations of throwing, and had a strangely barren first Ashes series in 2001 (nine wickets at 55). Three years later he was 12th man for nine successive Tests after his first bout of ankle surgery. He returned for the 2005 Ashes, displaying a never-say-die attitude with ball and bat, and nearly conjuring victory at Edgbaston with a battling 43: Andrew Flintoff's consoling of Lee at the end was the defining image of that epic series. And when Glenn McGrath struggled for impact, Lee became leader of the attack – a position he had craved since first crashing onto the Test scene. He claimed 20 wickets in the Ashes rematch, but picked up another ankle injury which kept him out of the 2007 World Cup. He bounced back in 2007-08, following 40 wickets in six home Tests with 18 in three in the Caribbean. Surgery on left ankle and foot spoiled his 2008-09 season, then his 2009 Ashes tour was spoiled by a rib strain that eventually kept him out of the Tests – although he showed what might have been with some incisive bowling in the one-day demolitions that followed.

THE FACTS Lee took a World Cup hat-trick against Kenya in 2002-03 ... His older brother Shane played 45 ODIs for Australia between 1995 and 2001 ... Lee averages 21.09 with the ball against New Zealand, but 40.61 v England ... He was on the winning side in each of his first ten Tests, a sequence ended by England's win at Leeds in 2001 ... Lee took 5 for 47 in his first Test innings, but did not improve on that until his 44th match ...

THE FIGURES *to 21.9.09*   www.cricinfo.com

Batting & Fielding	M	Inns	NO	Runs	HS	Avge	S/R	100	50	4s	6s	Ct	St
Tests	76	90	18	1451	64	20.15	52.97	0	5	182	18	23	0
ODIs	180	89	36	860	57	16.22	80.44	0	2	44	25	43	0
Twenty20 Ints	17	9	4	91	43*	18.20	144.44	0	0	8	4	5	0
First-class	116	139	25	2120	97	18.59	–	0	8	–	–	35	0

Bowling	M	Balls	Runs	Wkts	BB	Avge	RpO	S/R	5i	10m
Tests	76	16531	9554	310	5–30	30.81	3.46	53.32	10	0
ODIs	180	9220	7266	317	5–22	22.92	4.72	29.08	9	0
Twenty20 Ints	17	355	454	17	3–27	26.70	7.67	20.88	0	0
First-class	116	24194	13746	487	7–114	28.22	3.40	49.67	20	2

BRENDON McCULLUM

NEW ZEALAND

Full name **Brendon Barrie McCullum**
Born **September 27, 1981, Dunedin, Otago**
Teams **Otago, Kolkata Knight Riders**
Style **Right-hand bat, wicketkeeper**
Test debut **New Zealand v South Africa at Hamilton 2003-04**
ODI debut **New Zealand v Australia at Sydney 2001-02**

THE PROFILE Brendon McCullum stepped up to the national side as a wicketkeeper-batsman after an outstanding career in international youth cricket, where he proved capable of dominating opposition attacks. Not surprisingly he found it hard to replicate that at the highest level at first, although there were occasional fireworks in domestic cricket. But he finally made his mark in England in 2004, with 200 runs in the Tests, including an entertaining 96 at Lord's. He finally brought up his maiden century in Bangladesh in October, and added another hundred in the two-day victory over Zimbabwe in August 2005. He made his ODI debut as a batsman in 2001-02 in Australia, where he made the acquaintance of Brett Lee, who has since let him have more than one beamer, to widespread outrage. With some onlookers murmuring the name "Gilchrist", McCullum hammered 86 from 91 balls as New Zealand overhauled Australia's 346 at Hamilton in February 2007 with one wicket to spare. But he really made his mark in 2007-08, when he enlivened the opening match of the much-hyped Indian Premier League by smacking 158 not out from 73 balls for Kolkata Knight Riders. After that, he was a marked man in England in 2008, and although there were signs that he was having trouble tempering his attacking instincts in the longer game, he lit up Lord's again with 97, and also hit 71 at Trent Bridge. Then he walloped ten sixes in his 166 in a mismatch against Ireland. Early next year he showed he could do it in Tests, too, with successive innings of 84 and 115 against India in March 2009.

THE FACTS McCullum slammed 158 not out from only 73 balls (ten fours and 13 sixes) for Kolkata v Bangalore in the first match of the IPL ... He is the only man to be out twice in the nineties in Tests at Lord's without ever making a century there ... McCullum hit 166, and shared an opening stand of 274 with James Marshall, in an ODI against Ireland at Aberdeen in July 2008 ... His brother Nathan has also played one-day cricket for New Zealand ...

THE FIGURES to 21.9.09   www.cricinfo.com

Batting & Fielding	M	Inns	NO	Runs	HS	Avge	S/R	100	50	4s	6s	Ct	St
Tests	46	74	4	2283	143	31.70	62.61	3	13	281	27	139	9
ODIs	155	129	22	3004	166	28.07	87.99	1	15	258	85	165	13
Twenty20 Ints	28	28	4	747	69*	31.12	124.50	0	5	73	27	19	3
First-class	88	150	8	4732	160	33.32	–	7	27	–	–	244	17

Bowling	M	Balls	Runs	Wkts	BB	Avge	RpO	S/R	5i	10m
Tests	46	0	–	–	–	–	–	–	–	–
ODIs	155	0	–	–	–	–	–	–	–	–
Twenty20 Ints	28	0	–	–	–	–	–	–	–	–
First-class	88	0	–	–	–	–	–	–	–	–

TIM McINTOSH

Full name	**Timothy Gavin McIntosh**
Born	**December 4, 1979, Auckland**
Teams	**Auckland**
Style	**Left-hand bat**
Test debut	**New Zealand v West Indies at Dunedin 2008-09**
ODI debut	**No ODIs yet**

THE PROFILE Left-handed opener Tim McIntosh made his first-class debut for Auckland in March 1999. In December 2000 he hit 182 against Canterbury, and has been a consistent scorer at domestic level ever since, apart from a loss of form in 2004-05 when he moved to Canterbury but managed only 49 runs in six matches. Two years before that he had made 820 at 58 for Auckland, and soon returned there. Apart from his early days with New Zealand's Under-19s McIntosh had never aroused much interest from the selectors, but he made 268 against Canterbury in March 2008, then later that year hit 191 against Wellington and 78 against the touring West Indians, at a time when the Test openers were going through a bad trot. McIntosh made a nervous debut in Dunedin – it took him 38 balls to get off the mark – but he finished with 34 and 24 not out, then produced a classy 136 in the second Test at Napier. He batted for 455 minutes, and many of his 21 fours came square through point. It earned the stylish, steady McIntosh comparisons with another dogged left-handed New Zealand opener – Mark Richardson, who was also in his 30th year when he started what became a successful Test career in 2000. Slimmer pickings followed for McIntosh against India and Sri Lanka: he did make 69 in almost five hours in the first Test in Colombo in August 2009, but that was followed by three single-figure scores. He is unlikely to feature in the one-day team – he hasn't even played for Auckland in limited-overs cricket for four years.

THE FACTS McIntosh scored 268 for Auckland v Canterbury in March 2008: the next-highest score was 42 ... He made 205 v Otago at Lincoln in November 2006 ... McIntosh's hundred against West Indies at Napier in December 2008 was only the second by a New Zealand opener in a Test since 2004 ...

THE FIGURES to 21.9.09   www.cricinfo.com

Batting & Fielding	M	Inns	NO	Runs	HS	Avge	S/R	100	50	4s	6s	Ct	St
Tests	7	13	1	338	136	28.16	35.46	1	1	45	1	3	0
ODIs	0	0	–	–	–	–	–	–	–	–	–	–	–
Twenty20 Ints	0	0	–	–	–	–	–	–	–	–	–	–	–
First-class	88	147	10	4570	268	33.35	–	14	16	–	–	70	0

Bowling	M	Balls	Runs	Wkts	BB	Avge	RpO	S/R	5i	10m
Tests	7	0	–	–	–	–	–	–	–	–
ODIs	0	0	–	–	–	–	–	–	–	–
Twenty20 Ints	0	0	–	–	–	–	–	–	–	–
First-class	88	124	80	0	–	–	3.87	–	0	0

NEIL McKENZIE

SOUTH AFRICA

Full name	**Neil Douglas McKenzie**
Born	**November 24, 1975, Johannesburg, Transvaal**
Teams	**Lions**
Style	**Right-hand bat, occasional right-arm medium-pacer**
Test debut	**South Africa v Sri Lanka at Galle 2000**
ODI debut	**South Africa v Zimbabwe at Durban 1999-2000**

THE PROFILE Popular and unassuming, if mildly eccentric – one of his more bizarre superstitions was a liking for attaching bats to dressing-room ceilings – Neil McKenzie was a South African middle-order stalwart for four years in the early 2000s, despite a less-than-promising start as an opener in Sri Lanka in 2000. His father Kevin was a carefree middle-order batsman who represented South Africa during the rebel era, while Neil captained both the South African Schools and Under-19 sides. He made maiden Test and ODI centuries against New Zealand and Sri Lanka during 2000-01, and seemed to have established himself as a more or less permanent fixture in both teams. Questions were asked about his ability to cope with the very best spinners, which may account for his 3½-year exile from the side from March 2004, at a time when he ought to have been at the height of his career. Marriage and fatherhood calmed his superstitions a little, and McKenzie was eventually recalled to the Test side to face West Indies in January 2008 as an opener in place of Herschelle Gibbs, and cemented his place with 226 in a world-record opening stand with Graeme Smith against Bangladesh shortly afterwards. He did well in England, too, making 138 at Lord's and proving a calming influence in the dressing-room, but then a run of average scores found him out of favour again. Neat and economical at the crease, McKenzie is particularly strong on the leg side, although his judgment in leaving off-target balls was a feature of his restrained displays after his comeback.

THE FACTS McKenzie and Graeme Smith broke the 52-year-old Test record of India's Vinoo Mankad and Pankaj Roy (413) with an opening partnership of 415 against Bangladesh at Chittagong in 2007-08 ... McKenzie averages 60.42 in Tests against India, but 22.53 v Sri Lanka (although in ODIs he averages 54.40 v Sri Lanka) ... His father Kevin played for South African representative sides during the 1980s ...

THE FIGURES to 21.9.09   www.cricinfo.com

Batting & Fielding	M	Inns	NO	Runs	HS	Avge	S/R	100	50	4s	6s	Ct	St
Tests	58	94	7	3253	226	37.39	42.00	5	16	409	22	54	0
ODIs	64	55	10	1688	131*	37.51	69.40	2	10	142	8	21	0
Twenty20 Ints	2	1	1	7	7*	–	87.50	0	0	0	0	0	0
First-class	184	312	36	11823	226	42.83	–	29	59	–	–	155	0

Bowling	M	Balls	Runs	Wkts	BB	Avge	RpO	S/R	5i	10m
Tests	58	90	68	0	–	–	4.53	–	0	0
ODIs	64	46	27	0	–	–	3.52	–	0	0
Twenty20 Ints	2	0	–	–	–	–	–	–	–	–
First-class	184	672	369	7	2–13	52.71	3.29	96.00	0	0

MAHBUBUL ALAM

Full name **Mahbubul Alam**
Born **December 1, 1983, Faridpur, Dhaka**
Teams **Dhaka**
Style **Right-hand bat, right-arm fast-medium bowler**
Test debut **Bangladesh v New Zealand at Mirpur 2008-09**
ODI debut **Bangladesh v Zimbabwe at Mirpur 2008-09**

THE PROFILE Fast-medium bowler Mahbubul Alam was one of several players propelled into international cricket by the defection of a dozen senior internationals to the unauthorised Indian Cricket League late in 2008. Unusually for a Bangladeshi, "Robin" did not have a glittering youth career, although he was eventually signed up by the national academy, and was their leading wicket-taker on tours of South Africa and Sri Lanka in 2008. That followed a fine season for Dhaka in Bangladesh's National Cricket League, in which he took 39 first-class wickets at 20.68: only slow left-armer Mosharraf Hossain (44) and medium-pacer Tareq Aziz (43) took more, but at a higher cost. Mahbubul got the national call when New Zealand toured Bangladesh late in 2008: he sat out the one-dayers, but made a low-key debut in the rain-ruined second Test, dismissing Jamie How with his seventh ball. Soon after that he produced two stunning deliveries in South Africa to scupper Graeme Smith. In the first Test at Bloemfontein he angled one across the left-hander, but it nipped back to hit the off stump; in the second Test, at Centurion, the ball swung into Smith then jagged away to beat the bat and pin him lbw for 27. If Mahbubul could produce such deliveries at will he would be a world-beater: the trouble was these were isolated incidents, and he took only one other wicket as South Africa won both Tests easily. But the memory of those two deliveries to one of the world's leading batsmen may inspire Mahbubul to greater things as he contends with a number of similar bowlers for a regular place.

THE FACTS Mahbubul Alam took 5 for 47 (9 for 100 in the match) for Dhaka at Rajshahi in November 2007 ... He took a wicket (New Zealand's Jamie How) with his seventh ball in Test cricket in October 2008 ... Mahbubul took 5 for 57 for Bangladesh A v Ireland A in Dublin in June 2008 ...

THE FIGURES to 21.9.09   www.cricinfo.com

Batting & Fielding	M	Inns	NO	Runs	HS	Avge	S/R	100	50	4s	6s	Ct	St
Tests	4	7	3	5	2	1.25	6.94	0	0	0	0	0	0
ODIs	5	2	0	81	59	40.50	114.08	0	1	3	4	1	0
Twenty20 Ints	0	0	–	–	–	–	–	–	–	–	–	–	–
First-class	26	32	10	144	20	6.54	–	0	0	–	–	10	0

Bowling	M	Balls	Runs	Wkts	BB	Avge	RpO	S/R	5i	10m
Tests	4	587	314	5	2–62	62.80	3.20	117.40	0	0
ODIs	5	222	280	7	2–42	40.00	7.56	31.71	0	0
Twenty20 Ints	0	0	–	–	–	–	–	–	–	–
First-class	26	4143	2058	77	5–47	26.72	2.98	53.80	1	0

MAHMUDULLAH

Full name	**Mohammad Mahmudullah**
Born	**February 4, 1986, Mymensingh**
Teams	**Dhaka**
Style	**Right-hand bat, offspinner**
Test debut	**Bangladesh v West Indies at Kingstown 2009**
ODI debut	**Bangladesh v Sri Lanka at Colombo 2007**

THE PROFILE An offspinning allrounder who is also an assured close-in fielder, Mahmudullah was something of a surprise selection for Bangladesh's chastening tour of Sri Lanka in mid-2007 (all three Tests were lost by an innings, and all three ODIs ended in defeat too). He made his international debut in the second one-dayer, scoring 36 and picking up two wickets in his five overs. As a bowler he does turn the ball, and can also keep the runs down. Mahmudullah spent the summer of 2005 on the groundstaff at Lord's: MCC's head coach, Clive Radley, remembered him bowling "from quite wide of the crease – he spun it a lot and bowled a good *doosra*". Bangladesh have a lot of slow left-armers, but not many offspinners have made a mark yet. "Riyad" had a run in the one-day side in 2008, and although his bowling proved unpenetrative he contributed usefully down the order, making a maiden fifty against Pakistan at Faisalabad. He had a superb domestic season with the bat in 2008-09, making 710 runs at 54.61, including his first four centuries. Mahmudullah toured the West Indies in mid-2009, and made his Test debut when the pitch at St Vincent looked likely to take spin: he did better than even he might have expected, taking eight wickets, including 5 for 51 (his maiden first-class five-for) in the second innings, as Bangladesh pulled off only their second Test victory, against an admittedly weak West Indian team. He took four more wickets in another win in the second Test, and dismissed West Indies' stand-in captain, Floyd Reifer, in all four innings of the series.

THE FACTS Mahmudullah took 5 for 51 (and 8 for 110 in the match) on his Test debut, against West Indies in St Vincent in July 2009 ... His four first-class centuries all came within a month at the end of 2008, including 152 for Dhaka at Khulna ... He spent some time on the MCC groundstaff in 2005, playing alongside World Cup players in Daan van Bunge, Kevin O'Brien and William Porterfield ...

THE FIGURES to 21.9.09   www.cricinfo.com

Batting & Fielding	M	Inns	NO	Runs	HS	Avge	S/R	100	50	4s	6s	Ct	St
Tests	2	4	1	45	28	15.00	31.91	0	0	6	0	4	0
ODIs	32	26	8	519	58*	28.83	66.45	0	2	31	5	7	0
Twenty20 Ints	8	8	0	66	21	8.25	69.47	0	0	3	1	5	0
First-class	41	73	10	2196	152	34.85	–	4	9	–	–	42	0

Bowling	M	Balls	Runs	Wkts	BB	Avge	RpO	S/R	5i	10m
Tests	2	376	191	12	5–51	15.91	3.04	31.33	1	0
ODIs	32	1140	971	18	2–19	53.94	5.11	63.33	0	0
Twenty20 Ints	8	85	101	2	1–19	50.50	7.12	42.50	0	0
First-class	41	3282	1654	56	5–51	29.53	3.02	58.60	1	0

LASITH **MALINGA**

Full name	**Separamadu Lasith Malinga Swarnajith**
Born	**August 28, 1983, Galle**
Teams	**Nondescripts, Ruhuna, Mumbai Indians**
Style	**Right-hand bat, right-arm fast bowler**
Test debut	**Sri Lanka v Australia at Darwin 2004**
ODI debut	**Sri Lanka v United Arab Emirates at Dambulla 2004**

THE PROFILE A rare Sri Lankan cricketer from the south, whose ever-changing exotic hairstyles make him stand out on and off the park, Lasith Malinga played hardly any proper cricket until he was 17, preferring the softball version in the coconut groves near his home in Rathgama, a village near Galle. But after he was spotted by the former Test fast bowler Champaka Ramanayake, he was hurried into the Galle team, took 4 for 40 and 4 for 37 on his first-class debut, and has hardly looked back since. He bowls with a distinctive and explosive round-arm action, and generates genuine pace, often disconcerting batsmen who struggle to pick up the ball's trajectory. "Slinga" Malinga was a surprise selection for the 2004 tour of Australia, and soon showed his speed, starting with 6 for 90 in a warm-up game in Darwin. That paved the way for his inclusion in the Test team, and he acquitted himself well, with six wickets in his first match and four in the second: he added 5 for 80 (nine in the match) against New Zealand at Napier in April 2005. With a propensity for no-balls he was originally seen as too erratic for the one-day side, but buried that reputation with 13 wickets in the 5–0 whitewash of England in 2006. He continued his progress during 2006-07, collecting 18 wickets during the World Cup, including four in four balls against South Africa. Since then, in a reversal of his earlier career pattern, he has been largely overlooked in Tests but a fixture in ODIs and Twenty20 games, where his toe-crushing yorkers have proved hard to get away.

THE FACTS Malinga is the only bowler to take four wickets in four balls in international cricket, doing so against South Africa at Providence during the 2007 World Cup ... After he took 5 for 80 (9 for 210 in the match) with his low-slung action against New Zealand at Napier in April 2005, Stephen Fleming unsuccessfully asked the umpires to change their clothing: "There's a period there where the ball gets lost in their trousers" ... Malinga took 6 for 17 as Galle bowled out the Police for 51 in Colombo in November 2003 ...

THE FIGURES to 21.9.09   www.cricinfo.com

Batting & Fielding	M	Inns	NO	Runs	HS	Avge	S/R	100	50	4s	6s	Ct	St
Tests	28	34	13	192	42*	9.14	38.17	0	0	24	4	7	0
ODIs	59	28	12	96	15	6.00	51.06	0	0	5	1	11	0
Twenty20 Ints	18	9	6	60	27	20.00	120.00	0	0	3	3	8	0
First-class	80	97	41	501	42*	8.94	37.86	0	0	–	–	22	0

Bowling	M	Balls	Runs	Wkts	BB	Avge	RpO	S/R	5i	10m
Tests	28	4777	3076	91	5–68	33.80	3.86	52.49	2	0
ODIs	59	2842	2329	86	4–28	27.08	4.91	33.04	0	0
Twenty20 Ints	18	364	443	23	3–17	19.26	7.30	15.82	0	0
First-class	80	11321	7416	242	6–17	30.64	3.93	46.78	6	0

GRAHAM **MANOU**

AUSTRALIA

Full name	**Graham Allan Manou**
Born	**April 23, 1979, Modbury, South Australia**
Teams	**South Australia**
Style	**Right-hand bat, wicketkeeper**
Test debut	**Australia v England at Birmingham 2009**
ODI debut	**No ODIs yet**

THE PROFILE After years as a reliable domestic performer, South Australia's wicketkeeper Graham Manou suddenly found the kind of batting form which interested national selectors used to the performances of Adam Gilchrist. Manou made 596 first-class runs in 2007-08, and 647 more to go with 33 dismissals the following summer. That included four centuries, after only one in the previous eight seasons. This put him at the head of the queue behind Brad Haddin for national selection, and he made the Ashes tour in 2009. He looked set for a quiet time, until suddenly being propelled into the limelight when Haddin broke a finger just before the start of the third Test at Edgbaston. Manou was rushed into the side – the England management had to agree, as the toss had already taken place – and made a polished debut behind the stumps, settling any nerves when England batted with a good low catch to his left to remove Alastair Cook for a duck. It was all such a rush that Manou was not officially presented with his baggy green cap until the second morning. Tidy and athletic with the gloves, Manou had fought his way back into the South Australian side after being dropped in 2006-07, realising he needed to work harder and mature. He did it so well that by the end of the following season he was the state's leading runscorer – and captain. Manou had made his debut for South Australia in October 1999, the replacement for Tim Nielsen, who is now the national coach. In 2003-04 he won $A50,000 for hitting a sponsor's sign with a six in a one-day game.

THE FACTS Manou made his Test debut at Edgbaston in 2009, after not being named in the side at the toss, when Brad Haddin broke a finger: this was believed to be the first time in Test history that a team was changed after the coin had been spun ... Manou made 190 for South Australia v Tasmania at Hobart in October 2007, putting on 250 for the eighth wicket with Jason Gillespie ...

THE FIGURES to 21.9.09   www.cricinfo.com

Batting & Fielding	M	Inns	NO	Runs	HS	Avge	S/R	100	50	4s	6s	Ct	St
Tests	1	2	1	21	13*	21.00	53.84	0	0	3	0	3	0
ODIs	0	0	–	–	–	–	–	–	–	–	–	–	–
Twenty20 Ints	0	0	–	–	–	–	–	–	–	–	–	–	–
First-class	89	153	18	3340	190	24.74	58.05	5	16	–	–	282	20

Bowling	M	Balls	Runs	Wkts	BB	Avge	RpO	S/R	5i	10m
Tests	1	0	–	–	–	–	–	–	–	–
ODIs	0	0	–	–	–	–	–	–	–	–
Twenty20 Ints	0	0	–	–	–	–	–	–	–	–
First-class	89	12	8	0	–	–	4.00	–	0	0

SHAUN **MARSH**

Full name	**Shaun Edward Marsh**
Born	**July 9, 1983, Narrogin, Western Australia**
Teams	**Western Australia**
Style	**Left-hand bat, occasional left-arm spinner**
Test debut	**No Tests yet**
ODI debut	**Australia v West Indies at Kingstown 2007-08**

THE PROFILE As a child Shaun Marsh spent a lot of time in the Australian set-up travelling with his father Geoff, the former Test opener. That international grounding and a backyard net helped develop him into one of Australia's finest young batsmen. It also gave him a taste of what he could expect on his first trip with the national team when he was picked for the one-dayers in the West Indies in 2008. That came after his most consistent domestic season, which earned him his first national contract: he was also the surprise hit of the inaugural Indian Premier League, finishing as the top runscorer, which helped press his case for an Australian berth. More gifted than his father ("He's got a few more shots than me," Geoff once said), Shaun is a left-hander who impressed the Waugh twins during his maiden first-class century in 2003, which he reached with successive sixes over midwicket off Mark's offspin. The second century had to wait until 2004-05 as he struggled with concentration, the finest trait of his father's batting, and he was in and out of the state side for a while. After a subdued 2008-09 season, the highlights of which were successive ODI scores of 79 and 78 against South Africa in January, Marsh tore a hamstring while fielding against New Zealand. A lengthy recovery included a visit to the United States, where he traded hitting tips with baseballer Manny Ramirez, but when he returned to the Australian set-up in Dubai he hurt his leg again. That kept him out of the World Twenty20 in England in June 2009, and the one-sided one-dayers that followed the Ashes series.

THE FACTS Marsh was the leading scorer in the inaugural Indian Premier League season, with 616 runs for Kings XI Punjab ... He hit 81 on his ODI debut, against West Indies at Kingstown in June 2008 ... Marsh made 166 not out for Western Australia v Queensland at Perth in November 2007 ... His father, Geoff Marsh, played 50 Tests for Australia between 1985-86 and 1991-92, and his younger brother Mitchell (born October 1991) is a promising batsman too ...

THE FIGURES to 21.9.09   www.cricinfo.com

Batting & Fielding	M	Inns	NO	Runs	HS	Avge	S/R	100	50	4s	6s	Ct	St
Tests	0	0	–	–	–	–	–	–	–	–			
ODIs	15	15	1	582	81	41.57	75.09	0	5	58	3	1	0
Twenty20 Ints	3	3	0	53	29	17.66	110.41	0	0	3	3	0	0
First-class	51	94	13	2755	166*	34.01	46.20	4	13	–	–	39	0

Bowling	M	Balls	Runs	Wkts	BB	Avge	RpO	S/R	5i	10m
Tests	0	0	–	–	–	–	–	–	–	–
ODIs	15	0	–	–	–	–	–	–	–	–
Twenty20 Ints	3	0	–	–	–	–	–	–	–	–
First-class	51	144	120	2	2–20	60.00	5.00	72.00	0	0

NEW ZEALAND

CHRIS **MARTIN**

Full name	**Christopher Stewart Martin**
Born	**December 10, 1974, Christchurch, Canterbury**
Teams	**Auckland**
Style	**Right-hand bat, right-arm fast-medium bowler**
Test debut	**New Zealand v South Africa at Bloemfontein 2000-01**
ODI debut	**New Zealand v Zimbabwe at Taupo 2000-01**

THE PROFILE Chris Martin is an angular fast-medium bowler who receives almost as much attention for his inept batting as for his nagging bowling, which has produced more than 150 Test wickets, including 11 as New Zealand whipped South Africa at Auckland in March 2004. Seven more scalps followed in the next game. It was all the more remarkable as they were his first Tests in almost two years – he had been overlooked since Pakistan piled up 643 at Lahore in May 2002 (Martin 1 for 108). He got his original chance after a crop of injuries, but did not disgrace himself in the first portion of his Test career, taking 34 wickets at 34 in 11 Tests, including six as Pakistan were crushed by an innings at Hamilton in 2000-01. Since his return he has lowered that average a little, happy to bowl long spells *à la* Ewen Chatfield – he took 5 for 152 at Brisbane in November 2004, after a surprisingly unproductive England tour. Back in England in 2008, he again failed to make much impression in the Tests (four wickets at 58.75), but returned to form at home with 14 wickets in three Tests against India, including seven in a high-scoring draw at Wellington. But whatever Martin does with the ball he is likely to be remembered more for his clueless batting: 25 of his 35 Test dismissals have been for ducks, he finally reached double figures against Bangladesh in his 36th match (a Test record) in January 2008, and has bagged six pairs (no-one else has more than four). Mind you, he did once manage 25 for his former province, Canterbury, helping Chris Harris put on 75.

THE FACTS Very few Test players approach Martin's negative ratio of runs (82) to wickets (165): two that do are England's Bill Bowes (28 runs, 68 wickets) and David Larter (15, 37) ... Martin is the only man to have bagged six points in Tests ... Between March 2001 and October 2007 he played only two ODIs, but took six wickets in them ... In Tests Martin averages 24.59 with the ball against South Africa, but 74.14 v Australia ...

THE FIGURES *to 21.9.09*   www.cricinfo.com

Batting & Fielding	M	Inns	NO	Runs	HS	Avge	S/R	100	50	4s	6s	Ct	St
Tests	50	72	37	82	12*	2.34	19.29	0	0	12	0	11	0
ODIs	20	7	2	8	3	1.60	29.62	0	0	0	0	7	0
Twenty20 Ints	6	1	1	5	5*	–	83.33	0	0	0	0	1	0
First-class	143	178	88	353	25	3.92	–	0	0	–	–	28	0

Bowling	M	Balls	Runs	Wkts	BB	Avge	RpO	S/R	5i	10m
Tests	50	9773	5574	165	6–54	33.78	3.42	59.23	8	1
ODIs	20	948	804	18	3–62	44.66	5.08	52.66	0	0
Twenty20 Ints	6	138	193	7	2–14	27.57	8.39	19.71	0	0
First-class	143	27268	13995	444	6–54	31.52	3.07	61.41	18	1

DIMITRI **MASCARENHAS**

Full name **Adrian Dimitri Mascarenhas**
Born **October 30, 1977, Chiswick, Middlesex**
Teams **Hampshire, Rajasthan Royals**
Style **Right-hand bat, right-arm medium-pacer**
Test debut **No Tests yet**
ODI debut **England v West Indies at Lord's 2007**

THE PROFILE Dimitri Mascarenhas is just about the ultimate cosmopolitan cricketer: born in London, to Sri Lankan parents, he was brought up in Western Australia, and still returns there in the English winters (although he turned down a chance to join the WA state squad, to remain available for England). Charging in off a shortish run, large ear-rings jangling, he bends the ball about at just above medium-pace, and is hard to get away: he can also be a fierce striker of the ball. He made an immediate impact on his Hampshire debut in 1996, with 6 for 88 against Glamorgan, but has been more of a hit in one-day cricket. He made the first century at the new Rose Bowl, in 2001, and also took the first Twenty20 hat-trick. In 2004 Shane Warne, then his county captain, expressed surprise that England hadn't tried Mascarenhas in ODIs – and continued to push his case until he finally did get the call, in the middle of 2007, his benefit year. His early matches were unspectacular, although he did keep the runs down. But later that summer against India his rapid 52 nearly conjured an unlikely victory at Edgbaston, then he smacked five successive sixes at The Oval. Mascarenhas was the only Englishman to feature in the inaugural season of the Indian Premier League early in 2008, although in the end he played only once for Warne's title-winning Rajasthan side. After that he seemed to be an England outsider too: there were only two international appearances, and a few more in 2009 – although just as he seemed to have been forgotten he was called up to bolster the one-day side in the end-of-season series against Australia.

THE FACTS Mascarenhas took the first hat-trick in a Twenty20 match, for Hampshire v Sussex at Hove in July 2004, on his way to 5 for 14 ... He hit five successive sixes off India's Yuvraj Singh in a one-day international at The Oval in September 2007 ... Mascarenhas's 104 against Worcestershire in May 2001 was the first first-class century scored at the new Rose Bowl ground in Southampton ...

THE FIGURES to 21.9.09   www.cricinfo.com

Batting & Fielding	M	Inns	NO	Runs	HS	Avge	S/R	100	50	4s	6s	Ct	St
Tests	0	0	–	–	–	–	–	–	–	–	–	–	–
ODIs	20	13	2	245	52	22.27	95.33	0	1	12	13	4	0
Twenty20 Ints	14	13	5	123	31	15.37	123.00	0	0	8	5	7	0
First-class	180	270	30	6177	131	25.73	–	8	22	–	–	72	0

Bowling	M	Balls	Runs	Wkts	BB	Avge	RpO	S/R	5i	10m
Tests	0	0	–	–	–	–	–	–	–	–
ODIs	20	822	634	13	3–23	48.76	4.62	63.3	0	0
Twenty20 Ints	14	252	309	12	3–18	25.75	7.35	21.00	0	0
First-class	180	26049	11774	417	6–25	28.23	2.71	62.46	16	0

MASHRAFE MORTAZA

Full name	**Mashrafe bin Mortaza**
Born	**October 5, 1983, Norail, Jessore, Khulna**
Teams	**Khulna, Kolkata Knight Riders**
Style	**Right-hand bat, right-arm fast-medium bowler**
Test debut	**Bangladesh v Zimbabwe at Dhaka 2001-02**
ODI debut	**Bangladesh v Zimbabwe at Chittagong 2001-02**

THE PROFILE Quick and aggressive, Mashrafe Mortaza has been the standard-bearer for Bangladesh's pack of young pacemen, although injuries have long been a problem: he got through 2008 unscathed, but injured his right knee after bowling only 6.3 overs in the first Test in West Indies in July 2009, and had to undergo an operation (in fact both knees went under the knife). This was doubly disappointing as it was his first match as captain, and it ended in only Bangladesh's second Test victory – their first overseas, admittedly against a depleted West Indian side. Mashrafe won his first Test cap against Zimbabwe in 2001-02, in what was also his first-class debut. Though banging it in is his preferred style, "Koushik" proved adept at reining in his attacking instincts to concentrate on line and length. He excelled in the second Test against England in 2003-04, taking 4 for 60 in the first innings to keep Bangladesh in touch, but suffered a twisted knee that kept him out of Tests for over a year. He was recalled towards the end of 2004, and subsequently enhanced his reputation in England during an otherwise torrid early-season Test series. Mashrafe's 4 for 38 in the 2007 World Cup was key in a famous defeat of India, and the following year he became only the second Bangladeshi – and the first fast bowler – to take 100 wickets in ODIs. He is not a complete mug with the bat: he has a first-class century to his name, and over 20% of his ODI runs have come in sixes.

THE FACTS Mashrafe Mortaza was the first Bangladeshi (Nazmul Hossain in 2004-05 was the second) to make his first-class debut in a Test match: only three others have done this since 1899 – Graham Vivian of New Zealand (1964-65), Zimbabwe's Ujesh Ranchod (1992-93) and Yasir Ali of Pakistan (2003-04) ... Mashrafe started the famous ODI victory over Australia at Cardiff in 2005 by dismissing Adam Gilchrist second ball for 0 ... His 6 for 26 v Kenya in Nairobi in August 2006 are Bangladesh's best bowling figures in ODIs ... His record includes two ODIs for the Asia XI ...

THE FIGURES to 21.9.09   www.cricinfo.com

Batting & Fielding	M	Inns	NO	Runs	HS	Avge	S/R	100	50	4s	6s	Ct	St
Tests	36	67	5	797	79	12.85	67.20	0	3	95	22	9	0
ODIs	103	81	14	1046	51*	15.61	84.76	0	1	79	36	33	0
Twenty20 Ints	11	10	3	134	36	19.14	122.93	0	0	5	8	1	0
First-class	50	89	7	1327	132*	16.18	–	1	5	–	–	16	0

Bowling	M	Balls	Runs	Wkts	BB	Avge	RpO	S/R	5i	10m
Tests	36	5990	3239	78	4–60	41.52	3.24	76.79	0	0
ODIs	103	5280	4025	135	6–26	29.81	4.57	39.11	1	0
Twenty20 Ints	11	249	368	8	2–29	46.00	8.86	31.12	0	0
First-class	50	8277	4333	121	4–27	35.80	3.14	68.40	0	0

ANGELO **MATHEWS**

Full name	**Angelo Davis Mathews**
Born	**June 2, 1987, Colombo**
Teams	**Colts, Basnahira North, Kolkata Knight Riders**
Style	**Right-hand bat, right-arm fast-medium bowler**
Test debut	**Sri Lanka v Pakistan at Galle 2009**
ODI debut	**Sri Lanka v Zimbabwe at Harare 2008-09**

THE PROFILE Angelo Mathews first played for Sri Lanka Under-19s when he was just 16, and eventually won 23 one-day caps, many as captain. He also hit a defiant 123 in a youth Test in England in 2005. He was long seen as a potential international, as he is capable of batting anywhere in the top order and also bowls at a lively medium-pace. In first-class cricket he made a quiet start in 2006-07, but made big strides the following season, scoring 696 runs at 58 and earning an A-team trip to South Africa, where he made two centuries. His first internationals were against Zimbabwe – he made 52 not out in his third ODI, in Bangladesh in January 2009 – and shortly after that piled up 270 in a domestic match. He was picked for the World Twenty20 in England in June 2009, and helped Sri Lanka to the final, notably with three wickets against West Indies at The Oval, which effectively settled the semi-final in the first over. There was also some handy batting (35 not out in the final) and frenetic fielding, notably a gymnastic juggling effort at Trent Bridge, the legality of which MCC had to confirm: he caught the ball on the field but overbalanced, threw the ball up, patted it back while in mid-air behind the boundary, then picked it up again inside the rope. Mathews made his Test debut at home soon afterwards, and started with six innings of 27 or more. He is aiming to sharpen up his pace, as bowling improves his chances of a regular place, but it seems inevitable that it will be batting with which he makes his name in the long run.

THE FACTS Mathews made 270 for Basnahira North v Kandurata in Colombo in February 2009 ... He took 5 for 47 for Colts v Chilaw Marians in Colombo in March 2008, and 4 for 8 for Sri Lanka A v Andhra at Visakhapatnam in October 2008 ... Mathews scored 131 against South Africa A at Potchefstroom in September 2008, one of four centuries in Sri Lanka A's innings of 749 for 5 ...

THE FIGURES to 21.9.09   www.cricinfo.com

Batting & Fielding	M	Inns	NO	Runs	HS	Avge	S/R	100	50	4s	6s	Ct	St
Tests	4	6	1	230	64*	46.00	54.50	0	1	26	2	0	0
ODIs	13	11	1	231	52*	23.10	70.85	0	2	12	4	3	0
Twenty20 Ints	10	9	5	106	35*	26.50	129.26	0	0	9	2	2	0
First-class	33	51	6	2433	270	54.06	53.19	8	9	262	23	20	0

Bowling	M	Balls	Runs	Wkts	BB	Avge	RpO	S/R	5i	10m
Tests	4	234	138	4	1–13	34.50	3.53	58.50	0	0
ODIs	13	420	302	11	6–20	27.45	4.31	38.18	1	0
Twenty20 Ints	10	126	145	7	3–16	20.71	6.90	18.00	0	0
First-class	33	2637	1235	34	5–47	36.32	2.81	77.55	1	0

MEHRAB HOSSAIN

Full name **Mehrab Hossain**
Born **July 8, 1987, Dhaka**
Teams **Dhaka**
Style **Left-hand bat, slow left-arm orthodox spinner**
Test debut **Bangladesh v Sri Lanka at Colombo 2007**
ODI debut **Bangladesh v Zimbabwe at Jaipur 2006-07**

THE PROFILE Mehrab Hossain is a solid left-hand batsman who has already made four first-class hundreds, two of them in the same game against Zimbabwe A at Mutare in June 2006. He was opening in that match, but usually goes in at No. 4 or 5 for Dhaka, where he is sometimes the unwitting cause of confusion when batting with a team-mate who is also called Mehrab Hossain. The junior Mehrab is a resolute batsman, who rarely looks hurried, and is a good timer of the ball on the off side. He is also a handy left-arm orthodox spinner, although Bangladesh is not exactly short of those. Mehrab captained the national Academy side, then performed decently, without setting the world alight, when he had a run in the one-day team against Zimbabwe at the end of 2006. He finally made his Test debut in the second Test of Bangladesh's miserable tour of Sri Lanka in mid-2007. He took two wickets in three balls in his fourth over, but was among a host of batting failures as Bangladesh succumbed for 62, their lowest Test total. He made 83 against New Zealand at Chittagong in November 2008, and although he didn't feature in the successful West Indian tour the following July he returned to the one-day side in August 2009 when Abdur Razzak was injured, without much success. Mehrab was a handy musician – he played the drums in a pop group, and often strummed a guitar during team get-togethers – but since getting more seriously into religion during 2009 he has cut out the singing, as he feels it violates the Islamic code.

THE FACTS Mehrab Hossain took 6 for 80 (10 for 130 in the match) for Dhaka at Barisal in April 2005 ... He made 120 and 100 not out for Bangladesh A against Zimbabwe A at Mutare in June 2006 ... Mehrab made 196 for Dhaka at Barisal in March 2006 ... He is usually shown on scorecards as "Mehrab Hossain junior", to distinguish him from his Dhaka team-mate Mehrab Hossain, an opener (born 1978) who played nine Tests and 18 ODIs between 1998 and 2003 ... Thirteen of his 18 ODIs have been against Zimbabwe ...

THE FIGURES to 21.9.09   www.cricinfo.com

Batting & Fielding	M	Inns	NO	Runs	HS	Avge	S/R	100	50	4s	6s	Ct	St
Tests	7	13	1	243	83	20.25	51.05	0	1	32	1	2	0
ODIs	18	16	0	276	54	17.25	42.99	0	1	24	0	7	0
Twenty20 Ints	2	2	1	16	10	16.00	64.00	0	0	1	0	0	0
First-class	40	73	8	2084	196	32.06	–	4	9	–	–	20	0

Bowling	M	Balls	Runs	Wkts	BB	Avge	RpO	S/R	5i	10m
Tests	7	407	281	4	2–29	70.25	4.14	101.75	0	0
ODIs	18	253	214	4	2–30	53.50	5.07	63.25	0	0
Twenty20 Ints	2	17	20	0	–	–	7.05	–	0	0
First-class	40	3042	1753	41	6–80	42.75	3.45	74.19	2	1

BANGLADESH

AJANTHA **MENDIS**

Full name	**Balapuwaduge Ajantha Winslo Mendis**
Born	**March 11, 1985, Moratuwa**
Teams	**Army, Wayamba, Kolkata KR, S Australia, Hampshire**
Style	**Right-hand bat, right-arm off- and legspinner**
Test debut	**Sri Lanka v India at Colombo 2008**
ODI debut	**Sri Lanka v West Indies at Port-of-Spain 2007-08**

THE PROFILE Those batsmen who thought one Sri Lankan mystery spinner was enough found more on their plate during 2008, when Ajantha Mendis stepped up to join Muttiah Muralitharan in the national side. Mendis sends down a mesmerising mixture of offbreaks, legbreaks, top-spinners, googlies and flippers, plus his very own "carrom ball" – one flicked out using a finger under the ball, in the style of the old Australians Jack Iverson and John Gleeson. He is also very accurate. Mendis was a prolific wicket-taker in 2007-08 for the Army (he received not one but two promotions following his meteoric rise) and had taken 46 wickets in six matches when he was called up for the West Indian tour early in 2008. After doing well there he ran rings round the Indians – the supposed masters of spin bowling – in the Asia Cup, rather ruining the final by taking 6 for 13. He was the Man of the Series there, and did likewise in his first Test series – against the Indians again – with 26 wickets at 18.38 in three home Tests in July and August, including ten in the second Test at Galle and eight in each of the other two. He even achieved the rare feat of outperforming Murali (21 wickets at 22.23) in that series. There were signs in 2009, though, that batsmen were beginning to work Mendis out. He was instrumental in Sri Lanka reaching the World Twenty20 final in England with some tight spells, but shortly after that he was dropped for two of the home Tests against Pakistan and New Zealand. "The next six months will be huge for Ajantha," said Cricinfo's Charlie Austin in October 2009.

THE FACTS Mendis took 26 wickets in his first Test series, against India in 2008, the most by anyone in a debut series of three Tests, beating Alec Bedser's 24 for England against India in 1946 ... Mendis took 6 for 13 in the Asia Cup final against India at Karachi in July 2008 ... He took 7 for 27 for Army v Lankan CC at Panagoda in February 2008 ...

THE FIGURES *to 21.9.09*   **www.cricinfo.com**

Batting & Fielding	M	Inns	NO	Runs	HS	Avge	S/R	100	50	4s	6s	Ct	St
Tests	9	9	3	31	17	5.16	56.36	0	0	4	0	1	0
ODIs	33	16	8	73	15*	9.12	75.25	0	0	6	0	5	0
Twenty20 Ints	12	2	2	4	4*	–	200.00	0	0	1	0	1	0
First-class	30	40	3	429	37	11.59	60.00	0	0	42	3	10	0

Bowling	M	Balls	Runs	Wkts	BB	Avge	RpO	S/R	5i	10m
Tests	9	2358	1136	42	6–117	27.04	56.14	2	1	
ODIs	33	1533	1048	68	6–13	15.41	4.10	22.54	3	0
Twenty20 Ints	12	276	244	25	4–15	9.76	5.30	11.04	0	0
First-class	30	6312	2916	163	7–37	17.88	2.77	38.72	9	2

KYLE **MILLS**

Full name	**Kyle David Mills**
Born	**March 15, 1979, Auckland**
Teams	**Auckland**
Style	**Right-hand bat, right-arm fast-medium**
Test debut	**New Zealand v England at Nottingham 2004**
ODI debut	**New Zealand v Pakistan at Sharjah 2000-01**

THE PROFILE Injuries at inopportune times have hampered Kyle Mills, especially at the start of his international career. The likes of Shane Bond, Ian Butler and Jacob Oram seized their opportunities, making it harder for Mills, a genuine swing bowler of lively pace, to force his way back. In and out of the team after the 2003 World Cup, he marked another comeback, against Pakistan in 2003-04, by picking up a reprimand for excessive appealing. However, he did enough to tour England in 2004, and made his Test debut in the third match at Trent Bridge. But he suffered a side strain there, and missed the one-day series. That was a shame, as one-day cricket is really his forte: he played throughout 2005-06, chipping in with wickets in almost every game, even if his once-promising batting had diminished to the point that he managed double figures only once in 16 matches. A feisty temper remains, though: Stephen Fleming had to pull him away from Graeme Smith during a bad-tempered one-day series towards the end of 2005. Mills returned to South Africa early in 2006, and picked up eight wickets in his two Tests, almost doubling his career tally. But injuries impinged again: ankle surgery, then knee trouble – which necessitated another op – early in 2007. He missed the World Cup, but came back stronger, following up 5 for 25 in a one-dayer in South Africa with a Test-best 4 for 16 against England at Hamilton in March 2008. He lost his Test spot after some anaemic performances the following season, but remained a one-day force, starting the Chappell-Hadlee Series in Australia in February 2009 by taking the match award after claiming four prime scalps.

THE FACTS Mills spanked his only first-class century from No. 9 at Wellington in 2000-01, helping Auckland recover from 109 for 7 to reach 347 ... His 5 for 25 at Durban in November 2007 are NZ's best one-day figures against South Africa ... Mills achieved the first ten-wicket haul of his career, and in the process reached 100 first-class wickets, for Auckland against Canterbury in December 2004 ...

THE FIGURES *to 21.9.09*   www.cricinfo.com

Batting & Fielding	M	Inns	NO	Runs	HS	Avge	S/R	100	50	4s	6s	Ct	St
Tests	19	30	5	289	57	11.56	38.58	0	1	37	3	4	0
ODIs	103	57	23	551	54	16.20	74.05	0	1	37	18	27	0
Twenty20 Ints	15	11	3	117	33*	14.62	123.15	0	0	8	5	3	0
First-class	66	94	23	1840	117*	25.91	–	1	12	–	–	22	0

Bowling	M	Balls	Runs	Wkts	BB	Avge	RpO	S/R	5i	10m
Tests	19	2902	1453	44	4–16	33.02	3.00	65.95	0	0
ODIs	103	5075	3961	150	5–25	26.40	4.68	33.83	1	0
Twenty20 Ints	15	339	494	16	3–44	30.87	8.74	21.18	0	0
First-class	66	10456	5059	176	5–33	28.74	2.90	59.40	3	1

MISBAH-UL-HAQ

Full name	**Misbah-ul-Haq Khan Niazi**
Born	**May 28, 1974, Mianwali, Punjab**
Teams	**Faisalabad, Baluchistan, Sui Northern Gas**
Style	**Right-hand bat, occasional legspinner**
Test debut	**Pakistan v New Zealand at Auckland 2000-01**
ODI debut	**Pakistan v New Zealand at Lahore 2001-02**

THE PROFILE   An orthodox right-hander with a tight technique, Misbah-ul-Haq (no relation to Inzamam-ul-Haq) caught the eye with his unflappable temperament in a triangular one-day tournament in Nairobi in September 2002, making 50 against Kenya and repeating that in the rain-ruined final against Australia. But before Pakistan could hail him as a possible middle-order mainstay, Misbah's form slumped: his highest score in three Tests against Australia was 17. Pakistan's abysmal 2003 World Cup campaign – and the wholesale changes to the team in its aftermath – gave him another chance to redeem himself, but he did little of note in his limited opportunities, and seemed to have been forgotten forever afterwards, although he played quite a bit for the A team, often as captain. He remained a consistent domestic performer, making 951 runs at 50 in 2004-05, 882 the following season, and capping that with 1108 at 61 in 2006-07, but it was nonetheless a shock when he was given a national contract for 2007-08 and called up for the World Twenty20 championship in South Africa. However, he was a surprise hit there, and added 464 runs in three Tests against India, including two important centuries to ensure there was no danger of following on after India had twice totalled more than 600. Suddenly, in his mid-thirties but with a first-class average which remains above 50, Misbah was an automatic choice. He continued to contribute in all forms throughout 2009, and played his part in winning the World Twenty20 in England, although his batting wasn't needed in either the semi or the final.

THE FACTS   Misbah-ul-Haq has made five first-class double-centuries, the highest 247 for Sui Northern Gas v Southern at Sheikhupura in February 2009 ... He also made 208 not out (in a total of 723 for 4) for Punjab v Baluchistan at Sialkot in March 2008 ... He scored 161 and 133, both not out, in successive Tests against India in 2007-08 ... Misbah hit 87 not out, Pakistan's highest score in Twenty20 internationals, against Bangladesh in April 2008 ... He averages 50 in ODIs against Australia, but only 11.50 in Tests against them ...

THE FIGURES to 21.9.09   www.cricinfo.com

Batting & Fielding	M	Inns	NO	Runs	HS	Avge	S/R	100	50	4s	6s	Ct	St
Tests	15	25	2	871	161*	37.86	39.19	2	3	95	6	18	0
ODIs	54	48	11	1476	79*	39.89	82.00	0	9	108	24	31	0
Twenty20 Ints	23	19	8	509	87*	46.27	120.90	0	3	31	19	7	0
First-class	144	230	23	10527	247	50.85	–	31	50	–	–	138	0

Bowling	M	Balls	Runs	Wkts	BB	Avge	RpO	S/R	5i	10m
Tests	15	0	–	–	–	–	–	–	–	–
ODIs	54	24	30	0	–	–	7.50	–	0	0
Twenty20 Ints	23	0	–	–	–	–	–	–	–	–
First-class	144	318	242	3	1–2	80.66	4.56	106.00	0	0

AMIT **MISHRA**

INDIA

Full name **Amit Mishra**
Born **November 24, 1982, Delhi**
Teams **Haryana, Delhi Daredevils**
Style **Right-hand bat, legspinner**
Test debut **India v Australia at Mohali 2008-09**
ODI debut **India v South Africa at Dhaka 2002-03**

THE PROFILE Amit Mishra is a confident cricketer, but even he might have thought his international chance had passed when five years went by after he flirted with the one-day team early in 2003. The diminutive Mishra, who bowls big loopy legbreaks and has a fizzing googly, took only two wickets in three ODIs after several players were rested following the World Cup: pundits thought he was too slow through the air, and back he went to the domestic grind. But Mishra remained a consistent force for Haryana, taking 41 first-class wickets in all in 2004-05 and 46 in 2007-08, a season which he started by playing for the A team against the touring South Africans. He also did well in the inaugural IPL jamboree, the highlight a hat-trick against Adam Gilchrist's Deccan Chargers. Early the following season Mishra took 6 for 81 (and nine in the match) against New Zealand A, which earned him a Test call-up against Australia a fortnight later at Mohali when Anil Kumble rested a shoulder injury. Mishra grabbed his big chance, becoming the first Indian to take a debut five-for since Narendra Hirwani, one of the selectors who finally chose him. The googly accounted for three of his wickets, but the pick was arguably the legbreak which pinned top-scorer Shane Watson in front. Mishra took 14 Australian wickets in three Tests, then six more against England. He toured New Zealand early in 2009, although he didn't feature on the slower pitches there – but, with Kumble now in the commentary box, Mishra should win several more caps, especially at home.

THE FACTS Mishra took 5 for 71 against Australia at Mohali in October 2008: he was only the sixth Indian to take a five-for on Test debut ... He took a hat-trick in his 5 for 17 for Delhi Daredevils v Deccan Chargers in the first season of the IPL in May 2008 ... Mishra took 6 for 66 for Haryana v Jharkhand in Chandigarh in March 2005 ... He has twice scored 84 for Haryana – against Madhya Pradesh in November 2002 and Saurashtra in Jan 2007 ...

THE FIGURES to 21.9.09   www.cricinfo.com

Batting & Fielding	M	Inns	NO	Runs	HS	Avge	S/R	100	50	4s	6s	Ct	St
Tests	5	5	1	42	23	10.50	72.41	0	0	4	1	2	0
ODIs	3	0	–	–	–	–	–	–	–	–	–	0	0
Twenty20 Ints	0	0	–	–	–	–	–	–	–	–	–	–	–
First-class	86	114	15	1931	84	19.50	–	0	9	–	–	49	0

Bowling	M	Balls	Runs	Wkts	BB	Avge	RpO	S/R	5i	10m
Tests	5	1230	593	20	5–71	29.65	2.89	61.50	1	0
ODIs	3	84	67	2	1–29	33.50	4.78	42.00	0	0
Twenty20 Ints	0	0	–	–	–	–	–	–	–	–
First-class	86	18454	8743	337	6–66	25.94	2.84	54.75	18	1

MOHAMMAD AAMER

Full name	**Mohammad Aamer**
Born	**April 13, 1992, Gujjar Khan, Punjab**
Teams	**Rawalpindi, Sui Gas, North West Frontier Province**
Style	**Left-hand bat, left-arm fast-medium bowler**
Test debut	**Pakistan v Sri Lanka at Galle 2009**
ODI debut	**Pakistan v Sri Lanka at Dambulla 2009**

THE PROFILE Mohammad Aamer, a toothy left-arm pace bowler, reveres Wasim Akram – and like his hero he has emerged over the last couple of years as a genuine prospect. Even before he toured England with the Under-19s in 2007 he had been picked out as a special talent – by none other than Akram himself – at a pace camp in Lahore. He did well in England, taking eight wickets at 16 in the one-dayers, then he helped Pakistan win a triangular tournament in Sri Lanka. Aamer seemed set to be one of the stars of the Under-19 World Cup in Malaysia in 2008, only to go down with dengue fever. However, he was back the following season, when his career really took off. He took 55 wickets for National Bank in his debut season, impressing everyone with his pace and swing, and was a surprise selection for the World Twenty20 squad in England. It turned out to be an inspired choice: he replaced the out-of-sorts Sohail Tanvir and bowled with pace, accuracy and courage as Pakistan stormed to the title after an uncertain start. He bowled several nerveless death overs and one absolutely crucial opening one, in the final against Sri Lanka, when he dismissed the tournament's top-scorer Tillakaratne Dilshan for a five-ball duck, peppering him with short, quick balls. A Test debut followed in Sri Lanka, and he did well, taking a wicket in his first over and finishing with six in the match, before going unrewarded in the other two. But he was incisive in the ODIs that followed, taking 3 for 45 in the first match and 4 for 28 to set up a consolation victory in the last.

THE FACTS Mohammad Aamer took 7 for 61 (10 for 97 in the match) for National Bank v Lahore Shalimar at Lahore in February 2009 ... In his next match he took 6 for 95 against Khan Research Laboratories at Rawalpindi ... Aamer took a wicket (Sri Lanka's Malinda Warnapura) with his sixth ball in Test cricket in July 2009 ... He claimed 7 for 24 (against Jhelum) and 5 for 7 (v Chakwal) for Rawalpindi in an under-19 tournament in June 2007 ...

THE FIGURES to 21.9.09   www.cricinfo.com

Batting & Fielding	M	Inns	NO	Runs	HS	Avge	S/R	100	50	4s	6s	Ct	St
Tests	3	6	3	37	22*	12.33	39.78	0	0	3	1	0	0
ODIs	5	3	2	51	24*	51.00	78.46	0	0	5	0	3	0
Twenty20 Ints	8	1	0	0	0	0.00	–	0	0	0	0	2	0
First-class	13	17	5	141	23	11.75	49.47	0	0	16	1	2	0

Bowling	M	Balls	Runs	Wkts	BB	Avge	RpO	S/R	5i	10m
Tests	3	480	261	6	3–38	43.50	3.26	80.00	0	0
ODIs	5	259	183	9	4–28	20.33	4.23	28.77	0	0
Twenty20 Ints	8	162	197	7	1–16	28.14	7.29	23.14	0	0
First-class	13	2125	1116	62	7–61	18.00	3.15	34.27	3	1

MOHAMMAD ASHRAFUL

Full name **Mohammad Ashraful**
Born **July 7, 1984, Dhaka**
Teams **Dhaka, Mumbai Indians**
Style **Right-hand bat, legspinner**
Test debut **Bangladesh v Sri Lanka at Colombo 2001-02**
ODI debut **Bangladesh v Zimbabwe at Bulawayo 2000-01**

THE PROFILE On September 8, 2001, at the Sinhalese Sports Club in Colombo, Mohammad Ashraful turned a terrible mismatch into a slice of history by becoming the youngest man – or boy – to make a Test century. Just 17, he broke the long-standing record set by Mushtaq Mohammad (17 years 82 days) in 1960-61. Bangladesh still crashed to heavy defeat, but "Matin" was unbowed, repeatedly dancing down to hit Muttiah Muralitharan and his fellow spinners back over their heads. Inevitably, such a heady early achievement proved hard to live up to, and after a prolonged poor run Ashraful was dropped for England's first visit in October 2003. He returned a better player, but no less flamboyant, as he demonstrated with a glorious unbeaten 158 in defeat against India at Chittagong late in 2004. Still not 21 when Bangladesh made their maiden tour of England the following year, Ashraful confirmed his talent at Cardiff, when his brilliantly paced century set up an astonishing one-day victory over Australia. He continued to fire spasmodically, a superb 87 bringing victory over South Africa in the 2007 World Cup, but that was surrounded by more low scores. When Habibul Bashar stood down in May 2007 Ashraful took on the captaincy – but the results stayed the same and he looked careworn by the time he was replaced after a dismal World Twenty20 campaign in England in 2009. He celebrated his return to the ranks with a couple of fifties in the one-day portion of the successful West Indian tour, and a fine hundred against Zimbabwe at Bulawayo in August 2009.

THE FACTS Only 11 players have made their Test debuts when younger than Ashraful: three of them are from Bangladesh ... He scored 263, putting on 420 with Marshall Ayub, for Dhaka v Chittagong in November 2006 ... Ashraful averages 58.60 in Tests v India, but only 5.75 v England ... He took the catch that sealed Bangladesh's first Test win, over Zimbabwe at Chittagong in January 2005 ... Ashraful's highest ODI score is 109, against the UAE at Lahore in the 2008 Asia Cup ... His record includes two ODIs for the Asia XI ...

THE FIGURES *to 21.9.09* www.cricinfo.com

Batting & Fielding	M	Inns	NO	Runs	HS	Avge	S/R	100	50	4s	6s	Ct	St
Tests	50	97	4	2149	158*	23.10	45.86	5	7	264	21	22	0
ODIs	147	140	13	3049	109	24.00	72.13	3	18	308	26	29	0
Twenty20 Ints	12	12	0	189	61	15.75	167.25	0	1	22	6	3	0
First-class	94	177	5	4932	263	28.67	–	13	19	–	–	47	0

Bowling	M	Balls	Runs	Wkts	BB	Avge	RpO	S/R	5i	10m
Tests	50	1495	1114	19	2–42	58.63	4.47	78.68	0	0
ODIs	147	444	434	13	3–26	33.38	5.86	34.15	0	0
Twenty20 Ints	12	108	178	7	3–42	25.42	9.88	15.42	0	0
First-class	94	5938	3605	106	7–99	34.00	3.64	56.01	5	0

MOHAMMAD ASIF

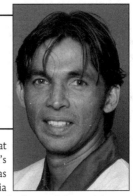

Full name	**Mohammad Asif**
Born	**December 20, 1982, Sheikhupura, Punjab**
Teams	**Sialkot, National Bank**
Style	**Left-hand bat, right-arm fast-medium bowler**
Test debut	**Pakistan v Australia at Sydney 2004-05**
ODI debut	**Pakistan v England at Rawalpindi 2005-06**

THE PROFILE When Mohammad Asif made his Test debut at Sydney in January 2005, there was little to suggest that Pakistan's long and happy tradition of unearthing blitzing fast bowlers was about to continue: he bowled 18 innocuous overs as Australia completed a whitewash. Towards the end of 2005, though, Asif caught the eye with ten wickets as Pakistan A embarrassed England at the start of their 2005-06 tour. He didn't feature in the Tests, but did make an impressive one-day debut the day after his 23rd birthday, dismissing Marcus Trescothick with his third ball and ending up with 2 for 14 from seven incisive overs. Tall and lean, and slightly more muscular these days, he generates good pace. His action isn't entirely classical, but it earned him seven plum wickets at Karachi as Pakistan clinched a famous win over India early in 2006, then 11 for 71 in a three-day win over Sri Lanka at Kandy. An elbow injury kept him out of the first three Tests in England in 2006, but he looked dangerous when he returned at The Oval, taking four wickets in England's first innings before the ball-tampering row blew up. But then he was embroiled in even worse scandals: he was banned (but subsequently cleared) after failing a drug test, was then arrested at Dubai Airport for allegedly possessing opium, and finally really was suspended after testing positive for nandrolone during the Indian Premier League. But such is his reputation that he was hustled back into national contention as soon as that ban expired in September 2009. If he can stay out of trouble, Asif still has a glittering future.

THE FACTS Mohammad Asif took 11 for 71 (6 for 44 and 5 for 27) against Sri Lanka at Kandy in April 2006 ... For Pakistan A against the England tourists in Lahore in November 2005 he took 7 for 62 in the first innings (10 for 106 in the match) ... At The Oval in 2006 Asif collected his fifth consecutive Test duck, equalling the unwanted record of Australia's Bob Holland and Ajit Agarkar of India ... Asif took 7 for 35 as Sialkot bowled Multan out for 67 in October 2004 ... His record includes three ODIs for the Asia XI ...

THE FIGURES *to 21.9.09*   www.cricinfo.com

Batting & Fielding	M	Inns	NO	Runs	HS	Avge	S/R	100	50	4s	6s	Ct	St
Tests	11	16	6	60	12*	6.00	26.90	0	0	6	0	2	0
ODIs	31	11	5	33	6	5.50	42.85	0	0	2	0	4	0
Twenty20 Ints	9	1	1	4	4*	–	400.00	0	0	1	0	3	0
First-class	70	94	37	468	42	8.21	–	0	0	–	–	26	0

Bowling	M	Balls	Runs	Wkts	BB	Avge	RpO	S/R	5i	10m
Tests	11	2334	1180	51	6–44	23.13	3.03	45.76	4	1
ODIs	31	1539	1198	36	3–28	33.27	4.67	42.75	0	0
Twenty20 Ints	9	209	269	12	4–18	22.41	7.72	17.41	0	0
First-class	70	12589	6907	282	7–35	24.49	3.29	44.64	17	5

MOHAMMAD YOUSUF

PAKISTAN

Full name	**Mohammad Yousuf Youhana**
Born	**August 27, 1974, Lahore, Punjab**
Teams	**Lahore, WAPDA**
Style	**Right-hand bat**
Test debut	**Pakistan v South Africa at Durban 1997-98**
ODI debut	**Pakistan v Zimbabwe at Harare 1997-98**

THE PROFILE Until his conversion to Islam in 2005, Mohammad Yousuf (formerly Yousuf Youhana) was one of the rare Christians to play for Pakistan. After a difficult debut, he quickly established himself as a stylish world-class batsman, and a middle-order pillar alongside Inzamam-ul-Haq and Younis Khan. After becoming a Muslim, he turned into a run machine, shattering Viv Richards's 30-year-old record for Test runs in a calendar year during a stellar 2006. Yousuf gathers his runs through composed, orthodox strokeplay: he is particularly strong driving through the covers and flicking wristily off his legs, and has a backlift as decadent and delicious as any, although a tendency to overbalance when playing across his front leg can get him into trouble. He is quick between the wickets, although not the best judge of a single, and there have recently been signs of increasing sluggishness in the field. Some initially questioned his temperament under pressure, but he began to silence those critics late in 2004. First came a spellbindingly languid century at Melbourne, when he ripped into Shane Warne as few Pakistanis have ever done. A century followed in the Kolkata cauldron, and he ended 2005 with an easy-on-the-eye 223 against England, eschewing the waftiness that had previously blighted him. His batting (and his beard) burgeoned in 2006, and it was a surprise when he jeopardised his international future the following year by signing for the unauthorised Indian Cricket League. But after an amnesty he returned to the traditional game in 2009, starting with a typically elegant century – his 24th in Tests – against Sri Lanka at Galle.

THE FACTS Since becoming a Muslim Mohammad Yousuf has averaged 72.39 in 23 Tests: in 59 matches beforehand he averaged 47.46 ... He scored 1788 Test runs in 2006, breaking Viv Richards's old calendar-year record of 1710 in 1976 ... Yousuf made double-centuries in successive Tests against England, 223 at Lahore in December 2005 and 202 at Lord's in July 2006 ... He has scored four Test double-centuries, but had not made another in first-class cricket until he hit 205 not out for Lancashire v Yorkshire in 2008 ...

THE FIGURES to 21.9.09   www.cricinfo.com

Batting & Fielding	M	Inns	NO	Runs	HS	Avge	S/R	100	50	4s	6s	Ct	St
Tests	82	140	12	7023	223	54.86	52.78	24	29	892	48	60	0
ODIs	272	257	40	9295	141*	42.83	75.30	15	62	752	87	53	0
Twenty20 Ints	1	1	0	20	20	20.00	105.26	0	0	2	1	0	0
First-class	125	208	20	9607	223	51.10	–		29	45	–	–	78	0

Bowling	M	Balls	Runs	Wkts	BB	Avge	RpO	S/R	5i	10m
Tests	82	6	3	0	–	–	3.00	–	0	0
ODIs	272	2	1	1	1-0	1.00	3.00	2.00	0	0
Twenty20 Ints	1	0	–	–	–	–	–	–	–	–
First-class	125	18	24	0	–	–	8.00	–	0	0

EOIN **MORGAN**

Full name **Eoin Joseph Gerard Morgan**
Born **September 10, 1986, Dublin, Ireland**
Teams **Middlesex**
Style **Left-hand bat, occasional right-arm medium-pacer**
Test debut **No Tests yet**
ODI debut **Ireland v Scotland at Ayr 2006**

THE PROFILE Eoin Morgan never hid his desire to play a higher level of cricket than his native country Ireland could offer. He skipped through the age groups in Ireland, seen as possibly more naturally gifted than Ed Joyce, the fellow Dubliner he joined at Middlesex in 2006. A compact left-hander with a full range of attractive strokes, Morgan captained Ireland in the 2006 Under-19 World Cup in Sri Lanka, finishing with an average of 67.60, and enjoyed plenty of success in the Intercontinental Cup (the ICC's first-class competition for non-Test countries), hitting 151 in the 2005 semi-final against the UAE, then scoring 209 not out – Ireland's first double-century – against the same opponents to put his side into the 2007 final. He was disappointing in the 2007 World Cup, managing just 91 runs from nine games, although there were fleeting glimpses of his class and potential. However, his development continued at county level: his inventive and audacious middle-order strokeplay helped Middlesex win the Twenty20 Cup in 2008, and he played for the England Lions. In 2009 he was named in England's squad for the ICC World Twenty20, effectively ending his career with Ireland. His early performances for his new side were modest, although his fielding did stand out – in Belfast in August, on as a substitute, he incurred the wrath of his former countrymen by nimbly preventing a final-over six which would have given Ireland a good chance of victory. He showed signs of settling in with 58 from just 41 balls against Australia at Trent Bridge in September.

THE FACTS Morgan is the only player ever to be out (run out, too!) for 99 in his first ODI, against Scotland in August 2006 ... His first 23 ODIs were for Ireland: he made 744 runs at 35.42 for them, including 115 v Canada in Nairobi in February 2007 ... Morgan scored 209 not out – the first double-century for Ireland – against the UAE in Abu Dhabi in February 2007 ... He made 161 for Middlesex v Kent at Canterbury in May 2009 ...

THE FIGURES to 21.9.09   www.cricinfo.com

Batting & Fielding	M	Inns	NO	Runs	HS	Avge	S/R	100	50	4s	6s	Ct	St
Tests	0	0	–	–	–	–	–	–	–	–	–	–	–
ODIs	31	31	4	905	115	33.51	73.51	1	6	76	22	10	0
Twenty20 Ints	1	1	0	6	6	6.00	75.00	0	0	0	0	0	0
First-class	48	81	11	2557	209*	36.52	50.07	6	11	–	–	43	1

Bowling	M	Balls	Runs	Wkts	BB	Avge	RpO	S/R	5i	10m
Tests	0	0	–	–	–	–	–	–	–	–
ODIs	31	0	–	–	–	–	–	–	–	–
Twenty20 Ints	1	0	–	–	–	–	–	–	–	–
First-class	48	79	46	2	2–24	23.00	3.49	39.50	0	0

SOUTH AFRICA

ALBIE **MORKEL**

Full name	**Johannes Albertus Morkel**
Born	**June 10, 1981, Vereeniging, Transvaal**
Teams	**Titans, Chennai Super Kings**
Style	**Left-hand bat, right-arm fast-medium bowler**
Test debut	**South Africa v Australia at Cape Town 2008-09**
ODI debut	**South Africa v New Zealand at Wellington 2003-04**

THE PROFILE Albie Morkel, a fast-medium bowler and big-hitting left-handed batsman, was lumbered with the tag of the "new Lance Klusener", and was touted early on by Ray Jennings (his provincial coach, and a former national coach too) as a potential world-class allrounder. It hasn't quite happened yet, although he does average over 40 in first-class cricket, with a double-century to his name, and Twenty20 seems to be tailor-made for his style of play. For Easterns (now the Titans) against the touring West Indians at Benoni in 2003-04 he defied food poisoning to score a century – putting on 141 for the ninth wicket with his brother, Morne, with whom he often opens the bowling too – and also took five wickets in the match. Albie was picked for the senior tour of New Zealand shortly after that, and made his ODI debut there early in 2004: he performed solidly, if unspectacularly, for a while until the selectors looked elsewhere. Morkel was back for the Afro-Asia Cup in June 2007. In the second match, at Chennai, Albie and Morne opened the bowling together for the African XI, the first instance of brothers sharing the new ball in an ODI since Kenya's Martin and Tony Suji did so during the 1999 World Cup. Shortly after that Albie hit 97 against the outclassed Zimbabweans. His huge sixes were a feature of the inaugural World Twenty20 championship late in 2007. He finally made his Test debut against Australia in March 2009, replacing his out-of-form brother and hitting 58, but the suspicion remains that he is better suited to the shorter formats.

THE FACTS Morkel made 204 not out, putting on 264 with Justin Kemp, as Titans drew with Western Province Boland in March 2005 after following on ... He took 6 for 36 for Easterns v Griqualand West in December 1999 ... Morkel's brother Morne has also played for South Africa, while another brother, Malan, played for SA Schools ... His record includes two ODIs for the Africa XI, in one of which he opened the bowling with Morne ...

THE FIGURES to 21.9.09   www.cricinfo.com

Batting & Fielding	M	Inns	NO	Runs	HS	Avge	S/R	100	50	4s	6s	Ct	St
Tests	1	1	0	58	58	58.00	81.69	0	1	10	1	0	0
ODIs	40	27	5	484	97	22.00	101.04	0	1	47	15	9	0
Twenty20 Ints	22	18	4	338	43	24.14	138.52	0	0	22	20	10	0
First-class	60	87	15	2992	204*	41.55	–	4	19	–	–	24	0

Bowling	M	Balls	Runs	Wkts	BB	Avge	RpO	S/R	5i	10m
Tests	1	192	132	1	1–44	132.00	4.12	192.00	0	0
ODIs	40	1600	1400	43	4–29	32.55	5.25	37.20	0	0
Twenty20 Ints	22	310	382	13	2–12	29.38	7.39	23.84	0	0
First-class	60	9139	4713	157	6–36	30.01	3.09	58.21	4	0

MORNE **MORKEL**

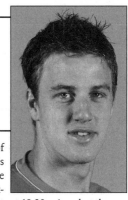

Full name	**Morne Morkel**
Born	**October 6, 1984, Vereeniging, Transvaal**
Teams	**Titans, Rajasthan Royals**
Style	**Left-hand bat, right-arm fast bowler**
Test debut	**South Africa v India at Durban 2006-07**
ODI debut	**Africa XI v Asia XI at Bangalore 2007**

THE PROFILE Morne Morkel, the taller, faster brother of Easterns allrounder Albie, has been a hot property ever since his first-class debut in 2003-04, when he and Albie put on 141 for the ninth wicket against the touring West Indians at Benoni. An out-and-out fast bowler, Morne did well in 2004-05, taking 20 wickets at 18.20 apiece, but then sat out most of the following season with injuries. But he had impressed Allan Donald: "He gets serious bounce, and he's got really great pace – genuine pace." Morkel used that to shake up the Indians for the Rest of South Africa in December 2006, bowling Virender Sehwag with his first ball and adding the wickets of Laxman, Tendulkar and Dhoni as the tourists lurched to 69 for 5. That got him into the national frame, and he played in the second Test at Durban when Dale Steyn was ruled out, although three wickets and some handy runs in a crushing victory weren't enough to keep him in for the final Test, when Steyn was fit again. Morkel played his first ODIs in the Afro-Asia Cup in India in June 2007, taking eight wickets in three games. A stress fracture early in the subsequent Pakistan tour halted the rapid rise, then a spell at Yorkshire was cut short by injury, but he bounced back later in 2008 to lead South Africa's attack in England, without ever quite being at his best as they won the Test series. Early the following year Morne had the unusual experience of being replaced in the Test side by his brother, but he remains a big part of South Africa's future plans.

THE FACTS Morkel took 6 for 43 and 6 for 48 for Titans v Eagles at Bloemfontein in March 2009, a week after being dropped from the Test side ... He took 5 for 50 against Bangladesh at Dhaka in February 2008 ... Morkel's first three ODIs were for the Africa XI: in one he opened the bowling with his brother Albie, the first instance of siblings sharing the new ball in an ODI since Kenya's Martin and Tony Suji did so during the 1999 World Cup ...

THE FIGURES *to 21.9.09*   www.cricinfo.com

Batting & Fielding	M	Inns	NO	Runs	HS	Avge	S/R	100	50	4s	6s	Ct	St
Tests	17	22	1	263	40	12.52	43.11	0	0	40	0	3	0
ODIs	21	8	3	81	25	16.20	101.25	0	0	8	2	6	0
Twenty20 Ints	9	1	1	1	1*	–	33.33	0	0	0	0	1	0
First-class	44	57	7	797	82*	15.94	45.25	0	3	–	–	19	0

Bowling	M	Balls	Runs	Wkts	BB	Avge	RpO	S/R	5i	10m
Tests	17	3101	1920	55	5–50	34.90	3.71	56.38	1	0
ODIs	21	1112	935	31	4–36	30.16	5.04	35.87	0	0
Twenty20 Ints	9	203	212	13	4–17	16.30	6.26	15.61	0	0
First-class	44	7598	4479	156	6–43	28.71	3.53	48.70	8	2

MUTTIAH **MURALITHARAN**

Full name **Muttiah Muralitharan**
Born **April 17, 1972, Kandy**
Teams **Tamil Union, Kandurata, Chennai Super Kings**
Style **Right-hand bat, offspinner**
Test debut **Sri Lanka v Australia at Colombo 1992-93**
ODI debut **Sri Lanka v India at Colombo 1993-94**

THE PROFILE Muttiah Muralitharan is the most successful
bowler the international game has seen, Sri Lanka's greatest player
... and the most controversial cricketer of the modern age.
Murali's rise from humble beginnings – the Tamil son of a hill-
country confectioner – to the top of the wicket-taking lists has divided opinion because of
his weird bent-armed delivery. From a loose-limbed, open-chested action, his chief weapons
are the big-turning offbreak and two top-spinners, one of which goes straight on and the
other, the *doosra*, which spins from a rubbery wrist in the opposite direction to his stock ball.
However, suspicions about his action surfaced when he was twice no-balled for throwing in
Australia in 1995-96. He was cleared after biomechanical analysis concluded that his action,
and a deformed elbow which he can't fully straighten, create the "optical illusion of
throwing". But the controversy would not die: Murali was called again in Australia in 1998-
99, had more tests, and was cleared again. Then his new *doosra* prompted further suspicion,
and he underwent yet more high-tech tests in 2004, which ultimately forced ICC to revise
their rules on chucking. On the field, Murali continued to pile up the wickets, overtaking
Courtney Walsh's Test-record 519 in May 2004: only shoulder trouble requiring surgery
allowed Shane Warne briefly to pass him and win the race to 700. Murali returned, potent
as ever, flummoxed England with 8 for 70 at Nottingham to square the 2006 series, and was
within touching distance of an astonishing 800 Test wickets by the end of 2009, the year in
which he also surpassed Wasim Akram (502) as the leading wicket-taker in ODIs.

THE FACTS Muralitharan was the second bowler (after Shane Warne) to take 700 Test
wickets, and the first to take 1,000 in all international cricket ... His 66 Test five-fors is
easily a record (Warne is next with 37) ... Murali has taken nine wickets in a Test innings
twice, and his 16 for 220 at The Oval in 1998 is the fifth-best haul in all Tests ... His record
includes a Test and three ODIs for the World XI, and four ODIs for the Asia XI ...

THE FIGURES *to 21.9.09*   www.cricinfo.com

Batting & Fielding	M	Inns	NO	Runs	HS	Avge	S/R	100	50	4s	6s	Ct	St
Tests	129	159	54	1203		11.45	70.06	0	1	138	27	70	0
ODIs	332	155	59	642	33*	6.68	75.79	0	0	47	10	128	0
Twenty20 Ints	9	2	0	1	1	0.50	20.00	0	0	0	0	0	0
First-class	228	271	81	2134	67	11.23	–	0	1	–	–	121	0

Bowling	M	Balls	Runs	Wkts	BB	Avge	RpO	S/R	5i	10m
Tests	129	42578	17398	783	9–51	22.21	2.44	54.60	66	22
ODIs	332	17893	11636	511	7–30	22.77	3.90	35.01	10	0
Twenty20 Ints	9	210	215	11	3–29	19.54	6.14	19.09	0	0
First-class	228	65652	26215	1357	9–51	19.31	2.39	48.38	118	34

MUSHFIQUR RAHIM

Full name	**Mohammad Mushfiqur Rahim**
Born	**September 1, 1988, Bogra**
Teams	**Sylhet**
Style	**Right-hand bat, wicketkeeper**
Test debut	**Bangladesh v England at Lord's 2005**
ODI debut	**Bangladesh v Zimbabwe at Harare 2006**

THE PROFILE A wild-card inclusion for Bangladesh's maiden tour of England in 2005, Mushfiqur Rahim was just 16 when he was selected for that daunting trip – two Tests in May, followed by six ODIs against England and Australia. Mushfiqur was principally chosen as understudy to long-serving wicketkeeper Khaled Mashud, but he had done well with the bat on an A-team tour of Zimbabwe earlier in 2005, scoring a century in the first Test at Bulawayo, and also enjoyed some success in England the previous year with the Under-19s, making 88 in the second Test at Taunton. He showed more evidence of grit with the full team, with a maiden first-class half-century to soften the pain of defeat against Sussex, followed by a hundred against Northamptonshire. That earned him a call-up – as a batsman – to become the youngest player to appear in a Test at Lord's. He was one of only three players to reach double figures in a disappointing first innings, but a twisted ankle kept him out of the second Test. Two years later Rahim supplanted Mashud for the 2007 World Cup, anchoring the win over India with 56 not out, and has since established himself as the first-choice keeper, with a short hiatus in 2008 after a run of low scores (four runs in five ODIs, including three successive ducks). He put that behind him in 2009, becoming one of Bangladesh's most consistent batsmen: ten successive double-figure scores in ODIs were allied to three solid contributions in the Tests in the Caribbean in July 2009, both of which were won against an under-strength West Indian side.

THE FACTS Mushfiqur Rahim's hundred for Bangladesh v Northamptonshire in 2005 made him the youngest century-maker in English first-class cricket, beating Sachin Tendulkar's record: Rahim was 16 years 261 days old, 211 days younger than Tendulkar in 1990; the youngest Englishman was 17-year-old Stephen Peters for Essex in 1996 ... Rahim was stumped for 98 in an ODI against Zimbabwe at Bulawayo in August 2009 ... He played two Tests before appearing in a first-class match at home ...

THE FIGURES to 21.9.09   www.cricinfo.com

Batting & Fielding	M	Inns	NO	Runs	HS	Avge	S/R	100	50	4s	6s	Ct	St
Tests	16	31	2	679	80	23.41	42.86	0	4	86	5	21	2
ODIs	54	47	9	837	98	22.02	60.65	0	3	66	6	33	9
Twenty20 Ints	12	10	4	57	14	9.50	82.60	0	0	3	0	6	7
First-class	37	66	9	1652	115*	28.98	–	2	10	–	–	63	6

Bowling	M	Balls	Runs	Wkts	BB	Avge	RpO	S/R	5i	10m
Tests	16	0	–	–	–	–	–	–	–	–
ODIs	54	0	–	–	–	–	–	–	–	–
Twenty20 Ints	12	0	–	–	–	–	–	–	–	–
First-class	37	0	–	–	–	–	–	–	–	–

NAEEM ISLAM

BANGLADESH

Full name	**Mohammed Naeem Islam**
Born	**December 31, 1986, Gaibandha**
Teams	**Rajshahi**
Style	**Right-hand bat, offspinner**
Test debut	**Bangladesh v New Zealand at Chittagong 2008-09**
ODI debut	**Bangladesh v New Zealand at Mirpur 2008-09**

THE PROFILE A batsman who is also a handy off-spinner, Naeem Islam was part of the Bangladesh Under-19 side which pulled off a famous triumph against their Australian counterparts in the 2004 Youth World Cup: eight of his team-mates that day have also made it into the full national team. In Naeem's case the senior call came late in 2008, in the wake of the defection of a dozen senior players to the unauthorised Indian Cricket League. He had just led the Academy side on a tour of Sri Lanka, ending up as the top-scorer with 304 runs in six matches. Naeem made his ODI debut against the touring New Zealanders in October 2008, taking 2 for 20 from four overs in his second match and making an adhesive 46 not out – he faced 106 balls in more than two hours as wickets tumbled around him – in the third. He made his Test debut shortly afterwards, contributing two more solid innings (14 from 46 balls and 19 from 70) in a low-scoring match ultimately decided by a remarkable allround display from Daniel Vettori. Naeem played another Test with less success in South Africa in November, and has since been confined to the one-day arena. He has sent down some tight spells, but the big haul continued to elude him, as did the breakthrough innings. He provided a rare highlight for Bangladesh in an otherwise dismal World Twenty20 campaign in England in June 2009 – they lost both their matches, to India and Ireland – by smacking three sixes in a defiant 28 against India, two of them successive balls from the pacy Ishant Sharma.

THE FACTS Naeem Islam scored 161 for the Bangladesh Academy against their South African counterparts at Khulna in April 2008: in the previous match, at Jessore, he made 136 ... He took a wicket (Daniel Flynn of New Zealand) with his fifth ball in Test cricket in October 2008 ... Naeem made 110 not out in his sixth first-class match, for Rajshahi v Dhaka at Fatullah in March 2005: his highest score is 126, for Rajshahi v Barisal in December 2006 ...

THE FIGURES *to 21.9.09*   www.cricinfo.com

Batting & Fielding	M	Inns	NO	Runs	HS	Avge	S/R	100	50	4s	6s	Ct	St
Tests	2	4	0	44	19	11.00	33.33	0	0	6	0	1	0
ODIs	19	15	7	204	46*	25.50	58.11	0	0	19	4	10	0
Twenty20 Ints	4	4	0	77	28	19.25	126.22	0	0	3	5	0	0
First-class	47	80	8	2518	126	34.97	43.82	4	17	–	–	35	1

Bowling	M	Balls	Runs	Wkts	BB	Avge	RpO	S/R	5i	10m
Tests	2	120	46	1	1–11	46.00	2.30	120.00	0	0
ODIs	19	781	587	16	3–32	36.68	4.50	48.81	0	0
Twenty20 Ints	4	54	81	2	2–32	40.50	9.00	27.00	0	0
First-class	47	1728	808	19	3–7	42.52	2.80	90.94	0	0

DIRK **NANNES**

Full name	**Dirk Peter Nannes**
Born	**May 16, 1976, Mount Waverly, Melbourne, Victoria**
Teams	**Victoria, Delhi Daredevils, the Netherlands**
Style	**Right-hand bat, left-arm fast-medium bowler**
Test debut	**No Tests yet**
ODI debut	**Australia v Scotland at Edinburgh 2009**

THE PROFILE   For most of Dirk Nannes's adult life, cricket has been an afterthought. A self-confessed "accidental cricketer", he used to play a couple of games for his Melbourne club Fitzroy at the start of the season, a handful at the end, and in between travel the world pursuing his other passion, skiing. He was no run-of-the-mill ski bum – he competed for several years in World Cup events and narrowly missed selection for Australia's Winter Olympics team in the late 1990s. But when he started to take his cricket seriously, he quickly grabbed the attention of Victoria's selectors. It led to a first-class debut at 29, and some impressive performances at state level – especially in the shorter games, in which he has become something of a specialist. A genuinely quick left-armer who can swing the ball late, Nannes destroyed Western Australia with 4 for 23 in the Twenty20 final in 2007-08, then headed to England, where an impressive season included helping Middlesex win their domestic 20-over title too. After keeping Glenn McGrath out of Delhi's IPL starting line-up early in 2009 Nannes was an outsider for Australia's World Twenty20 side in England in June, and when he was eventually excluded his Dutch parentage allowed him to turn out for the Netherlands: he was a gleeful participant in their defeat of England at Lord's. A couple of months later Nannes was facing England again – this time for Australia. In between he made his one-day international debut for Australia against Scotland, taking his first wicket the ball after being swiped for six. Anything but a typical fast bowler, Nannes studied the saxophone at university and runs a successful ski-travel company.

THE FACTS   Nannes played for the Netherlands in the World Twenty20 in England in June 2009, dismissing Shahid Afridi at Lord's, and two months later appeared for Australia against England ...Nannes took 7 for 50 (11 for 95 in the match) for Victoria v Queensland at Brisbane in October 2008 ... The previous month he took 6 for 32 for Middlesex v Worcestershire at Kidderminster ...

THE FIGURES *to 21.9.09*   www.cricinfo.com

Batting & Fielding	M	Inns	NO	Runs	HS	Avge	S/R	100	50	4s	6s	Ct	St
Tests	0	0	–	–	–	–	–	–	–	–	–	–	–
ODIs	1	1	0	1	1	1.00	50.00	0	0	0	0	0	0
Twenty20 Ints	3	1	0	6	6	6.00	85.71	0	0	0	0	0	0
First-class	22	24	8	108	31*	6.75	33.12	0	0	14	2	6	0

Bowling	M	Balls	Runs	Wkts	BB	Avge	RpO	S/R	5i	10m
Tests	0	0	–	–	–	–	–	–	–	–
ODIs	1	42	20	1	1–20	20.00	2.85	42.00	0	0
Twenty20 Ints	3	48	56	1	1–26	56.00	7.00	48.00	0	0
First-class	22	3947	2205	89	7–50	24.77	3.35	44.34	2	1

BRENDAN **NASH**

Full name	**Brendan Paul Nash**
Born	**December 14, 1977, Attadale, Western Australia**
Teams	**Jamaica**
Style	**Left-hand bat, left-arm medium-pacer**
Test debut	**West Indies v New Zealand at Dunedin 2008-09**
ODI debut	**West Indies v Bermuda at King City 2008**

THE PROFILE A smallish (5ft 8ins/173cm) but solid left-hander, Brendan Nash played in three Pura Cup finals for Queensland, scoring 96 in one of them, before losing his state contract after a patchy 2006-07 season. After that he decided to try his luck in Jamaica, where his father Paul was born (he swam for Jamaica in the 1968 Mexico Olympics, but emigrated to Australia while his wife was pregnant with Brendan). Nash had a fine first season for his new team, helping Jamaica win the Carib Beer Cup title: he was left stranded on 91 against Guyana, but made no mistake in the next game, against Trinidad & Tobago, making 102. In the Carib Beer Challenge final, also against T&T, he made another century, to finish with 422 runs in seven first-class matches. Although he was less prolific in limited-overs games, it was no great surprise when he was called up to the West Indian squad, although there were murmurs about an Australian "mercenary" muscling his way in after being jettisoned by his state. After a low-key debut in a one-day series in Canada, Nash won his first Test cap in New Zealand in December 2008, then proved a reliable middle-order buttress in the home series against England, making a four-hour 55 in the first Test at Kingston, which West Indies won, and adding a maiden century (batting for 330 minutes in all) at Port-of-Spain, when a draw clinched the series victory. He added 81 in an otherwise disappointing team display at Lord's a couple of months later. He is a handy containing medium-pacer, and remains a fine fielder: earlier in his career he was Australia's substitute fielder in a Test against West Indies (and dropped a catch).

THE FACTS Nash was the first white man to play for West Indies since Geoff Greenidge in 1972-73 ... Nash hit 176 for Queensland v New South Wales at Brisbane in October 2002 ... He averaged 27 with the bat for Queensland, 30 for Jamaica – and 38 for West Indies ... Nash scored 96 in Australia's Pura Cup final in 2001-02, and 117 in West Indies' Carib Beer Challenge final in April 2008 ...

THE FIGURES *to 21.9.09*   www.cricinfo.com

Batting & Fielding	M	Inns	NO	Runs	HS	Avge	S/R	100	50	4s	6s	Ct	St
Tests	9	13	0	497	109	38.23	40.80	1	4	71	2	3	0
ODIs	9	7	3	104	39*	26.00	73.75	0	0	11	1	1	0
Twenty20 Ints	0	0	–	–	–	–	–	–	–	–	–	–	–
First-class	54	91	7	2568	176	30.57	–	6	10	–	–	25	0

Bowling	M	Balls	Runs	Wkts	BB	Avge	RpO	S/R	5i	10m
Tests	9	330	178	1	1–34	178.00	3.23	330.00	0	0
ODIs	9	294	224	5	3–56	44.80	4.57	58.80	0	0
Twenty20 Ints	0	0	–	–	–	–	–	–	–	–
First-class	54	822	380	10	2–7	38.00	2.77	82.20	0	0

NASIR JAMSHED

Full name	**Nasir Jamshed**
Born	**December 6, 1989, Lahore, Punjab**
Teams	**Lahore, National Bank**
Style	**Left-hand bat**
Test debut	**No Tests yet**
ODI debut	**Pakistan v Zimbabwe at Karachi 2007-08**

THE PROFILE A hard-hitting left-hand opener prone to ugly hoicks but also capable of some lovely drives and pulls, Nasir Jamshed jumped to national prominence early in 2008, forcing his way into the squad for the one-day series against the touring Zimbabweans after flaying them for 182 from 240 balls in a warm-up game. Jamshed kick-started his international career with a Man of the Match-winning 61 (from 48 balls) in the first game, and 74 (from 64 balls with 14 fours) in the second. Leaner pickings followed, almost inevitably, until he peeled off successive unbeaten scores of 53 and 52 against India and Bangladesh in the Asia Cup in July, to suggest that he had found a permanent place. Jamshed had long been tipped for stardom. He made his first-class debut shortly after turning 15, and made 74: that won him a place in Pakistan's Under-19 team, and he responded with 44 and 204 in his first match, against Sri Lanka. He remained in the Under-19s long enough to ensure they retained their World Cup title early in 2006, with victory in an astonishing final in Colombo (Pakistan were bowled out for 109, but humbled India for 71). He consolidated after that before breaking out in 2007-08, a season in which he topped the runscoring lists with 1353 runs – 800 of them in the Quaid-e-Azam Trophy – including six centuries, which was more than enough to earn him a run in the national team, although there have been murmurs about his weight.

THE FACTS Nasir Jamshed made 74 on his first-class debut for National Bank against Defence Housing Authority at Faisalabad in February 2005, two months after his 15th birthday ... The following month he made 204 for Pakistan Under-19s in the first Test against Sri Lanka in Karachi ... Jamshed scored 61 and 74 in his first two ODIs, against Zimbabwe in January 2008 ...

THE FIGURES *to 21.9.09*   www.cricinfo.com

Batting & Fielding	M	Inns	NO	Runs	HS	Avge	S/R	100	50	4s	6s	Ct	St
Tests	0	0	–	–	–	–	–	–	–	–	–	–	–
ODIs	12	12	2	353	74	35.30	101.14	0	4	49	6	4	0
Twenty20 Ints	0	0	–	–	–	–	–	–	–	–	–	–	–
First-class	35	59	5	2598	182	48.11	–	10	9	–	–	29	0

Bowling	M	Balls	Runs	Wkts	BB	Avge	RpO	S/R	5i	10m
Tests	0	0	–	–	–	–	–	–	–	–
ODIs	12	0	–	–	–	–	–	–	–	–
Twenty20 Ints	0	0	–	–	–	–	–	–	–	–
First-class	35	6	8	0	–	–	8.00	–	0	0

RANA **NAVED-UL-HASAN**

Full name **Rana Naved-ul-Hasan**
Born **February 28, 1978, Sheikhupura, Punjab**
Teams **WAPDA, Yorkshire**
Style **Right-hand bat, right-arm fast-medium bowler**
Test debut **Pakistan v Sri Lanka at Karachi 2004-05**
ODI debut **Pakistan v Sri Lanka at Sharjah 2002-03**

PAKISTAN

THE PROFILE Naved-ul-Hasan made his debut in Sharjah immediately after the disastrous 2003 World Cup. Few backed him then, despite some impressive early performances, and he was dropped soon after, supposedly because of some unspecified disciplinary problems. But, helped by the continuing doubts about Shoaib Akhtar's fitness and injuries to other bowlers, Naved worked his way up to become the one-day team's spearhead. He can bowl a reverse-swinging yorker almost at will, and his change of pace, as Virender Sehwag would testify, is another useful weapon. But his nous, control over line and length, and commitment in the field stood out. He was Pakistan's leading one-day bowler in 2005, impressing first in the triangular series in Australia and then on the flatter, less responsive pitches of India and the Caribbean. It has been a different story in Tests, although he was badly missed in 2006 in England – where he had starred in county cricket for Sussex – when a troublesome groin injury kept him out of the Test series. During a spell out of favour Naved signed for the unauthorised Indian Cricket League in 2007-08, which seemed to have ended his international career – but after an amnesty he returned, complete with a new head of hair, and took 4 for 44 in an ODI in Sri Lanka in August 2009. He is a hard-hitting lower-order batsman, with centuries for Sheikhupura and Sussex, although he hasn't had much chance to display this skill at international level yet, despite his insistence that he is, in fact, a natural wicketkeeper/batsman. He gave up his first love, hockey, for cricket.

THE FACTS Naved-ul-Hasan has taken 31 wickets at 23.67 in ODIs against India – and two at 96.00 against South Africa ... He took 6 for 27 against India at Jamshedpur in April 2005 ... Naved made his highest score of 139 for Sussex v Middlesex at Lord's in 2005, and then took seven wickets, including four in one over in the second innings ... He took 91 wickets in Pakistan in 2000-01: the following season he took 7 for 49, still his best figures, for Sheikhupura against Sialkot at Muridke ...

THE FIGURES *to 21.9.09*   www.cricinfo.com

Batting & Fielding	M	Inns	NO	Runs	HS	Avge	S/R	100	50	4s	6s	Ct	St
Tests	9	15	3	239	42*	19.91	84.15	0	0	32	5	3	0
ODIs	65	43	15	422	33	15.07	79.17	0	0	30	12	14	0
Twenty20 Ints	3	1	1	17	17*	–	242.85	0	0	0	2	2	0
First-class	115	162	18	3263	139	22.65	–	4	9	–	–	56	0

Bowling	M	Balls	Runs	Wkts	BB	Avge	RpO	S/R	5i	10m
Tests	9	1565	1044	18	3–30	58.00	4.00	86.94	0	0
ODIs	65	2986	2761	100	6–27	27.61	5.54	29.86	1	0
Twenty20 Ints	3	61	74	4	3–19	18.50	7.27	15.25	0	0
First-class	115	21362	12027	494	7–49	24.34	3.37	43.24	27	4

ASHISH **NEHRA**

INDIA

Full name	**Ashish Nehra**
Born	**April 29, 1979, Delhi**
Teams	**Delhi, Delhi Daredevils**
Style	**Right-hand bat, left-arm fast-medium bowler**
Test debut	**India v Sri Lanka at Colombo 1998-99**
ODI debut	**India v Zimbabwe at Harare 2001**

THE PROFILE   For a short time Ashish Nehra looked the best of India's crop of left-arm pacemen – but injuries, notably several ankle operations after a breakdown late in 2005, seemed to have scuppered his international career. But Nehra sparkled in the IPL, especially in the second season in South Africa early in 2009, when his 19 wickets was exceeded only by RP Singh (another left-armer) and Anil Kumble. That brought Nehra back into national contention, and when Zaheer Khan was rested for the one-day series in the West Indies in June Nehra was recalled after almost four years out. He took three wickets in his comeback at Kingston then three more in the third match, and with Zaheer's shoulder injury still giving cause for concern Nehra looked set for more opportunities. He knew the reason for his renaissance: "The IPL is as good as international cricket. Every team has about eight or nine international cricketers so the standard is really high." Nehra has most of the virtues of a classical left-arm fast bowler: pace (admittedly slightly reduced since his various injuries), accuracy, an ability to move the ball off the pitch, and a devastating late inswinger that can harass the best. On his first full tour – to Zimbabwe in 2000-01 – he took five wickets at Bulawayo to help India win a Test outside the subcontinent for the first time in 15 years. But inconsistency and injuries held him back, although there were occasional signs of a rare talent, notably when he demolished England in the 2003 World Cup, taking six wickets with what *Wisden* called "searing pace and swing".

THE FACTS   Nehra took 6 for 23 against England at Durban during the 2003 World Cup: he also took 6 for 59 v Sri Lanka in Colombo in August 2005 ... He took 7 for 14 for North Zone v East Zone at Guwahati in the 2000–01 Duleep Trophy ... Nehra took 19 wickets (18.21) in the second season of the IPL in 2008–09: only RP Singh (23) and Anil Kumble (21) took more ...

THE FIGURES to 21.9.09   www.cricinfo.com

Batting & Fielding	M	Inns	NO	Runs	HS	Avge	S/R	100	50	4s	6s	Ct	St
Tests	17	25	11	77	19	5.50	30.07	0	0	8	3	5	0
ODIs	79	28	15	88	24	6.76	67.17	0	0	8	2	12	0
Twenty20 Ints	0	0	–	–	–	–	–	–	–	–	–	–	–
First-class	78	92	30	515	43	8.30	–	0	0	–	–	24	0

Bowling	M	Balls	Runs	Wkts	BB	Avge	RpO	S/R	5i	10m
Tests	17	3447	1866	44	4–72	42.40	3.24	78.34	0	0
ODIs	79	3841	3103	102	6–23	30.42	4.84	37.65	2	0
Twenty20 Ints	0	0	–	–	–	–	–	–	–	–
First-class	78	14829	7677	257	7–14	29.87	3.10	57.70	12	4

MARCUS **NORTH**

AUSTRALIA

Full name	**Marcus James North**
Born	**July 28, 1979, Pakenham, Melbourne, Victoria**
Teams	**Western Australia, Hampshire**
Style	**Left-hand bat, offspinner**
Test debut	**Australia v South Africa at Johannesburg 2009**
ODI debut	**Australia v Pakistan at Abu Dhabi 2008-09**

THE PROFILE Marcus North seemed destined to be remembered as a nomad who played for no fewer than five English first-class counties – but finally, after years on the fringe, he was selected at 29 for Australia's tour of South Africa early in 2009. A tall, well-organised left-hander with a peachy cover-drive, North is also a handy containing offspinner. He made 117 on debut at the Wanderers while the other batsmen struggled, and although he missed the final Test with a stomach bug he was a certainty for the Ashes tour that followed. He started that with another neat hundred at Cardiff, and added another in the fourth Test after making 96 in the third: when he failed, so did Australia – he managed only 24 runs in the two Tests they lost as the Ashes slipped away. North has long been a key player for Western Australia, in all three formats, latterly as captain (although his first season in charge, 2007-08, was disrupted by knee trouble). He first gained widespread notice in 2003-04, when he made 1074 first-class runs in Australia, although he had made a double-century for WA two years before that. He added another in October 2006, during an Australian-record third-wicket stand of 459 with Chris Rogers against Victoria at the WACA. Always a dangerous one-day player as well, North blasted 115 from 85 balls against Tasmania in 2006-07. Before that he had a successful youth career, notably making 200 not out and 132 in an Under-19 Test against Pakistan at Sheikhupura early in 1997. He found it difficult at first to make the transition from star youth player to serious first-class performer, but has made up for that since.

THE FACTS North made 239 not out for WA v Victoria at Perth in October 2006, sharing an Australian-record third-wicket stand of 459 with Chris Rogers ... North was the 18th man to score a century on Test debut for Australia ... He was the second player to appear in first-class cricket for five English counties (Durham, Lancashire, Derbyshire, Gloucestershire and, in 2009, Hampshire): fast bowler AJ Harris beat him to the distinction by a week ...

THE FIGURES to 21.9.09   www.cricinfo.com

Batting & Fielding	M	Inns	NO	Runs	HS	Avge	S/R	100	50	4s	6s	Ct	St
Tests	7	12	1	527	125*	47.90	48.04	3	1	64	1	5	0
ODIs	2	2	0	6	5	3.00	31.57	0	0	0	0	1	0
Twenty20 Ints	1	1	0	20	20	20.00	95.23	0	0	1	0	0	0
First-class	136	239	24	9653	239*	44.89	–	26	52	–	–	104	0

Bowling	M	Balls	Runs	Wkts	BB	Avge	RpO	S/R	5i	10m
Tests	7	633	302	6	4–98	50.33	2.86	105.5	0	0
ODIs	2	18	16	0	–	–	5.33	–	0	0
Twenty20 Ints	1	0	–	–	–	–	–	–	–	–
First-class	136	8590	4433	103	6–69	43.03	3.09	83.3	1	0

MAKHAYA **NTINI**

Full name	**Makhaya Ntini**
Born	**July 6, 1977, Mdingi, Cape Province**
Teams	**Warriors, Chennai Super Kings**
Style	**Right-hand bat, right-arm fast bowler**
Test debut	**South Africa v Sri Lanka at Cape Town 1997-98**
ODI debut	**South Africa v New Zealand at Perth 1997-98**

THE PROFILE Makhaya Ntini has had a fair bit to contend with during his life. A product of the South African Board's development programme, Ntini was discovered as a cattle-herd in the Eastern Cape, given a pair of boots and packed off to Dale College, one of the country's best-regarded cricketing nurseries. With an action consciously modelled on Malcolm Marshall's, Ntini made his ODI debut in Australia in 1997-98, bowling well in helpful conditions at Perth, and his first Test – he was the first black African to play for South Africa – came a couple of months later. He was then convicted of rape, but cleared on appeal. After that ordeal he returned for the Sharjah tournament in 2000, exhibiting greater control than before. Although a little short of the pace of a Brett Lee or a Shoaib Akhtar, he steadily improved, getting a little closer to the stumps but maintaining his high pace and occasional dangerous late inswing, and in 2003 became the first South African to take ten wickets in a Test at Lord's, before devastating West Indies in Trinidad in 2005 with 13 for 132. Ntini steamed on, relishing his new role as the pace spearhead, and hurtled past 300 Test wickets during a destructive 6 for 59 against Pakistan at Port Elizabeth in January 2007. Shortly after that, though, he failed to spark at the World Cup, and was dropped for the last two games. He laboured through the following home season, then struggled at first in England in 2008, before perking up with seven wickets at The Oval, after taking his 350th wicket in the previous match. He remains a role model for black youth in South Africa, but faces a battle to stay in the Test side as he approaches his 100th cap and his 400th wicket.

THE FACTS Ntini's 13 for 132 (6 for 95 and 7 for 37) at Port-of-Spain in April 2005 are South Africa's best match figures in Tests, surpassing Hugh Tayfield's 13 for 165 at Melbourne in 1952-53 ... He has taken 68 Test wickets against England, and 63 v West Indies ... Ntini has taken 247 (63.6%) of his Test wickets in 51 matches at home ... Only 24 (6.1%) of his Test wickets have been lbws ... Ntini's record includes one ODI for the World XI ...

THE FIGURES *to 21.9.09*   www.cricinfo.com

Batting & Fielding	M	Inns	NO	Runs	HS	Avge	S/R	100	50	4s	6s	Ct	St
Tests	99	113	42	688	32*	9.69	49.17	0	0	103	8	25	0
ODIs	173	47	24	199	42*	8.65	66.77	0	0	16	6	30	0
Twenty20 Ints	9	3	1	9	5	4.50	100.00	0	0	2	0	1	0
First-class	172	198	70	1215	34*	9.49	–	0	0	–	–	40	0

Bowling	M	Balls	Runs	Wkts	BB	Avge	RpO	S/R	5i	10m
Tests	99	20414	11009	388	7–37	28.37	3.23	52.61	18	4
ODIs	173	8687	6559	266	6–22	24.65	4.53	32.65	4	0
Twenty20 Ints	9	168	252	6	2–22	42.00	9.00	28.00	0	0
First-class	172	32051	17452	611	7–37	28.56	3.26	52.45	25	4

IAIN **O'BRIEN**

NEW ZEALAND

Full name	**Iain Edward O'Brien**
Born	**July 10, 1976, Lower Hutt, Wellington**
Teams	**Wellington, Leicestershire**
Style	**Right-hand bat, right-arm fast-medium bowler**
Test debut	**New Zealand v Australia at Christchurch 2004-05**
ODI debut	**New Zealand v England at Napier 2007-08**

THE PROFILE A tenacious seamer who doesn't mind bowling into the wind (essential if your home team is Wellington), Iain O'Brien earned his first Test cap in March 2005 after a solid domestic season (20 wickets at 26.55), when New Zealand's attack was hit by injuries. He managed only two wickets in two matches against Australia, and disappeared until 2006-07, when he made the squad when Sri Lanka toured. He wasn't used, however, and had to settle for being the leading wicket-taker in the State Championship with 34 at 20.85. Those figures were enough to keep him in the frame, and he finally added to his Test caps in South Africa in November 2007. Still his bowling looked a bit short of the required class, but he made the most of Shane Bond's absence with the disapproved Indian Cricket League: first he took seven wickets in two Tests against Bangladesh, then took over Bond's national contract when it was controversially cancelled. O'Brien missed the home series against England, but toured there later in 2008. He was rather surprisingly preferred to the promising Tim Southee in the last two Tests, but justified his selection with four wickets in each game, running in enthusiastically and looking more of a genuine Test bowler than before. The improvement continued: at home he took seven West Indian wickets in the drawn Napier Test in December 2008, including a Test-best 6 for 75 in the first innings: "That's as consistent as I've ever been out in the middle, pace-wise as well," he said. O'Brien then performed enthusiastically against India and Sri Lanka, sandwiched by an effective county stint with Leicestershire.

THE FACTS O'Brien took 8 for 55 (13 for 117 in the match) for Wellington against Auckland at Wellington in 2006–07 ... He took a hat-trick in a two-day game for Wellington against the New Zealand Academy in November 2004 ... O'Brien took 6 for 39 (9 for 68 in the match) for Leicestershire v Middlesex at Grace Road in July 2009 ...

THE FIGURES *to 21.9.09*   www.cricinfo.com

Batting & Fielding	M	Inns	NO	Runs	HS	Avge	S/R	100	50	4s	6s	Ct	St
Tests	19	29	4	152	19*	6.08	33.77	0	0	19	1	6	0
ODIs	10	2	2	3	3*	–	27.27	0	0	0	0	1	0
Twenty20 Ints	4	0	–	–	–	–	–	–	–	–	–	0	0
First-class	80	98	25	649	44	8.89	–	0	0	–	–	15	0

Bowling	M	Balls	Runs	Wkts	BB	Avge	RpO	S/R	5i	10m
Tests	19	3533	1981	58	6–75	34.15	3.36	60.91	1	0
ODIs	10	453	488	14	3–68	34.85	6.46	32.35	0	0
Twenty20 Ints	4	78	116	6	2–30	19.33	8.92	13.00	0	0
First-class	80	14483	7205	278	8–55	25.91	2.98	52.09	12	1

PRAGYAN OJHA

Full name	**Pragyan Prayash Ojha**
Born	**September 5, 1986, Bhubaneshwar**
Teams	**Hyderabad, Deccan Chargers**
Style	**Left-hand bat, left-arm orthodox spinner**
Test debut	**No Tests yet**
ODI debut	**India v Bangladesh at Karachi 2008**

THE PROFILE A left-arm spinner with teasing flight and pleasing loop, Pragyan Ojha made a stunning start in first-class cricket: for Hyderabad in the Ranji Trophy semi-final at Jaipur in March 2005, he took the first five wickets to fall in eventual champions Railways' first innings, starting with the Test allrounder Sanjay Bangar. He became a persistent wicket-taker, his best return so far being 39 in 2007-08. He won an A-team place in 2007, and spun them to an innings victory over South Africa A with 3 for 29 and 5 for 56 in the first Test at Delhi that September. Ojha showed his control with some decent performances for Deccan Chargers in the inaugural Indian Premier League season early in 2008, finishing with 11 wickets, and added 18 more in South Africa in 2009. His one-day international debut came in the Asia Cup in Pakistan in June 2008. He made an immediate impact with three outfield catches and an absolute ripper which foxed Bangladesh's Raqibul Hasan, his maiden wicket. A couple of tidy performances followed against Sri Lanka, which helped him win a place on the tour of Sri Lanka which came afterwards. Still seen by the national selectors as a one-day performer, Ojha started the 2009 World Twenty20 in England well, taking a wicket with his first ball and finishing with 4 for 21 against Bangladesh, but he was omitted later in the tournament, then missed out on the one-day Compaq Cup in Sri Lanka in September as the selectors tried out legspinner Amit Mishra as Harbhajan Singh's partner.

THE FACTS Ojha took a wicket (Bangladesh's Shakib Al Hasan) with his first ball in Twenty20 internationals, at Trent Bridge in June 2009, and finished with 4 for 21 ... He took 7 for 114 for Hyderabad v Rajasthan at Jaipur in December 2006: the previous week he took 6 for 84 v Maharashtra ... On his first-class debut, against Railways at Delhi in March 2005, Ojha took the first five wickets to fall, finishing with 5 for 55 ...

THE FIGURES to 21.9.09   www.cricinfo.com

Batting & Fielding	M	Inns	NO	Runs	HS	Avge	S/R	100	50	4s	6s	Ct	St
Tests	0	0	–	–	–	–	–	–	–	–	–	–	–
ODIs	9	4	3	27	16*	27.00	49.09	0	0	2	0	5	0
Twenty20 Ints	3	0	–	–	–	–	–	–	–	–	–	1	0
First-class	32	44	14	299	35	9.96	33.63	0	0	34	0	13	0

Bowling	M	Balls	Runs	Wkts	BB	Avge	RpO	S/R	5i	10m
Tests	0	0	–	–	–	–	–	–	–	–
ODIs	9	480	336	12	4–38	28.00	4.20	40.00	0	0
Twenty20 Ints	3	66	68	7	4–21	9.71	6.18	9.42	0	0
First-class	32	7006	3387	126	7–114	26.88	2.90	55.60	8	0

GRAHAM **ONIONS**

ENGLAND

Full name	**Graham Onions**
Born	**September 9, 1982, Gateshead**
Teams	**Durham**
Style	**Right-hand bat, right-arm fast-medium bowler**
Test debut	**England v West Indies at Lord's 2009**
ODI debut	**England v Australia at Chester-le-Street 2009**

THE PROFILE A brisk seam bowler, with a name that is a headline-writer's dream (especially when Durham's wicketkeeper Phil Mustard does the catching), Graham Onions first caught the eye during 2006, taking 54 wickets. He maintained an impressive workload for Durham, and didn't just take wickets on helpful surfaces at Chester-le-Street. He was called up for the late-season ODIs against Pakistan when Darren Gough was injured, although he didn't actually play, but he later toured Bangladesh with England A. The following two seasons were more of a struggle – Ottis Gibson (now England's bowling coach) sometimes kept him out of the Durham side in 2007, and the following year he had injury problems – but Onions started 2009 in rare form and was called up for the Tests against West Indies. He started in fairytale fashion, mopping up the tail with four wickets in seven balls to finish with 5 for 38 and his name on the Lord's honours board at his first attempt, bowling at a lively pace and swinging the ball away. He played in three of the Ashes Tests without quite recapturing this form, although he did enliven the second morning at Edgbaston by taking wickets with the first two balls of the day. Although he was left out for the final Test he was at The Oval as the Ashes were recaptured, then returned to Durham as they clinched the Championship for the second year running. Onions replaced Andrew Flintoff in the squad for the Champions Trophy in South Africa in September 2009, although oddly the selectors ignored him until the very last game of the dispiriting 6-1 thrashing by Australia just beforehand.

THE FACTS Onions took 8 for 101 for Durham v Warwickshire at Edgbaston in May 2007: two years later he took 7 for 38 in the same fixture ... At Edgbaston in July 2009 Onions took wickets with the first two balls of the second day's play against Australia: this is believed to have happened only once before in Test history, when Australia's "Chuck" Fleetwood-Smith did it against England at Melbourne in 1936-37 ...

THE FIGURES to 21.9.09   www.cricinfo.com

Batting & Fielding	M	Inns	NO	Runs	HS	Avge	S/R	100	50	4s	6s	Ct	St
Tests	5	5	2	19	17*	6.33	36.53	0	0	2	0	0	0
ODIs	1	0	–	–	–	–	–	–	–	–	–	0	0
Twenty20 Ints	0	0	–	–	–	–	–	–	–	–	–	–	–
First-class	48	20	5	106	19	7.06	72.10	0	0	–	–	7	0

Bowling	M	Balls	Runs	Wkts	BB	Avge	RpO	S/R	5i	10m
Tests	5	739	503	20	5–38	25.15	4.08	36.95	1	0
ODIs	1	54	28	1	1–28	28.00	3.11	54.00	0	0
Twenty20 Ints	0	0	–	–	–	–	–	–	–	–
First-class	68	10868	6557	222	8–101	29.53	3.61	48.95	9	0

JACOB **ORAM**

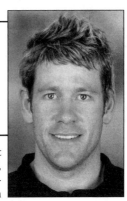

Full name	**Jacob David Philip Oram**
Born	**July 28, 1978, Palmerston North, Manawatu**
Teams	**Central Districts, Chennai Super Kings**
Style	**Left-hand bat, right-arm fast-medium bowler**
Test debut	**New Zealand v India at Wellington 2002-03**
ODI debut	**New Zealand v Zimbabwe at Wellington 2000-01**

THE PROFILE It's hard to miss Jacob Oram, and not just because of his height of 6ft 6ins (198cm). He is agile in the field, especially at gully, and he complements that with solid fast-medium bowling and aggressive batting. Foot problems cost him a season at a vital stage, but he came back strongly in 2002-03 to seal a regular international place. He narrowly missed a century against Pakistan in the Wellington Boxing Day Test of 2003, but made up for that by carving 119 not out against South Africa, then 90 in the second Test, which earned him an England tour in 2004. By then his bowling was starting to lose its sting, and he went down with back trouble shortly after pounding 126 against Australia at Brisbane in November 2004. After nearly 18 months out Oram showed what New Zealand's middle order had been missing, coming in at 38 for 4 at Centurion and making 133, still his highest score. He missed the start of the 2006-07 Australian one-day series with a hamstring injury, but bucked the team up with some stirring performances when he did get there, including a 71-ball century – NZ's fastest, and his first in ODIs – against Australia at Perth. A badly broken finger threatened to keep him out of the 2007 World Cup, but he made it (he said he'd have the finger amputated if that would help: luckily it wasn't necessary) and played his part in the march to the semi-finals. He continued to be a regular member of all New Zealand's sides, although a strange diffidence crept into his batting in England in 2008, when many thought he should have been moved up the order in an inexperienced line-up.

THE FACTS Oram averages 62.00 in Tests against Australia, 52.50 v South Africa – and 10.25 v India ... With the ball in ODIs he averages 14.75 v Bangladesh, but 79.30 v Australia ... Oram scored his maiden century in only his fourth first-class match, for Central Districts v Canterbury at Christchurch in 1998-99, and his 155 remains his highest score ...

THE FIGURES to 21.9.09   www.cricinfo.com

Batting & Fielding	M	Inns	NO	Runs	HS	Avge	S/R	100	50	4s	6s	Ct	St
Tests	33	59	10	1780	133	36.32	50.38	5	6	209	21	15	0
ODIs	132	96	12	2050	101*	24.40	82.92	1	11	151	64	40	0
Twenty20 Ints	20	19	5	377	66*	26/92	141.72	0	2	29	18	9	0
First-class	85	136	18	3992	155	33.83	–	8	18	–	–	36	0

Bowling	M	Balls	Runs	Wkts	BB	Avge	RpO	S/R	5i	10m
Tests	33	4964	1983	60	4–41	33.05	2.39	82.73	0	0
ODIs	132	5584	4091	132	5–26	30.99	4.39	42.30	2	0
Twenty20 Ints	20	282	420	7	3–33	60.00	8.93	40.28	0	0
First-class	85	10670	4158	155	6–45	26.82	2.33	68.83	3	0

TIM **PAINE**

AUSTRALIA

Full name	**Timothy David Paine**
Born	**December 8, 1984, Hobart, Tasmania**
Teams	**Tasmania**
Style	**Right-hand bat, wicketkeeper**
Test debut	**No Tests yet**
ODI debut	**Australia v Scotland at Edinburgh 2009**

THE PROFILE A talented top-order batsman and wicket-keeper, Tasmania's Tim Paine was earmarked as next in line behind Brad Haddin, for the one-day team at least, when he joined the squad for the ODIs that followed the Ashes series in England in 2009. In the event Paine ended up playing throughout, as Haddin had to have surgery on the finger he broke before the Edgbaston Test. And he did not disappoint, pulling off some quicksilver stumpings to go with some forthright batting from the top of the order, the highlight a fine century at Trent Bridge which included several whips off the pads – stork-like, with the back foot in the air – which fizzed down to fine leg. His call-up came soon after a strong showing for Australia A, including a six-studded 134 against Pakistan A in July 2009, which followed a season in which he finally elbowed his way past the highly rated Sean Clingeleffer as Tasmania's wicketkeeper in all formats. In the Sheffield Shield Paine made 445 runs at a touch under 30, and added 42 dismissals. He had made headlines early on in his career, extending his maiden first-class century against Western Australia at Perth to 215 in only his fifth match in October 2006. He was playing then as a specialist opening batsman, and a short-lived experiment with keeping as well was not a success (six innings brought only one double-figure score). It was a different story in one-dayers, though, where Paine instantly seemed able to handle both roles, and eventually he got the gloves back in first-class cricket.

THE FACTS Paine made 215 for Tasmania v Western Australia at Perth in October 2006 ... He made 134 (with five sixes) for Australia A v Pakistan A in Brisbane in July 2009 ... Paine captained Australia at the Under-19 World Cup in Bangladesh in 2003-04, and signed his first contract with Tasmania when he was 16 ...

THE FIGURES to 21.9.09   www.cricinfo.com

Batting & Fielding	M	Inns	NO	Runs	HS	Avge	S/R	100	50	4s	6s	Ct	St
Tests	0	0	–	–	–	–	–	–	–	–	–	–	–
ODIs	8	8	1	266	111	38.00	72.47	1	1	34	1	9	3
Twenty20 Ints	1	0	–	–	–	–	–	–	–	–	–	0	0
First-class	31	57	5	1611	215	30.98	43.16	1	12	167	5	85	2

Bowling	M	Balls	Runs	Wkts	BB	Avge	RpO	S/R	5i	10m
Tests	0	0	–	–	–	–	–	–	–	–
ODIs	8	0	–	–	–	–	–	–	–	–
Twenty20 Ints	1	0	–	–	–	–	–	–	–	–
First-class	31	6	3	0	–	–	3.00	–	0	0

MONTY **PANESAR**

Full name **Mudhsuden Singh Panesar**
Born **April 25, 1982, Luton, Bedfordshire**
Teams **Northamptonshire**
Style **Left-hand bat, slow left-arm orthodox spinner**
Test debut **England v India at Nagpur 2005-06**
ODI debut **England v Australia at Melbourne 2006-07**

THE PROFILE Monty Panesar quickly made himself a cult hero to English crowds enchanted by his enthusiastic wicket celebrations and endearingly erratic fielding. That, and equally amateurish batting, had threatened to hold him back, but when Ashley Giles was ruled out of the 2005-06 Indian tour Panesar received a late summons. He's a throwback to an earlier Northamptonshire slow left-armer, Bishan Bedi, who also twirled away in a *patka*, teasing and tempting with flight and guile, although Panesar gives it more of a rip than Bedi did. Panesar's arrival was delayed while he finished university but, finally free from studies, he took 46 Championship wickets at 21.54 in 2005. He made his Test debut at Nagpur that winter, picking up Sachin Tendulkar as his first wicket. He captivated crowds at home in 2006, sending down the ball of the season to bowl Younis Khan and set up victory at Leeds. Next season he claimed 31 wickets in seven home Tests, and remained the crowd's favourite as Montymania showed no sign of stopping. But, lacking variety, he struggled in Sri Lanka at the end of 2007 (eight Test wickets cost more than 50 each), and laboured a little in England too, while his antics and frequent appealing rubbed some up the wrong way. By the start of 2009 he had lost his place as England's No. 1 spinner to Graeme Swann (ironically, since Panesar's arrival had hastened Swann's departure from Northamptonshire), and his only contribution to the Ashes series was an unlikely match-saving display with the bat, in the first Test at Cardiff. After that, with Adil Rashid's star on the rise, Panesar lost his England contract and faced an uncertain future.

THE FACTS Panesar took 7 for 181 for Northamptonshire v Essex at Chelmsford in July 2005 ... He was the first Sikh to play Test cricket for anyone other than India: when Panesar opposed Harbhajan Singh during his debut at Nagpur in 2005-06 it was the first instance of Sikh bowling to Sikh in a Test ... He averages 25.00 with the ball in Tests against West Indies – but 53.57 v India ...

THE FIGURES to 21.9.09   www.cricinfo.com

Batting & Fielding	M	Inns	NO	Runs	HS	Avge	S/R	100	50	4s	6s	Ct	St
Tests	39	51	17	187	26	5.50	29.44	0	0	20	1	9	0
ODIs	26	8	3	26	13	5.20	28.57	0	0	2	0	3	0
Twenty20 Ints	1	1	0	1	1	1.00	50.00	0	0	0	0	0	0
First-class	109	141	48	789	39*	8.48	33.01	0	0	–	–	25	0

Bowling	M	Balls	Runs	Wkts	BB	Avge	RpO	S/R	5i	10m
Tests	39	9042	4331	126	6–37	34.37	2.87	71.76	8	1
ODIs	26	1308	980	24	3–25	40.83	4.49	54.50	0	0
Twenty20 Ints	1	24	40	2	2–40	20.00	10.00	12.00	0	0
First-class	109	24393	11640	352	7–181	33.06	2.86	69.29	19	3

THARANGA **PARANAVITANA**

SRI LANKA

Full name	**Nishad Tharanga Paranavitana**
Born	**April 15, 1982, Kegalle**
Teams	**Sinhalese Sports Club, Kandurata**
Style	**Left-hand bat, offspinner**
Test debut	**Sri Lanka v Pakistan at Karachi 2008-09**
ODI debut	**No ODIs yet**

THE PROFILE   Tharanga Paranavitana is a tall, upright left-handed opener who first made a name for himself in the Emerging Team tournament in Sri Lanka late in 2003. A run of consistent scores on the domestic scene followed, but it was a stellar 2007–08 season – which followed a brief trip to Zimbabwe with the A team – that established him as a real Test prospect. Paranavitana was the leading runscorer in the top tier of the Premier League with 893, and his 236 against Colombo CC in the last match helped the Sinhalese Sports Club clinch the title. That was his third century of the summer (and the second double of his career), and he added another in the regional competition for Kandurata to finish the first-class season with 1059 runs at 81. All that – and 159 in a representative match against South Africa A – meant he had to be given a chance in the national team, and he eventually won his first Test cap at Karachi early in 2009. The disappointment of a first-ball duck was followed by a chest wound in the terrorist attack on the Sri Lankan team bus in Lahore. Thankfully, Paranavitana was back to full fitness in time for the return series in Sri Lanka, and made his mark with 72 and 49 in a narrow victory at Galle, then 73 in the final Test in Colombo. Leaner times followed in the series against New Zealand, and he was also fined half his match fee for claiming a catch which replays showed had clearly bounced in front of him.

THE FACTS   Paranavitana scored 236 (and 80 not out) for Sinhalese Sports Club v Colombo CC in March 2008 ... He made 232 not out for Sinhalese v Tamil Union in February 2007 ... Paranavitana started his Test career (against Pakistan at Karachi in February 2009) with a first-ball duck – just like his opening partner that day, Malinda Warnapura (against Bangladesh in June 2007) ...

THE FIGURES to 21.9.09   www.cricinfo.com

Batting & Fielding	M	Inns	NO	Runs	HS	Avge	S/R	100	50	4s	6s	Ct	St
Tests	7	13	0	330	73	25.38	51.96	0	2	37	0	4	0
ODIs	0	0	–	–	–	–	–	–	–	–	–	–	–
Twenty20 Ints	0	0	–	–	–	–	–	–	–	–	–	–	–
First-class	86	142	15	5225	236	41.14	52.10	14	20	–	–	93	0

Bowling	M	Balls	Runs	Wkts	BB	Avge	RpO	S/R	5i	10m
Tests	7	84	69	1	1–26	69.00	4.92	84.00	0	0
ODIs	0	0	–	–	–	–	–	–	–	–
Twenty20 Ints	0	0	–	–	–	–	–	–	–	–
First-class	86	1268	640	20	4–39	32.00	3.02	63.40	0	0

WAYNE **PARNELL**

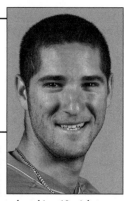

Full name	**Wayne Dillon Parnell**
Born	**July 30, 1989, Port Elizabeth, Cape Province**
Teams	**Warriors, Kent**
Style	**Left-hand bat, left-arm fast-medium bowler**
Test debut	**No Tests yet**
ODI debut	**South Africa v Australia at Perth 2008-09**

THE PROFILE Tall, slim, and waspishly fast, left-armer Wayne Parnell can also bat well, and exhibited strong leadership qualities during a glittering junior career which included captaining South Africa in the Under-19 World Cup in Malaysia in 2008 (he had already played in the 2006 event at 16). In Malaysia he led by example, taking 18 wickets – the most in the tournament – and scoring useful middle-order runs to steer South Africa into the final, where they lost a rain-affected game to India. The national selectors were already on alert, and after testing out the conditions Down Under during an Emerging Players tournament Parnell was called up for the one-day series in Australia early in 2009. He played only one ODI there, proving a little expensive in a victory over Australia at Perth, but began to make his presence felt in the return series back home, taking 4 for 25 as the Aussies were rolled for 131 at Centurion. He was rewarded by becoming the youngest South African to be awarded a national contract. Then, after warming up with some useful spells for Kent, Parnell was one of the stars of the World Twenty20 in England in 2009, derailing England (3 for 16) and West Indies (4 for 13) inside 48 hours. He bowled with pace and accuracy during the powerplays and the final overs, and still finished with an economy rate of less than six an over. He was outstanding in the semi-final against eventual champions Pakistan: after conceding 14 runs in his first over, he bounced back strongly to give away only 12 off his next three.

THE FACTS In the quarter-final of the 2008 Under-19 World Cup in Kuala Lumpur Parnell top-scored with 57 from No. 7, and then took 6 for 8 as Bangladesh were bowled out for 41 ... He scored 90 for Kent v Glamorgan at Canterbury in May 2009, putting on 151 for the seventh wicket with James Tredwell ... Parnell's best first-class bowling figures of 4 for 7 came in his second match, for Eastern Province v KwaZulu/Natal at Port Elizabeth in November 2006 ...

THE FIGURES *to 21.9.09*   www.cricinfo.com

Batting & Fielding	M	Inns	NO	Runs	HS	Avge	S/R	100	50	4s	6s	Ct	St
Tests	0	0	–	–	–	–	–	–	–	–	–	–	–
ODIs	4	0	–	–	–	–	–	–	–	–	–	1	0
Twenty20 Ints	8	0	–	–	–	–	–	–	–	–	–	0	0
First-class	16	21	3	347	90	19.27	52.10	0	2	38	4	2	0

Bowling	M	Balls	Runs	Wkts	BB	Avge	RpO	S/R	5i	10m
Tests	0	0	–	–	–	–	–	–	–	–
ODIs	4	216	188	6	4–25	31.33	5.22	36.00	0	0
Twenty20 Ints	8	173	192	11	4–13	17.45	6.65	15.72	0	0
First-class	16	2861	1427	44	4–7	32.43	2.99	65.02	0	0

NEW ZEALAND

JEETAN **PATEL**

Full name	**Jeetan Shashi Patel**
Born	**May 7, 1980, Wellington**
Teams	**Wellington, Warwickshire**
Style	**Right-hand bat, offspinner**
Test debut	**New Zealand v South Africa at Cape Town 2005-06**
ODI debut	**New Zealand v Zimbabwe at Harare 2005-06**

THE PROFILE The son of Indian parents, but born and brought up in Wellington's eastern suburbs, offspinner Jeetan Patel was fast-tracked into the New Zealand one-day side after being identified as the sort of slow bowler who could be effective at the death. Patel first played for Wellington in 1999-2000, bowling 59 overs and taking 5 for 145 against Auckland on debut. Three middling seasons followed, and he seemed to be heading nowhere, with an average in the mid-forties. But then he took 6 for 32 against Otago in 2004-05, propelling Wellington into the final against Auckland, which they lost. Suddenly good judges were noting his ability to make the ball loop and drift, not unlike a right-handed Daniel Vettori. Patel was chosen to tour Zimbabwe in August 2005, and has been a one-day regular since. At home his 2 for 23 from ten overs throttled Sri Lanka at Wellington, then three wickets at Christchurch helped subdue West Indies too. All this put Patel in line for a first Test cap, which came against South Africa in April 2006: he wheeled away for 42 overs and removed Graeme Smith, Boeta Dippenaar and AB de Villiers at a cost of 117 runs. Since then Patel has often been used as a foil to Vettori on spinning tracks, winkling out six West Indians at Napier in December 2008, and six Sri Lankans in Colombo late in 2009. He usually succeeds in keeping the runs down, not least in most of his six outings in the 2007 World Cup. His batting, initially underwhelming, has improved: he more than doubled his highest score during a county stint with Warwickshire, hitting 120 from No. 10 against Yorkshire.

THE FACTS Patel won the Man of the Match award for 2 for 23 in ten overs against Sri Lanka at Wellington in 2005-06 after being super-subbed into the game ... He also won the match award in his first Twenty20 international, after taking 3 for 20 v South Africa at Johannesburg in October 2005 ... Patel made 120 for Warwickshire v Yorkshire at Edgbaston in May 2009, sharing a county-record ninth-wicket stand of 233 with Jonathan Trott ...

THE FIGURES to 21.9.09   www.cricinfo.com

Batting & Fielding	M	Inns	NO	Runs	HS	Avge	S/R	100	50	4s	6s	Ct	St
Tests	9	12	2	131	27*	13.10	43.52	0	0	13	0	5	0
ODIs	38	12	6	72	34	12.00	54.96	0	0	4	2	11	0
Twenty20 Ints	11	4	1	9	5	3.00	64.28	0	0	1	0	4	0
First-class	81	96	34	1224	120	19.74	–	1	3	–	–	28	0

Bowling	M	Balls	Runs	Wkts	BB	Avge	RpO	S/R	5i	10m
Tests	9	2556	1289	33	5–110	39.06	3.02	77.45	1	0
ODIs	38	1766	1469	42	3–11	34.97	4.99	42.04	0	0
Twenty20 Ints	11	199	269	16	3–20	16.81	8.11	12.43	0	0
First-class	81	14656	7159	171	6–32	41.86	2.93	85.70	5	0

MUNAF **PATEL**

Full name **Munaf Musa Patel**
Born **July 12, 1983, Ikhar, Gujarat**
Teams **Baroda, Rajasthan Royals**
Style **Right-hand bat, right-arm fast-medium bowler**
Test debut **India v England at Mohali 2005-06**
ODI debut **India v England at Goa 2005-06**

THE PROFILE Few fast men generated as much hype before bowling a ball in first-class – let alone international – cricket as Munaf Patel, from the little town of Ikhar in Gujarat, did early in 2003. Kiran More spotted him: soon Patel was being hailed as the fastest bowler in India, although at first he spent more time recovering from injuries than actually playing. He's strongly built, though not overly tall, and bustles up to the crease, gathering momentum before releasing in a windmill-whirl of hands. He has a well-directed yorker, and can reverse-swing the ball. In March 2006 he finally received a call from the selectors – now chaired by his old pal More – after taking 10 for 91 in a match for the Board President's XI against the England tourists. He finished his first Test with 7 for 97, and continued to strike consistently in the West Indies later in 2006. Things got harder after that. He picked up an ankle niggle in South Africa, and was criticised when it bothered him in the final Test – but he regained full fitness in time for the World Cup. Then it was a back injury, and Patel returned to the Chennai academy – which he calls his "second home" – to remodel his action. In Australia in 2007-08 he sometimes seemed uninterested, and certainly didn't make the batsmen hop about much. He played his first Test for 16 months in New Zealand in March 2009, taking five wickets in a comfortable victory at Hamilton, although his bowling after that was unspectacular, and lacked the fiery pace that earned him those early rave reviews.

THE FACTS Patel's match figures of 7 for 97 were the best on Test debut by an Indian fast bowler, beating Mohammad Nissar's 6 for 135 v England at Lord's in 1932 (Abid Ali, more of a medium-pacer, took 7 for 116 on debut against Australia in 1967–68) ... Patel's best first-class figures are 6 for 50, for Maharashtra v Railways at Delhi in January 2006 ...

THE FIGURES to 21.9.09   www.cricinfo.com

Batting & Fielding	M	Inns	NO	Runs	HS	Avge	S/R	100	50	4s	6s	Ct	St
Tests	12	13	5	56	15*	7.00	40.87	0	0	7	1	6	0
ODIs	41	15	8	52	15	7.42	66.66	0	0	5	1	6	0
Twenty20 Ints	0	0	–	–	–	–	–	–	–	–	–	–	–
First-class	42	47	14	485	78	14.69	69.68	0	1	–	–	11	0

Bowling	M	Balls	Runs	Wkts	BB	Avge	RpO	S/R	5i	10m
Tests	12	2394	1230	34	4–25	36.17	3.08	70.41	0	0
ODIs	41	1825	1464	46	4–49	31.82	4.81	39.67	0	0
Twenty20 Ints	0	0	–	–	–	–	–	–	–	–
First-class	42	7646	3635	148	6–50	24.56	2.85	51.66	5	1

IRFAN **PATHAN**

INDIA

Full name	**Irfan Khan Pathan**
Born	**October 27, 1984, Baroda, Gujarat**
Teams	**Baroda, Kings XI Punjab**
Style	**Left-hand bat, left-arm fast-medium bowler**
Test debut	**India v Australia at Adelaide 2003-04**
ODI debut	**India v Australia at Melbourne 2003-04**

THE PROFILE Irfan Pathan was initially rated the most talented swing and seam bowler to emerge from India since Kapil Dev, and he was soon being thought of as a possible successor for Kapil in the allround department too. He was strikingly composed in his Test debut at 19: his instinct is not just what to bowl to whom and when, but also to keep learning new tricks. A potent left-armer's outswinger helped him to a hat-trick in the first over of the Karachi Test in January 2006, and he's adept at reverse-swing too, although his pace has reduced in recent years. When batting, he was regularly pushed up the order, sometimes even opening in one-dayers, although his batting graph has also slowed down of late. At No. 3 he produced a spectacular 83 against Sri Lanka – and he often bailed India out in Tests as well, with 93 and 82 against Sri Lanka late in 2005, and 90 as India piled up 603 against Pakistan at Faisalabad early in 2006. But he struggled after that with shoulder trouble. Pathan returned to the one-day side later in 2007, and was handed a Test recall against Pakistan at Bangalore in December. He celebrated his first Test for 19 months by clubbing his first century, reaching it with his fourth six. Early in 2008 he played two important innings and took five wickets as Australia were beaten at Perth, but since then the advent of other left-arm pacemen has shoved him down the queue a little, although he remains a regular in both limited-overs squads.

THE FACTS Pathan was the first bowler to take a hat-trick in the first over of a Test match, when he dismissed Salman Butt, Younis Khan and Mohammad Yousuf at Karachi in January 2006: from 0 for 3, Pakistan recovered to win by 341 runs ... Pathan took 12 for 126 in the match against Zimbabwe at Harare in September 2005 ... He is one of only five players to have scored a century and taken a hat-trick in Tests ... His half-brother Yusuf Pathan has also played for India ...

THE FIGURES *to 21.9.09*   www.cricinfo.com

Batting & Fielding	M	Inns	NO	Runs	HS	Avge	S/R	100	50	4s	6s	Ct	St
Tests	29	40	5	1105	102	31.57	53.22	1	6	131	18	8	0
ODIs	107	78	18	1368	83	22.80	77.68	0	5	127	33	18	0
Twenty20 Ints	16	12	7	133	33*	26.60	125.47	0	0	6	6	2	0
First-class	80	106	23	2481	111*	29.89	–	2	14	–	–	25	0

Bowling	M	Balls	Runs	Wkts	BB	Avge	RpO	S/R	5i	10m
Tests	29	5884	3226	100	7–59	32.26	3.28	58.84	7	2
ODIs	107	4194	4547	152	5–27	29.91	5.25	34.17	1	0
Twenty20 Ints	16	306	395	16	3–16	24.68	7.74	19.12	0	0
First-class	80	15328	8079	270	7–35	29.92	3.16	56.77	13	3

YUSUF **PATHAN**

Full name **Yusuf Khan Pathan**
Born **November 17, 1982, Baroda, Gujarat**
Teams **Baroda, Rajasthan Royals**
Style **Right-hand bat, offspinner**
Test debut **No Tests yet**
ODI debut **India v Pakistan at Dhaka 2008**

THE PROFILE   A hard-hitting batsman and handy offspinner, Yusuf Pathan made his Ranji Trophy debut in 2001-02. But it wasn't for another three years – by which time his younger half-brother Irfan was already a Test player – that Yusuf established himself as a regular. Over the next three seasons he scored plenty of runs and took a fair few wickets for Baroda, but didn't do himself justice when called up for two of the Challenger Trophy tournaments which help the selection process for India's one-day side. Eventually, though, his ability to score runs quickly – he had the highest strike rate in the Ranji Trophy in 2006-07 – and some impressive performances in the one-day Deodhar Trophy and Twenty20 domestic tournament were rewarded with a place in India's squad for the inaugural World Twenty20 championship in South Africa, alongside his brother. He didn't play in the qualifying matches, but was drafted in for the final, when he opened and smote his second ball into the stands. He followed that with an impressive showing for the Rajasthan Royals in the inaugural Indian Premier League season early in 2008, finishing with 435 runs at a heady strike rate of 179, boosted by a 21-ball fifty (the IPL's fastest) against the Deccan Chargers. In the final, he helped Shane Warne's team to the title by following up three important wickets with a 39-ball 56. After all that, he was a shoo-in for India's limited-overs teams, where he has maintained his impressive batting strike-rate, often proving devastating in the closing overs.

THE FACTS   Yusuf Pathan made his international debut in the final of the inaugural World Twenty20 championship in South Africa in September 2007: he hit his second ball, from Mohammad Asif, for six ... Pathan scored 183 for Baroda v Bengal at Baroda in November 2007 ... He took 6 for 47 for Baroda v Tamil Nadu in Chennai in January 2007, and 10 for 119 in the match against Bengal at Baroda in November 2007 ...

THE FIGURES to 21.9.09   www.cricinfo.com

Batting & Fielding	M	Inns	NO	Runs	HS	Avge	S/R	100	50	4s	6s	Ct	St
Tests	0	0	–	–	–	–	–	–	–	–	–	–	–
ODIs	29	19	8	242	59*	22.00	100.83	0	2	18	11	6	0
Twenty20 Ints	9	8	3	122	33*	24.40	171.83	0	0	6	9	5	0
First-class	35	54	6	1774	183	36.95	86.07	4	8	–	–	36	0

Bowling	M	Balls	Runs	Wkts	BB	Avge	RpO	S/R	5i	10m
Tests	0	0	–	–	–	–	–	–	–	–
ODIs	29	608	584	16	3–56	36.50	5.76	38.00	0	0
Twenty20 Ints	9	89	118	4	2–23	29.50	7.95	22.25	0	0
First-class	35	6473	2854	89	6–47	32.06	2.64	72.73	7	1

ROBIN **PETERSON**

SOUTH AFRICA

Full name	**Robin John Peterson**
Born	**August 4, 1979, Port Elizabeth, Cape Province**
Teams	**Warriors**
Style	**Left-hand bat, slow left-arm orthodox spinner**
Test debut	**South Africa v Bangladesh at Dhaka 2002-03**
ODI debut	**South Africa v India at Colombo 2002-03**

THE PROFILE Spin bowlers of genuine potential are rare in South Africa, more so the jewels who can bat and field well, but on the face of it Robin Peterson ticks all three boxes. He has five centuries and nearly 250 first-class wickets, and is a lurking presence square of the wicket in the field. At first glance his left-arm spin looks a little too plain, but he does turn it given help from the pitch. He also has a *doosra*, which turns in to the right-hander. After a glittering youth career Peterson made his Test debut against Bangladesh in May 2003, taking five wickets and scoring 61, but since then has been seen mainly as a one-day specialist – especially after Brian Lara carted him for a Test-record 28 in an over at the end of 2003 – although he did take 5 for 33 against Bangladesh on a helpful Chittagong track early in 2008. That got him on the plane for the England tour that followed, but Paul Harris was preferred in the Tests. Peterson had played some one-dayers in India late in 2005, but had little success, a pattern repeated when the Australians toured early the following year, when he managed only one wicket in three matches. Still, he was the only specialist spinner chosen for the 2006 Champions Trophy and, despite continuing modest returns, for the 2007 World Cup. Again he contributed little with the ball, although his thick-edged four did complete a last-gasp victory over Sri Lanka after Lasith Malinga's four wickets in four balls had derailed what seemed a routine run-chase. The suspicion remains, though, that Peterson doesn't do enough with the ball in international cricket.

THE FACTS Peterson's unlucky 13th over against West Indies at Johannesburg in December 2003 was the most expensive in Test history: Brian Lara hit it for 28 (466444) ... The highest of Peterson's five centuries is 130, for Eastern Province v Gauteng at Johannesburg in October 2002 ... He also made 108 for South Africa A v India A at Bloemfontein in April 2002 ... Peterson took 6 for 67 for Eastern Province v Border at East London in December 1999, and 6 for 16 in a one-day game for EP v Namibia in November 2002 ...

THE FIGURES *to 21.9.09* www.cricinfo.com

Batting & Fielding	M	Inns	NO	Runs	HS	Avge	S/R	100	50	4s	6s	Ct	St
Tests	6	7	1	163	61	27.16	71.80	0	1	19	1	5	0
ODIs	35	15	4	147	36	13.36	75.77	0	0	14	2	7	0
Twenty20 Ints	5	2	0	42	34	21.00	107.69	0	0	3	2	2	0
First-class	91	143	18	3164	130	25.31	–	5	10	–	–	40	0

Bowling	M	Balls	Runs	Wkts	BB	Avge	RpO	S/R	5i	10m
Tests	6	959	497	14	5–33	35.50	3.10	68.50	1	0
ODIs	35	1252	992	17	2–26	58.35	4.75	73.64	0	0
Twenty20 Ints	5	65	86	6	3–30	14.33	7.93	10.83	0	0
First-class	91	16309	8271	240	6–67	34.46	3.04	67.95	11	1

KEVIN **PIETERSEN**

Full name	**Kevin Peter Pietersen**
Born	**June 27, 1980, Pietermaritzburg, Natal, South Africa**
Teams	**Hampshire, Bangalore Royal Challengers**
Style	**Right-hand bat, offspinner**
Test debut	**England v Australia at Lord's 2005**
ODI debut	**England v Zimbabwe at Harare 2004-05**

THE PROFILE Expansive with bat and explosive with bombast, Kevin Pietersen is not one for the quiet life. Bold-minded and big-hitting, he first ruffled feathers by quitting South Africa – he was disenchanted with the race-quota system – in favour of England, his eligibility coming courtesy of an English mother. He never doubted he would play Test cricket: he has self-confidence in spades and, fortunately, sackfuls of talent too. Sure enough, as soon as he was eligible, he was chosen for England's one-day series in Zimbabwe, where he averaged 104. Then, in South Africa, and undeterred by hostile crowds, he hammered a robust century in the second match. Test cricket was next on the to-do list. In 2005 he replaced Graham Thorpe, against Australia, at Lord's ... and coolly blasted a couple of fifties in a losing cause, then, with the Ashes at stake, hit 158 on the final day at The Oval. "KP" had arrived – and how. The runs kept coming: 158 at Adelaide and 226 against West Indies at Headingley sandwiched two tons in the 2007 World Cup, where he was the star of England's lame campaign. Late in 2008 he succeeded Michael Vaughan as captain, and started in his usual fairytale fashion, biffing a hundred as South Africa were beaten in the Oval Test, then inspiring a landslide in the one-day series. But his captaincy ended in tears after a fallout with the coach, then his form dipped as he battled a persistent Achilles injury. That eventually needed an operation, which kept him out of the last three Ashes Tests in 2009. But no-one was writing off the man who Ricky Ponting once said could be "the next superstar of world cricket".

THE FACTS Pietersen reached 100 against South Africa at East London in February 2005 from 69 balls, the fastest for England in ODIs ... After 25 Tests he had made 2448 runs, more than anyone else except Don Bradman (3194) ... He averages 98.66 in ODIs v South Africa – and 16.50 v Bangladesh ... Pietersen was out for 158 three times in Tests before going on to 226 against West Indies in May 2007 ... His record includes two ODIs for the World XI ...

THE FIGURES *to 21.9.09*   www.cricinfo.com

Batting & Fielding	M	Inns	NO	Runs	HS	Avge	S/R	100	50	4s	6s	Ct	St
Tests	54	97	4	4647	226	49.96	62.76	16	15	537	48	32	0
ODIs	92	82	15	3127	116	46.67	87.41	7	20	290	58	32	0
Twenty20 Ints	19	19	1	529	79	29.38	146.53	0	2	58	12	7	0
First-class	140	233	16	11026	254*	50.81	–	38	44	–	–	112	0

Bowling	M	Balls	Runs	Wkts	BB	Avge	RpO	S/R	5i	10m
Tests	54	735	518	4	1–0	129.50	4.22	183.75	0	0
ODIs	92	214	201	5	2–22	40.20	5.63	42.80	0	0
Twenty20 Ints	19	6	9	0	–	–	9.00	–	0	0
First-class	140	5539	3229	61	4–31	52.93	3.49	90.80	0	0

RICKY **PONTING**

AUSTRALIA

Full name	**Ricky Thomas Ponting**
Born	**December 19, 1974, Launceston, Tasmania**
Teams	**Tasmania, Kolkata Knight Riders**
Style	**Right-hand bat, right-arm medium-pace bowler**
Test debut	**Australia v Sri Lanka at Perth 1995-96**
ODI debut	**Australia v South Africa at Wellington 1994-95**

THE PROFILE Ricky Ponting began with Tasmania at 17 and Australia at 20, and was unluckily given out for 96 on his Test debut. He remains the archetypal modern cricketer, playing all the shots with a full flourish and knowing only attack – and his dead-eye fielding is another plus. A gambler and a buccaneer, Ponting has had setbacks, against probing seam and high-class finger-spin, which he plays with hard hands when out of form. In the '90s there were off-field indiscretions, but his growing maturity was acknowledged when he succeeded Steve Waugh as one-day captain in 2002. It was a seamless transition: Ponting led the 2003 World Cup campaign from the front, clouting a coruscating century in the final, and acceded to the Test crown when Waugh finally stepped down early in 2004. But things changed in 2005. A humiliating one-day defeat by Bangladesh caused the first ripples of dissent against his leadership style, and more followed as the Ashes series progressed. The loss of the urn hurt, and the pain lingered. Ponting bounced back by winning 11 of 12 Tests in 2005-06, which was just a warm-up for the Ashes rematch. He led that off with 196 at Brisbane – and was furious to miss his double-century – and remained tight-lipped until the 5-0 whitewash was sealed. His batting never wavered, and not long after retaining the World Cup in 2007 he sailed past 20,000 international runs during another successful season. The runs continued to flow – he became his country's leading Test runscorer in 2009 – but another Ashes defeat (Billy Murdoch, in the 1890s, was the last Australian captain to lose two series in England) reopened those old wounds.

THE FACTS The only Australian with a higher Test average is Don Bradman (99.94) ... Ponting uniquely scored two hundreds in his 100th Test, v South Africa at Sydney in Jan 2006 ... His 242 v India at Adelaide in 2003-04 is the highest by a player on the losing side in a Test (in the next game he made 257, and they won) ... When he was 8, Ponting's grandmother gave him a T-shirt that read "Under this shirt is a Test player" ... His record includes one ODI for the World XI ...

THE FIGURES to 21.9.09   www.cricinfo.com

Batting & Fielding	M	Inns	NO	Runs	HS	Avge	S/R	100	50	4s	6s	Ct	St
Tests	136	229	26	11345	257	55.88	59.37	38	48	1280	66	159	0
ODIs	319	310	35	11756	164	42.74	80.66	27	68	1042	141	138	0
Twenty20 Ints	17	16	2	401	98*	28.64	132.78	0	2	41	11	8	0
First-class	236	400	53	20192	257	58.19	–	72	86	–	–	248	0

Bowling	M	Balls	Runs	Wkts	BB	Avge	RpO	S/R	5i	10m
Tests	136	539	242	5	1–0	48.40	2.69	107.80	0	0
ODIs	319	150	104	3	1–12	34.66	4.16	50.00	0	0
Twenty20 Ints	17	–	–	–	–	–	–	–	–	–
First-class	236	1434	768	14	2–10	54.85	3.21	102.42	0	0

DAMMIKA **PRASAD**

Full name	**Kariyawasam Tirana Gamage Dammika Prasad**
Born	**May 30, 1983, Ragama**
Teams	**Sinhalese Sports Club, Basnahira North**
Style	**Right-hand bat, right-arm fast-medium bowler**
Test debut	**Sri Lanka v India at Colombo 2008**
ODI debut	**Sri Lanka v Bangladesh at Chittagong 2005-06**

THE PROFILE A prosperous international career looked on the cards when Dammika Prasad took two wickets in his first over in a one-day international, against Bangladesh in February 2006. However, he played only two more games before a back injury kept him on the sidelines for six months. He returned with the A team in India, and also toured England with them in 2007. The following year he returned to the full side, and made his Test debut against India at the Sara Stadium in Colombo, in a match Sri Lanka won to take the series. Prasad, bustling in and occasionally moving the ball away at a fair pace, ended up with five wickets, including the wicket of Virender Sehwag – India's best batsman in the series – in both innings. He has long had the ability to bowl at the death in one-dayers, having worked hard to develop subtle variations including a good yorker. He can also work up a fair head of steam, and pushed the speedo over 90mph at times during his Test debut. He proved expensive in his next Test, against Bangladesh, but that pacy promise got him restored to the side late in 2009 against New Zealand. Interestingly, at school Prasad was a No. 3 batsman (and has a few first-class fifties under his belt to prove it). When he was 17 he had to try his hand at fast bowling as the school had no-one to take the new ball. He was an instant success, gaining selection for the Under-19 World Cup in 2002 and also winning a six-month scholarship to play in England.

THE FACTS Prasad took the wicket of Shahriar Nafees with his third ball in international cricket, against Bangladesh in Chittagong in February 2006 – and dismissed Aftab Ahmed with his next delivery ... Prasad took 6 for 25 (10 for 98 in the match) for Southern Province against Uva at Galle in January 2004 ... He scored 89 for Sri Lanka A v Durham at Chester-le-Street in August 2007 ...

THE FIGURES to 21.9.09   www.cricinfo.com

Batting & Fielding	M	Inns	NO	Runs	HS	Avge	S/R	100	50	4s	6s	Ct	St
Tests	3	3	0	45	36	15.00	52.32	0	0	6	0	0	0
ODIs	5	3	0	17	8	5.66	34.00	0	0	0	0	0	0
Twenty20 Ints	0	0	–	–	–	–	–	–	–	–	–	–	–
First-class	49	53	6	857	89	18.23	57.67	0	6	–	–	11	0

Bowling	M	Balls	Runs	Wkts	BB	Avge	RpO	S/R	5i	10m
Tests	3	524	405	11	3–82	36.81	4.63	47.63	0	0
ODIs	5	216	217	5	2–29	43.40	6.02	43.20	0	0
Twenty20 Ints	0	0	–	–	–	–	–	–	–	–
First-class	49	6503	4020	155	6–25	25.93	3.70	41.95	3	1

ASHWELL **PRINCE**

SOUTH AFRICA

Full name **Ashwell Gavin Prince**
Born **May 28, 1977, Port Elizabeth, Cape Province**
Teams **Warriors, Lancashire**
Style **Left-hand bat, occasional left-arm spinner**
Test debut **South Africa v Australia at Johannesburg 2001-02**
ODI debut **South Africa v Bangladesh at Kimberley 2002-03**

THE PROFILE A crouching left-hander with a high-batted stance and a Gooch-like grimace, Ashwell Prince was helped into the national team by South Africa's controversial race-quota system, although he quickly justified his selection by top-scoring with a gutsy debut 49 against Australia in 2001-02. That, and a matchwinning 48 in the third Test, seemed to have buried an early reputation as a one-day flasher. But a run of low scores saw him left out for a while, before he bounced back with Test hundreds against outclassed Zimbabwe and almost-outclassed West Indies early in 2005. However, his 119 at Sydney in January 2006 was an altogether better performance. Prince had previously struggled against Shane Warne, and although he eventually succumbed again it was only after an important stand of 219 with Jacques Kallis. He did well in the Tests in England in 2008, with centuries at Lord's and Leeds, but by then he was a back number in ODIs, having been left out following a largely anonymous World Cup. He made a Test-best 162 not out against Bangladesh at Centurion in November 2008, but was then sidelined by a broken thumb. Jean-Paul Duminy's stellar arrival meant there was no automatic return for Prince, and he showed what he thought of that by grafting 150 when he was recalled and asked to open instead of the injured Graeme Smith against Australia at Cape Town in March 2009. Long rated highly by Ali Bacher, Prince is strong through the off side, and although his throwing has been hampered by a long-term shoulder injury, he remains a fine fielder in the covers.

THE FACTS Prince became South Africa's first black captain when the injured Graeme Smith missed the series in Sri Lanka in 2006 ... Prince averages 77.00 in Tests against West Indies, but 27.57 v Sri Lanka ... In his first 18 Test innings against Australia, Prince was dismissed 11 times by Shane Warne ... Prince made 254 for Warriors v Titans at Centurion in March 2009, a week before being recalled to the Test side against Australia and hitting 150 ... His record includes three ODIs for the Africa XI ...

THE FIGURES *to 21.9.09*   www.cricinfo.com

Batting & Fielding	M	Inns	NO	Runs	HS	Avge	S/R	100	50	4s	6s	Ct	St
Tests	48	77	12	3074	162*	47.29	44.38	11	8	341	11	29	0
ODIs	52	41	12	1018	89*	35.10	67.77	0	3	77	4	26	0
Twenty20 Ints	1	1	0	5	5	5.00	83.33	0	0	0	0	0	0
First-class	166	265	37	10204	254	44.75	–	25	48	–	–	108	0

Bowling	M	Balls	Runs	Wkts	BB	Avge	RpO	S/R	5i	10m
Tests	48	96	47	1	1–2	47.00	2.93	96.00	0	0
ODIs	52	12	3	0	–	–	1.50	–	0	0
Twenty20 Ints	1	0	–	–	–	–	–	–	–	–
First-class	166	276	166	4	2–11	41.50	3.60	69.00	0	0

MATT **PRIOR**

Full name	**Matthew James Prior**
Born	**February 26, 1982, Johannesburg, South Africa**
Teams	**Sussex**
Style	**Right-hand bat, wicketkeeper**
Test debut	**England v West Indies at Lord's 2007**
ODI debut	**England v Zimbabwe at Bulawayo 2004-05**

THE PROFILE Sussex wicketkeeper Matt Prior represented England at several junior levels, and completed his set by making his Test debut in May 2007, against West Indies at Lord's. He repaid the faith of Peter Moores, his former county boss turned national coach, with a cracking century – the first by a keeper on debut for England. It was full of solid drives and clumping pulls, and seemed to announce a readymade star, especially when Prior added some acrobatic takes behind the stumps. He finished that series with 324 runs – but there were already rumbles about his keeping technique, which didn't seem to matter while England were winning. But then India arrived, and Prior's fumbles were magnified as the visitors stole the series: he dropped Sachin Tendulkar and VVS Laxman as India made 664 at The Oval. The runs dried up, too, and suddenly Prior's talkativeness behind the stumps, and his footwork, were called into question. Another uninspiring series followed in Sri Lanka and Prior was dropped, in favour of his old Sussex team-mate Tim Ambrose. Prior went back to Hove and sharpened up his technique, and was ready when Ambrose in turn faltered during 2008: Prior returned for the one-dayers against South Africa, and pouched a record-equalling six catches (one of them a one-handed flying stunner) at Trent Bridge. By 2009 he looked even more the part – and even more like his mentor, Alec Stewart – making several smart catches and another century against West Indies to secure his place. Prior was born in South Africa, moved to England at 11 – he says he lost his accent within a week – and he soon joined Sussex, making his debut in 2001.

THE FACTS Prior was the 17th man to score a century on Test debut for England: he was the fifth person to score a century on Test debut at Lord's, after Australia's Harry Graham, John Hampshire and Andrew Strauss of England, and India's Sourav Ganguly ... Prior equalled the ODI wicketkeeping record with six catches against South Africa at Nottingham in August 2008 ... He made 201 not out for Sussex v Loughborough UCCE at Hove in May 2004 ...

THE FIGURES to 21.9.09   www.cricinfo.com

Batting & Fielding	M	Inns	NO	Runs	HS	Avge	S/R	100	50	4s	6s	Ct	St
Tests	23	37	7	1326	131*	44.20	64.33	2	10	157	5	51	2
ODIs	48	46	6	950	87	23.75	74.16	0	2	105	5	50	4
Twenty20 Ints	6	5	0	116	32	23.20	128.88	0	0	10	5	4	2
First-class	154	243	25	8785	201*	40.29	67.40	20	50	–	–	354	24

Bowling	M	Balls	Runs	Wkts	BB	Avge	RpO	S/R	5i	10m
Tests	23	0	–	–	–	–	–	–	–	–
ODIs	48	0	–	–	–	–	–	–	–	–
Twenty20 Ints	6	0	–	–	–	–	–	–	–	–
First-class	154	0	–	–	–	–	–	–	–	–

SURESH **RAINA**

Full name **Suresh Kumar Raina**
Born **November 27, 1986, Ghaziabad, Uttar Pradesh**
Teams **Uttar Pradesh, Chennai Super Kings**
Style **Left-hand bat, occasional offspinner**
Test debut **No Tests yet**
ODI debut **India v Sri Lanka at Dambulla 2005**

THE PROFILE Suresh Raina puts people in mind of Yuvraj Singh, another powerful left-hander. A string of fine performances at junior level landed him a place in the national Under-19 side, and in April 2005 Raina strolled in to bat in the domestic one-day final spanked nine fours and a six in 48 from 33 balls as Uttar Pradesh tied with Tamil Nadu and shared the title, then left to catch the flight home for his school exams. The following season his 620 runs in six matches helped UP win the Ranji Trophy for the first time. His electric fielding added zing to India's one-day side, and it came as no surprise when, even before he'd managed an ODI fifty, he was fast-tracked into the Test squad against England in March 2006, although he didn't actually play a Test – and still hasn't. However, despite three fifties in five one-day knocks against England, the early promise turned out to be a false dawn – he couldn't manage another in 16 more attempts before being dropped early in 2007. It was more than a year before Raina won his place back. In June 2008 he hit two centuries in the Asia Cup, against Hong Kong and Bangladesh, then made 53 and 76 in Sri Lanka in August as India fought back to win the one-day series there. In New Zealand at the start of 2009 he slammed 61 not out from 43 balls in a Twenty20 international then 66 from 39 in an ODI, but was underwhelming with the bat in the World Twenty20 in England in June.

THE FACTS Raina scored 203 for Uttar Pradesh against Orissa at Cuttack in November 2007 ... His first ODI century, against Hong Kong at Karachi in June 2008, came from 66 balls and included five sixes ... Raina scored 72 in the first Under-19 Test and 63 in the third in England in 2002, when Irfan Pathan was a team-mate ...

THE FIGURES *to 21.9.09*   www.cricinfo.com

Batting & Fielding	M	Inns	NO	Runs	HS	Avge	S/R	100	50	4s	6s	Ct	St
Tests	0	0	–	–	–	–	–	–	–	–	–	–	–
ODIs	68	58	12	1611	116*	35.02	86.05	2	10	137	36	31	0
Twenty20 Ints	9	8	2	119	61*	19.83	111.21	0	1	8	6	3	0
First-class	46	79	3	3392	203	44.63	59.15	6	22	–	–	49	0

Bowling	M	Balls	Runs	Wkts	BB	Avge	RpO	S/R	5i	10m
Tests	0	0	–	–	–	–	–	–	–	–
ODIs	68	206	162	3	1–14	54.00	4.71	68.66	0	0
Twenty20 Ints	9	6	6	1	1–6	6.00	6.00	6.00	0	0
First-class	46	756	322	9	3–40	35.77	2.55	84.00	0	0

DENESH **RAMDIN**

Full name	**Denesh Ramdin**
Born	**March 13, 1985, Couva, Trinidad**
Teams	**Trinidad & Tobago**
Style	**Right-hand bat, wicketkeeper**
Test debut	**West Indies v Sri Lanka at Colombo 2005**
ODI debut	**West Indies v India at Dambulla 2005**

THE PROFILE Wicketkeeper-batsman Denesh Ramdin has long been viewed in the Caribbean as the solution to the void which has never really been satisfactorily filled since the retirement of Jeff Dujon in 1991. Originally a fast bowler who kept wicket when he had finished with the ball, at 13 Ramdin decided to concentrate on keeping, honing his reflexes and working on his agility. He led both the Trinidad and West Indies Under-19 sides before being selected, still only 19 and with just 13 first-class games behind him, as the first-choice keeper for the senior tour of Sri Lanka in 2005. He impressed everyone with his work behind and in front of the stumps, and continued to do so in Australia later in 2005, when his best moment was a plucky 71 – he shared a fine partnership of 182 in the second Test with his fellow Trinidadian Dwayne Bravo, just after they'd heard that T&T had qualified for the football World Cup. Carlton Baugh was preferred for some of the home one-dayers early in 2006, and it was something of a surprise when Ramdin returned for the Tests against India. But he justified his selection with some smooth keeping, and a gritty unbeaten 62 that took West Indies frustratingly close to victory in the series-deciding fourth Test in Jamaica. He started the 2007 series in England with a bright 60 at Lord's, but then struggled with the bat; his keeping was patchy, but he put that right, then ended his fallow period with the bat by cashing in on a Bridgetown featherbed to make a seven-hour 166 against England early in 2009.

THE FACTS Ramdin's 166 against England at Bridgetown in 2008-09 was the second-highest score by a West Indian wicketkeeper in a Test, after Clyde Walcott's 168 not out at Lord's in 1950 ... Ramdin played in the West Indies side that won the Under-15 World Challenge in 2000, beating Pakistan in the final at Lord's; four years later he captained West Indies in the Under-19 World Cup, when they lost the final at Dhaka – to Pakistan ...

THE FIGURES *to 21.9.09*   www.cricinfo.com

Batting & Fielding	M	Inns	NO	Runs	HS	Avge	S/R	100	50	4s	6s	Ct	St
Tests	36	62	7	1323	166	24.05	47.01	1	7	177	2	103	2
ODIs	67	51	14	740	74*	20.00	81.40	0	2	63	3	91	5
Twenty20 Ints	16	11	2	137	30	15.22	125.68	0	0	18	2	10	1
First-class	71	118	14	2807	166	26.99	–	5	13	–	–	188	19

Bowling	M	Balls	Runs	Wkts	BB	Avge	RpO	S/R	5i	10m
Tests	36	0	–	–	–	–	–	–	–	–
ODIs	67	0	–	–	–	–	–	–	–	–
Twenty20 Ints	16	0	–	–	–	–	–	–	–	–
First-class	71	0	–	–	–	–	–	–	–	–

RAVI **RAMPAUL**

WEST INDIES

Full name	**Ravindranath Rampaul**
Born	**October 15, 1984, Preysal, Trinidad**
Teams	**Trinidad & Tobago**
Style	**Left-hand bat, right-arm fast-medium bowler**
Test debut	**No Tests yet**
ODI debut	**West Indies v Zimbabwe at Bulawayo 2003-04**

THE PROFILE Ravi Rampaul is a tall, well-built fast bowler, but his career has been hamstrung by injuries and ill-luck. He made his Trinidad debut in 2002, and 18 wickets in six matches the following year – and some impressive performances for West Indies Under-19s – propelled him to the verge of full international selection. It was his aggressive approach that really caught the eye: in a one-dayer against Antigua & Barbuda he unleashed four successive bouncers at the opener, then finished him off with an unplayable yorker. Just 19, he made his ODI debut late in 2003: he was rarely collared, but hardly ran through sides either – in 14 matches in Africa and the Caribbean that season he took nine wickets, only once managing more than one. Nonetheless he was retained for the 2004 England tour, and played three more ODIs before he broke down and returned home ahead of the Tests. Shin splints sidelined him for more than a year, and he did not play another first-class match until 2006-07, taking 7 for 51 as T&T beat Barbados in the Carib Beer final. That won him another England tour, but restricted by a groin tear, he again missed the Tests, before helping to turn the one-day series around with 4 for 41 in the pivotal second match at Edgbaston. After a chastening time in South Africa early in 2008 he was back early the next year, taking four wickets at Kingston to square West Indies' one-day series against India, but still a Test cap proved elusive: he was named to play Bangladesh in July 2009, only for the whole squad to withdraw as a long-running contracts dispute came to a head.

THE FACTS Rampaul took 7 for 51 as Trinidad & Tobago beat Barbados in the final of the Carib Beer Challenge at Pointe-à-Pierre in February 2007 ... His highest score of 64 not out was for West Indies A v Sri Lanka A at Basseterre in December 2006 ... In the World Under-15 Challenge in 2000, Rampaul took 7 for 11 against Holland, and opened both the bowling and the batting in the final at Lord's, as West Indies beat Pakistan ... Rampaul played for Ireland in the Friends Provident Trophy in 2008 ...

THE FIGURES to 21.9.09   www.cricinfo.com

Batting & Fielding	M	Inns	NO	Runs	HS	Avge	S/R	100	50	4s	6s	Ct	St
Tests	0	0	–	–	–	–	–	–	–	–	–	–	–
ODIs	36	12	2	111	26*	11.10	74.49	0	0	9	4	4	0
Twenty20 Ints	5	1	1	0	0*	–	0.00	0	0	0	0	0	0
First-class	33	45	5	584	64*	14.60	–	0	2	–	–	11	0

Bowling	M	Balls	Runs	Wkts	BB	Avge	RpO	S/R	5i	10m
Tests	0	0	–	–	–	–	–	–	–	–
ODIs	36	1277	1053	30	4–37	35.10	4.94	42.56	0	0
Twenty20 Ints	5	120	177	5	2–35	35.40	8.85	24.00	0	0
First-class	33	4913	2889	109	7–51	26.50	3.52	45.07	6	1

RAQIBUL HASAN

Full name	**Mohammad Raqibul Hasan**
Born	**October 8, 1987, Jamalpur**
Teams	**Barisal**
Style	**Right-hand bat, legspinner**
Test debut	**Bangladesh v South Africa at Centurion 2008-09**
ODI debut	**Bangladesh v South Africa at Chittagong 2007-08**

THE PROFILE Another of Bangladesh's young achievers, Raqibul Hasan toured with Bangladesh A before he had played a first-class match, made a hundred on his first-class debut, and hit a triple-century – the first in Bangladesh domestic cricket – before he was 20 years old. It was clearly only a matter of time until he was given a chance in the full national team, and he duly made his ODI debut in March 2008, scoring 63 in his second match and adding 89 against India in the Kitply Cup and 52 against Sri Lanka in the Asia Cup. "Nirala" is a complete batsman, with a fine cover-drive, and although he started as more of an accumulator than a dasher, he showed signs in 2009 of being able to up the tempo to claim a regular spot in one-day international cricket. His best innings in the shorter format have been 63 against South Africa, in only his second ODI, and a patient 89 against India at Mirpur in June 2008. He looks a natural for Tests, though – that triple-century, an innings of 313 not out in a Barisal total of 712 for 7 (another domestic record) against Sylhet, occupied 11 hours. He made a slow start in the five-day game, though, until a well-played double of 44 and 65 in Grenada helped seal a 2-0 series victory over a depleted West Indian side in July 2009. In the second innings Bangladesh, chasing 215, were reeling at 67 for 4 before Raqibul and Shakib Al Hasan steadied the nerves with a stand of 106.

THE FACTS Raqibul Hasan scored 313 not out for Barisal v Sylhet at Fatullah in March 2007: he was 19 years 161 days old, the third-youngest triple-centurion in first-class history after Javed Miandad and Wasim Jaffer … He was selected for the Bangladesh A tour of Zimbabwe in 2004-05 before he had played first-class cricket: on his debut, against Zimbabwe A at Bulawayo, he scored 100 …

THE FIGURES to 21.9.09   www.cricinfo.com

Batting & Fielding	M	Inns	NO	Runs	HS	Avge	S/R	100	50	4s	6s	Ct	St
Tests	5	10	0	229	65	22.90	44.12	0	1	30	1	4	0
ODIs	31	30	3	799	89	29.59	63.21	0	6	67	3	8	0
Twenty20 Ints	4	4	0	33	16	8.25	67.34	0	0	1	0	1	0
First-class	30	54	2	1860	313*	35.76	–	2	10	–	–	21	0

Bowling	M	Balls	Runs	Wkts	BB	Avge	RpO	S/R	5i	10m
Tests	5	12	5	0	–	–	2.50	–	0	0
ODIs	31	0	–	–	–	–	–	–	–	–
Twenty20 Ints	4	0	–	–	–	–	–	–	–	–
First-class	30	300	207	4	1–4	51.75	4.14	75.00	0	0

ENGLAND

ADIL **RASHID**

Full name	**Adil Usman Rashid**
Born	**February 17, 1988, Bradford, Yorkshire**
Teams	**Yorkshire**
Style	**Right-hand bat, legspinner**
Test debut	**No Tests yet**
ODI debut	**England v Ireland at Belfast 2009**

THE PROFILE Yorkshire have rarely had much truck with legspinners, but a funny thing happened in 2006: they suddenly started playing two of them. The first was Mark Lawson, and he was joined towards the end of the season by 18-year-old Adil Rashid, a product of the young-spinner programme set up by Terry Jenner, Shane Warne's Australian mentor. Rashid, who bowls with a high action and has all the legspin variations, plus the priceless virtue of accuracy, bowled Yorkshire to victory over Warwickshire in his first match, then had purists licking their lips as he and Lawson shared all ten Middlesex wickets in an innings at Scarborough. The first home-grown player of Asian descent to appear regularly for Yorkshire, Rashid finished his first season with 25 wickets in six matches – plus 14 in three Under-19 Tests against India, traditionally good players of spin – then toured Bangladesh with England A. He consolidated in 2007, then had his best season so far in 2008, finishing with 65 wickets. Rashid is also a wristy middle-order batsman with four first-class centuries under his belt, the highest an unbeaten 157 against Lancashire in 2009. That was the year he played for England for the first time: after trundling around the Caribbean without playing, he kept things reasonably quiet during England's up-and-down World Twenty20 campaign, then made a promising start in ODIs. He did well with bat and ball against Australia at The Oval before perplexingly being left out for the next two matches. The only major fly in the ointment so far has been a stress fracture of the back, which forced him to remodel his action over the winter of 2006-07: he is now more side-on.

THE FACTS Rashid took 6 for 67 on his first-class debut, for Yorkshire v Warwickshire at Scarborough in July 2006 ... He scored 114, and then took 8 for 157, for England Under-19s v India at Taunton in August 2006 ... Rashid made 157 not out against Lancashire at Headingley in August 2009 (Yorkshire made 429 after being 144 for 6 when he came in) ... Rashid was the Cricket Writers' Club's Young Cricketer of the Year in 2007 ...

THE FIGURES to 21.9.09   www.cricinfo.com

Batting & Fielding	M	Inns	NO	Runs	HS	Avge	S/R	100	50	4s	6s	Ct	St
Tests	0	0	–	–	–	–	–	–	–	–	–	–	–
ODIs	4	4	1	60	31*	20.00	111.11	0	0	8	0	2	0
Twenty20 Ints	4	1	1	9	9*	–	52.94	0	0	0	0	0	0
First-class	53	73	13	2205	157*	36.75	51.12	4	13	288	5	23	0

Bowling	M	Balls	Runs	Wkts	BB	Avge	RpO	S/R	5i	10m
Tests	0	0	–	–	–	–	–	–	–	–
ODIs	4	186	164	3	1–16	54.66	5.29	62.00	0	0
Twenty20 Ints	4	78	95	3	1–11	31.66	7.30	26.00	0	0
First-class	53	9828	5809	171	7–107	33.97	3.54	57.47	10	0

AARON **REDMOND**

Full name	**Aaron James Redmond**
Born	**September 23, 1979, Auckland**
Teams	**Otago**
Style	**Right-hand bat, legspinner**
Test debut	**New Zealand v England at Lord's 2008**
ODI debut	**No ODIs yet**

THE PROFILE Aaron Redmond learned his cricket on the hard tracks of Western Australia after his father – the ultimate one-cap wonder Rodney, who scored 107 and 56 in his only Test, in 1972-73 – moved the family moved there when Aaron was a youngster. Back in New Zealand he started with Canterbury, primarily as a legspinner, before establishing himself as a top-order batsman with Otago. He was earmarked as a potential international early on, touring England with New Zealand A in 2000 (and making 92 against Sussex) after only seven first-class matches. But it took him a long time to reach the highest rung of the ladder: his first Test cap came at Lord's in May 2008 after four solid domestic seasons with the bat. But he struggled on the early-season English pitches, especially against the swing of James Anderson, and made only 54 runs in six innings. A 79 followed in Bangladesh, then an attacking 83 at Adelaide in what, oddly, was his last Test to date. With Tim McIntosh and Martin Guptill making their marks at the top of the order, Redmond seemed to have been forgotten – until a clutch of injuries led to an emergency call-up from club cricket in Lancashire to reinforce the side for the World Twenty20 in June 2009. Redmond borrowed a shirt from his Otago opening partner Brendon McCullum, and proceeded to bat like him, belting 13 fours in 63 from 30 balls against Ireland at Trent Bridge. He missed the tour of Sri Lanka that followed, but had done enough to ensure his name remained in the selectors' minds.

THE FACTS Redmond made 146 for the touring New Zealanders against England Lions at Southampton in May 2008 ... He rarely bowls his legspin now, but did take 4 for 30 for New Zealand A v India A at Chennai in October 2008 ... Redmond's father, Rodney, played one Test for New Zealand in 1972-73, scoring 107 and 56, but never played again: he had trouble adjusting from glasses to contact lenses and eventually retired ...

THE FIGURES to 21.9.09   www.cricinfo.com

Batting & Fielding	M	Inns	NO	Runs	HS	Avge	S/R	100	50	4s	6s	Ct	St
Tests	7	14	1	299	83	23.00	38.08	0	2	42	2	5	0
ODIs	0	0	–	–	–	–	–	–	–	–	–	–	–
Twenty20 Ints	3	3	0	101	63	33.66	177.19	0	1	18	1	0	0
First-class	84	145	10	4380	146	32.44	–	7	27	–	–	65	0

Bowling	M	Balls	Runs	Wkts	BB	Avge	RpO	S/R	5i	10m
Tests	7	75	62	3	2–27	20.66	4.96	25.00	0	0
ODIs	0	0	–	–	–	–	–	–	–	–
Twenty20 Ints	3	0	–	–	–	–	–	–	–	–
First-class	84	7862	4283	98	4–30	43.70	3.26	80.22	0	0

FLOYD **REIFER**

Full name	**Floyd Lamonte Reifer**
Born	**July 23, 1972, Parish Land, Christ Church, Barbados**
Teams	**Combined Campuses & Colleges**
Style	**Right-hand bat, occasional right-arm medium-pacer**
Test debut	**West Indies v Sri Lanka at St John's 1997**
ODI debut	**West Indies v Sri Lanka at Port-of-Spain 1997**

THE PROFILE A tall left-hander, Floyd Reifer, a member of a famous cricketing family – three of his uncles played for Barbados – first made the West Indian side in mid-1997, after making 940 runs in the home season, including a maiden double-century. He played twice against Sri Lanka at home then twice in South Africa in 1998-99, failing to reach 30 and collecting three ducks, looking especially insecure against South Africa's fast bowlers. That seemed to be that: Reifer returned to domestic cricket, and also turned out for Scotland during a spell as a professional there. He continued to score consistently at home, latterly as captain of the new Combined Campuses & Colleges team which was added to the West Indian first-class competition in 2007-08. Around that time, Reifer told a reporter: "I notice you always write that I'm a former West Indies player. I have not retired. I believe I am batting the best I have for a long time and I can make it back to the top again." And he did, in the most unexpected of circumstances, in July 2009, when the original squad to face Bangladesh decided to pull out a day before the first Test started as a divisive contracts dispute rumbled on. Reifer was named as captain of a replacement squad cobbled together in a matter of hours, and resumed his Test career after more than ten years. There was no fairytale ending, though: he again struggled with the bat as Bangladesh won both Tests and all three ODIs before Reifer and his inexperienced side salvaged a scrap of pride with a Twenty20 victory.

THE FACTS West Indies played 109 Tests between Reifer's fourth cap, in 1998-99, and his fifth in 2009: only Martin Bicknell, who missed 114 England Tests between 1993 and 2003, has had a longer gap between appearances ... Reifer scored 200 for Barbados v Windward Islands in May 1997, putting on 275 with Philo Wallace ... Reifer hit six sixes in an over in a Twenty20 club game in Barbados in August 2008, exactly 40 years to the day since another Barbadian, Garry Sobers, became the first to achieve the feat in a first-class match ...

THE FIGURES to 21.9.09   www.cricinfo.com

Batting & Fielding	M	Inns	NO	Runs	HS	Avge	S/R	100	50	4s	6s	Ct	St
Tests	6	12	0	111	29	9.25	32.17	0	0	12	0	6	0
ODIs	5	5	0	81	40	16.20	55.86	0	0	7	2	3	0
Twenty20 Ints	1	1	0	22	22	22.00	110.00	0	0	2	1	1	0
First-class	125	214	19	6737	200	34.54	–	13	37	–	–	130	0

Bowling	M	Balls	Runs	Wkts	BB	Avge	RpO	S/R	5i	10m
Tests	6	0	–	–	–	–	–	–	–	–
ODIs	5	0	–	–	–	–	–	–	–	–
Twenty20 Ints	1	0	–	–	–	–	–	–	–	–
First-class	125	252	156	1	1–19	156.00	3.71	252.00	0	0

KEMAR **ROACH**

Full name **Kemar Andre Jamal Roach**
Born **June 30, 1988, St Lucy, Barbados**
Teams **Barbados**
Style **Right-hand bat, right-arm fast-medium bowler**
Test debut **West Indies v Bangladesh at Kingstown 2009**
ODI debut **West Indies v Bermuda at King City 2008**

THE PROFILE A right-arm fast bowler, Kemar Roach had played only four first-class matches, all of them in 2008, when he was called into the squad for the third Test against Australia at Bridgetown in June. He was only 19, and slightly fortunate still to be around: he had agreed to play in the Birmingham League, but was deemed ineligible as he had played one fewer than the five first-class games required of overseas players by the league's rules. Roach didn't play – he was mature enough to realise that he was only there for the experience – but he was included for the Twenty20 international shortly afterwards at the Kensington Oval, and took two of the three wickets to fall, dismissing the Australian openers Shaun Marsh and Luke Ronchi after starting with a nervous beamer. He made his ODI debut in the tri-series in Canada later in 2008. The following year he was drafted in when the senior players withdrew from the series against Bangladesh, and was one of West Indies' few successes, taking 13 wickets in the two Tests. Floyd Reifer, his captain, observed: "He does a lot, especially with the old ball, getting it to move in and out." Roach hit trouble during the ODIs, when he let loose two beamers and was taken off and fined, but overall he displayed enough pace to show that he would still be a factor when the seniors returned. Roach has a nice flowing action: he suffered a bit with no-balls for a while, but claims to have put that behind him after lots of hard work.

THE FACTS Roach took 6 for 48 in the second Test against Bangladesh at St George's in July 2009, and followed that with 5 for 44 in the first ODI at Roseau (he had Tamim Iqbal caught behind off the first ball in international cricket in Dominica) ... Roach took a hat-trick against Sri Lanka Under-19s in a warm-up match before the 2006 Youth World Cup in Colombo ...

THE FIGURES *to 21.9.09*   www.cricinfo.com

Batting & Fielding	M	Inns	NO	Runs	HS	Avge	S/R	100	50	4s	6s	Ct	St
Tests	2	4	2	14	6	7.00	21.21	0	0	2	0	2	0
ODIs	5	2	0	10	10	5.00	71.42	0	0	1	0	1	0
Twenty20 Ints	2	0	–	–	–	–	–	–	–	–	–	0	0
First-class	17	21	4	215	52*	12.64	–	0	1	–	–	11	0

Bowling	M	Balls	Runs	Wkts	BB	Avge	RpO	S/R	5i	10m
Tests	2	519	229	13	6–48	17.61	2.64	39.92	1	0
ODIs	5	274	240	13	5–44	18.46	5.25	21.07	1	0
Twenty20 Ints	2	42	44	2	2–29	22.00	6.28	21.00	0	0
First-class	17	2317	1452	48	6–48	30.25	3.76	48.27	2	0

RUBEL HOSSAIN

BANGLADESH

Full name	**Mohammad Rubel Hossain**
Born	**January 1, 1990, Bagerhat**
Teams	**Chittagong**
Style	**Right-hand bat, right-arm fast-medium bowler**
Test debut	**Bangladesh v West Indies at Kingstown 2009**
ODI debut	**Bangladesh v Sri Lanka at Mirpur 2008-09**

THE PROFILE A right-arm fast bowler with a slingy action not unlike Lasith Malinga's, Rubel Hossain began by playing tape-ball cricket in his home town of Bagerhat (in Khulna), before he was discovered during a national search for fast bowlers after getting the highest reading on the speed-gun. He made his first-class debut in October 2007 against Khulna, whose side included his hero Mashrafe Mortaza – not that that had stopped him bouncing Mortaza in their previous encounters. He remains raw – his debut Test was only his 11th first-class match – but is pacier than most of his contemporaries. Rubel played in the Under-19 World Cup in Malaysia in February 2008, and later that year was called into the full national squad after several senior players joined the unauthorised Indian Cricket League. In his first ODI, a rain-affected game against Sri Lanka at Mirpur in January 2009, he helped set up a rare Bangladesh victory with 4 for 33. He toured the Caribbean later in the year, playing in both Tests as Bangladesh pulled off a clean sweep against a depleted West Indian side. Rubel again made a decent start, taking three first-innings wickets in St Vincent – his three victims (Ryan Austin, Omar Phillips and Nikita Miller) were, like himself, making their Test debut. He didn't strike again in the Tests, and proved expensive in the subsequent one-dayers: he was left out of the side that played five ODIs in Zimbabwe shortly afterwards. If he can improve his accuracy he could make a name for himself as Bangladesh's fastest bowler. Rubel's love of speed also runs to a fascination with motor-bikes.

THE FACTS Rubel Hossain took 5 for 60 for Chittagong at Sylhet in December 2008 ... He took 4 for 33 on his ODI debut as Bangladesh beat Sri Lanka at Mirpur in January 2009 ... Rubel took 4 for 19 against the Netherlands and 5 for 16 against Scotland on successive days in warm-up games for the World Twenty20 in England in May 2009 ...

THE FIGURES *to 21.9.09*   www.cricinfo.com

Batting & Fielding	M	Inns	NO	Runs	HS	Avge	S/R	100	50	4s	6s	Ct	St
Tests	2	3	2	5	3*	5.00	10.41	0	0	0	0	0	0
ODIs	7	3	2	1	1*	1.00	11.11	0	0	0	0	2	0
Twenty20 Ints	3	1	1	8	8*	–	160.00	0	0	1	0	1	0
First-class	12	17	5	35	14*	2.91	–	0	0	–	–	3	0

Bowling	M	Balls	Runs	Wkts	BB	Avge	RpO	S/R	5i	10m
Tests	2	240	182	3	3–76	60.66	4.55	80.00	0	0
ODIs	7	255	217	9	4–33	24.11	5.10	28.33	0	0
Twenty20 Ints	3	62	93	2	1–13	46.50	9.00	31.00	0	0
First-class	12	1671	1158	23	5–60	50.34	4.15	72.65	1	0

JESSE **RYDER**

Full name	**Jesse Daniel Ryder**
Born	**August 6, 1984, Masterton, Wellington**
Teams	**Wellington, Bangalore Royal Challengers**
Style	**Left-hand bat, right-arm medium-pacer**
Test debut	**New Zealand v Bangladesh at Chittagong 2008-09**
ODI debut	**New Zealand v England at Wellington 2007-08**

THE PROFILE Jesse Ryder had a troubled childhood, and latterly battled with his weight and demons of his own: just after establishing himself in the one-day side after a series of promising performances early in 2008, he injured tendons in his hand when he smashed a window in a bar at 5.30 in the morning shortly after celebrating a tight series victory over England. He missed the Tests, and the England tour which followed. But Ryder, who can also bowl useful seamers at a gentle pace, is seriously talented: New Zealand Cricket had already forgiven him for refusing to play for their A team (he briefly threatened to try to qualify for England), and gave him yet another chance despite continued concerns about his drinking habits. Ryder gives the ball a good thump: he biffed 79 not out in the second game of that series against England at Hamilton, going run for run with Brendon McCullum in a rollicking opening stand of 165 which won the game with half the overs unused. He finally made his Test debut in Bangladesh in November 2008, and was an instant success, with 91 in his second match then three successive fifties against West Indies at home. Against India he hit his maiden century in the first Test at Hamilton, then cracked a superb 201 in the second at Napier, setting up a massive total of 619 after entering at 23 for 3. A groin strain ruined his World Twenty20 campaign in June 2009, but he was back for the Sri Lankan tour that followed, where he again scored consistently in the Tests and one-dayers.

THE FACTS Ryder scored 236 for Wellington v Central Districts at Palmerston North in March 2005 ... When he scored 201 against India at Napier in March 2009 it was the second time "J. Ryder" had made 201 in a Test – Jack of Australia made 201 not out v England at Adelaide in 1924-25 ... Ryder played two one-day games for Ireland in 2007 before being dumped after missing the plane to the next match ...

THE FIGURES to 21.9.09   www.cricinfo.com

Batting & Fielding	M	Inns	NO	Runs	HS	Avge	S/R	100	50	4s	6s	Ct	St
Tests	11	20	2	898	201	49.88	55.50	2	4	103	3	8	0
ODIs	19	17	1	555	105	34.68	90.53	1	2	60	19	5	0
Twenty20 Ints	9	9	0	231	62	25.66	132.75	0	2	25	10	5	0
First-class	52	84	6	3411	236	43.73	–	7	17	–	–	43	0

Bowling	M	Balls	Runs	Wkts	BB	Avge	RpO	S/R	5i	10m
Tests	11	378	212	4	2–7	53.00	3.36	94.50	0	0
ODIs	19	244	267	8	3–29	33.37	6.56	30.50	0	0
Twenty20 Ints	9	60	68	2	1–2	34.00	6.80	30.00	0	0
First-class	52	2743	1283	45	4–23	28.51	2.80	60.95	0	0

PAKISTAN

SAEED AJMAL

Full name	**Saeed Ajmal**
Born	**October 14, 1977, Faisalabad, Punjab**
Teams	**Faisalabad, Khan Research Laboratories**
Style	**Right-hand bat, offspinner**
Test debut	**Pakistan v Sri Lanka at Galle 2009**
ODI debut	**Pakistan v India at Karachi 2008**

THE PROFILE Offspinner Saeed Ajmal had been a first-class player for more than ten years when the selectors came calling. Given Pakistan's usual propensity for plucking teenagers from obscurity, he must have thought, at 30, that his chance had gone. However, another impressive domestic season – 38 wickets at 28.63 in 2007-08, plus some decent one-day performances, which followed 62 wickets at 24.29 the previous term – earned him a place at the Asia Cup in Pakistan in mid-2008. He started reasonably well, taking 1 for 47 against India and strangling Bangladesh with two late strikes in his second match. Ajmal is very much a modern offspinner, tossing in a handy *doosra* from a high action. His stock ball remains the offie, although it doesn't turn much, but he has a nice rhythmic delivery, and can get a good loop on the ball. He received a jolting setback when the umpires reported his action as suspect during the one-day series against Australia in Abu Dhabi early in 2009 – he was also fined after he complained about being complained about – but tests found any elbow flexion was within the permitted 15-degree limit, and he was cleared to resume bowling. "I was carrying a 50-kilo bag on my head," said Ajmal of the verdict, "but this decision has allowed me to throw that bag off." He showed his delight by bowling with guile and maturity as Pakistan swept to the World Twenty20 title in England in June, taking 12 wickets (only Umar Gul, with 13, took more) and often bottling up the middle overs. He was retained for the Test tour of Sri Lanka that followed, making his mark with 14 wickets in three matches there.

THE FACTS Saeed Ajmal took 7 for 63 for Khan Research Laboratories v Zarai Taraqiati Bank in Rawalpindi in December 2008 ... He took 7 for 220 in 63 overs in only his second first-class match, for Faisalabad v Karachi Whites in Karachi in November 1996 ... Ajmal had figures of 4.5-3-4-5 for Faisalabad v Karachi Blues at Karachi in January 1998 ... In 2006-07, his best season, he took 62 wickets at 24.29 in Pakistan ...

THE FIGURES to 21.9.09   www.cricinfo.com

Batting & Fielding	M	Inns	NO	Runs	HS	Avge	S/R	100	50	4s	6s	Ct	St
Tests	3	6	3	13	8	4.33	43.33	0	0	1	0	0	0
ODIs	15	7	4	22	16	7.33	52.38	0	0	2	0	2	0
Twenty20 Ints	9	1	1	0	0*	–	–	0	0	0	0	2	0
First-class	83	109	36	847	53	11.60	–	0	2	–	–	27	0

Bowling	M	Balls	Runs	Wkts	BB	Avge	RpO	S/R	5i	10m
Tests	3	880	421	14	4–87	30.07	2.87	62.85	0	0
ODIs	15	788	516	13	2–19	39.69	3.92	60.61	0	0
Twenty20 Ints	9	215	200	16	4–19	12.50	5.58	13.43	0	0
First-class	83	15980	7379	269	7–63	27.43	2.77	59.40	17	1

SALMAN BUTT

Full name	**Salman Butt**
Born	**October 7, 1984, Lahore, Punjab**
Teams	**Lahore, National Bank**
Style	**Left-hand bat, occasional offspinner**
Test debut	**Pakistan v Bangladesh at Multan 2003-04**
ODI debut	**Pakistan v West Indies at Southampton 2004**

THE PROFILE Because he's left-handed, with supple wrists, it's easy to compare Salman Butt with Saeed Anwar. His drives and cuts through extra cover and backward point are flicked or scooped: it is a high-scoring region for him, as it was for Anwar. He doesn't mind pulling, and off his toes he's efficient, rather than whippy as Anwar was. But in attitude and temperament – a confident air and a touch of spikiness – he's more like Anwar's long-time opening partner, Aamer Sohail. Butt's breakthrough at the highest level came late in 2004. After a maiden one-day century at Eden Gardens, he made 70 at Melbourne and 108 in the New Year Test at Sydney. Then came the fall: he failed to consolidate during 2005, despite another one-day hundred against India, and was dropped as doubts crept in about his defence and his dash. He responded by unveiling startling restraint against England late in the year, grinding out a hundred and two fifties in the Tests, followed by another ton at India's expense. He was dropped again after an uninspiring England tour, and did not feature in 2006-07, which at least meant he was spared the misery of the World Cup. Back in favour (briefly as vice-captain) he made 74 in a one-dayer against Sri Lanka in Abu Dhabi in May 2007. He continued his good form with three one-day hundreds in the first six months of 2008, but a slump the following year – no fifties in three Tests, and an indifferent run in ODIs after an early century against Sri Lanka – found him out of the side again by July.

THE FACTS Salman Butt's first four ODI hundreds – and his seventh – all came against India: he averages 51.00 against them, but only 13.33 against West Indies (and 1.00 v Scotland) ... His highest score is 290, for Punjab v Federal Areas at Lahore in February 2008 ... Butt captained Pakistan in the Under-19 World Cup in New Zealand early in 2002 ...

THE FIGURES to 21.9.09   www.cricinfo.com

Batting & Fielding	M	Inns	NO	Runs	HS	Avge	S/R	100	50	4s	6s	Ct	St
Tests	22	40	0	1146	122	28.65	47.19	2	6	168	1	9	0
ODIs	68	68	4	2459	136	38.42	76.34	8	11	307	7	19	0
Twenty20 Ints	16	15	1	328	74	23.42	96.75	0	1	33	6	3	0
First-class	74	129	6	5092	290	41.39	–	14	20	–	–	28	0

Bowling	M	Balls	Runs	Wkts	BB	Avge	RpO	S/R	5i	10m
Tests	22	137	106	1	1–36	106.00	4.64	137.00	0	0
ODIs	68	69	90	0	–	–	7.82	–	0	0
Twenty20 Ints	16	0	–	–	–	–	–	–	–	–
First-class	74	926	646	11	4–82	58.72	4.18	84.18	0	0

THILAN **SAMARAWEERA**

Full name	**Thilan Thusara Samaraweera**
Born	**September 22, 1976, Colombo**
Teams	**Sinhalese Sports Club, Kandurata**
Style	**Right-hand bat, offspinner**
Test debut	**Sri Lanka v India at Colombo 2001-02**
ODI debut	**Sri Lanka v India at Sharjah 1998-99**

THE PROFILE   Early in 2009, cricket seemed insignificant for Thilan Samaraweera as he lay in hospital, the most badly injured of the Sri Lankan players subjected to terrorist attack in Pakistan. A bullet was lodged in his left thigh, and a distinguished career hung in the balance – all the more galling as he was in the form of his life, having scored 231 in the first Test at Karachi and 214 in the ongoing one at Lahore. Mercifully, he was soon back to his best, scoring 159 and 143 in successive Tests against New Zealand at home in August before settling a few scores with his first one-day international century, after long being branded too slow for the limited-overs side. In all he made 1083 runs in his first eight Tests in 2009 at an average of 83: not bad for a man who started out as an offspinner, seemingly destined to play the odd Test in the shadow of Muttiah Muralitharan. Realising he was on a hiding to nothing there, Samaraweera reinvented himself as a specialist batsman, starting with a century on Test debut against India in August 2001, helping Sri Lanka to a 2-1 series win. The departure of Aravinda de Silva and Hashan Tillekeratne allowed him to secure a middle-order place, where his patient approach makes him a valuable foil for his more flamboyant colleagues. An adhesive and well-organised player, Samaraweera has a particular liking for his home ground, the Sinhalese Sports Club, where he scored three centuries in his first six Tests. His steady offspin is rarely used now, although he has a reputation as a partnership-breaker and clearly has the talent to become a useful support bowler.

THE FACTS   Samaraweera was the third Sri Lankan, after Brendon Kuruppu and Romesh Kaluwitharana, to score a century on Test debut, against India in August 2001 ... Five of his Test centuries have come at the Sinhalese Sports Club, his home ground in Colombo, where he averages 76.86 ... He averages 75.00 in Tests against New Zealand, but 24.66 v South Africa ... Samaraweera's brother Dulip played seven Tests for Sri Lanka in the early 1990s ...

THE FIGURES *to 21.9.09*   www.cricinfo.com

Batting & Fielding	M	Inns	NO	Runs	HS	Avge	S/R	100	50	4s	6s	Ct	St
Tests	54	85	12	3787	231	51.87	47.49	11	19	453	5	35	0
ODIs	22	18	2	353	104	22.06	58.93	1	0	28	0	5	0
Twenty20 Ints	0	0	–	–	–	–	–	–	–	–	–	–	–
First-class	207	285	51	11233	231	48.00	–	29	56	–	–	170	0

Bowling	M	Balls	Runs	Wkts	BB	Avge	RpO	S/R	5i	10m
Tests	54	1291	679	14	4–49	48.50	3.15	92.21	0	0
ODIs	22	672	509	10	3–34	50.90	4.54	67.20	0	0
Twenty20 Ints	0	0	–	–	–	–	–	–	–	–
First-class	207	17458	8132	348	6–55	23.36	2.79	50.16	15	2

DARREN **SAMMY**

Full name	**Darren Julius Garvey Sammy**
Born	**December 20, 1983, Micoud, St Lucia**
Teams	**Windward Islands**
Style	**Right-hand bat, right-arm medium-pacer**
Test debut	**West Indies v England at Manchester 2007**
ODI debut	**West Indies v New Zealand at Southampton 2004**

THE PROFILE Darren Julius Garvey Sammy has names invoking images of great leadership. He was the first Test cricketer to emerge from St Lucia, an island rediscovering its cricket culture as the new Beausejour Stadium has captured imaginations, and is also believed to be the only Seventh Day Adventist to have played a Test. Sammy, who spent some time at Lord's with the MCC cricket staff, is a handy batsman and a tall, nagging medium-pacer. He joined the regional one-day squad in 2004, and was a late call-up to the Champions Trophy squad in England that September after Jermaine Lawson pulled out with a stress fracture of the back. In July 2006 Sammy captained St Lucia in the inaugural Stanford 20/20 tournament, and a decent first-class season – 269 runs at 44 in five matches, plus 16 wickets at less than 20 – earned him a recall for the 2007 England tour. He was drafted into the side for the third Test at Old Trafford, and celebrated with seven wickets in the second innings – three of them in one over. His pace is unthreatening, but he brings the ball down from quite a height and wobbles it around. He was overlooked for a while in Tests, perceived to be short of the requisite pace, but when the senior players withdrew from the series against Bangladesh in mid-2009 as a divisive contracts dispute rumbled on Sammy imposed himself with five-fors in both Tests. A virtuoso performance in the second match at St George's nearly brought victory as Bangladesh chased 215: he took five of the six wickets to fall and caught the other one.

THE FACTS Sammy took 7 for 66 in his first Test, against England at Old Trafford in 2007: only Alf Valentine, with 8 for 104 against England at Old Trafford in 1950, has returned better figures on Test debut for West Indies ... Sammy made 121 for Windward Islands v Barbados at Bridgetown in March 2009 ... No play was possible in his first ODI, against New Zealand at Southampton in July 2004, but because the toss took place it counts as an appearance ...

THE FIGURES to 21.9.09   www.cricinfo.com

Batting & Fielding	M	Inns	NO	Runs	HS	Avge	S/R	100	50	4s	6s	Ct	St
Tests	7	13	0	237	48	18.23	50.96	0	0	30	0	8	0
ODIs	26	19	5	283	51	20.21	93.09	0	1	20	6	13	0
Twenty20 Ints	9	5	2	29	14*	9.66	93.54	0	0	1	2	2	0
First-class	58	97	7	2285	121	25.38	–	1	16	–	–	75	0

Bowling	M	Balls	Runs	Wkts	BB	Avge	RpO	S/R	5i	10m
Tests	7	1324	649	25	7–66	25.96	2.94	52.96	3	0
ODIs	26	1028	801	15	2–2	53.40	4.67	68.53	0	0
Twenty20 Ints	9	180	184	10	3–21	18.40	6.13	18.00	0	0
First-class	58	8041	3611	140	7–66	25.79	2.69	57.43	9	0

KUMAR **SANGAKKARA**

Full name	**Kumar Chokshanada Sangakkara**
Born	**October 27, 1977, Matale**
Teams	**Nondescripts, Kandurata, Kings XI Punjab**
Style	**Left-hand bat, wicketkeeper**
Test debut	**Sri Lanka v South Africa at Galle 2000**
ODI debut	**Sri Lanka v Pakistan at Galle 2000**

THE PROFILE Within months of making the side at 22, Kumar Sangakkara had become one of Sri Lanka's most influential players: a talented left-hand strokemaker, a slick wicketkeeper, and a sharp-eyed strategist with an even sharper tongue. His success was unexpected, for his domestic performances had been relatively modest, but the selectors were immediately justified when he starred in his first one-day tournament, in July 2000. From the start his effortless batting oozed class: he possesses the grace of David Gower, but the attitude of an Aussie. At the outset he was happier on the back foot, but a fierce work ethic and a deep interest in the theory of batsmanship helped him, and he is now as comfortable driving through the covers as cutting behind point. He was briefly relieved of keeping duties after the 2003 World Cup: he made more runs, but soon got the gloves back. The extra burden had no obvious effect on his batting: he made 185 against Pakistan in March 2006, and scored consistently in England too. But there was a change of thinking after that, and Prasanna Jayawardene was given the gloves in Tests. Sangakkara responded with seven centuries, among them three doubles, in his next nine Tests, including 287 as he and Mahela Jayawardene put on a world-record 624 against South Africa, successive double-centuries against Bangladesh, and a magnificent 192 against Australia at Hobart in November 2007. An astute thinker, he took over as captain early in 2009, and led the side to the final of the World Twenty20 in England. His batting seemed unaffected, as he peeled off Test centuries against Pakistan and New Zealand later in the year.

THE FACTS Sangakkara scored 287, and put on 624 (the highest stand in first-class cricket) with Mahela Jayawardene against South Africa in Colombo in July 2006 ... He also made 270, adding 438 with Marvan Atapattu, v Zimbabwe at Bulawayo in May 2004 ... Sangakkara averages 76.20 in Tests when he is not the designated wicketkeeper, but 40.48 when lumbered with the gloves ... Against Bangladesh in 2007 he became only the fourth man to score back-to-back double-centuries in Tests ... His record includes three ODIs for the World XI and four for the Asia XI ...

THE FIGURES to 21.9.09   www.cricinfo.com

Batting & Fielding	M	Inns	NO	Runs	HS	Avge	S/R	100	50	4s	6s	Ct	St
Tests	85	142	10	7308	287	55.36	55.94	20	32	946	21	156	20
ODIs	254	237	26	7594	138*	35.99	73.98	10	48	750	30	242	64
Twenty20 Ints	18	17	2	435	69	29.00	113.57	0	3	43	4	9	7
First-class	170	271	20	11692	287	46.58	–	38	56	–	–	317	33

Bowling	M	Balls	Runs	Wkts	BB	Avge	RpO	S/R	5i	10m
Tests	85	66	38	0	–	–	3.45	–	0	0
ODIs	254	–	–	–	–	–	–	–	–	–
Twenty20 Ints	18	0	–	–	–	–	–	–	–	–
First-class	170	192	108	1	1–13	108.00	3.37	192.00	0	0

RAMNARESH **SARWAN**

Full name	**Ramnaresh Ronnie Sarwan**
Born	**June 23, 1980, Wakenaam Island, Essequibo, Guyana**
Teams	**Guyana**
Style	**Right-hand bat, legspinner**
Test debut	**West Indies v Pakistan at Bridgetown 1999-2000**
ODI debut	**West Indies v England at Nottingham 2000**

THE PROFILE A light-footed right-hander, Ramnaresh Sarwan was brought up in the South American rainforest around the Essequibo River. After his first Test innings – 84 against Pakistan – the former England captain Ted Dexter was moved to predict a Test average of 50. And on his first tour, to England in 2000, Sarwan lived up to the hype by topping the averages: his footwork was strikingly confident and precise, and it was a surprise when a horror run of three runs in five innings followed in Australia. He soon put that behind him, although his maiden Test century still took 28 matches. He has scored consistently since: 392 runs in four Tests against South Africa in 2003-04 then, after a lean run at home against England, an unbeaten 261 against Bangladesh in June 2004. Then came another England tour: he began and ended it on low notes, but was prolific in between. He also played a big part as West Indies reached the final of the one-day series then won the Champions Trophy, and carried on his good form in Australia. After Brian Lara's retirement, "Reggie" Sarwan took on the captaincy for the 2007 England tour – but that ended in tears with an injured shoulder during the second Test, which seems to have permanently affected his throwing. Then a groin strain restricted him, as Chris Gayle took over as captain, but Sarwan was in peerless form in the home series against England in 2009, collecting 626 runs at 104.33, with three centuries – one of them a monumental 291 on a Bridgetown featherbed – plus a 94. Another silky hundred followed at Chester-le-Street in the return series.

THE FACTS Sarwan scored 291 at Bridgetown in 2008-09: only Brian Lara (twice) and Lawrence Rowe (302) have made higher Test scores for West Indies against England (Viv Richards also made 291, at The Oval in 1976) ... Sarwan made 107, 94 and 106 in his previous three Test innings against England in the series ... In ODIs Sarwan averages 65.00 v India – but only 22.40 v Sri Lanka ... Sarwan made 100 and 111 for the West Indies Board President's XI against the touring Zimbabweans at Pointe-à-Pierre in March 2000 ...

THE FIGURES *to 21.9.09*   www.cricinfo.com

Batting & Fielding	M	Inns	NO	Runs	HS	Avge	S/R	100	50	4s	6s	Ct	St
Tests	81	142	8	5671	291	42.32	46.84	15	31	727	14	47	0
ODIs	152	142	28	4907	115*	43.04	77.08	3	33	408	50	39	0
Twenty20 Ints	11	10	3	201	59	28.71	118.93	0	2	12	6	4	0
First-class	183	307	22	11396	291	39.98	–	30	60	–	–	131	0

Bowling	M	Balls	Runs	Wkts	BB	Avge	RpO	S/R	5i	10m
Tests	81	2022	1163	23	4–37	50.56	3.45	87.91	0	0
ODIs	152	581	586	16	3–31	36.62	6.05	36.31	0	0
Twenty20 Ints	11	12	10	2	2–10	5.00	5.00	6.00	0	0
First-class	183	4175	2208	54	6–62	40.88	3.17	77.31	1	0

VIRENDER **SEHWAG**

INDIA

Full name	**Virender Sehwag**
Born	**October 20, 1978, Delhi**
Teams	**Delhi, Delhi Daredevils**
Style	**Right-hand bat, offspinner**
Test debut	**India v South Africa at Bloemfontein 2001-02**
ODI debut	**India v Pakistan at Mohali 1998-99**

THE PROFILE   Soon after his Test-debut century late in 2001 Virender Sehwag was being compared to Tendulkar. It is half-true: Sehwag is also short and square, and plays the straight drive, back-foot punch and whip off the hips identically – but he leaves even Sachin standing when it comes to audacity. He also bowls effective, loopy offspin. Asked to open in England in 2002, Sehwag proved an instant hit, and many pivotal innings followed, including India's first triple-century (brought up, characteristically, with a six), in Pakistan early in 2004. Surprisingly, he struggled in ODIs after an electric start, enduring a run of 60 games from January 2004 in which he averaged below 30. His fitness levels also dropped, but he continued to sparkle in Tests, making 254 – in an opening stand of 410 with Rahul Dravid – at Lahore in January 2006. Then in St Lucia he came excruciatingly close (99 not out) to a century before lunch on the first day, a feat no Indian has yet managed. Sehwag was dropped after the 2007 World Cup, but practised hard, lost a stone, and in March 2008 bounced back with another triple-century, against South Africa. Later in the year he carried his bat for 201 at Galle, and added 66 and 92 in a series-clinching victory over Australia at Nagpur in November. Overall he scored 1462 runs in the calendar year, at a strike-rate (85.84 per 100 balls) unprecedented for an opener. His mould-breaking efforts earned him recognition as *Wisden's* Leading Cricketer in the World for 2008. The following year, though, was disrupted when he injured his shoulder in the IPL and missed the World Twenty20 in England.

THE FACTS   Sehwag's 319 v South Africa at Chennai in March 2008 is India's highest Test score: he reached 300 in 278 balls, the fastest-known Test triple-century (he is third on the list too) ... No other Indian has made a Test triple-century, while Sehwag has two ... He made 105 on his Test debut, v South Africa in November 2001 ... Sehwag carried his bat (201 out of 329, the lowest Test total to include a double-century) v Sri Lanka at Galle in mid–2008 ... His record includes a Test and three ODIs for the World XI, and seven ODIs for the Asia XI ...

THE FIGURES *to 21.9.09*   www.cricinfo.com

Batting & Fielding	M	Inns	NO	Runs	HS	Avge	S/R	100	50	4s	6s	Ct	St
Tests	69	119	4	5757	319	50.06	78.72	15	18	817	66	55	0
ODIs	205	200	8	6592	130	34.33	101.85	11	35	902	107	79	0
Twenty20 Ints	12	11	0	223	68	20.27	144.80	0	1	24	10	1	0
First-class	131	218	8	10234	319	48.73	–	29	36	–	–	114	0

Bowling	M	Balls	Runs	Wkts	BB	Avge	RpO	S/R	5i	10m
Tests	69	2455	1265	29	5–104	43.62	3.09	84.65	1	0
ODIs	205	4015	3531	87	3–25	40.58	5.27	46.14	0	0
Twenty20 Ints	12	6	20	0	–	–	20.00	–	0	0
First-class	131	7086	3698	93	5–104	39.76	3.13	76.19	1	0

OWAIS **SHAH**

Full name	**Owais Alam Shah**
Born	**October 22, 1978, Karachi, Pakistan**
Teams	**Middlesex**
Style	**Right-hand bat, occasional offspinner**
Test debut	**England v India at Mumbai 2005-06**
ODI debut	**England v Australia at Bristol 2001**

THE PROFILE Owais Shah was a schoolboy prodigy, making 64 for Middlesex in a one-dayer against Yorkshire when only 16, and captaining England to victory in the Under-19 World Cup in February 1998. A silky strokemaker, strong on the leg side, he seemed set for a stellar career, and after a couple of low-key seasons played for England in 2001, scoring 62 against Pakistan in his second ODI. So far, so good ... but then he dropped off the radar, amid suggestions that his fielding wasn't up to scratch. He was in and out of the one-day side until the 2002-03 Australian tri-series, when he made only one decent contribution, and was then forgotten for three years. It seemed to be a classic case of wasted talent, but he was revitalised by Twenty20 cricket, and finished 2005 with more first-class runs than anyone else. When England had personnel problems in India that winter Shah lit up his Test debut with two cocky innings of 88 and 38 ... before being forgotten again. He got another chance early in 2007, but struggled, although he kept his name in the frame with a sparkling Twenty20 innings against West Indies. That guaranteed him another run in the one-day side, and a place in the inaugural World Twenty20 championship in September 2007, just after he scored a fine maiden ODI century against India. He remained in the frame in 2009, the highlight a brisk 75 against West Indies at Edgbaston, although later in the year against Australia his rabbit-in-the-headlights running between wickets reduced Shah – and some of his batting partners – to nervous wrecks.

THE FACTS Shah scored 203 for Middlesex v Derbyshire at Southgate in 2001 ... He captained England to victory in the Under-19 World Cup in South Africa in February 1998: his team-mates included Robert Key and Chris Schofield ... Shah hit 55 from 35 balls as England won their Twenty20 international against West Indies at The Oval in June 2007 ... He hit hundreds on successive days against Lancashire at Old Trafford in 2006, in different competitions ...

THE FIGURES to 21.9.09   www.cricinfo.com

Batting & Fielding	M	Inns	NO	Runs	HS	Avge	S/R	100	50	4s	6s	Ct	St
Tests	6	10	0	269	88	26.90	41.90	0	2	35	3	2	0
ODIs	67	62	6	1689	107*	30.16	78.33	1	11	136	19	20	0
Twenty20 Ints	17	15	1	347	55*	24.78	122.18	0	1	26	13	5	0
First-class	209	356	33	13717	203	42.46	–	37	69	–	–	160	0

Bowling	M	Balls	Runs	Wkts	BB	Avge	RpO	S/R	5i	10m
Tests	6	30	31	0	–	–	6.20	–	0	0
ODIs	67	187	173	7	3–15	24.71	5.55	26.71	0	0
Twenty20 Ints	17	0	–	–	–	–	–	–	–	–
First-class	209	1974	1356	22	3–33	61.63	4.12	89.72	0	0

SHAHADAT HOSSAIN

Full name	**Kazi Shahadat Hossain**
Born	**August 7, 1986, Dhaka**
Teams	**Dhaka**
Style	**Right-hand bat, right-arm fast-medium bowler**
Test debut	**Bangladesh v England at Lord's 2005**
ODI debut	**Bangladesh v Kenya at Bogra 2005-06**

THE PROFILE Shahadat Hossain was discovered during a talent-spotting camp in Narayanganj, and whisked away to the Institute of Sports for refinement. In the 2004 Under-19 World Cup he stood out as a promising fast bowler in a tournament which generally lacked firepower, and made rapid progress after that. "Rajib" has all the necessary attributes for a genuine fast bowler: he is tall and strong, and doesn't put unnecessary pressure on his body with a slightly open-chested delivery position after a smooth run-up. He is naturally aggressive and, above everything, has raw pace. His Test debut at Lord's in 2005 was a chastening experience, as his 12 overs disappeared for 101. But he was just 18: after that he did well against Sri Lanka, taking four wickets in an innings in Colombo and again at Chittagong before going one better in Bogra's inaugural Test in March 2006 with 5 for 86. And he excelled against South Africa early in 2008, when 6 for 27 at Mirpur gave his side a rare first-innings lead – and an even rarer (if illusory) sniff of victory. In one-day internationals, despite a hat-trick against Zimbabwe, he was in and out of the side: he played only once in the 2007 World Cup (and was hit around in the sobering defeat by Ireland), and by 2009 he was seemingly seen as too expensive for the shorter games. In Tests he remained a regular, although eight matches between October 2008 and July 2009 produced only 11 wickets. He was, however, part of the side which won an overseas series for the first time, when a severely depleted West Indies were walloped 2-0 in the Caribbean.

THE FACTS Shahadat Hossain's 6 for 27 against South Africa at Mirpur in February 2008 are the best by a Bangladesh fast bowler in Tests ... He took Bangladesh's first hat-trick in ODIs, against Zimbabwe at Harare in August 2006 ... Shahadat took only two wickets – both against Kenya – in his first six ODIs: in six ODIs against New Zealand he has taken 1 for 201 ...

THE FIGURES to 21.9.09   www.cricinfo.com

Batting & Fielding	M	Inns	NO	Runs	HS	Avge	S/R	100	50	4s	6s	Ct	St
Tests	23	43	13	231	33	7.70	38.69	0	0	32	1	4	0
ODIs	43	22	14	58	12*	7.25	47.54	0	0	5	0	5	0
Twenty20 Ints	4	4	3	7	4*	7.00	77.77	0	0	0	0	0	0
First-class	43	73	26	479	37*	10.19	–	0	0	–	–	8	0

Bowling	M	Balls	Runs	Wkts	BB	Avge	RpO	S/R	5i	10m
Tests	23	3344	2316	53	6–27	43.69	4.15	63.09	2	0
ODIs	43	1797	1691	41	3–34	41.24	5.64	43.82	0	0
Twenty20 Ints	4	78	116	4	2–22	29.00	8.92	19.50	0	0
First-class	43	6231	4191	114	6–27	36.76	4.03	54.65	5	0

SHAHID AFRIDI

Full name	**Sahibzada Mohammad Shahid Khan Afridi**
Born	**March 1, 1980, Khyber Agency**
Teams	**Karachi, Sind, Habib Bank**
Style	**Right-hand bat, legspinner**
Test debut	**Pakistan v Australia at Karachi 1998-99**
ODI debut	**Pakistan v Kenya at Nairobi 1996-97**

THE PROFILE A flamboyant allrounder introduced to international cricket as a 16-year-old legspinner, Shahid Afridi astonished everyone except himself by pinch-hitting the fastest one-day hundred, from 37 balls in his maiden innings. He's a compulsive shotmaker, and although until 2004 that was too often his undoing, he eventually blossomed. A string of incisive contributions culminated in a violent century against India in April 2005: the only faster ODI hundred was Afridi's own. A few weeks before, he had smashed 58 in 34 balls, and also grabbed three crucial wickets, as Pakistan memorably squared the Test series at Bangalore. And so it continued: a Test ton against West Indies, important runs against England, then, early in 2006, he went berserk on some flat tracks against India. An Afridi assault is laced with lofted drives and short-arm jabs over midwicket. He's at his best when forcing straight, and at his weakest pushing just outside off. But perhaps the biggest improvement has been in his legspin. When conditions suit, he gets turn as well as lazy drift, but variety is the key: there's a vicious faster ball and an offbreak too. He shocked everyone when, after finally establishing himself, he announced his retirement from Tests in 2006. To less surprise, he recanted a fortnight later and toured England, but has not played a five-day game since. After an uncertain start in Twenty20 cricket – a format which might have been invented with him in mind – he roared back to form in the World Twenty20 in England in 2009 with important runs and wickets, including a ferocious 51 as Pakistan romped to victory in the final at Lord's.

THE FACTS In his second match (he hadn't batted in the first) Shahid Afridi hit the fastest hundred in ODIs, from only 37 balls, v Sri Lanka in Nairobi in October 1996 ... Afridi has the highest strike rate – 110.99 runs per 100 balls – of anyone with more than 20 innings in ODIs ... In successive Tests against India in 2006 he hit 103 (from 80 balls) at Lahore, and 156 (128 balls, six sixes) at Faisalabad ... Only Sanath Jayasuriya (270) has hit more sixes in ODIs ... Afridi's record includes three ODIs for the Asia XI and two for the World XI ...

THE FIGURES *to 21.9.09*   www.cricinfo.com

Batting & Fielding	M	Inns	NO	Runs	HS	Avge	S/R	100	50	4s	6s	Ct	St
Tests	26	46	1	1683	156	37.40	86.13	5	8	216	50	10	0
ODIs	281	263	17	5715	109	23.23	110.99	4	29	528	250	96	0
Twenty20 Ints	24	22	2	421	54*	21.05	147.71	0	3	37	14	7	0
First-class	109	180	4	5598	164	31.80	–	12	30	–	–	75	0

Bowling	M	Balls	Runs	Wkts	BB	Avge	RpO	S/R	5i	10m
Tests	26	3092	1640	47	5–52	34.89	3.18	65.78	1	0
ODIs	281	11664	8993	259	6–38	34.72	4.62	45.03	3	0
Twenty20 Ints	24	561	535	34	4–11	15.73	5.72	16.50	0	0
First-class	109	13391	6954	257	6–101	27.05	3.11	52.10	8	0

SHAKIB AL HASAN

Full name **Shakib Al Hasan**
Born **March 24, 1987, Magura, Khulna**
Teams **Khulna**
Style **Left-hand bat, slow left-arm orthodox spinner**
Test debut **Bangladesh v India at Chittagong 2006-07**
ODI debut **Bangladesh v Zimbabwe at Harare 2006**

THE PROFILE Shakib Al Hasan first came to prominence late in 2005, when he blasted 83 from only 62 balls to take Bangladesh's Under-19s to victory over England in Dhaka. A fortnight later he was at it again, with an 82-ball century against Sri Lanka, after taking three wickets. A full debut was not far off, and it duly came against Zimbabwe in August 2006: he took a wicket and then strolled in at No. 4 to make 30 not out in the matchwinning partnership. A stylish left-hander, Shakib proved remarkably consistent at first, being dismissed in single figures only once in 18 one-dayers leading up to the 2007 World Cup: that run included 134 not out against Canada. The heady start continued in the Caribbean with a half-century in the famous win over India, and another against England. After the World Cup came his first taste of personal failure – only 17 runs in three innings in Sri Lanka – but he soon returned to form. He sealed Bangladesh's 2-0 triumph over a depleted West Indies side in July 2009, finishing just short of a maiden Test century in Grenada: by then he had taken over from the injured Mashrafe Mortaza as captain. Shakib's flattish left-arm spin – always effective in ODIs, where he has an impressive economy-rate – suddenly blossomed in Tests. After only three wickets in his first six matches, he took 7 for 36 against New Zealand in October 2008, then claimed five-fors in three successive games against South Africa and Sri Lanka: finally he rubber-stamped his arrival as a true international-class allrounder with 13 wickets in those two Tests in West Indies.

THE FACTS Shakib Al Hasan took 7 for 36, Bangladesh's best bowling figures in Tests, against New Zealand at Chittagong in October 2008 ... He made 134 not out v Canada at St John's in February 2007 ... In his first Test as captain (against West Indies in Grenada in July 2009), Shakib took 3 for 59 and 5 for 70, and finished the match with 96 not out ... He averages 38.40 with the bat in ODIs against Pakistan – and 4.00 v Ireland ...

THE FIGURES *to 21.9.09*　　　　　　　　　www.cricinfo.com

Batting & Fielding	M	Inns	NO	Runs	HS	Avge	S/R	100	50	4s	6s	Ct	St
Tests	14	26	2	715	96*	29.79	53.47	0	3	90	2	8	0
ODIs	70	67	12	1904	134*	34.61	74.90	3	12	169	14	14	0
Twenty20 Ints	11	11	0	129	26	11.72	106.61	0	0	14	1	4	0
First-class	38	70	7	2164	129	34.34	–	3	11	–	–	24	0

Bowling	M	Balls	Runs	Wkts	BB	Avge	RpO	S/R	5i	10m
Tests	14	2991	1357	48	7–36	28.27	2.72	62.31	5	0
ODIs	70	3489	2378	76	3–11	31.28	4.08	45.90	0	0
Twenty20 Ints	11	234	261	13	4–34	20.07	6.69	18.00	0	0
First-class	38	7024	3035	102	7–36	29.75	2.59	68.86	7	0

ISHANT **SHARMA**

Full name	**Ishant Sharma**
Born	**September 2, 1988, Delhi**
Teams	**Delhi, Kolkata Knight Riders**
Style	**Right-hand bat, right-arm fast-medium bowler**
Test debut	**India v Bangladesh at Dhaka 2006-07**
ODI debut	**India v South Africa at Belfast 2007**

THE PROFILE Tall fast bowlers have always been a much-prized rarity in Indian cricket. Their earliest Tests featured Mohammad Nissar, a few years ago Abey Kuruvilla flitted across the international scene ... and now there's Ishant Sharma, a lofty 6ft 4ins (193cm). He's regularly above 80mph, and possesses a sharp and deceptive bouncer, delivered from a high arm action. He started to play seriously at 14, rose quickly, and played one-dayers for Delhi in 2005-06 when only 17. The following season he took 4 for 65 from 34 overs on his first-class debut and finished his first term with 29 wickets at 20.10. Early in 2007 he was on the verge of reinforcing the national team in South Africa – flights had been booked and visa arrangements made – but in the end he was left to concentrate on domestic cricket and a youth tour. However, when Munaf Patel was injured again in Bangladesh in May, Sharma finally did get on the plane, and took a wicket in a landslide victory at Dhaka. In Australia at the end of 2007 he looked the real deal, especially in the Perth Test, when he dismissed Ricky Ponting during a sensational spell, and again in the one-dayers as India surprised the hosts to snaffle the series. Then, later in 2008, he took three crucial wickets to settle the Galle Test, and 15 more in the successful home series against Australia. He has been one of the faces of the IPL, if not one of its greatest successes, and – if a worryingly frail-looking physique holds up – he is set for a long and successful career.

THE FACTS Ishant Sharma took 7 for 24 (11 for 51 in the match) for Delhi v Orissa at Delhi in November 2008 ... He has taken 20 of his 42 ODI wickets against Sri Lanka: his average against them is 23.05, but 108.50 v Pakistan ... In 2006-07, his first season of first-class cricket, Sharma took 29 wickets at 20.10 for Delhi, then made his Test debut in only his seventh match ...

THE FIGURES to 21.9.09   www.cricinfo.com

Batting & Fielding	M	Inns	NO	Runs	HS	Avge	S/R	100	50	4s	6s	Ct	St
Tests	18	24	12	142	23	11.83	31.41	0	0	15	0	6	0
ODIs	33	9	4	33	13	6.60	43.42	0	0	3	0	9	0
Twenty20 Ints	9	1	1	3	3*	–	50.00	0	0	0	0	1	0
First-class	36	40	22	175	23	9.72	30.54	0	0	18	0	9	0

Bowling	M	Balls	Runs	Wkts	BB	Avge	RpO	S/R	5i	10m
Tests	18	3234	1724	52	5–118	33.15	3.19	62.19	1	0
ODIs	33	1533	1447	46	4–38	31.45	5.66	33.32	0	0
Twenty20 Ints	9	158	227	4	2–34	56.75	8.62	39.50	0	0
First-class	36	6649	3332	128	7–24	26.03	3.00	51.94	3	1

ROHIT **SHARMA**

Full name **Rohit Gurunathan Sharma**
Born **April 30, 1987, Bansod, Nagpur, Maharashtra**
Teams **Mumbai, Deccan Chargers**
Style **Right-hand bat, offspinner**
Test debut **No Tests yet**
ODI debut **India v Ireland at Belfast 2007**

INDIA

THE PROFILE Rohit Sharma made a stellar start to his first-class career in December 2006, hitting 205 against Gujarat in only his fourth match for Mumbai, after a near-miss (95) in his previous game. Earlier that year he had made his first-class debut for India A, and also exuded class in the Youth World Cup, cracking three half-centuries in six days in mid-tournament before missing out in the low-scoring final. Sharma was at No. 3 then, which may well turn out to be his best position as he is an adaptable batsman, strong off the back foot, equally happy as accumulator or aggressor. He finished 2006-07 with 600 runs at 40, plus 356 in one-dayers and a 49-ball Twenty20 century against Gujarat, which all earned him a national call as the dust settled on India's disastrous World Cup campaign. He made his ODI debut in Ireland, retained his place for the one-day leg of the tour of England that followed, then had a couple of useful innings in the World Twenty20 championship in South Africa. Since then he has been a one-day regular (the Test call still awaits), with solid if unspectacular results – his best innings to date was an undefeated 70 against Sri Lanka at Canberra in February 2008 during the successful tri-series campaign in Australia. During the second edition of the IPL in 2009 Sharma's Deccan Chargers entered the last over against Kolkata needing 21 to win – and Sharma hit 26, including a six off the final ball, off Bangladesh's Mashrafe bin Mortaza. A few matches previously Sharma's seldom-seen offspin had claimed an unlikely hat-trick to derail the Mumbai Indians.

THE FACTS Rohit Sharma extended his maiden first-class century to 205, for Mumbai v Gujarat in December 2006... He took a hat-trick (and four wickets in five balls) as Deccan Chargers beat Mumbai Indians in the IPL at Centurion in May 2009 ... He hit 101 not out, off only 45 balls, against Gujarat in a Twenty20 match in April 2007 ... Sharma made 404 runs at a strike rate of 147.98 in the inaugural IPL season in 2008 ...

THE FIGURES *to 21.9.09*   www.cricinfo.com

Batting & Fielding	M	Inns	NO	Runs	HS	Avge	S/R	100	50	4s	6s	Ct	St
Tests	0	0	–	–	–	–	–	–	–	–	–	–	–
ODIs	41	38	10	695	70*	24.82	72.24	0	4	51	5	18	0
Twenty20 Ints	13	11	4	238	52*	34.00	122.68	0	2	22	8	2	0
First-class	28	42	3	1923	205	49.39	–	5	9	–	–	21	0

Bowling	M	Balls	Runs	Wkts	BB	Avge	RpO	S/R	5i	10m
Tests	0	0	–	–	–	–	–	–	–	–
ODIs	41	185	132	2	2–27	66.00	4.28	92.50	0	0
Twenty20 Ints	13	12	15	0	–	–	7.50	–	0	0
First-class	28	378	206	2	1–1	103.00	3.26	189.00	0	0

SHOAIB AKHTAR

Full name	**Shoaib Akhtar**
Born	**August 13, 1975, Rawalpindi, Punjab**
Teams	**Islamabad, Federal Areas, Khan Research Laboratories**
Style	**Right-hand bat, right-arm fast bowler**
Test debut	**Pakistan v West Indies at Rawalpindi 1997-98**
ODI debut	**Pakistan v Zimbabwe at Harare 1997-98**

THE PROFILE Shoaib Akhtar electrified the 1999 World Cup with his spectacular run-up and blistering speed. But it was too much, too young, for the "Rawalpindi Express": breaking the 100mph barrier seemed more important than cementing his place. He was twice sidelined after throwing allegations, and although his action was cleared – tests showed a hyper-extensible elbow – injuries often impinged. He shook up the Aussies in 2002, and promised much in the following year's World Cup, but came a cropper, especially in a needle encounter with Sachin Tendulkar. Then Pakistan lost a series to India, and Shoaib felt the heat as his commitment was questioned. He blew hot and cold in Australia in 2004-05, by turns Pakistan's most incisive threat and their most disinterested player. He bounced back at the end of 2005 with 17 England wickets, mixing yorkers and bouncers with lethal slower balls. But there were further whispers about his action, ankle trouble kept him out of most of the 2006 England tour, then he was banned for two years after a positive drug test. The ban was lifted on appeal, but it and various injuries kept him out of the 2007 World Cup. He was back later that year – briefly, being sent home from the World Twenty20 championship after a dressing-room spat left Mohammad Asif with a bat-bruised thigh – then copped a five-year ban early in 2008 for criticising the board. The end? No ... it was later reduced to 18 months, then suspended. Shoaib isn't quite finished yet, although the emergence of bowlers like Mohammad Aamer – who is half his age – means the last-chance saloon is not far off.

THE FACTS Shoaib was clocked at 100.04mph by an unofficial speed-gun during a one-dayer v New Zealand in April 2002: he also recorded 100.23mph (161.3kph) at the 2003 World Cup ... His best figures in Tests and ODIs both came against New Zealand ... Against England in the 2003 World Cup Shoaib was the fifth No. 11 to top-score in an ODI innings, with 43 ... His record includes three ODIs for the Asia XI and two for the World XI ...

THE FIGURES to 21.9.09   www.cricinfo.com

Batting & Fielding	M	Inns	NO	Runs	HS	Avge	S/R	100	50	4s	6s	Ct	St
Tests	46	67	13	544	47	10.07	41.43	0	0	53	22	12	0
ODIs	144	70	32	373	43	9.81	75.05	0	0	26	11	17	0
Twenty20 Ints	7	1	1	1	1*	–	100.00	0	0	0	0	2	0
First-class	133	186	50	1670	59*	12.27	–	0	1	–	–	41	0

Bowling	M	Balls	Runs	Wkts	BB	Avge	RpO	S/R	5i	10m
Tests	46	8143	4574	178	6–11	25.69	3.37	45.74	12	2
ODIs	144	6798	5321	223	6–16	23.86	4.69	30.48	4	0
Twenty20 Ints	7	138	183	8	2–11	22.87	7.95	17.25	0	0
First-class	133	20460	12265	467	6–11	26.26	3.59	43.81	28	2

SHOAIB MALIK

Full name	**Shoaib Malik**
Born	**February 1, 1982, Sialkot, Punjab**
Teams	**Sialkot, Pakistan International Airlines**
Style	**Right-hand bat, offspinner**
Test debut	**Pakistan v Bangladesh at Multan 2001-02**
ODI debut	**Pakistan v West Indies at Sharjah 1999-2000**

THE PROFILE Short of wicketkeeping, there are few roles Shoaib Malik hasn't tried. He has batted everywhere from 1 to 10 in one-dayers, though he has now settled at 3 or 4. He began in Tests in the lower order, then tried opening. As an offspinner, everything about his bowling, from the short-stepping run-up to the *doosra*, bears a striking similarity to Saqlain Mushtaq's. But his action was reported twice, and he now bowls less after two bouts of elbow surgery. Finally, in the wake of the disasters of the 2007 World Cup, came his biggest challenge ... captaincy. It didn't start well: after surrendering a short series to South Africa he lost the first Test in India, then picked up an injury and had to watch as his battered side was labelled by some as Pakistan's worst ever to tour the old enemy. It was a slightly different story in ODIs, although he was flattered to be in charge for a national-record run of 11 consecutive victories early in 2008, since ten of them came against Zimbabwe and Bangladesh. Shoaib is an uncomplicated batsman, free with checked drives and cuts, or slogging when needed. Probably his finest performance in Tests came when he defied Murali with an unbeaten eight-hour 148 to earn a draw in Colombo in March 2006. Heavy defeat to Sri Lanka in a one-day series in January 2009 spelt the end of his spell as captain: seemingly rather relieved to be back in the ranks, he contributed to victory in the World Twenty20 in England in June, then hit another important century in the drawn third Test in Colombo the following month.

THE FACTS Shoaib Malik extended his first Test century, against Sri Lanka in Colombo in March 2006, to 148 not out in 448 minutes as Pakistan forced a draw ... He made 90, 95 and 106 in successive one-day innings against India in February 2006 ... Shoaib has batted in every position except No. 11 in ODIs, averaging 52.80 from No. 2, 45.61 from No. 4, and 41.40 at No. 3 (and 7.50 at No. 10) ... He took 7 for 81 for Pakistan International Airlines v WAPDA at Faisalabad in February 2001 ...

THE FIGURES to 21.9.09   www.cricinfo.com

Batting & Fielding	M	Inns	NO	Runs	HS	Avge	S/R	100	50	4s	6s	Ct	St
Tests	26	42	6	1394	148*	38.72	44.16	2	7	179	12	13	0
ODIs	181	161	21	4858	143	34.70	79.04	6	31	401	57	63	0
Twenty20 Ints	25	24	6	541	57	30.05	118.12	0	2	44	13	8	0
First-class	86	130	16	3503	148*	30.72	–	8	16	–	–	41	0

Bowling	M	Balls	Runs	Wkts	BB	Avge	RpO	S/R	5i	10m
Tests	26	2010	1153	17	4-42	67.82	3.44	118.23	0	0
ODIs	181	6150	4675	128	4-19	36.52	4.56	48.04	0	0
Twenty20 Ints	25	204	208	12	2-14	17.33	6.11	17.00	0	0
First-class	86	10615	5312	168	7-81	31.61	3.00	63.18	5	1

PETER **SIDDLE**

Full name **Peter Matthew Siddle**
Born **November 25, 1984, Traralgon, Victoria**
Teams **Victoria**
Style **Right-hand bat, right-arm fast bowler**
Test debut **Australia v India at Mohali 2008-09**
ODI debut **Australia v New Zealand at Brisbane 2008-09**

THE PROFILE Peter Siddle has long been considered one of the most dangerous fast bowlers in Australia – but also one of the most fragile. A shoulder reconstruction sidelined him for most of 2006-07, then he dislocated the joint at the start of the following season, and aggravated it again later on. Despite this he finished 2007-08 with 33 wickets in just five matches. That included nine victims in the Pura Cup final against New South Wales, although by then Siddle's shoulder was very sore, and he underwent reconstructive surgery only a week later. He emerged fitter than ever, and was a surprise inclusion for the Test tour of India in October 2008, after visiting there with the A team the previous month. His first Test wicket was the plum one of Sachin Tendulkar. The burly Siddle has elements of two illustrious predecessors in his run-up and general attitude: the approach is reminiscent of Craig McDermott's, while the bustling delivery reminds some of Merv Hughes – and he has a touch of the old Hughes banter, too. In England in 2009 he fought off the challenges of other pacemen to play throughout the series, moving the ball at pace, and finishing second in the averages with 20 wickets. That included a decisive first-day spell of 5 for 21 to put England on the ropes in the fourth Test at Headingley, which Australia won easily. Siddle grew up in Morwell in rural Victoria, and was a promising competitive wood-chopper before he eventually took up cricket at 14. "I did it between the ages of 11 and 13 but thought if I was going to play competitive sport I should give it away because I didn't want to chop any toes off!"

THE FACTS Siddle took 6 for 57 for Victoria v South Australia at St Kilda in January 2008 ... He took 9 for 167 in the match in the Pura Cup final against New South Wales at Sydney in March 2008, although Victoria still lost ... Siddle took a wicket (New Zealand's Kyle Mills) with his sixth ball in one-day internationals, at Brisbane in February 2009 ...

THE FIGURES to 21.9.09   www.cricinfo.com

Batting & Fielding	M	Inns	NO	Runs	HS	Avge	S/R	100	50	4s	6s	Ct	St
Tests	12	18	4	197	35	14.07	54.12	0	0	25	1	7	0
ODIs	3	1	1	8	8*	–	266.66	0	0	1	0	1	0
Twenty20 Ints	1	1	1	1	1*	–	100.00	0	0	0	0	0	0
First-class	27	36	9	374	38	13.85	44.52	0	0	42	2	12	0

Bowling	M	Balls	Runs	Wkts	BB	Avge	RpO	S/R	5i	10m
Tests	12	2837	1418	49	5–21	28.93	2.99	57.89	2	0
ODIs	3	126	85	3	1–13	28.33	4.04	42.00	0	0
Twenty20 Ints	1	24	24	2	2–24	12.00	6.00	12.00	0	0
First-class	27	5136	2662	98	6–57	27.16	3.10	52.40	6	0

RYAN **SIDEBOTTOM**

Full name	**Ryan Jay Sidebottom**
Born	**January 15, 1978, Huddersfield, Yorkshire**
Teams	**Nottinghamshire**
Style	**Left-hand bat, left-arm fast-medium bowler**
Test debut	**England v Pakistan at Lord's 2001**
ODI debut	**England v Zimbabwe at Harare 2001-02**

THE PROFILE Although Ryan Sidebottom's long curly hair made him one of the most recognisable faces on the county circuit, for six years he seemed destined to be a one-cap wonder, just like his father, Arnie. The junior Sidebottom (who like his dad was also a useful footballer, having trials for Sheffield United) did well for England A in the Caribbean in 2001, and made his Test debut at Lord's later that year: he didn't move it much, failed to strike, and was promptly returned to county cricket. A move from Yorkshire to Nottinghamshire in 2004 revitalised him. He took 50 wickets for the first time in 2005, repeated the dose the following year, and when Matthew Hoggard was injured early in 2007 Sidebottom was the selectors' surprise packet. He was an instant success back at Headingley, taking eight wickets (five of them lbw) as West Indies were torpedoed. Crucially for a bowler who rarely exceeds 80mph, he now swung the ball in, as well as away – the first left-armer to do this regularly for England since John Lever a generation or two earlier. Sidebottom collected 24 wickets in six Tests, then in six more against New Zealand in 2008, home and away, he starred with 41 victims, including a hat-trick at Hamilton. However, a heavy workload began to tell: he started snapping at team-mates, and missed some matches with strains. An Achilles problem clouded the start of 2009, and the nearest he got to the Ashes series was a squad place in the final two Tests. He did play in the disheartening one-dayers that followed, keeping the runs down without taking many wickets, but faces an important winter of re-establishment.

THE FACTS Sidebottom took 7 for 47 against New Zealand at Napier in March 2008: two Tests earlier, at Hamilton, his ten wickets in the match included a hat-trick ... His father, Arnie, played one Test for England against Australia in 1985 ... He took 6 for 16 (and 5 for 27) for Yorkshire against Kent at Leeds in June 2000 ... One of his nicknames is "Sexual Chocolate", after a fictional band in an Eddie Murphy film who all had long flowing hair ...

THE FIGURES to 21.9.09   www.cricinfo.com

Batting & Fielding	M	Inns	NO	Runs	HS	Avge	S/R	100	50	4s	6s	Ct	St
Tests	21	29	11	298	31	16.55	33.86	0	0	35	0	5	0
ODIs	23	17	8	113	24	12.55	73.85	0	0	8	0	6	0
Twenty20 Ints	8	1	1	5	5*	–	125.00	0	0	1	0	3	0
First-class	137	175	52	1511	54	12.28	–	0	1	–	–	46	0

Bowling	M	Balls	Runs	Wkts	BB	Avge	RpO	S/R	5i	10m
Tests	21	4626	2133	77	7-47	27.70	2.76	60.07	5	1
ODIs	23	1195	961	27	3-19	35.59	4.82	44.25	0	0
Twenty20 Ints	8	172	202	11	3-16	18.36	7.04	15.63	0	0
First-class	137	24302	11378	443	7-47	25.68	2.80	54.85	19	2

LENDL **SIMMONS**

Full name	**Lendl Mark Platter Simmons**
Born	**January 25, 1985, Port-of-Spain, Trinidad**
Teams	**Trinidad & Tobago**
Style	**Right-hand bat, right-arm medium-pace bowler**
Test debut	**West Indies v England at Port-of-Spain 2008-09**
ODI debut	**West Indies v Pakistan at Faisalabad 2006-07**

THE PROFILE Like his fellow Trinidadians Denesh Ramdin and Ravi Rampaul, Lendl Simmons (the nephew of the former Test opener Phil) first made a mark at the Under-15 World Challenge event in England in 2000, which West Indies won. He made a steady rise through the junior ranks, playing in the Youth World Cups of 2002 and 2004 (losing in the final). An opener, and a fine fielder who sometimes keeps wicket, Simmons – who is named after the top 1980s tennis player Ivan Lendl – made his first-class debut six weeks after his 17th birthday. He passed 500 runs in the 2004-05 and 2005-06 West Indian seasons, and toured England with the West Indian A team later in 2006. He stepped up to the full ODI side in Pakistan later that year, collecting a duck in his first match but a mature 70 in his second. He struggled after that, collecting only 42 runs in four innings, but retained his place for the 2007 World Cup. He made only one appearance, though, in rather peculiar circumstances: called up in place of a fast bowler for the vital Super Eight match against New Zealand, he batted No. 8 and didn't bowl. Finally a massive 282 for West Indies A against the England tourists early in 2009 ensured him a Test place, but in three matches at home and away against England he failed to set the world alight. Shortly afterwards Simmons hammered 77 off 50 balls against South Africa in the World Twenty20 in England (he had earlier taken four wickets against Sri Lanka), but was then surprisingly omitted from the squad for the home one-dayers against India.

THE FACTS Simmons made 282 for West Indies A against England in St Kitts in January 2009 ... He made 200 (his maiden century) for Trinidad & Tobago against Jamaica at Scarborough in Tobago in February 2006, after being out for 0 in the first innings ... Simmons hit 108 not out for West Indies A against the Pakistan tourists at Shenley in August 2006 ... His uncle, Phil Simmons, won 26 Test caps for West Indies between 1988 and 1997 ...

THE FIGURES *to 21.9.09*   www.cricinfo.com

Batting & Fielding	M	Inns	NO	Runs	HS	Avge	S/R	100	50	4s	6s	Ct	St
Tests	3	6	0	87	24	14.50	38.32	0	0	10	1	3	0
ODIs	14	14	2	248	70	20.66	57.80	0	2	26	2	4	0
Twenty20 Ints	7	7	1	182	77	30.33	118.95	0	1	25	1	4	0
First-class	62	108	9	3372	282	34.06	–	7	15	–	–	75	4

Bowling	M	Balls	Runs	Wkts	BB	Avge	RpO	S/R	5i	10m
Tests	3	180	139	1	1–60	139.00	4.63	180.00	0	0
ODIs	14	6	9	0	–	–	9.00	–	0	0
Twenty20 Ints	7	36	55	6	4–19	9.16	9.16	6.00	0	0
First-class	62	486	313	10	3–6	31.30	3.86	48.60	0	0

RP **SINGH**

INDIA

Full name	**Rudra Pratap Singh**
Born	**December 6, 1985, Rae Bareli, Uttar Pradesh**
Teams	**Uttar Pradesh, Deccan Chargers**
Style	**Right-hand bat, left-arm fast-medium bowler**
Test debut	**India v Pakistan at Faisalabad 2005-06**
ODI debut	**India v Zimbabwe at Harare 2005-06**

THE PROFILE   One of India's several left-arm seamers, Rudra Pratap Singh first made the headlines at the Under-19 World Cup in 2004, chiefly for some intelligent bowling at the death. After 34 Ranji Trophy wickets for Uttar Pradesh in 2004-05, the joint-highest for the summer, Singh made the national one-day squad at the end of 2005, and took two wickets in his second over of international cricket, against Zimbabwe at Harare in September. He took four wickets (and the match award) against Sri Lanka in his third game, and three more in his fourth, before four barren outings cost him his place in May 2006. He had also won the match award on his Test debut on a shirtfront at Faisalabad, where Pakistan ran up 588. He was overlooked for a while, but put an early-season stint with Leicestershire to good use in 2007, forcing his way into the side for the three-Test series in England. He took 5 for 59 in a tidy display of swing bowling at Lord's, knocking over Michael Vaughan in both innings, troubling him from round the wicket. An up-and-down time followed: after four-fors in the Sydney and Perth Tests, he lost his place after three wicketless matches later in 2008, and hasn't played a Test since – although he remains in the one-day shake-up, and was the leading wicket-taker in the second IPL tournament in South Africa early in 2009. Virender Sehwag has long been an admirer: "RP is a very talented bowler – his specialty is that he can bring the ball in to the right-handers and swing it both ways."

THE FACTS   RP Singh won the Man of the Match award on his Test debut – even though there were six centuries in the match, at Faisalabad in January 2006: Singh took 4 for 89 in Pakistan's first innings of 588 ... He averages 22.07 with the ball in ODIs against Sri Lanka, but 77.66 v West Indies ... Singh was the leading wicket-taker (23) in the second IPL tournament, in South Africa early in 2009 ...

THE FIGURES *to 21.9.09*   www.cricinfo.com

Batting & Fielding	M	Inns	NO	Runs	HS	Avge	S/R	100	50	4s	6s	Ct	St
Tests	13	17	3	91	30	6.50	36.40	0	0	11	1	6	0
ODIs	54	19	10	102	23	11.33	43.22	0	0	5	1	12	0
Twenty20 Ints	10	2	2	3	2*	–	100.00	0	0	0	0	2	0
First-class	45	60	12	444	41*	9.25	–	0	0	–	–	19	0

Bowling	M	Balls	Runs	Wkts	BB	Avge	RpO	S/R	5i	10m
Tests	13	2330	1564	40	5–59	39.10	4.02	58.25	1	0
ODIs	54	2379	2142	64	4–35	33.46	5.40	37.17	0	0
Twenty20 Ints	10	198	225	15	4–13	15.00	6.81	13.20	0	0
First-class	45	8049	4556	156	5–33	29.20	3.39	51.59	7	1

DEVON **SMITH**

Full name	**Devon Sheldon Smith**
Born	**Oct 21, 1981, Hermitage, Sauteurs, St Patrick, Grenada**
Teams	**Windward Islands**
Style	**Left-hand bat, occasional offspinner**
Test debut	**West Indies v Australia at Georgetown 2002-03**
ODI debut	**West Indies v Australia at Kingston 2002-03**

THE PROFILE A belligerent left-handed opener whose eye makes up for a lack of footwork, Grenada's Devon Smith was drafted into the Test squad for the home series against India early in 2002, after making 750 runs in the Busta Cup. He didn't play, though, and made his debut against Australia the following year. Smith blazed 62 in his first Test, but bagged a pair in the next one. Early in 2004 he dragged West Indies out of a hole with a stroke-filled century against England on the first day of the series at Kingston. But just as he began to settle in, he fractured a thumb in the nets: he missed the next two Tests, then was dropped after three failures in the return series in England. He started the 2005-06 Australian tour well, making a hundred against Queensland then 88 in the first Test at Brisbane, but five single-figure scores followed, and the axe fell again. In one-dayers he was originally overshadowed by another Smith, the unrelated Dwayne, but both played in the 2007 World Cup, Devon making 61 in West Indies' last match, the thriller against England, which ensured him another English tour. He made several starts in the Tests there, crunching some classy cover-drives, but got out too often when set, making five scores between 16 and 42 before a double failure at The Oval. A maiden double-century for the Windwards Islands early in 2009 ensured his selection for the Tests against England that followed, but his best score in seven matches was just 55. He remains another underachiever in a West Indian side rather too full of them.

THE FACTS Smith scored 61 (in 34 balls) in his first Twenty20 international, against England at The Oval in June 2007 ... His highest first-class score is 212 for Windward Islands v Guyana at St George's in January 2009 ... He made 181 for West Indies A against Lancashire at Liverpool in July 2002 ... He has never played an ODI against Pakistan ...

THE FIGURES *to 21.9.09*   www.cricinfo.com

Batting & Fielding	M	Inns	NO	Runs	HS	Avge	S/R	100	50	4s	6s	Ct	St
Tests	31	55	2	1315	108	24.81	47.18	1	4	188	0	27	0
ODIs	29	27	2	625	91	25.00	68.83	0	3	60	5	10	0
Twenty20 Ints	6	6	0	203	61	33.83	126.08	0	2	22	5	1	0
First-class	119	211	8	7254	212	35.73	–	15	34	–	–	101	0

Bowling	M	Balls	Runs	Wkts	BB	Avge	RpO	S/R	5i	10m
Tests	31	6	3	0	–	–	3.00	–	0	0
ODIs	29	0	–	–	–	–	–	–	–	–
Twenty20 Ints	6	0	–	–	–	–	–	–	–	–
First-class	119	426	211	2	1–2	105.50	2.97	213.00	0	0

GRAEME **SMITH**

SOUTH AFRICA

Full name	**Graeme Craig Smith**
Born	**February 1, 1981, Johannesburg, Transvaal**
Teams	**Cape Cobras, Rajasthan Royals**
Style	**Left-hand bat, occasional offspinner**
Test debut	**South Africa v Australia at Cape Town 2001-02**
ODI debut	**South Africa v Australia at Bloemfontein 2001-02**

THE PROFILE   In March 2003, Graeme Smith became South Africa's youngest captain at 22, when Shaun Pollock was dumped after a disastrous World Cup. A tall, aggressive left-hand opener, Smith had few leadership credentials – and only a handful of caps – but the selectors' faith was instantly justified: in England in 2003 he collected back-to-back double-centuries. Reality bit back the following year, with Test-series defeats in Sri Lanka and India. There was also a run of 11 losses in 12 ODIs, a mixed time in New Zealand, and the start of an ultimately fruitless series against England. Yet Smith continued to crunch runs aplenty: his 125 to square the New Zealand series was a minor epic. He yields to no-one physically, but can be subdued by more insidious means: by the end of 2004, as Matthew Hoggard's inswinger had him frequently fumbling around his front pad, even the runs started to dry up. But he roared back in the Caribbean in 2005, with hundreds in three successive Tests. Smith did well at the 2007 World Cup, except when it really mattered – a wild stroke gifted Nathan Bracken his wicket as South Africa subsided in the semi. A baton-charge to 85 squared the home Test series against West Indies at the start of 2008, and later that year Smith achieved what he narrowly missed in 2003 – winning a Test series in England, his unbeaten 154 in a stiff run-chase at Edgbaston being one of the great captain's innings. In 2008-09 he presided over South Africa's first Test-series victory in Australia, although his own contribution to that and the return rubber was hampered by two hand fractures courtesy of Mitchell Johnson.

THE FACTS   In the first Test against England in 2003 Smith scored 277 at Birmingham, the highest score by a South African in Tests: in the second he made 259, the highest Test score by a visiting player at Lord's, beating Don Bradman's 254 in 1930 ... He averages 71.88 in Tests against West Indies, but only 32.73 against Australia ... Smith played four matches for Somerset in 2005, scoring 311 against Leicestershire in one of them ... His record includes one Test for the World XI (as captain) and one ODI for the Africa XI ...

THE FIGURES *to 21.9.09*   www.cricinfo.com

Batting & Fielding	M	Inns	NO	Runs	HS	Avge	S/R	100	50	4s	6s	Ct	St
Tests	77	135	9	6342	277	50.33	61.20	18	25	824	18	104	0
ODIs	141	139	9	5251	134*	40.39	82.08	7	38	612	32	72	0
Twenty20 Ints	18	18	2	513	89*	32.06	121.27	0	3	73	8	9	0
First-class	114	197	14	9293	311	50.78	–	26	35	–	–	159	0

Bowling	M	Balls	Runs	Wkts	BB	Avge	RpO	S/R	5i	10m
Tests	77	1319	801	8	2–145	100.12	3.64	164.87	0	0
ODIs	141	1026	951	18	3–30	52.83	5.56	57.00	0	0
Twenty20 Ints	18	24	57	0	–	–	14.25	–	0	0
First-class	114	1687	1048	11	2–145	95.27	3.72	153.36	0	0

SOHAIL TANVIR

Full name	**Sohail Tanvir**
Born	**December 12, 1984, Rawalpindi, Punjab**
Teams	**Rawalpindi, KRL, Rajasthan Royals, South Australia**
Style	**Left-hand bat, left-arm fast-medium bowler**
Test debut	**Pakistan v India at Delhi 2007-08**
ODI debut	**Pakistan v South Africa at Lahore 2007-08**

THE PROFILE Sohail Tanvir made an immediate mark in first-class cricket, scoring 97 not out in only his second match for Rawalpindi in October 2004, when he shared a last-wicket stand of 173 with Yasir Ali that more than doubled the score. And when he was called up to replace Shoaib Akhtar (sent home in disgrace) at the World Twenty20 championship in South Africa in September 2007, Tanvir made an impression again – not with the bat, initially, although he did swipe the first ball he received in international cricket for six, but with his bowling. He bustles in and delivers brisk left-arm off the wrong foot, and is a bit faster than he looks. He developed quickly, adding good changes of pace – helped by the fact that he can also bowl respectable left-arm spin if required – and has a deceptive yorker. He took four key wickets as Pakistan won the decisive one-dayer of their five-match series in India in November 2007, and five more in vain against Sri Lanka at the Asia Cup in mid-2008. In between he returned the best figures of the inaugural Indian Premier League, 6 for 14, for the eventual champions Rajasthan Royals. Tanvir was tried in Tests, too, but although he kept it tight he struggled to make much impression in two matches on batsmen's pitches in India at the end of 2007. Two years later, though, he found himself supplanted by the 17-year-old Mohammad Aamer during the World Twenty20 in England, and faced an uncertain future, not helped when a planned stint with Surrey fell through after visa troubles.

THE FACTS Sohail Tanvir hit sixes off the first and third balls he received in international cricket – from Sreesanth of India in the World Twenty20 final at Johannesburg in September 2007 ... Tanvir took 6 for 14 for Rajasthan Royals against Chennai Super Kings at Jaipur in May 2008, the best bowling figures in any Twenty20 match, and the best in the first season of the IPL ... He has made three first-class hundreds, the highest 132 for Federal Areas v Baluchistan at Karachi in February 2008 ...

THE FIGURES to 21.9.09   www.cricinfo.com

Batting & Fielding	M	Inns	NO	Runs	HS	Avge	S/R	100	50	4s	6s	Ct	St
Tests	2	3	0	17	13	5.66	38.63	0	0	4	0	2	0
ODIs	31	18	5	182	59	14.00	95.78	0	1	17	2	8	0
Twenty20 Ints	13	4	1	17	12	5.66	100.00	0	0	0	2	3	0
First-class	33	54	9	1350	132	30.00	–	3	7	–	–	15	0

Bowling	M	Balls	Runs	Wkts	BB	Avge	RpO	S/R	5i	10m
Tests	2	504	316	5	3–83	63.20	3.76	100.80	0	0
ODIs	31	1542	1272	44	5–48	28.90	4.94	35.04	1	0
Twenty20 Ints	13	264	329	9	3–31	36.55	7.47	29.33	0	0
First-class	33	7186	3954	144	8–54	27.45	3.30	49.90	9	2

TIM **SOUTHEE**

Full name	**Timothy Grant Southee**
Born	**December 11, 1988, Whangarei**
Teams	**Northern Districts**
Style	**Right-hand bat, right-arm fast-medium bowler**
Test debut	**New Zealand v England at Napier 2007-08**
ODI debut	**New Zealand v England at Chester-le-Street 2008**

THE PROFILE Few players have made such a remarkable Test debut as 19-year-old Tim Southee in March 2008. First, swinging the ball at a healthy pace, he took 5 for 55 as England were restricted to 253, his victims including Andrew Strauss for 0 and Kevin Pietersen for 129. Later, with New Zealand in a hopeless position on the final day, he strolled in and smashed 77 not out from just 40 balls, with nine sixes, five of them off an unamused Monty Panesar. His second Test, at Lord's in May 2008, was rather more mundane – one run, no wickets – then he fell ill and lost his place to Iain O'Brien. Southee made his first-class debut for Northern Districts at 18 in February 2007, and the following season showed significant promise, claiming 6 for 68 in a particularly impressive effort against Auckland. He was chosen for the Under-19 World Cup, but had to interrupt his preparations when he was drafted into the senior set-up for the Twenty20 games against England in early 2008. He ended the Under-19 World Cup as the second-highest wicket-taker, with 17, and was named Player of the Tournament. After that he barely had time to unpack when that Test call came. Later in 2008 he shook up the Australians with three wickets in his first four overs at Brisbane, but leaner times almost inevitably followed, and he was sidelined after ten expensive overs in a one-dayer against India in March 2009. But Southee remains very much one for the future: "He's still growing, actually," said New Zealand's chief selector Glenn Turner, "and we think he has probably been a bit rushed."

THE FACTS Southee hit nine sixes in his first Test innings, a number only ever exceeded by four players, none of whom was making his debut: he had earlier become only the sixth New Zealander to take a five-for on Test debut ... He conceded 105 runs in ten overs against India at Christchurch in March 2009, a number exceeded in ODIs only by Australia's Mick Lewis, with 10–0–113–0 v South Africa at Johannesburg in 2005-06 ... Southee took 6 for 68 for Northern Districts in Auckland in December 2007 ...

THE FIGURES to 21.9.09   www.cricinfo.com

Batting & Fielding	M	Inns	NO	Runs	HS	Avge	S/R	100	50	4s	6s	Ct	St
Tests	5	9	2	127	77*	18.14	79.37	0	1	8	12	1	0
ODIs	21	10	3	96	32	13.71	124.67	0	0	7	5	1	0
Twenty20 Ints	7	3	1	15	12*	7.50	100.00	0	0	2	0	3	0
First-class	25	32	5	360	77*	13.33	66.91	0	2	30	18	4	0

Bowling	M	Balls	Runs	Wkts	BB	Avge	RpO	S/R	5i	10m
Tests	5	927	575	12	5–55	47.91	3.72	77.25	1	0
ODIs	21	1026	923	26	4–38	35.50	5.39	39.46	0	0
Twenty20 Ints	7	168	252	8	2–22	31.50	9.00	21.00	0	0
First-class	25	4999	2509	83	6–68	30.22	3.01	60.22	4	0

SREESANTH

Full name **Shanthakumaran Sreesanth**
Born **February 6, 1983, Kothamangalam, Kerala**
Teams **Kerala, Warwickshire, Kings XI Punjab**
Style **Right-hand bat, right-arm fast-medium bowler**
Test debut **India v England at Nagpur 2005-06**
ODI debut **India v Sri Lanka at Nagpur 2005-06**

THE PROFILE For three seasons, Sreesanth was little more than a quiz question, as the only Kerala bowler to take a Ranji Trophy hat-trick. He started as a legspinner, idolising Anil Kumble, then once he turned to pace his rise was rapid but, since he played for a weak side, almost unnoticed. Not many bowlers play in the Duleep Trophy in their first season, but Sreesanth did, after taking 22 wickets in his first seven games in 2002-03. A couple of years later, now equipped with a more side-on action and increased pace, a superb display at the 2005 Challenger Trophy (trial matches for the national squad) propelled him into the side for the Sri Lanka series. Later he snapped up 6 for 55 against England, still the best one-day figures by an Indian fast bowler at home. Idiosyncratic, with an aggressive approach – to the stumps and the game – he can be expensive, but is also a wicket-taking bowler: in Antigua in June 2006 he fired out Ramnaresh Sarwan and Brian Lara (both for 0) in successive overs. He sometimes rubs opponents up the wrong way, but there is talent among the tantrums: Sreesanth took 19 wickets in the inaugural Indian Premier League season in 2007-08, although his international form tailed off a little, and he has been overlooked since April 2008. A back injury in the second IPL didn't help his chances of a recall, although a stint with Warwickshire – during which he took 5 for 93 against Yorkshire – formed part of his rehabilitation.

THE FACTS Sreesanth took a hat-trick for Kerala v Himachal Pradesh in the Ranji Trophy in November 2004 ... He is only the second man from Kerala to play for India, after Tinu Yohannan, another fast-medium bowler ... Sreesanth did not score a run in ODIs until his 16th match, although that was only his fourth innings ... He took 19 wickets in the first IPL season, the same as Shane Warne and exceeded only by Sohail Tanvir (22) ...

THE FIGURES to 21.9.09   www.cricinfo.com

Batting & Fielding	M	Inns	NO	Runs	HS	Avge	S/R	100	50	4s	6s	Ct	St
Tests	14	21	7	217	35	15.50	64.97	0	0	29	4	2	0
ODIs	41	16	8	34	10*	4.25	36.17	0	0	1	0	6	0
Twenty20 Ints	10	3	2	20	19*	20.00	142.85	0	0	4	0	2	0
First-class	50	69	21	477	35	9.93	46.94	0	0	–	–	10	0

Bowling	M	Balls	Runs	Wkts	BB	Avge	RpO	S/R	5i	10m
Tests	14	2873	1573	50	5–40	31.46	3.28	57.46	1	0
ODIs	41	1925	1856	59	6–55	31.45	5/78	32.62	1	0
Twenty20 Ints	10	204	288	7	2–12	41.14	8.47	29.14	0	0
First-class	50	8993	5052	156	5–40	32.21	3.35	57.64	4	0

SOUTH AFRICA

DALE **STEYN**

Full name	**Dale Willem Steyn**
Born	**June 27, 1983, Phalaborwa, Limpopo Province**
Teams	**Titans, Bangalore Royal Challengers**
Style	**Right-hand bat, right-arm fast bowler**
Test debut	**South Africa v England at Port Elizabeth 2004-05**
ODI debut	**Africa XI v Asia XI at Centurion 2005-06**

THE PROFILE Dale Steyn's rise to the South African side was as rapid as his bowling: he was picked for his first Test little more than a year after his first-class debut. A rare first-class cricketer from the far north of South Africa, from the Limpopo province close to the Kruger National Park and the Zimbabwe border, Steyn is genuinely fast, and moves the ball away. He sprints up and hurls the ball down aggressively, often following up with a snarl for the batsman, *à la* Allan Donald. He took eight wickets in three Tests against England in 2004-05 before returning to the finishing school of domestic cricket, but was recalled in April 2006 and claimed 5 for 47 as New Zealand were routed at Centurion. He couldn't quite nail down a regular spot, though, despite six wickets in a win over India at Cape Town the following January. He had half a season of county cricket with Essex in 2005, and also rattled a few helmets for Warwickshire in 2007. But Steyn really came of age in 2007-08, taking 40 wickets in five home Tests against New Zealand and West Indies, then 14 in two matches on Bangladesh's traditionally slow tracks. Finally he blew India away with 5 for 23 as they subsided to 76 all out and defeat at Ahmedabad in April. After a subdued time in England in 2008 – he broke his thumb and missed the last two Tests – Steyn confirmed his rise to world class with 34 victims in the home-and-away series against Australia in 2008-09, including ten wickets – and a rollicking 76 during a match-turning stand of 180 with J-P Duminy – in the win at Melbourne that sealed South Africa's first-ever series win Down Under.

THE FACTS Steyn took 8 for 41 (14 for 110 in the match) for Titans v Eagles at Bloemfontein in December 2007 ... He took 10 for 93 and 10 for 91 in successive home Tests against New Zealand in November 2007 ... Steyn improved his highest first-class score by 745% by scoring 82 for Essex v Durham in July 2005: his previous-best was 11 ... He made his ODI debut for the Africa XI, and his record includes two matches for them ...

THE FIGURES *to 21.9.09*   www.cricinfo.com

Batting & Fielding	M	Inns	NO	Runs	HS	Avge	S/R	100	50	4s	6s	Ct	St
Tests	33	41	8	393	76	11.90	42.39	0	1	43	6	9	0
ODIs	29	8	3	20	6	4.00	50.00	0	0	1	0	5	0
Twenty20 Ints	12	2	1	2	1*	2.00	66.66	0	0	0	0	3	0
First-class	73	85	19	870	82	13.18	50.52	0	3	–	–	14	0

Bowling	M	Balls	Runs	Wkts	BB	Avge	RpO	S/R	5i	10m
Tests	33	6676	4029	170	6–49	23.70	3.62	39.27	11	3
ODIs	29	1365	1196	43	4–16	27.81	5.25	31.74	0	0
Twenty20 Ints	12	258	290	20	4–9	14.50	6.74	12.90	0	0
First-class	73	13963	7937	320	8–41	24.80	3.41	43.63	19	5

ANDREW **STRAUSS**

Full name	**Andrew John Strauss**
Born	**March 2, 1977, Johannesburg, South Africa**
Teams	**Middlesex**
Style	**Left-hand bat**
Test debut	**England v New Zealand at Lord's 2004**
ODI debut	**England v Sri Lanka at Dambulla 2003-04**

THE PROFILE Andrew Strauss, a fluid and attractive left-hand opener, was born in Johannesburg, but – schooled at Radley College and Durham University – is a very English product. At the crease, there is something of Graham Thorpe about his ability to accumulate runs without recourse to big shots, and it was this that first earned him a one-day place in 2003-04 after he made 1400 runs in 2003, his first full season as Middlesex's captain. He confirmed his star quality – and his affinity for Lord's – with a century on Test debut against New Zealand (hastening Nasser Hussain's retirement) in May 2004, and added another in his first ODI there. In South Africa that winter, Strauss won the first Test almost single-handedly with 126 and 94 not out, and added two further hundreds on his way to 656 runs in the series. In 2005 he overcame initial uncertainties against McGrath and Warne to record two more tons in England's Ashes victory. But after seven hundreds in his first 19 Tests, the next 34 produced only five, as bowlers probed outside off and fed a penchant for a rather uppish pull/hook: the one-day runs dried up, too. He probably saved his Test career with 177 at Napier in March 2008 – but soon after that everything changed. He started the 2008-09 winter with twin centuries against India – and ended it entrenched as England's captain, after the Pietersen–Moores fallout. Strauss showed his liking for the top job with punchy centuries in three successive Tests in the Caribbean, then topped the Ashes runscorers with 474, including a sublime 161 to set up victory at Lord's, then 55 and 75 to seal the deal at The Oval.

THE FACTS Strauss was the 15th England player to score a century on Test debut, with 112 v New Zealand at Lord's in May 2004 ... In July 2006 he became only the third man to make a century on debut as England captain, following Archie MacLaren (1897-98) and Allan Lamb (1989-90); Kevin Pietersen followed suit in 2008 ... England never lost a Test in which Strauss scored a century, until he made two at Chennai in December 2008 (his 15th and 16th hundreds) but India won by six wickets ...

THE FIGURES *to 21.9.09*   www.cricinfo.com

Batting & Fielding	M	Inns	NO	Runs	HS	Avge	S/R	100	50	4s	6s	Ct	St
Tests	67	123	5	5266	177	44.62	49.49	18	17	655	8	75	0
ODIs	92	91	8	2766	152	33.32	76.87	3	18	294	9	33	0
Twenty20 Ints	4	4	0	73	33	18.25	114.06	0	0	9	0	1	0
First-class	181	321	16	13090	177	42.91	–	35	56	–	–	148	0

Bowling	M	Balls	Runs	Wkts	BB	Avge	RpO	S/R	5i	10m
Tests	67	0	–	–	–	–	–	–	–	–
ODIs	92	6	3	0	–	–	3.00	–	0	0
Twenty20 Ints	4	0	–	–	–	–	–	–	–	–
First-class	181	102	89	2	1–16	44.50	5.23	51.00	0	0

GRAEME **SWANN**

Full name	**Graeme Peter Swann**
Born	**March 24, 1979, Northampton**
Teams	**Nottinghamshire**
Style	**Right-hand bat, offspinner**
Test debut	**England v India at Chennai 2008-09**
ODI debut	**South Africa v England at Bloemfontein 1999-2000**

THE PROFILE Self-confident and gregarious, Graeme Swann is an aggressive offspinner, not afraid to give the ball a real tweak, and a hard-hitting lower-order batsman. He claimed a place in the revamped England squad which toured South Africa in 1999-2000 under new coach Duncan Fletcher, but Swann found life outside the Test side frustrating, although he did play an ODI, in which he bravely continued to give the ball a rip. However, he was less impressive off the field – what some saw as confidence, others interpreted as arrogance or cheek – and slid out of the international reckoning. After marking time with Northamptonshire for a while, not helped by Monty Panesar's arrival, Swann moved to Trent Bridge in 2005 – a decision immediately justified when he helped Nottinghamshire win the Championship. He was recalled for the Sri Lankan tour late in 2007, and took 4 for 34 in a one-day win at Dambulla, but more modest performances followed against New Zealand, home and away, and he was soon on the outer again. However, with Panesar in something of a slump, Swann finally won his first Test cap in India in December 2008, making up for lost time by dismissing Gautam Gambhir and Rahul Dravid in his first over. He soon developed a reputation for troubling left-handers – by September 2009, 32 of his 48 Test victims were lefties, with 15 of those falling lbw. Swann played throughout the 2009 Ashes, although his returns were modest and he failed to shine when he might have bowled England to victory on the final day at Edgbaston. Still, he had the last laugh by removing Michael Hussey to secure the urn at The Oval, and remained an upbeat character throughout.

THE FACTS Swann took two wickets in his first over in Test cricket: the only other bowler ever to do this was England's Richard Johnson (v Zimbabwe at Chester-le-Street in 2003) ... Swann took 7 for 33 (after not bowling in the first innings) for Northamptonshire v Derbyshire in June 2003 ... He made 183 for Northants v Gloucestershire at Bristol in August 2002, helping Michael Hussey (310 not out) put on 318 for the sixth wicket ...

THE FIGURES *to 21.9.09*   www.cricinfo.com

Batting & Fielding	M	Inns	NO	Runs	HS	Avge	S/R	100	50	4s	6s	Ct	St
Tests	12	14	4	354	63*	35.40	78.31	0	3	47	2	7	0
ODIs	23	16	1	181	34	12.26	73.89	0	0	14	0	10	0
Twenty20 Ints	8	5	3	33	15*	16.50	117.85	0	0	2	0	0	0
First-class	187	258	21	6440	183	27.17	–	4	34	–	–	134	0

Bowling	M	Balls	Runs	Wkts	BB	Avge	RpO	S/R	5i	10m
Tests	12	2941	1459	48	5–57	30.39	2.97	61.27	2	0
ODIs	23	1008	767	30	5–28	25.56	4.56	33.60	1	0
Twenty20 Ints	8	162	188	10	2–21	18.80	6.96	16.20	0	0
First-class	187	32002	15978	486	7–33	32.87	2.99	65.84	17	3

SYED RASEL

BANGLADESH

Full name	**Syed Rasel**
Born	**July 3, 1984, Jessore, Khulna**
Teams	**Khulna**
Style	**Left-hand bat, left-arm medium-pacer**
Test debut	**Bangladesh v Sri Lanka at Colombo 2005-06**
ODI debut	**Bangladesh v Sri Lanka at Colombo 2005-06**

THE PROFILE A sensational spell of swing bowling for Bangladesh A at Canterbury in August 2005 propelled Syed Rasel into the international reckoning at the age of 21. He had missed the senior tour earlier in the season, but, having steadily developed his trade on a difficult five-week trip, Rasel tore through Kent's defences with 7 for 50 in the first innings, and finished with 10 for 91 in the match. It wasn't enough to win the game, but he was immediately drafted into the senior squad for the tour of Sri Lanka that followed in September, and he made his Test and one-day debuts there. With shades of Chaminda Vaas in his left-arm approach, Rasel took six wickets in his first two matches, including 4 for 129 in the second Test, which Bangladesh lost by an innings. Nevertheless, he soon had his revenge on home soil, taking 2 for 28 at Bogra the following February as Sri Lanka slumped to their first-ever one-day defeat at Bangladesh's hands. He rose through the ranks from divisional cricket in his home province of Khulna, and his ability to swing the ball at a modest pace sets him apart from many of his rivals. He injured his foot in a motorbike accident shortly before the Champions Trophy in India in October 2006, but recovered to play, and did enough over the season to claim a World Cup place. He troubled many batsmen in the Caribbean with his left-arm approach, only once failing to take a wicket in seven starts, but took a step backwards in 2008, not helped when he dislocated his collarbone while fielding in New Zealand then injured his back in South Africa. He remained in the one-day mix throughout 2009, but hasn't played a Test since July 2007.

THE FACTS Fourteen of Syed Rasel's ODI wickets have come against Kenya (at 15.21), and 16 (at 28.25) against Sri Lanka ... He took 7 for 55 (11 for 109 in the match) for Khulna in Dhaka, and 8 for 67 at Barisal, both in 2003-04 ... Rasel's first four Tests – and his sixth – were all against Sri Lanka ... He became Muttiah Muralitharan's 700th Test wicket, at Kandy in July 2007 ...

THE FIGURES *to 21.9.09*   www.cricinfo.com

Batting & Fielding	M	Inns	NO	Runs	HS	Avge	S/R	100	50	4s	6s	Ct	St
Tests	6	12	4	37	19	4.62	38.94	0	0	6	0	0	0
ODIs	46	23	8	72	15	4.80	43.63	0	0	6	0	8	0
Twenty20 Ints	8	3	1	7	6	3.50	77.77	0	0	1	0	1	0
First-class	42	65	22	445	33	10.34	41.20	0	0	–	–	7	0

Bowling	M	Balls	Runs	Wkts	BB	Avge	RpO	S/R	5i	10m
Tests	6	879	573	12	4–129	47.75	3.91	73.25	0	0
ODIs	46	2390	1780	59	4–22	30.16	4.46	40.50	0	0
Twenty20 Ints	8	174	202	4	1–10	50.50	6.96	43.50	0	0
First-class	42	7083	3463	119	8–67	29.10	2.93	59.52	3	2

179

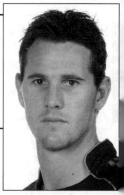

AUSTRALIA

SHAUN **TAIT**

Full name	**Shaun William Tait**
Born	**Feb 22, 1983, Bedford Park, Adelaide, South Australia**
Teams	**South Australia**
Style	**Right-hand bat, right-arm fast bowler**
Test debut	**Australia v England at Nottingham 2005**
ODI debut	**Australia v England at Sydney 2006-07**

THE PROFILE   Shaun Tait's shoulder-strong action slung him on to the 2005 Ashes tour, where he played in two of the Tests, but it soon disrupted his quest for further impact. With a muscular but unrefined method that seems to invite pain, Tait returned from England only to hurt himself in a grade match. Shoulder surgery forced him out for the rest of the year, but fortunately there seemed to be no reduction in his frightening pace. An abbreviated 2005-06 featured 6 for 41 in the domestic one-day final, an amazing combination of spot-on speed and 14 wides. His old-fashioned approach of yorkers and bumpers, mixed with a modern dose of reverse-swing, produced 65 wickets in 2004-05, his first full home season, earning him that Ashes trip. A hamstring twang delayed Tait's one-day entry until February 2007, but despite mixed results (much speed, less accuracy) at first he was bravely taken to the World Cup, and was one of the stars in the Caribbean, blowing away 23 batsmen, more than anyone except Glenn McGrath. Again there was a cost: he needed elbow surgery later in 2007, and eventually withdrew from cricket altogether, citing physical and emotional exhaustion. He did not bowl a ball for six months, but returned determined to regain his mojo. However, after sticking with him during his emotional troubles, Cricket Australia upset Tait by not offering him another contract in March 2009. He took out his frustration on some unsuspecting Surrey clubbies, and returned home raring to go again: he even got his contract back after Andrew Symonds lost his.

THE FACTS   Tait took 8 for 43 for South Australia v Tasmania at Adelaide in January 2004, the best figures in Australian domestic one-day cricket ... He played for Durham in 2004, bowling 21 no-balls in his first match, against Somerset, in figures of 12-0-113-0: in his second (and last) game the damage was 6-0-63-0 ... Tait took 23 wickets in the 2007 World Cup, equal with Muttiah Muralitharan and behind only Glenn McGrath (26) ... Tait took 7 for 29 (10 for 98 in the match) for South Australia v Queensland at Brisbane in December 2007 ...

THE FIGURES *to 21.9.09*   www.cricinfo.com

Batting & Fielding	M	Inns	NO	Runs	HS	Avge	S/R	100	50	4s	6s	Ct	St
Tests	3	5	2	20	8	6.66	43.47	0	0	4	0	1	0
ODIs	22	4	2	24	11	12.00	88.88	0	0	3	1	2	0
Twenty20 Ints	3	1	1	1	1*	–	100.00	0	0	0	0	1	0
First-class	50	70	29	509	68	12.41	51.36	0	2	–	–	15	0

Bowling	M	Balls	Runs	Wkts	BB	Avge	RpO	S/R	5i	10m
Tests	3	414	302	5	3–97	60.40	4.37	82.80	0	0
ODIs	22	1080	961	38	4–39	25.28	5.33	28.42	0	0
Twenty20 Ints	3	72	95	4	2–22	23.75	7.91	18.00	0	0
First-class	50	9263	5661	198	7–29	28.59	3.66	46.78	7	1

TAMIM IQBAL

Full name	**Tamim Iqbal Khan**
Born	**March 20, 1989, Chittagong**
Teams	**Chittagong**
Style	**Left-hand bat**
Test debut	**Bangladesh v New Zealand at Dunedin 2007-08**
ODI debut	**Bangladesh v Zimbabwe at Harare 2006-07**

THE PROFILE A flamboyant left-hander, Tamim Iqbal is one of Bangladesh's most assured young batsmen, and one of their hardest hitters. He is particularly strong square of the wicket, and has a good flick shot, but his almost premeditated charges down the track – while spectacular – sometimes bring his downfall. Selected for the 2007 World Cup after just four ODIs – in which he amassed only 57 runs against the might of Zimbabwe, Bermuda and Canada – Tamim proceeded to light up the start of the competition with 51 off 53 balls to ensure Bangladesh's pursuit of India's modest 191 got off to a flying start. Shrugging off a blow on the neck when he missed a hook at Zaheer Khan, Tamim jumped down the wicket and smashed him over midwicket for six. Bangladesh duly administered the victory which virtually ensured that they, not India, would progress to the Super Eights. All this came three days before the 18th birthday of a player with cricket in his veins (his brother and uncle played for Bangladesh as well). Tamim struggled to reproduce this form afterwards: it wasn't until his 18th ODI, in Sri Lanka in July 2007, that he reached 50 again. But the following year he made a hundred against Ireland, then in August 2009 rounded off a consistent run by hammering 154 – a Bangladesh ODI record – against Zimbabwe. It was a similar story in Tests: great start (53 and 84 against New Zealand in January 2008), quieter phase (17 innings with a highest of 47), exciting flowering (128 as West Indies were beaten in St Vincent in July 2009).

THE FACTS Tamim Iqbal hit 154, Bangladesh's highest score in ODIs, against Zimbabwe at Bulawayo in August 2009 ... He scored 53 and 84 on his Test debut, against New Zealand in Dunedin in January 2008, sharing a national-record opening stand of 161 in the second innings with Junaid Siddique ... His brother, Nafis Iqbal, has played 11 Tests and 18 ODIs for Bangladesh, while their uncle, Akram Khan, played eight Tests and 44 ODIs, and captained them in pre-Test days ...

THE FIGURES *to 21.9.09*   www.cricinfo.com

Batting & Fielding	M	Inns	NO	Runs	HS	Avge	S/R	100	50	4s	6s	Ct	St
Tests	12	22	0	608	128	27.63	46.23	1	2	87	1	5	0
ODIs	61	61	0	1729	154	28.34	72.28	2	10	196	21	20	0
Twenty20 Ints	12	12	0	160	32	13.33	89.38	0	0	23	0	2	0
First-class	32	57	1	2036	128	36.35	–	3	14	–	–	13	0

Bowling	M	Balls	Runs	Wkts	BB	Avge	RpO	S/R	5i	10m
Tests	12	12	4	0	–	–	2.00	–	0	0
ODIs	61	1	6	0	–	–	36.00	–	0	0
Twenty20 Ints	12	0	–	–	–	–	–	–	–	–
First-class	32	120	71	0	–	–	3.55	–	0	0

WEST INDIES

JEROME **TAYLOR**

Full name	**Jerome Everton Taylor**
Born	**June 22, 1984, St Elizabeth, Jamaica**
Teams	**Jamaica**
Style	**Right-hand bat, right-arm fast bowler**
Test debut	**West Indies v Sri Lanka at Gros Islet 2002-03**
ODI debut	**West Indies v Sri Lanka at Kingstown 2002-03**

THE PROFILE Jerome Taylor was just 18, with a solitary limited-overs game for Jamaica to his name, when he was called into the squad for the final one-dayer of West Indies' home series against Sri Lanka in June 2003. It was the culmination of an explosive first season: 21 wickets at 20.14 in six first-class matches included 8 for 59 (and ten in the match) in Jamaica's five-wicket victory over Trinidad & Tobago. After a persistent back injury, he returned with 26 wickets at 16.61 in 2004-05, which helped him force his way back into international contention. The inexperienced Zimbabweans found Taylor too hot to handle in the Caribbean early in 2006: he took six wickets in the first two games, winning the match award in both. He continued his good form when the Indians arrived, taking three wickets in a consolation victory at the end of the one-day series, then collecting nine – including his first five-wicket haul – in vain in the deciding Test at Kingston. He impressed in one-dayers in 2006-07, his 13 wickets in the Champions Trophy including a hat-trick against Australia, and showed occasional signs of fire in England in 2007, without much success; but he looked good in taking 19 wickets in four home Tests in 2008. He also blasted a maiden Test century in New Zealand later in the year (rather a surprise given his previous-best first-class score was just 40). By the time England arrived early in 2009 Taylor was the most menacing of the bowlers, starting the series with 5 for 11 as England crashed for 51 at Kingston, gifting West Indies the victory which ultimately won them the series.

THE FACTS Taylor was 18 years 363 days old when he made his Test debut in June 2003 ... He scored his maiden first-class century in a Test, against New Zealand in Dunedin in December 2008: 34 people had previously done this, but only one other (New Zealander Bruce Taylor in 1964-65) had never even passed 50 before ... Taylor took an ODI hat-trick against Australia in the Champions Trophy in Mumbai in October 2006 ... He took 8 for 59 in only his third first-class game, for Jamaica v Trinidad & Tobago at Port-of-Spain in March 2003 ...

THE FIGURES *to 21.9.09*   www.cricinfo.com

Batting & Fielding	M	Inns	NO	Runs	HS	Avge	S/R	100	50	4s	6s	Ct	St
Tests	28	44	6	621	106	16.34	57.98	1	1	86	12	5	0
ODIs	62	27	7	198	43*	9.90	90.00	0	0	20	4	16	0
Twenty20 Ints	12	5	3	20	11*	10.00	105.26	0	0	1	1	3	0
First-class	63	95	17	1077	106	13.80	–	1	1	–	–	15	0

Bowling	M	Balls	Runs	Wkts	BB	Avge	RpO	S/R	5i	10m
Tests	28	4881	2880	81	5–11	35.55	3.54	60.25	3	0
ODIs	62	3070	2442	92	5–48	26.54	4.77	33.36	1	0
Twenty20 Ints	12	252	344	17	3–6	20.23	8.19	14.82	0	0
First-class	63	9941	5378	202	8–59	26.62	3.24	49.21	11	2

ROSS **TAYLOR**

Full name	**Luteru Ross Poutoa Lote Taylor**
Born	**March 8, 1984, Lower Hutt, Wellington**
Teams	**Central Districts, Bangalore Royal Challengers**
Style	**Right-hand bat, offspinner**
Test debut	**New Zealand v South Africa at Johannesburg 2007-08**
ODI debut	**New Zealand v West Indies at Napier 2005-06**

THE PROFILE Ross Taylor was singled out for attention from an early age – he captained New Zealand in the 2001-02 Under-19 World Cup – but it was some time before he made the big breakthrough. In March 2005 he extended his maiden first-class century to 184, then began the following season with a bang: five sixes in a century in a warm-up game against Otago were followed by 107 in a one-dayer, also against Otago, in January 2006. He then cracked 121 against Wellington, 114 off long-suffering Otago in the semi, then 50 in the final against Canterbury. Taylor rounded off a fine season with 106 as CD won the State Championship final at Wellington. It all led to a call-up for the final two ODIs of West Indies' tour early in 2006, and a regular place the following season. He flogged Sri Lanka – Murali and all – for an unbeaten 128 in only his third match, and showed that was no fluke with an equally muscular 117 against Australia at Auckland in February 2007. A belated Test debut followed against South Africa in November, and he hit 120 against England in his third match, before entrancing Old Trafford with an unbeaten 154 in the return series, during which he also took some fine catches in the slips. Taylor started 2008-09 in good one-day touch, then found his feet in Tests again with a fine 151 against India at Napier in March 2009, followed by 107 in the next Test at Wellington. He carried on his good form in the IPL, and for New Zealand in Sri Lanka later in the year.

THE FACTS Only two New Zealanders – Martin Donnelly and Bevan Congdon (twice) – have made higher Test scores in England than Taylor's 154 not out at Manchester in 2008 ... He and Jesse Ryder put on 271, a record for New Zealand's fourth wicket, against India at Napier in March 2009 ... Taylor made 217 for Central Districts v Otago at Napier in December 2006 ... He hit 66 from 22 balls in a Twenty20 match against Otago in January 2006 ...

THE FIGURES to 21.9.09   www.cricinfo.com

Batting & Fielding	M	Inns	NO	Runs	HS	Avge	S/R	100	50	4s	6s	Ct	St
Tests	19	35	1	1343	154*	39.50	58.98	4	5	191	9	34	0
ODIs	65	59	11	1783	128*	37.14	83.39	3	10	166	39	38	0
Twenty20 Ints	22	21	2	450	63	23.68	123.28	0	3	29	22	18	0
First-class	64	107	3	4081	217	39.24	–	9	21	–	–	75	0

Bowling	M	Balls	Runs	Wkts	BB	Avge	RpO	S/R	5i	10m
Tests	19	32	14	0	–	–	2.62	–	0	0
ODIs	65	30	32	0	–	–	6.40	–	0	0
Twenty20 Ints	22	0	–	–	–	–	–	–	–	–
First-class	64	602	330	4	2–34	82.50	3.28	150.50	0	0

SACHIN **TENDULKAR**

INDIA

Full name	**Sachin Ramesh Tendulkar**
Born	**April 24, 1973, Bombay (now Mumbai)**
Teams	**Mumbai, Mumbai Indians**
Style	**Right-hand bat, occasional medium-pace/legspin**
Test debut	**India v Pakistan at Karachi 1989-90**
ODI debut	**India v Pakistan at Gujranwala 1989-90**

THE PROFILE You only have to attend a one-dayer at the Wankhede Stadium, and watch the lights flicker and the floor tremble as the massive wave of applause echoes around the ground when he comes in, to realise what Sachin Tendulkar means to Mumbai ... and India. Age, and niggling injuries, may have dimmed the light a little – he's now more of an accumulator than an artist – but he is still light-footed with bat in hand, the nearest thing to Bradman, as The Don himself recognised before his death. Sachin seems to have been around for ever: that's because he made his Test debut at 16, shrugging off a blow on the head against Pakistan; captivated England in 1990, with a maiden Test century; and similarly enchanted Australia in 1991-92. Two more big hundreds lit up the 2007-08 series Down Under, while at Christchurch in March 2009 a massive 163 filled one of the few remaining gaps on his CV – an ODI hundred in New Zealand. Indeed, he leads the list of ODI runscorers by a country mile, and owns the records for most runs and centuries in Tests too. Fitness and desire permitting, he could reach 100 international hundreds before he's done. Until he throttled back in his thirties, Tendulkar usually looked to attack, but his wicket still remains the one the opposition wants most. Small, steady at the crease before a decisive move forward or back, he remains a master, and his whipped flick to fine leg is an object of wonder. He could have starred as a bowler, as he can do offbreaks, legbreaks, or dobbly medium-pacers, and remains a handy option, especially in one-dayers.

THE FACTS Tendulkar passed his childhood idol Sunil Gavaskar's record of 34 Test centuries in December 2005: in seven Tests afterwards his highest score was 34 ... No-one is close to his 44 ODI centuries (Sanath Jayasuriya is next with 28) ... Tendulkar has hit ten Test centuries against Australia, and eight in ODIs ... His first mention in *Wisden* came when he was 14, in a stand of 664 with another future Test batsman, Vinod Kambli, in a school game ...

THE FIGURES *to 21.9.09*   www.cricinfo.com

Batting & Fielding	M	Inns	NO	Runs	HS	Avge	S/R	100	50	4s	6s	Ct	St
Tests	159	261	27	12773	248*	54.58	–	42	53	–	51	102	0
ODIs	428	418	39	16895	186*	44.57	85.77	44	91	1839	177	129	0
Twenty20 Ints	1	1	0	10	10	10.00	83.33	0	0	2	0	1	0
First-class	261	412	43	21662	248*	58.70	–	69	99	–	–	170	0

Bowling	M	Balls	Runs	Wkts	BB	Avge	RpO	S/R	5i	10m
Tests	159	3934	2272	44	3–10	51.63	3.46	89.40	0	0
ODIs	428	8015	6806	154	5–32	44.19	5.09	52.04	2	0
Twenty20 Ints	1	15	12	1	1–12	12.00	4.80	15.00	0	0
First-class	261	7299	4164	69	3–10	60.34	3.42	105.78	0	0

UPUL **THARANGA**

Full name	**Warushavithana Upul Tharanga**
Born	**February 2, 1985, Balapitiya**
Teams	**Nondescripts, Ruhuna**
Style	**Left-hand bat, occasional wicketkeeper**
Test debut	**Sri Lanka v India at Ahmedabad 2005-06**
ODI debut	**Sri Lanka v West Indies at Dambulla 2005-06**

THE PROFILE Upul Tharanga's call-up to Sri Lanka's one-day squad in July 2005 brightened a year marred by the Indian Ocean tsunami, which washed away his family home in Ambalangoda, a fishing town on the west coast. Tharanga, a wispy left-hander blessed with natural timing, had long been tipped for the big time, playing premier-league cricket at 15 and passing seamlessly through the national age-group squads. He first caught the eye during the Under-19 World Cup in 2004, with 117 against South Africa and 61 in 42 balls against India in the next game. In August 2005 he won his first one-day cap, and hit 105 against Bangladesh in only his fifth match – he celebrated modestly, aware that stiffer challenges lay ahead – then pummelled 165 against them in his third Test. During 2006 he lit up Lord's with 120 in the first of what became five successive defeats of England: he added 109 in the fifth of those, at Headingley, sharing a record opening stand with Sanath Jayasuriya. The feature of those innings was the way he made room to drive through the off side. A bright future beckoned for Tharanga, and he scored consistently during 2006-07, playing throughout the World Cup and scoring 73 in the semi-final against New Zealand, before struggling the following season and losing his place. He emerged from the doldrums in 2008-09, passing 150 twice for the A team in South Africa then making his maiden double-century in a domestic match. In August 2009 he scored 76 in a one-dayer against New Zealand – his first international fifty for more than two years – and celebrated with 80 in the next game.

THE FACTS Tharanga and Sanath Jayasuriya put on 286 in 31.5 overs against England at Leeds in July 2006, a first-wicket record for all ODIs ... He averages 47.60 in ODIs against England, but 11 v Australia (and 0 v Ireland) ... Tharanga carried his bat for 265 for Ruhuna v Basnahira South in March 2009 ... He scored 165 and 71 not out in the ten-wicket defeat of Bangladesh at Bogra in March 2006 ... His record includes one ODI for the Asia XI ...

THE FIGURES to 21.9.09   www.cricinfo.com

Batting & Fielding	M	Inns	NO	Runs	HS	Avge	S/R	100	50	4s	6s	Ct	St
Tests	15	26	1	713	165	28.52	49.51	1	3	99	5	11	0
ODIs	82	78	1	2361	120	30.66	70.66	6	11	278	6	15	0
Twenty20 Ints	8	8	0	114	37	14.25	116.32	0	0	10	3	1	0
First-class	69	119	4	4033	265*	35.06	–	8	17	–	–	56	1

Bowling	M	Balls	Runs	Wkts	BB	Avge	RpO	S/R	5i	10m
Tests	15	0	–	–	–	–	–	–	–	–
ODIs	82	0	–	–	–	–	–	–	–	–
Twenty20 Ints	8	0	–	–	–	–	–	–	–	–
First-class	69	18	4	0	–	–	1.33	–	0	0

SRI LANKA

DEVON **THOMAS**

WEST INDIES

Full name   **Devon Cuthbert Thomas**
Born   **November 12, 1989, Bethesda, Antigua**
Teams   **Leeward Islands**
Style   **Right-hand bat, wicketkeeper, occ. medium-pacer**
Test debut   **No Tests yet**
ODI debut   **West Indies v Bangladesh at Roseau 2009**

THE PROFILE Devon "Boobie" Thomas set Antiguan cricket alight in 2007, smashing two double-centuries for his club side Bethesda at the tender age of 17. One of them was an innings of 277, while the other – a round 200 – came after he was joined by the last man when only 85: the tenth wicket added 130. He later slammed 224 in a 50-over game for Antigua's Under-19s against the British Virgin Islands. Thomas made his first-class debut in January 2008, and the following month kept wicket in the Under-19 World Cup. His keeping is tidy, but his batting may turn out to be his stronger suit. After playing for West Indies A against the England tourists early in 2009 (he made a neat 38 in a total of 574 dominated by Lendl Simmons's 282), Thomas hit his maiden first-class hundred for the A team against Bangladesh at Bridgetown in July. When the senior players withdrew as a divisive dispute over contracts rumbled on, Thomas was overlooked for the reserve side which played the Tests – but he was called up for the one-dayers and made his debut in the second game at Roseau. Oddly, it was not as a batsman (he didn't get to the crease) or a wicketkeeper that he made his mark, but as a bowler. Called into service when Kemar Roach was removed from the attack for bowling beamers, Thomas dismissed Mahmudullah with his second ball and Mushfiqur Rahim with his seventh (it wasn't quite enough: Bangladesh still won by three wickets, with six balls left). However, Thomas's batting talent is such that if he can improve his wicketkeeping he could challenge Denesh Ramdin for a regular place.

THE FACTS Thomas scored 105 for West Indies A against Bangladesh at Bridgetown in July 2009 ... After starting the match as wicketkeeper, he took a wicket with his second ball in ODIs, against Bangladesh at Roseau in July 2009 ... Thomas opened for Antigua against the Indian tourists in May 2006, aged 16, and scored 30 ... He made 53 against South Africa in the Under-19 World Cup in Kuala Lumpur in 2008 ...

THE FIGURES to 21.9.09   www.cricinfo.com

Batting & Fielding	M	Inns	NO	Runs	HS	Avge	S/R	100	50	4s	6s	Ct	St
Tests	0	0	–	–	–	–	–	–	–	–	–	–	–
ODIs	2	1	1	29	29*	–	90.62	0	0	2	0	3	0
Twenty20 Ints	1	0	–	–	–	–	–	–	–	–	–	0	0
First-class	17	24	0	617	105	25.70	–	1	2	–	–	43	1

Bowling	M	Balls	Runs	Wkts	BB	Avge	RpO	S/R	5i	10m
Tests	0	0	–	–	–	–	–	–	–	–
ODIs	2	7	11	2	2–11	5.50	9.42	3.50	0	0
Twenty20 Ints	1	0	–	–	–	–	–	–	–	–
First-class	17	0	–	–	–	–	–	–	–	–

THILAN **THUSHARA**

Full name	**Magina Thilan Thushara Mirando**
Born	**March 1, 1981, Balapitiya**
Teams	**Sinhalese Sports Club, Kandurata, Chennai Super Kings**
Style	**Left-hand bat, left-arm fast-medium bowler**
Test debut	**West Indies v Sri Lanka at Kingston, 2003**
ODI debut	**West Indies v Sri Lanka at Gros Islet, 2007-08**

THE PROFILE A left-arm seam bowler who bats a bit, Thilan Thushara Mirando served a long international apprenticeship behind the evergreen Chaminda Vaas. And in 2009, with Vaas finally creaking into well-earned retirement, Thushara seemed to have sealed a regular Test place at last. He took 12 wickets in the home series against Pakistan in July 2009, including 5 for 83 – his first five-for – in the third Test in Colombo (Vaas's farewell game). Six more wickets followed in the defeat of New Zealand at Galle in August. He hasn't yet matched Vaas's tenacity with the bat, although he does have a first-class century to his name and can give the ball a thump. Thushara hails from the coastal town of Balapitiya, and made his first-class debut as long ago as August 1999. After a few years of steady improvement, including a spell with the Sri Lankan Board's Fast Bowling Unit, he made his Test debut against West Indies in June 2003, but failed to take a wicket and dropped off the international radar for five years. In 2007-08 he was the leading wicket-taker as Kandurata shared the inter-provincial one-day title, and won a recall for another West Indian tour. This time he took five wickets in the Test victory in Guyana, and three more (including Chris Gayle in both innings) as West Indies squared the series in Trinidad. He also made his ODI debut there, and has been a regular ever since, latterly forming an incisive new-ball pairing with Nuwan Kulasekara. Thushara took 5 for 47 in vain against India in Colombo in August 2008.

THE FACTS Thushara took 6 for 50 (10 for 868 in the match) for Sinhalese Sports Club v Chilaw Marians in Colombo in March 2008 ... He scored 103 not out (from 81 balls, after coming in at 98 for 7) for Nondescripts against Burgher RC in Colombo in January 2003 ... Thushara took his first Test wicket almost five years after his debut ...

THE FIGURES to 21.9.09   www.cricinfo.com

Batting & Fielding	M	Inns	NO	Runs	HS	Avge	S/R	100	50	4s	6s	Ct	St
Tests	9	13	2	90	15*	8.18	45.68	0	0	12	0	3	0
ODIs	31	24	6	346	54*	19.22	96.64	0	1	29	7	3	0
Twenty20 Ints	5	2	0	4	3	2.00	50.00	0	0	0	0	2	0
First-class	98	144	15	1968	103*	15.25	–	1	5	–	–	38	0

Bowling	M	Balls	Runs	Wkts	BB	Avge	RpO	S/R	5i	10m
Tests	9	1542	961	28	5–83	34.32	3.73	55.07	1	0
ODIs	31	1335	1048	42	5–47	24.95	4.71	31.78	1	0
Twenty20 Ints	5	108	138	5	2–37	27.60	7.66	21.60	0	0
First-class	98	126868	7531	256	6–50	29.41	3.56	49.55	8	1

JONATHAN **TROTT**

Full name	**Ian Jonathan Leonard Trott**
Born	**April 22, 1981, Cape Town, South Africa**
Teams	**Warwickshire**
Style	**Right-hand bat, right-arm medium-pacer**
Test debut	**England v Australia at The Oval 2009**
ODI debut	**England v Ireland at Belfast 2009**

ENGLAND

THE PROFILE The story sounds familiar: aggressive right-hander, born in South Africa, reputation for cockiness on the county circuit. But no, we're not talking Kevin Pietersen here, rather Jonathan Trott, who moved to England (after playing for South Africa in the Under-19 World Cup) in 2003. His grandparents were British, which meant he could play as a non-overseas player for Warwickshire, although he didn't actually become eligible for England until 2006. He was consistent from the start, following up 763 runs from ten matches in 2003 by passing 1000 in each of the next three seasons. His form dipped in 2007 – only 473 runs at 22 – although, contrarily, he was a left-field pick for England's two Twenty20 games against West Indies that summer. Trott managed only 9 and 2, and returned post haste to county cricket. But he was back to form in 2008 (1240 runs at 62), and when he continued to make runs in 2009, in an eye-catchingly forthright manner, he was named in the squad for the fourth Ashes Test. He didn't play there, but retained his place – despite the clamour for a Mark Ramprakash recall – for the vital final Test at The Oval after Ravi Bopara was dropped. The selectors' bravery in sticking with Trott (the first Englishman to make his debut in an Ashes decider since 1896) was repaid in spades with a nerveless century, which followed a promising 41, cut short by a reflex run-out. Trott has all the shots, even if a propensity for the off side suggests he might be an lbw candidate. He has also done well in one-day cricket for Warwickshire – he was the leading domestic Twenty20 runs cover in 2009 – and it was astonishing that England ignored him throughout their dispiriting series of thrashings by Australia in the one-day series that followed the Tests.

THE FACTS Trott was the 18th batsman to score a century on Test debut for England: the previous three (Alistair Cook, Matt Prior and Andrew Strauss) were also playing against Australia at The Oval in 2009 ... Trott made 210 for Warwickshire v Sussex at Edgbaston in August 2005 ... He took 7 for 39 for Warwickshire v Kent at Canterbury in September 2003 ...

THE FIGURES *to 21.9.09*　　　　　　　　　　　　www.cricinfo.com

Batting & Fielding	M	Inns	NO	Runs	HS	Avge	S/R	100	50	4s	6s	Ct	St
Tests	1	2	0	160	119	80.00	58.39	1	0	17	0	1	0
ODIs	1	1	0	0	0	0.00	0.00	0	0	0	0	0	0
Twenty20 Ints	3	3	1	11	9	5.50	61.11	0	0	0	0	0	0
First-class	134	223	29	8728	210	44.98	–	20	44	–	–	131	0

Bowling	M	Balls	Runs	Wkts	BB	Avge	RpO	S/R	5i	10m
Tests	1	0	–	–	–	–	–	–	–	–
ODIs	1	0	–	–	–	–	–	–	–	–
Twenty20 Ints	3	0	–	–	–	–	–	–	–	–
First-class	134	4128	2310	51	7–39	45.29	3.35	80.94	1	0

LONWABO **TSOTSOBE**

Full name	**Lonwabo Lopsy Tsotsobe**
Born	**March 7, 1984, Port Elizabeth**
Teams	**Warriors**
Style	**Right-hand bat, left-arm fast-medium**
Test debut	**No Tests yet**
ODI debut	**South Africa v Australia at Perth 2008-09**

THE PROFILE A tall left-arm swing bowler, Lonwabo Tsotsobe had a dream start to his ODI career in Australia in January 2009, when he had Shaun Marsh caught at midwicket, and a couple of overs later removed Ricky Ponting to a catch behind. Later on he nabbed Mike Hussey and Mitchell Johnson as well, to finish with debut figures of 4 for 50 as South Africa romped to a 4-1 series victory which helped them pinch the No. 1 one-day ranking from the Aussies. This put him in the frame for a Test cap when the Australians visited South Africa shortly afterwards, but after being named in the 12 for the second Test Tsotsobe was forced to withdraw with knee-cartilage damage, which kept him on the sidelines for the rest of the season. In his absence his Warriors team-mate Wayne Parnell, who is a bit quicker through the air and a better batsman, took the chance to claim a one-day place, and also did well at the World Twenty20 in England. Still, Tsotsobe was rewarded with a national contract, although Parnell could well prove a formidable obstacle to a regular place. Tsotsobe made his first-class debut for Eastern Province in 2004-05, taking 7 for 44 in his first match, against Boland. He moved up a notch to play for Warriors in 2006-07, and again did well, following a solid debut season for them with 49 wickets at 23.59 the following summer, before 12 wickets in two matches against Sri Lanka A in September 2008 earned him that trip to Australia.

THE FACTS Tsotsobe took 7 for 44 (9 for 96 in the match) on his first-class debut for Eastern Province against Boland at Paarl in November 2004, and took 10 for 72 in the match for EP against South Western Districts in Port Elizabeth in October 2006 ... He took 7 for 39 for Warriors v Lions at Johannesburg in October 2007 ... Tsotsobe's first victim in both Twenty20 internationals and ODIs was the Australian batsman Shaun Marsh ...

THE FIGURES to 21.9.09   www.cricinfo.com

Batting & Fielding	M	Inns	NO	Runs	HS	Avge	S/R	100	50	4s	6s	Ct	St
Tests	0	0	–	–	–	–	–	–	–	–	–	–	–
ODIs	1	0	–	–	–	–	–	–	–	–	–	2	0
Twenty20 Ints	1	1	0	1	1	1.00	14.28	0	0	0	0	0	0
First-class	35	47	20	174	27*	6.44	29.79	0	0	21	3	8	0

Bowling	M	Balls	Runs	Wkts	BB	Avge	RpO	S/R	5i	10m
Tests	0	0	–	–	–	–	–	–	–	–
ODIs	1	54	50	4	4–50	12.50	5.55	13.50	0	0
Twenty20 Ints	1	12	16	1	1–16	16.00	8.00	12.00	0	0
First-class	35	6102	3024	142	7–39	21.29	2.97	42.97	5	1

DARYL **TUFFEY**

Full name **Daryl Raymond Tuffey**
Born **June 11, 1978, Milton, Otago**
Teams **Auckland**
Style **Right-hand bat, right-arm fast-medium bowler**
Test debut **New Zealand v Australia at Hamilton 1999-2000**
ODI debut **New Zealand v Zimbabwe at Harare 2000-01**

THE PROFILE Big Daryl Tuffey has made a surprising comeback to New Zealand colours, resurrecting an international career that looked over after the 2007 World Cup. Tuffey seemed to have burned his bridges by joining the unauthorised Indian Cricket League, but when an amnesty was declared in mid-2009 he was suddenly back in the national reckoning, following 27 wickets in the 2008-09 domestic season for Auckland, his best return since 34 in 2000-01. "I'd like to think I'm a little wiser after a couple of years out. I think I'm physically stronger than I was when I was playing a few years ago," he said. He was chosen for the tour of Sri Lanka in September, although in the end he sat out the Tests and the one-dayers, despite taking 5 for 53 against Sri Lanka A in a one-day warm-up game (Shane Bond, the other ICL returnee, did make his international comeback in the one-day series). In the first part of his international career Tuffey, a strapping fast-medium bowler in the style of Richard Hadlee's long-time partner Ewen Chatfield, had proved an admirable foil for Bond – slower, but more durable. He also established a happy knack of taking wickets in the first over of a new spell. His best Test performance was a probing 6 for 54 at Auckland, which helped New Zealand square the home series against England in 2001-02. After that Tuffey was a regular member of both the Test and one-day sides for a while, before injuries started to impinge, notably a serious shoulder problem which kept him out for almost two years.

THE FACTS Tuffey took 7 for 12 (11 for 66 in the match) for Northern Districts v Wellington at Hamilton in February 2001: he took the first six wickets as Wellington stumbled to 29 for 6 ... His best Test figures are 6 for 54, against England at Auckland in March 2002: the previous week he took 7 for 60 for ND against Canterbury at Christchurch ...

THE FIGURES to 21.9.09   www.cricinfo.com

Batting & Fielding	M	Inns	NO	Runs	HS	Avge	S/R	100	50	4s	6s	Ct	St
Tests	22	30	7	263	35	11.43	36.52	0	0	28	1	12	0
ODIs	81	42	20	156	20*	7.09	60.46	0	0	14	1	19	0
Twenty20 Ints	1	1	1	5	5*	–	250.00	0	0	1	0	0	0
First-class	79	93	22	1012	89*	14.25	–	0	4	–	–	33	0

Bowling	M	Balls	Runs	Wkts	BB	Avge	RpO	S/R	5i	10m
Tests	22	4110	2057	66	6–54	31.16	3.00	62.27	2	0
ODIs	81	3728	2945	92	4–24	32.01	4.73	40.52	0	0
Twenty20 Ints	1	24	50	1	1–50	50.00	12.50	24.00	0	0
First-class	79	14705	6813	267	7–12	25.51	2.77	55.07	10	1

MAHELA **UDAWATTE**

Full name	**Mahela Lakmal Udawatte**
Born	**July 19, 1986, Colombo**
Teams	**Chilaw Marians, Wayamba**
Style	**Left-hand bat, occasional offspinner**
Test debut	**No Tests yet**
ODI debut	**Sri Lanka v West Indies at Port-of-Spain 2007-08**

THE PROFILE Mahela Udawatte was a prolific runmaker for Ananda College, but his talents were initially overlooked by the Sri Lankan selectors, who ignored him when they chose the national Under-19 team in 2003, even though he had made more than 1000 runs at school level that season. Undaunted, Udawatte joined Chilaw Marians straight from school, and was soon opening the batting (he'd usually gone in at No. 3 before). After he reeled off three hundreds in five matches in the national under–23 tournament in 2004-05 the powers-that-be could ignore him no longer, and he joined the development squad. He progressed to the A team for the tour of England in 2007, after top-scoring for Chilaw Marians in the Premier Championship final against Sinhalese Sports Club in March 2006, with 67 out of 172 against an attack which included the Test fast bowlers Dilhara Fernando and Nuwan Zoysa. A powerful and attacking left-hander who likes to take on the quicks, Udawatte is seen by some as the eventual replacement for Sanath Jayasuriya. He went to the West Indies early in 2008, where he made 73 in his third one-day international. An innings of 67 followed in his only outing in the Asia Cup, then he made a mature 43 against India at the Premadasa Stadium in Colombo to help set up a winning total in a rain-affected match. He was left out after a modest run in a one-day series in Zimbabwe at the end of 2008, but in July 2009 thumped 161 for Sri Lanka A against the Pakistan tourists to keep his name in the frame.

THE FACTS Udawatte hit 168 for Chilaw Marians v Bloomfield in Colombo in February 2008 ... He was out for a duck in his first ODI, against West Indies in Trinidad in April 2008, but made 73 in his third, in St Lucia, and 67 in his fourth, against the UAE in the Asia Cup ... Udawatte hit 161 as Sri Lanka A beat the touring Pakistanis in a one-day game at Kurunegala in July 2009 ...

THE FIGURES to 21.9.09   www.cricinfo.com

Batting & Fielding	M	Inns	NO	Runs	HS	Avge	S/R	100	50	4s	6s	Ct	St
Tests	0	0	–	–	–	–	–	–	–	–	–	–	–
ODIs	9	9	0	257	73	28.55	67.10	0	2	25	3	0	0
Twenty20 Ints	5	5	0	77	25	15.40	122.22	0	0	8	2	0	0
First-class	52	95	25	2812	168	31.24	–	3	18	–	–	25	0

Bowling	M	Balls	Runs	Wkts	BB	Avge	RpO	S/R	5i	10m
Tests	0	0	–	–	–	–	–	–	–	–
ODIs	9	0	–	–	–	–	–	–	–	–
Twenty20 Ints	5	0	–	–	–	–	–	–	–	–
First-class	52	210	144	5	2–31	28.80	4.11	42.00	0	0

UMAR AKMAL

Full name	**Mohammad Umar Akmal**
Born	**May 26, 1990, Lahore, Punjab**
Teams	**Lahore, Sui Northern Gas**
Style	**Right-hand batsman**
Test debut	**No Tests yet**
ODI debut	**Pakistan v Sri Lanka at Dambulla 2009**

THE PROFILE Umar Akmal, the youngest brother of Pakistan's wicketkeeper Kamran Akmal, started his international career with a flourish in 2009. Only 19, he hit a run-a-ball 66 in only his second match, against Sri Lanka at Dambulla, and bettered that with a superb maiden century to earn a consolation victory in the fourth match in Colombo. An attacking right-hander, he entered in that innings with Pakistan a wobbly 130 for 4 in the 26th over, and hurtled to his hundred from just 70 balls. He outscored Younis Khan, his captain, in a stand of 176, and appeared comfortable from the start. He refused to be tied down, swinging his seventh delivery – from Ajantha Mendis – over long-on for the first of four sixes. He pierced minute gaps in the field, and sprinted his runs (not always a Pakistani strength) as the total mounted. His international start mirrored his domestic one. In a triumphant 2007-08 season, Umar amassed 855 runs from nine Quaid-e-Azam Trophy matches, at an average of 77.72 and an impressive strike-rate of 90.18. He extended his maiden century – in his sixth match – to 248 (off 225 balls) against Karachi Blues, and two matches later clattered 186 not out from 170 balls against Quetta. Three centuries followed for Pakistan A in Australia before he joined Kamran in the Pakistan line-up. Intikhab Alam, the national coach, said: "The good thing about him is that he is not afraid to play his shots. He accepts challenges, and to hit Lasith Malinga over his head for a six is not a joke. You've got to have a lot of ability to do that."

THE FACTS Umar Akmal made 248 for Sui Northern Gas v Karachi Blues in Karachi in December 2007, and later that month hit 186 not out against Quetta at Lahore ... He hit a century, from only 70 balls, in his fourth one-day international, against Sri Lanka in Colombo in August 2009 ... Umar and Kamran Akmal were the first brothers to play together in an ODI for Pakistan since Moin and Nadeem Khan in 1994-95 ...

THE FIGURES to 21.9.09   www.cricinfo.com

Batting & Fielding	M	Inns	NO	Runs	HS	Avge	S/R	100	50	4s	6s	Ct	St
Tests	0	0	–	–	–	–	–	–	–	–	–	–	–
ODIs	4	4	1	192	102*	64.00	110.34	1	1	13	6	2	0
Twenty20 Ints	1	1	0	30	30	30.00	150.00	0	0	4	0	2	0
First-class	26	42	5	1930	248	52.16	75.24	5	12	242	26	25	0

Bowling	M	Balls	Runs	Wkts	BB	Avge	RpO	S/R	5i	10m
Tests	0	0	–	–	–	–	–	–	–	–
ODIs	4	0	–	–	–	–	–	–	–	–
Twenty20 Ints	1	0	–	–	–	–	–	–	–	–
First-class	26	0	–	–	–	–	–	–	–	–

UMAR GUL

Full name	**Umar Gul**
Born	**April 14, 1984, Peshawar, North-Western Frontier Province**
Teams	**Peshawar, Habib Bank, Western Australia**
Style	**Right-hand bat, right-arm fast-medium bowler**
Test debut	**Pakistan v Bangladesh at Karachi 2003-04**
ODI debut	**Pakistan v Zimbabwe at Sharjah 2002-03**

THE PROFILE Umar Gul was called up by Pakistan at 19, after their miserable 2003 World Cup campaign. He usually keeps a good line, and obtains appreciable outswing with the new ball, while he can also nip the ball back in. He had a gentle introduction to Test cricket, collecting 15 wickets against Bangladesh, then he starred in his only Test of India's tour in April 2004, at Lahore. Gul, disparaged by some as the "Peshawar Rickshaw" to Shoaib Akhtar's "Rawalpindi Express", tore through India's imposing top order, moving the ball both ways off the seam at a sharp pace. His 5 for 31 gave Pakistan the early initiative, and they went on to level the series. Stress fractures in the back kept him out after that, and it was two years before he returned. In the absence of several senior seamers in England in 2006 he looked the best of the rest, particularly enjoying the conditions at Headingley, with five first-innings wickets as the others struggled. He maintained his progress in 2006-07, taking nine wickets in the first Test against West Indies at Lahore before missing the South African tour with a knee injury. He was back for the World Cup, and was one of the few to return with reputation intact, but more injuries restricted him before he started 2009 in fine fettle with a six-for against Sri Lanka on a batting paradise at Lahore. He has proved a Twenty20 star, usually coming on after the initial overs and firing in yorkers on demand. He was the leading wicket-taker at both the 2007 and 2009 world championships, and was the first to take a five-for in Twenty20 internationals.

THE FACTS Umar Gul was the first bowler to take five wickets in a Twenty20 international, with 5 for 6 v New Zealand at The Oval in June 2009: he also took 4 for 8 v Australia in Dubai in May 2009 ... He took 8 for 78 for Peshawar v Karachi Urban at Peshawar in October 2005 ... Gul claimed 5 for 46 on his first-class debut, for Pakistan International Airlines v ADBP at Karachi in his only match in 2000-01, then took 45 wickets at 18.62 in 2001-02, his first full season of domestic cricket ...

THE FIGURES to 21.9.09   www.cricinfo.com

Batting & Fielding	M	Inns	NO	Runs	HS	Avge	S/R	100	50	4s	6s	Ct	St
Tests	21	26	2	203	46	8.45	41.59	0	0	22	7	5	0
ODIs	60	24	8	178	33	11.12	71.48	0	0	17	4	6	0
Twenty20 Ints	21	6	5	19	9*	19.00	146.15	0	0	1	1	7	0
First-class	48	55	7	548	46	11.41	–	0	0	–	–	12	0

Bowling	M	Balls	Runs	Wkts	BB	Avge	RpO	S/R	5i	10m
Tests	21	4452	2690	83	6–135	32.40	3.62	53.63	4	0
ODIs	60	2861	2352	90	5–17	26.13	4.93	31.78	1	0
Twenty20 Ints	21	457	410	37	5–6	11.08	5.38	12.35	1	0
First-class	48	9647	5623	216	8–78	26.03	3.49	44.66	14	1

SOUTH AFRICA

ROELOF **VAN DER MERWE**

Full name	**Roelof Erasmus van der Merwe**
Born	**December 31, 1984, Johannesburg, Transvaal**
Teams	**Titans, Bangalore Royal Challengers**
Style	**Right-hand bat, slow left-arm orthodox spinner**
Test debut	**No Tests yet**
ODI debut	**South Africa v Australia at Centurion 2008-09**

THE PROFILE Roelof van der Merwe is that modern phenomenon, a limited-overs specialist – and his particular specialty is Twenty20 cricket. He is a curious mix: a blacksmith of a batsman, whose main idea is to smash the ball as far as possible, but a tidy left-arm spinner who keeps it tight. He played in the Under-19 World Cup in 2004 before starting a modest first-class career with Northerns (he started with a duck, and still hasn't managed a hundred or a five-for). But he soon made his presence felt in one-day cricket, topping the wickets list in the domestic 45-over championship after moving to Titans for 2007-08. Titans won that and the Standard Bank Pro20 series, and van der Merwe was named player of the year, among a clutch of other awards. The following season he took 30 wickets – 14 more than anyone else – as Titans retained their 45-over title, and was called up for the two Twenty20 games against Australia at home in March 2009. In the first one, at Centurion, he picked up the match award after biffing 48 from 30 balls, with four sixes, and taking a wicket. He also played in four of the ODIs which followed, then played a big part in South Africa's march to the semi-finals of the World Twenty20 in England, keeping his economy rate down below six an over, although his big hitting was more hit and miss. Before that he had helped Bangalore Royal Challengers to the final of the second IPL tournament, held in South Africa. After all this he edged out Wayne Parnell and Lonwabo Tsotsobe to be named South Africa's international newcomer of the year for 2009.

THE FACTS van der Merwe scored 48, took a wicket and effected a run-out to clinch the match award on his Twenty20 international debut against Australia at Centurion in March 2009 ... He made 81 for Northerns v North West in February 2009 ... In a Twenty20 game for Titans v Zimbabwe at Centurion in April 2008 van der Merwe took 3 for 18 then scored 70 not out ... He took 5 for 31, and then made 64 not out from 42 balls, as Titans beat Cape Cobras in a 45-over semi-final at Centurion in January 2009 ...

THE FIGURES to 21.9.09   www.cricinfo.com

Batting & Fielding	M	Inns	NO	Runs	HS	Avge	S/R	100	50	4s	6s	Ct	St
Tests	0	0	–	–	–	–	–	–	–	–	–	–	–
ODIs	4	2	1	9	6*	9.00	112.50	0	0	0	1	1	0
Twenty20 Ints	7	3	0	49	48	16.33	125.64	0	0	2	4	4	0
First-class	14	20	5	511	81	34.06	62.77	0	2	56	4	8	0

Bowling	M	Balls	Runs	Wkts	BB	Avge	RpO	S/R	5i	10m
Tests	0	0	–	–	–	–	–	–	–	–
ODIs	4	210	149	8	3–37	18.62	4.25	26.25	0	0
Twenty20 Ints	7	168	165	11	2–14	15.00	5.89	15.27	0	0
First-class	14	2051	1063	28	4–59	37.96	3.10	73.25	0	0

VAUGHN **VAN JAARSVELD**

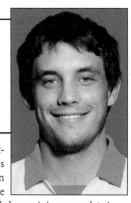

Full name	**Vaughn Bernard van Jaarsveld**
Born	**February 2, 1985, Johannesburg, Transvaal**
Teams	**Lions**
Style	**Left-hand bat, occasional right-arm medium-pacer**
Test debut	**No Tests yet**
ODI debut	**South Africa v Australia at Melbourne 2008-09**

THE PROFILE Vaughn van Jaarsveld is a hard-hitting left-hander who has enjoyed considerable success in South Africa's Pro20 competition. A consistent scorer in all formats, he was chosen for South Africa's one-day squad in Australia in 2008-09. In the event he arrived in Australia quicker than expected, after being called up as injury cover late in the Test portion of that triumphant tour. He didn't make the five-day side in the end, but did make his one-day debut Down Under, playing two ODIs without reaching double figures. He also played three Twenty20 games in Australia and at home without overly troubling the scorers, and missed out on the World Twenty20 in England that followed. No relation to the former South African batsman Martin, who now plies his trade for Kent, this van Jaarsveld also flirted with a career in English county cricket. He signed a two-year deal with Warwickshire as a Kolpak player in 2007. "I am now committed to playing for England," he said at the time, "I have made my intentions clear. I'm here to qualify as an Englishman. I'm going to be spending at least 210 days a year over in England and the aim is to play for England." However, in the winter of 2007-08 he breached his contract by returning home, and Warwickshire terminated the deal. "It's a disappointing situation," said Ashley Giles, the former England spinner who is now Warwickshire's director of cricket. "He's signed a contract, a lucrative one for a young guy, and we're paying him. He was in our plans but now he tells us he doesn't want to come back."

THE FACTS van Jaarsveld hit 159 (and 68) for Lions v Dolphins at Pietermaritzburg in November 2006 ... Three of his first-class hundreds have been scored against the Dolphins, and the other two against the Warriors ... van Jaarsveld played for South Africa's Under-15s in the world challenge in England in 2000 ... He hit five sixes (and two fours) in his 65 not out from 37 balls for Lions v Zimbabwe in a Twenty20 game at Johannesburg in March 2008 ...

THE FIGURES to 21.9.09   www.cricinfo.com

Batting & Fielding	M	Inns	NO	Runs	HS	Avge	S/R	100	50	4s	6s	Ct	St
Tests	0	0	–	–	–	–	–	–	–	–	–	–	–
ODIs	2	2	0	9	5	4.50	60.00	0	0	0	0	1	0
Twenty20 Ints	3	3	0	15	12	5.00	656.21	0	0	0	0	0	0
First-class	42	74	5	2638	159	38.23	60.36	5	21	–	–	43	0

Bowling	M	Balls	Runs	Wkts	BB	Avge	RpO	S/R	5i	10m
Tests	0	0	–	–	–	–	–	–	–	–
ODIs	2	0	–	–	–	–	–	–	–	–
Twenty20 Ints	3	0	–	–	–	–	–	–	–	–
First-class	42	18	11	0	–	–	3.66	–	0	0

DANIEL **VETTORI**

Full name **Daniel Luca Vettori**
Born **January 27, 1979, Auckland**
Teams **Northern Districts, Delhi Daredevils**
Style **Left-hand bat, left-arm orthodox spinner**
Test debut **New Zealand v England at Wellington 1996-97**
ODI debut **New Zealand v Sri Lanka at Christchurch 1996-97**

THE PROFILE Daniel Vettori is probably the best left-arm spinner around – an assessment reinforced by his selection for the World XI in Australia late in 2005 – and the only cloud on his horizon is a susceptibility to injury, particularly in the bowler's danger area of the back. He seemed to have recovered from one stress fracture, which led to a dip in form in 2003, but after a couple of matches for Warwickshire in 2006 he was on the plane home nursing another one. Vettori has usually been fit since, though, which is just as well as he carries a huge burden these days as New Zealand's captain, handy batsman and senior bowler (he passed 300 Test wickets in Sri Lanka late in 2009). His early Tests in charge, after succeeding Stephen Fleming, were notable for some superb personal performances – two fifties and nine wickets to stave off embarrassing defeat by Bangladesh in October 2008, and two similar allround efforts which could not prevent defeat in Sri Lanka the following August. Vettori still has the enticing flight and guile that made him New Zealand's youngest Test player at 18 in 1996-97, and he remains economical in 50- and 20-over games. After his mini-slump he returned to form in England in 2004, then butchered Bangladesh with 20 wickets in two Tests. He has improved his batting – after starting at No. 11, blinking nervously through his glasses – to the point that his four centuries include New Zealand's fastest in Tests, an 82-ball effort against the admittedly hopeless Zimbabweans at Harare in August 2005.

THE FACTS Vettori made his first-class debut in 1996-97, for Northern Districts against the England tourists: his maiden first-class victim was Nasser Hussain ... Three weeks later Vettori became NZ's youngest-ever Test player, at 18 years 10 days: his first wicket was Hussain again ... Vettori has taken 57 Test wickets against Australia and 51 v Sri Lanka, but only 4 at 100.25 v Pakistan ... His record includes a Test and four ODIs for the World XI ...

THE FIGURES *to 21.9.09*   www.cricinfo.com

Batting & Fielding	M	Inns	NO	Runs	HS	Avge	S/R	100	50	4s	6s	Ct	St
Tests	94	141	23	3492	140	29.59	56.59	4	20	440	12	48	0
ODIs	241	146	46	1532	83	15.32	79.17	0	3	115	8	65	0
Twenty20 Ints	18	13	3	67	17*	6.70	106.34	0	0	7	0	7	0
First-class	146	209	31	5339	140	29.99	–	7	30	–	–	72	0

Bowling	M	Balls	Runs	Wkts	BB	Avge	RpO	S/R	5i	10m
Tests	94	23125	10156	303	7–87	33.51	2.63	76.32	18	3
ODIs	241	11342	7883	244	5–7	32.30	4.17	46.48	2	0
Twenty20 Ints	18	426	390	27	4–20	14.44	5.49	15.77	0	0
First-class	146	33850	15069	477	7–87	31.59	2.67	70.96	28	3

MURALI **VIJAY**

Full name	**Murali Vijay Krishna**
Born	**April 1, 1984, Chennai**
Teams	**Tamil Nadu, Chennai Super Kings**
Style	**Right-hand bat, occasional offspinner**
Test debut	**India v Australia at Nagpur 2008-09**
ODI debut	**No ODIs yet**

THE PROFILE All batsmen want to go into their Test debut in good form, and Murali Vijay was in better nick than most: when Gautam Gambhir was banned from the final Test against Australia in November 2008, Vijay was hoicked out of Tamil Nadu's Ranji Trophy game against Maharashtra not long after making 243 in an opening stand of 462 with Abhinav Mukund. While the Ranji game went on without him, Vijay made a very sound debut at Nagpur, sharing useful opening stands of 98 and 116 with Virender Sehwag as India set about what became a series-clinching 172-run victory. Vijay helped in the field too, running out Matthew Hayden (an IPL team-mate) and Michael Hussey, and also taking a catch at short leg. Once Gambhir returned Vijay sat out the Tests in New Zealand early in 2009, but he is clearly next in line if the Gambhir-Sehwag combination misfires. Tall and solid, Vijay was an instant success in first-class cricket, despite being a late starter (he only switched to "proper" cricket from the soft-ball variety at 17, so missed the usual age-group progression): he hit 179 against Andhra in his second match, and finished his first season (2006-07) with 628 runs at 52 – only two others made more. An indication of his class came when there was no second-season dip: 2007-08 brought him 667 runs, including a double-century against Saurashtra during another big opening stand with Mukund. Vijay also averages 44 in one-day cricket, and although he has not yet played an ODI he was part of the squad which went to the West Indies in June 2009.

THE FACTS Vijay made 243 for Tamil Nadu v Maharashtra at Nasik in November 2008, sharing an opening stand of 462 with Abhinav Mukund, who made 300 not out ... Vijay also made 230 not out for Tamil Nadu v Saurashtra at Chennai in December 2007: this time his opening stand with Mukund was worth 256 ... Vijay made 179 against Andhra in his second first-class match, at Chennai in December 2006 ...

THE FIGURES to 21.9.09   www.cricinfo.com

Batting & Fielding	M	Inns	NO	Runs	HS	Avge	S/R	100	50	4s	6s	Ct	St
Tests	1	2	0	74	41	37.00	55.22	0	0	7	0	1	0
ODIs	0	0	–	–	–	–	–	–	–	–	–	–	–
Twenty20 Ints	0	0	–	–	–	–	–	–	–	–	–	–	–
First-class	26	45	2	2134	243	49.62	46.90	5	8	250	32	31	0

Bowling	M	Balls	Runs	Wkts	BB	Avge	RpO	S/R	5i	10m
Tests	1	0	–	–	–	–	–	–	–	–
ODIs	0	0	–	–	–	–	–	–	–	–
Twenty20 Ints	0	0	–	–	–	–	–	–	–	–
First-class	26	108	71	1	1–16	71.00	3.94	108.00	0	0

VIRAT KOHLI

INDIA

Full name	**Virat Kohli**
Born	**November 5, 1988, Delhi**
Teams	**Delhi, Bangalore Royal Challengers**
Style	**Right-hand bat, occasional medium-pacer**
Test debut	**No Tests yet**
ODI debut	**India v Sri Lanka at Dambulla 2008**

THE PROFILE An attacking player with a cool head and the hint of a swagger that suggests he knows he's pretty good, Virat Kohli has been making big scores from a young age. He made three double-centuries for Delhi's Under-17s, then captained the Indian side that won the Under-19 World Cup in Malaysia in 2008, scoring 235 runs including a round 100 against West Indies. By then Kohli had already made his Ranji Trophy debut, making 90 (after Delhi had been 14 for 4) against Karnataka in his fourth match. The upward curve continued in 2007-08, his second season, with a maiden century against Rajasthan and a superb 169 against Karnataka in December 2007. He was consistent in limited-overs cricket without making big scores (that came later, with four one-day hundreds in a fortnight in February 2009), and was called up for a one-day series in Sri Lanka in August 2008. He wasn't expected to play, but an injury to Virender Sehwag gave Kohli a chance: he reached double figures in all five of his innings with 54 in the fourth game. He kept his name in the selectors' minds with another good domestic season (613 runs at 55, with a career-best 197 against Pakistan's national champions), then improved his IPL form after a disappointing first campaign. He remains one for the future: "He is a very physical type of player. He likes to impose himself on the game," said Dav Whatmore, India's Under-19 coach. Kohli agrees that it is calculated aggression: "I can't be bogged down by a bowler. I just like to give it back."

THE FACTS Kohli scored 197 for Delhi against Pakistan's champions Sui Northern Gas in the Mohammad Nissar Trophy match at Delhi in September 2008: he and Aakash Chopra (182) put on 385 for the second wicket ... Kohli made 105 for the Board President's XI against the Australian tourists at Hyderabad in October 2008 ... He made 251 not out for Delhi Under-17s v Himachal Pradesh at Una in December 2004 ...

THE FIGURES *to 21.9.09*   www.cricinfo.com

Batting & Fielding	M	Inns	NO	Runs	HS	Avge	S/R	100	50	4s	6s	Ct	St
Tests	0	0	–	–	–	–	–	–	–	–	–	–	–
ODIs	6	6	1	161	54	32.20	66.80	0	1	21	1	3	0
Twenty20 Ints	0	0	–	–	–	–	–	–	–	–	–	–	–
First-class	21	29	4	1243	197	49.72	51.68	4	4	173	6	14	0

Bowling	M	Balls	Runs	Wkts	BB	Avge	RpO	S/R	5i	10m
Tests	0	0	–	–	–	–	–	–	–	–
ODIs	6	0	–	–	–	–	–	–	–	–
Twenty20 Ints	0	0	–	–	–	–	–	–	–	–
First-class	21	66	66	1	1–23	66.00	6.00	66.00	0	0

ADAM **VOGES**

Full name	**Adam Charles Voges**
Born	**October 4, 1979, Subiaco, Perth, Western Australia**
Teams	**Western Australia, Nottinghamshire**
Style	**Right-hand bat, left-arm unorthodox spinner**
Test debut	**No Tests yet**
ODI debut	**Australia v New Zealand at Hamilton 2006-07**

THE PROFILE Part of Western Australia's big-hitting middle order, Adam Voges (it's pronounced Vo-jes) is most famous for his maiden one-day century, against New South Wales in October 2004 – batting at No. 3, he didn't enter until the 30th over, but reached three figures in 62 balls, the fastest in Australian domestic history at the time. He also clattered a sponsor's sign with one of his seven sixes. Voges collected many plaudits for that innings, and a $50,000 bonus for his superb aim ... but was left out for the next Pura Cup match. He returned later that season, and produced his first hundred. Next summer he passed 600 first-class runs: the only blemish was a brief suspension for missing a training session, but that was forgotten when, after Damien Martyn's sudden retirement, Voges was called into Australia's squad for the third Ashes Test of 2006-07 on his home turf at the WACA. He didn't play – Andrew Symonds got the place instead, and made it his own for a while – but Voges kept his name in the frame by ending the season with 630 runs at 57. He made his ODI debut in New Zealand, but didn't quite do enough to win a World Cup spot. He is a fine fielder, but his left-arm wrist-spin hasn't had much chance yet. Despite pulling out of the one-day series in South Africa early in 2009 to get married, Voges played against Scotland later that summer, scoring 72 and putting on 114 with David Hussey, who made a century – but neither of them could get into the team for the one-sided series against England that followed.

THE FACTS Voges's 100 not out in 62 balls for Western Australia against NSW in October 2004 was the fastest century in Australian domestic one-day cricket at the time ... He made 180 for WA v Tasmania at Hobart in December 2007 ... Voges learnt of his call-up to the Australian Test squad in 2006-07 while playing for a Cricket Australia XI against the England tourists: he was tapped on the shoulder and asked to leave the field, and admitted "I thought I was in trouble" ...

THE FIGURES *to 21.9.09*   www.cricinfo.com

Batting & Fielding	M	Inns	NO	Runs	HS	Avge	S/R	100	50	4s	6s	Ct	St
Tests	0	0	–	–	–	–	–	–	–	–	–	–	–
ODIs	2	2	1	88	72	88.00	118.91	0	1	0	5	1	0
Twenty20 Ints	4	3	1	63	26	31.50	121.15	0	0	6	0	2	0
First-class	73	122	15	4176	180	39.02	50.61	8	22	–	–	96	0

Bowling	M	Balls	Runs	Wkts	BB	Avge	RpO	S/R	5i	10m
Tests	0	0	–	–	–	–	–	–	–	–
ODIs	2	36	51	0	–	–	8.50	–	0	0
Twenty20 Ints	4	12	5	2	2–5	2.50	2.50	6.00	0	0
First-class	73	2273	1228	34	4–92	36.11	3.24	66.85	0	0

MALINDA **WARNAPURA**

SRI LANKA

Full name	**Basnayake Shalith Malinda Warnapura**
Born	**May 26, 1979, Colombo**
Teams	**Colts, Basnahira South**
Style	**Left-hand bat, offspinner**
Test debut	**Sri Lanka v Bangladesh at Colombo 2007**
ODI debut	**Sri Lanka v Pakistan at Abu Dhabi 2007**

THE PROFILE A nuggety left-hander strong on the off side, Malinda Warnapura took his time to make his mark in international cricket, despite an impressive pedigree (his uncle, Bandula Warnapura, captained Sri Lanka). This Warnapura – more of an accumulator than a dasher – started his first-class career in 1998, but it was not until late in 2006 that he really arrived. Chosen for the Sri Lanka A side that took part in India's Duleep Trophy tournament, he made 421 runs in three matches, including 65 and 149 not out in the final, won by North Zone. Despite this he missed the senior tour of New Zealand that followed, then struggled with illness when the A team visited the West Indies. But when Bangladesh A toured Sri Lanka early in 2007 he was back to his best, stroking a career-best 242 in the first unofficial Test, and he followed that with a hundred in one of the one-dayers to show he was adept at the shorter game as well. At 28, he was handed a first Test cap against Bangladesh in June 2007 ... and was dismissed by the only ball he received. But in the absence of Upul Tharanga (injured foot) and Marvan Atapattu (injured pride, after being kept on the bench throughout the World Cup), Warnapura retained his place, and made an assured 82 in another innings victory in the second Test. Next he scored 120 against West Indies in Guyana, and started the Indian series in July 2008 with 115 in Colombo, before a modest run against Pakistan a year later cost him his place.

THE FACTS Warnapura scored 242 for Sri Lanka A v Bangladesh A in Colombo in March 2007, sharing a stand of 376 with Thilan Samaraweera ... On his Test debut, against Bangladesh in Colombo three months later, he was out first ball ... In March 2008 Warnapura scored the first Test century at Providence in Guyana ... His uncle, Bandula Warnapura, captained Sri Lanka in their inaugural Test, against England in 1981–82 ...

THE FIGURES *to 21.9.09* www.cricinfo.com

Batting & Fielding	M	Inns	NO	Runs	HS	Avge	S/R	100	50	4s	6s	Ct	St
Tests	14	24	1	821	120	35.69	58.14	2	7	98	2	14	0
ODIs	3	3	0	35	30	11.66	46.05	0	0	5	0	3	0
Twenty20 Ints	0	0	–	–	–	–	–	–	–	–	–	–	–
First-class	143	219	22	7098	242	36.06	–	16	36	–	–	98	0

Bowling	M	Balls	Runs	Wkts	BB	Avge	RpO	S/R	5i	10m
Tests	14	54	40	0	–	–	4.44	–	0	0
ODIs	3	0	–	–	–	–	–	–	–	–
Twenty20 Ints	0	0	–	–	–	–	–	–	–	–
First-class	143	6798	3211	116	6–22	27.68	2.83	58.60	4	0

DAVID **WARNER**

Full name	**David Andrew Warner**
Born	**October 27, 1986, Paddington, Sydney**
Teams	**New South Wales, Durham, Delhi Daredevils**
Style	**Left-hand bat, occasional legspinner**
Test debut	**No Tests yet**
ODI debut	**Australia v South Africa at Hobart 2008-09**

THE PROFILE   A diminutive and dangerous opening batsman, David Warner exploded onto the international scene in January 2009. His astonishing 89 from 43 balls, wielding the bat more like a baseball one, on his Twenty20 debut against South Africa at the MCG was all the more remarkable as he was the first man to play for the full Australian side before playing first-class cricket since 1877. His surprise call-up capped an eventful couple of months in which he also earned an IPL contract and a deal to use a two-sided bat. The rewards had come after he began the season by smashing nine sixes in 165 not out – a NSW one-day record – against Tasmania in Sydney, and showed it was no fluke with 97 from 54 balls against the luckless islanders the following week. He finished with 390 FR Cup runs at a strike-rate of 129. Promoted to the Australian one-day team after his Twenty20 heroics, Warner struggled after a muscular 69 in his second game, although he remained in the squad for the World Twenty20 in England. Despite the attention of the national selectors, he did not make his first-class debut until a late reshuffle enabled him to play in NSW's final match of the season. He picked up 42 off 48 balls in a satisfying start. An excellent fieldsman, Warner was used as a substitute in the Perth Test against South Africa in 2005-06. That same season he was the leading run-scorer on the Under-19 tour of India, and went on to play at the Under-19 World Cup. A keen surfer, he was sent home from the Australian academy in 2007 for general untidiness.

THE FACTS   Warner was the first man since John Hodges and Tom Kendall in the first Test of all in 1876-77 to represent Australia in a full international without previously having played a first-class match ... He made his only first-class appearance so far for New South Wales in March 2009 ... Warner won the match award for his 89 from 43 balls (seven fours and six sixes) on Twenty20 international debut against South Africa in January 2009 ...

THE FIGURES *to 21.9.09*   www.cricinfo.com

Batting & Fielding	M	Inns	NO	Runs	HS	Avge	S/R	100	50	4s	6s	Ct	St
Tests	0	0	–	–	–	–	–	–	–	–	–	–	–
ODIs	7	7	0	106	69	15.14	77.37	0	1	8	3	1	0
Twenty20 Ints	8	8	0	273	89	34.12	139.28	0	2	26	9	1	0
First-class	1	1	0	42	42	42.00	87.50	0	0	6	1	2	0

Bowling	M	Balls	Runs	Wkts	BB	Avge	RpO	S/R	5i	10m
Tests	0	0	–	–	–	–	–	–	–	–
ODIs	7	0	–	–	–	–	–	–	–	–
Twenty20 Ints	8	0	–	–	–	–	–	–	–	–
First-class	1	12	7	0	–	–	3.50	–	0	0

SHANE **WATSON**

AUSTRALIA

Full name	**Shane Robert Watson**
Born	**June 17, 1981, Ipswich, Queensland**
Teams	**Queensland**
Style	**Right-hand bat, right-arm fast-medium bowler**
Test debut	**Australia v Pakistan at Sydney 2004-05**
ODI debut	**Australia v South Africa at Centurion 2001-02**

THE PROFILE Hulking, blond and spiky-haired, Shane Watson should be the shiny embodiment of modern-day Australian cricket ... if only that body didn't keep cracking up. He started young: Queensland Under-17s at 15, the Academy, nipping off at 19 to Tasmania, where he hit his maiden hundred in his fifth match. He missed the 2003 World Cup with stress fractures of the back: until then his batting lacked nothing in swagger, if a little in artifice, while his medium-pace bowling was willing. He bounced back in 2003-04 with four hundreds for Tasmania. Back home in Queensland (Tassie was too cold) he was tipped to become Australia's next champion allrounder by their last one, Alan Davidson, but it hasn't quite happened like that. Instead Watson has become a change bowler, handy in ODIs, and has been concentrating on his batting. A clean hitter, he had a spell opening in ODIs; then in England in 2009, with Phillip Hughes struggling, Watson was a surprising choice to go in first instead in the Tests. But he did well, contributing five solid innings, the lowest of which was 34, despite a tendency to whip across the line that resulted in several confident lbw shouts. The first right-hander to open for Australia since Michael Slater in 2001, Watson will start 2009-10 in pole position at the top of the order, as long as he steers clear of injury. In 2005-06 it was his shoulder, then a persistent hamstring injury kept him out of the Ashes rematch, but he bounced back to play an allround role in the defence of the World Cup.

THE FACTS Watson hit 201 in the 2005-06 Pura Cup final demolition of Victoria before retiring hurt: uniquely, four batsmen passed 150 in Queensland's 900 for 6 ... He averaged 145 at the 2007 World Cup, thanks to five not-outs, and scored at a rollicking 170.58 runs per 100 balls ... Watson played for Hampshire, alongside Shane Warne: in 2005 he scored 203 not out for them against Warwickshire at the Rose Bowl ...

THE FIGURES to 21.9.09   www.cricinfo.com

Batting & Fielding	M	Inns	NO	Runs	HS	Avge	S/R	100	50	4s	6s	Ct	St
Tests	11	18	0	497	78	27.61	47.37	0	4	74	1	2	0
ODIs	85	67	20	1755	126	37.34	80.91	2	9	159	23	22	0
Twenty20 Ints	7	6	1	86	33	17.20	117.80	0	0	8	2	2	0
First-class	75	129	15	5190	203*	45.52	–	13	27	–	–	56	0

Bowling	M	Balls	Runs	Wkts	BB	Avge	RpO	S/R	5i	10m
Tests	11	1018	547	14	4–42	39.07	3.22	72.71	0	0
ODIs	85	3115	2497	83	4–39	30.08	4.80	37.53	0	0
Twenty20 Ints	7	75	108	3	1–17	36.00	8.64	25.00	0	0
First-class	75	6895	3977	135	7–69	29.45	3.46	51.07	3	1

CAMERON **WHITE**

Full name	**Cameron Leon White**
Born	**August 18, 1983, Bairnsdale, Victoria**
Teams	**Victoria**
Style	**Right-hand bat, legspinner**
Test debut	**Australia v India at Bangalore 2008-09**
ODI debut	**Australia v World XI at Melbourne 2005-06**

THE PROFILE Cameron "Bear" White long seemed destined to play a significant role for Australia. Only the precise nature of that role baffled admirers. Nagging legspinner? Solid middle-order bat? Intuitive skipper? Or a bit of all three? The over-eager Shane Warne comparisons that accompanied his arrival have long since died away. Indeed, White is a peculiarly unAustralian leggie – tall and robust, relying on changes of pace and a handy wrong'un rather than prodigious turn or flight. He has a neat line in self-deprecation: "There's no flippers or anything exciting like that," he once admitted. What is not in doubt is his cricket sense, nor his maturity. Victoria's youngest-ever captain at 20, he won rave reviews for his handling of more experienced colleagues. White played his first ODIs against the World XI late in 2005. He made little impact, and lost his national contract after a mediocre season. But he had a wonderful time with the bat for Somerset in 2006 (David Hookes, the late Victorian coach, always felt White's best chance of representing Australia was to earn a top-six spot). He feasted on county bowlers, and smashed a Twenty20 ton in 55 balls. That preceded a better home summer, and he was recalled for the one-day series at the start of 2007: his bowling lacked control, and batting opportunities were limited. He missed the World Cup, but toured India at the end of 2008. He did little in four Tests there, and returned even more firmly pigeonholed as a one-day player. More modest returns threatened that place too, until back in England late in 2009 he followed mature innings of 53 and 42 with a fine maiden century at the Rose Bowl.

THE FACTS White made 260 not out for Somerset v Derbyshire in August 2006, the highest individual score in the fourth innings of any first-class match, beating a record formerly held by Hansie Cronje and Denis Compton ... White took 6 for 66 (10 for 136 in the match) for Victoria v Western Australia at Melbourne in March 2003 ... Ten of his 15 first-class centuries were scored in 24 matches for Somerset ...

THE FIGURES to 21.9.09   www.cricinfo.com

Batting & Fielding	M	Inns	NO	Runs	HS	Avge	S/R	100	50	4s	6s	Ct	St
Tests	4	7	2	146	46	29.20	44.24	0	0	15	1	1	0
ODIs	36	26	7	594	105	31.26	89.86	1	1	46	14	19	0
Twenty20 Ints	8	8	3	207	55	41.40	150.00	0	1	10	12	6	0
First-class	103	172	21	6351	260*	42.05	–	15	28	–	–	97	0

Bowling	M	Balls	Runs	Wkts	BB	Avge	RpO	S/R	5i	10m
Tests	4	558	342	5	2–71	68.40	3.67	111.60	0	0
ODIs	36	325	345	12	3–5	28.75	6.36	27.08	0	0
Twenty20 Ints	8	24	25	1	1–11	25.00	6.25	24.00	0	0
First-class	103	11562	6773	170	6–66	39.84	3.51	68.01	2	1

LUKE **WRIGHT**

ENGLAND

Full name	**Luke James Wright**
Born	**March 7, 1985, Grantham, Lincolnshire**
Teams	**Sussex**
Style	**Right-hand bat, right-arm fast-medium bowler**
Test debut	**No Tests yet**
ODI debut	**England v India at The Oval 2007**

THE PROFILE He's an attacking batsman who can bowl medium-fast, so it's no great surprise that Luke Wright admires Andrew Flintoff, or that he hoped to follow him into the England side. That ambition was realised when Flintoff, among others, was injured, and Wright was called up against India in September 2007. Like Freddie, Wright marked his ODI debut by scoring 50, an exciting innings which started with a four and a six. But he made little impression after that, although his strike-rate was impressive. He continued in the one-day mix throughout 2009 – at least until a ball from a bowling machine broke his toe during the miserable one-day series against Australia in September – although he hadn't done anything terribly spectacular beyond a rapid 71 in the World Twenty20 opener against the Netherlands at Lord's, and even that ended in embarrassment when England lost off the last ball. Wright made his first-class debut for Leicestershire against Sussex in 2003, and although Mushtaq Ahmed nabbed him for a duck Sussex signed him up for the following season. Wright repaid them with a debut century, and had played only ten first-class games when he went to the Caribbean with England A early in 2006. His career really took off the following year, when he was the leading Twenty20 Cup runscorer with 346, including a pyrotechnic 103 in just 45 balls against Kent. That earned him his county cap – and that national call, which he celebrated by hammering 125 in 73 balls in a 40-over game against Gloucestershire. He also made a dramatic start to the 2008 season, with an undefeated 155 for Sussex against MCC, but so far his bowling has made less of a mark.

THE FACTS Wright made 103 from 45 balls (11 fours, six sixes) in a Twenty20 Cup match against Kent at Canterbury in June 2007 ... He hit 155 not out for Sussex v MCC at Lord's in the first match of the 2008 season ... Wright scored 100 on his debut for Sussex (his second first-class match), v Loughborough UCCE in May 2004 ... He took a hat-trick for England Under-19s v South Africa in a one-day game at Hove in August 2003 ...

THE FIGURES *to 21.9.09*   www.cricinfo.com

Batting & Fielding	M	Inns	NO	Runs	HS	Avge	S/R	100	50	4s	6s	Ct	St
Tests	0	0	–	–	–	–	–	–	–	–	–	–	–
ODIs	21	16	1	344	52	22.93	103.61	0	2	35	11	7	0
Twenty20 Ints	14	13	0	211	71	16.23	131.05	0	1	27	4	7	0
First-class	57	81	14	2402	155*	35.85	63.93	7	12	–	–	26	0

Bowling	M	Balls	Runs	Wkts	BB	Avge	RpO	S/R	5i	10m
Tests	0	0	–	–	–	–	–	–	–	–
ODIs	21	330	260	6	2–34	43.33	4.72	55.00	0	0
Twenty20 Ints	14	78	109	2	1–24	54.50	8.38	39.00	0	0
First-class	57	5742	3351	78	5–66	42.96	3.50	73.61	2	0

YOUNIS KHAN

Full name	**Mohammad Younis Khan**
Born	**Nov 29, 1977, Mardan, North-West Frontier Province**
Teams	**NWFP, Peshawar, Habib Bank, South Australia**
Style	**Right-hand bat, occasional legspinner**
Test debut	**Pakistan v Sri Lanka at Rawalpindi 1999-2000**
ODI debut	**Pakistan v Sri Lanka at Karachi 1999-2000**

THE PROFILE Younis Khan is a fearless middle-order batsman, as befits his Pathan ancestry. He plays with a flourish, and is especially strong in the arc from backward point to extra cover, and he is prone to getting down on one knee and driving extravagantly. But this flamboyance is coupled with grit. He started with a century on Test debut, against Sri Lanka early in 2000, and scored well in bursts after that, with 153 against West Indies in Sharjah the highlight. Younis was one of the few batsmen who retained his place after Pakistan's disastrous 2003 World Cup, but he lost it soon afterwards after a string of low scores. Another century against Sri Lanka finally cemented that Test place, and he has been a heavy runmaker ever since, especially against India: in March 2005 he made 147 and 267 in successive Tests against them, and continued in that vein early in 2006, with 199, 83, 194, 0 and 77, before scoring consistently in England too, making 173 at Leeds, which became his home ground the following year during a successful spell with Yorkshire. He flirted with the captaincy – once theatrically resigning – before finally taking over full-time early in 2009. He started by making 313 in 760 minutes against Sri Lanka on a Karachi featherbed, then later in the year led his side to victory in the World Twenty20 in England, overcoming a lackadaisical start ... but immediately afterwards retired from 20-over cricket. Younis remained in charge in the longer formats, though, despite a disappointing series defeat in Sri Lanka, and seemed set for a long run – as long as the theatricals are held in check.

THE FACTS Younis Khan scored 313, Pakistan's third triple-century in Tests, against Sri Lanka at Karachi in February 2009 ... He averages 88.06 in Tests against India – and more than 31 against everyone else ... Younis was the seventh of ten Pakistanis to score a century on Test debut, with 107 v Sri Lanka at Rawalpindi in February 2000 ... Against India at home early in 2006 he shared successive stands of 319, 142, 242, 0 and 158 with Mohammad Yousuf ... At Lahore in that series Younis became the sixth batsman to be out for 199 in a Test ...

THE FIGURES to 21.9.09   www.cricinfo.com

Batting & Fielding	M	Inns	NO	Runs	HS	Avge	S/R	100	50	4s	6s	Ct	St
Tests	63	112	7	5260	313	50.09	53.73	16	21	638	24	67	0
ODIs	191	185	19	5623	144	33.87	76.68	6	37	456	50	101	0
Twenty20 Ints	22	20	3	432	51	25.41	124.85	0	2	31	12	11	0
First-class	145	235	27	10689	313	51.38	–	34	43	–	–	151	0

Bowling	M	Balls	Runs	Wkts	BB	Avge	RpO	S/R	5i	10m
Tests	63	540	341	7	2–23	48.71	3.78	77.14	0	0
ODIs	191	224	224	2	1–3	112.00	6.00	112.00	0	0
Twenty20 Ints	22	22	18	3	3–18	6.00	4.90	7.33	0	0
First-class	145	2347	1382	31	4–52	44.58	3.53	75.70	0	0

YUVRAJ SINGH

Full name	**Yuvraj Singh**
Born	**December 12, 1981, Chandigarh**
Teams	**Punjab, Kings XI Punjab**
Style	**Left-hand bat, left-arm orthodox spinner**
Test debut	**India v New Zealand at Mohali 2003-04**
ODI debut	**India v Kenya at Nairobi 2000-01**

THE PROFILE Generously gifted, Yuvraj Singh made a lordly entry into international cricket when still only 18, toppling Australia in the ICC Knockout of October 2000 with a blistering 84 in his first innings and some scintillating fielding. He supplements those skills with some clever, loopy left-arm spin, with which he took two hat-tricks in the second season of the IPL in 2009. While his ability to hit the ball long and clean was instantly recognised, at first he was troubled by quality spin, and temporarily lost his place. But he returned early in 2002, and swung the series against Zimbabwe India's way with two matchwinning innings, then went to England and played key roles in three one-day run-chases, culminating at Lord's where his 69, and stand of 121 with Mohammad Kaif, set up a memorable victory over England. It still took another 15 months, and an injury to Sourav Ganguly, for Yuvraj to get a Test look-in. But in his third match, against Pakistan on a Lahore greentop, he stroked a stunning first-day century off 110 balls. A troublesome knee injury briefly threatened to keep him out of the 2007 World Cup, but later in the year he smashed Stuart Broad for six sixes in an over during the inaugural World Twenty20 championship. A scintillating 169 against Pakistan at Bangalore in December 2007 seemed to have nailed down a Test place at last – but a string of modest scores followed, and he was out again by the middle of 2008, although he remains marvellously consistent in one-dayers and a fearsome sight (for bowlers, at least) in Twenty20 games.

THE FACTS Yuvraj hit England's Stuart Broad for six sixes in an over during the World Twenty20 championships at Durban in September 2007 ... He played 73 ODIs before winning his first Test cap ... He averages 63.55 in Tests against Pakistan, but 9.14 v Australia ... Yuvraj has the highest strike-rate in Twenty20 internationals of anyone with more than 350 runs ... His father, fast bowler Yograj Singh, played one Test in 1980–81 ... Yuvraj's record includes three ODIs for the Asia XI ...

THE FIGURES *to 21.9.09*　　　　www.cricinfo.com

Batting & Fielding	M	Inns	NO	Runs	HS	Avge	S/R	100	50	4s	6s	Ct	St
Tests	28	45	6	1387	169	35.56	57.76	3	6	196	13	27	0
ODIs	239	219	31	7098	139	37.75	89.46	12	41	726	130	70	0
Twenty20 Ints	15	14	2	415	70	34.58	160.85	0	4	26	30	5	0
First-class	84	136	17	5153	209	43.30	–	16	23	–	–	85	0

Bowling	M	Balls	Runs	Wkts	BB	Avge	RpO	S/R	5i	10m
Tests	28	561	316	7	2–9	45.14	3.37	80.14	0	0
ODIs	239	3458	2977	76	4–6	39.17	5.16	45.50	0	0
Twenty20 Ints	15	78	121	2	1–17	60.50	9.30	39.00	0	0
First-class	84	1617	861	18	3–25	47.83	3.19	89.83	0	0

MONDE **ZONDEKI**

Full name	**Monde Zondeki**
Born	**July 25, 1982, King William's Town, Cape Province**
Teams	**Cape Cobras**
Style	**Right-hand bat, right-arm fast-medium bowler**
Test debut	**South Africa v England at Leeds 2003**
ODI debut	**South Africa v Sri Lanka at Bloemfontein 2002-03**

THE PROFILE Monde Zondeki is cut straight from the modern history of the new South Africa, and spent a year of his childhood in Zambia living with his exiled uncle, the late ANC cabinet minister Steve Tshwete. He eventually returned home and attended Dale College, a fine cricketing nursery which also claims Makhaya Ntini as an old boy. Although he initially tried legspin, Zondeki was soon bowling fast – and later, very fast. He became the latest young paceman to attempt to fill Allan Donald's boots, and could hardly have made a more stunning impact, taking a wicket with his first ball in international cricket – Marvan Atapattu caught in the slips in a one-dayer at Bloemfontein in 2002. Predictably, Zondeki struggled to make much impression at the 2003 World Cup, but was still selected for that year's England tour. He starred on his Test debut at Headingley ... with bat not ball: South Africa were struggling at 142 for 7 before Zondeki made 59 and helped Gary Kirsten add 150 for the eighth wicket. However, a side strain restricted him to just 4.5 overs, and bad luck with injuries meant he did not get back into the Test side until March 2005, against Zimbabwe. It was an impressive comeback: nine wickets booked him a place to the Caribbean, but he managed just seven wickets in three Tests there, then injuries impinged again. But the amusingly nicknamed "All Hands" Zondeki was the leading domestic wicket-taker in 2007-08, with 62 at 19.16, which earned him a national contract, and another Test cap when Bangladesh turned up for their customary thrashing at Centurion in November 2008.

THE FACTS Zondeki took the wicket of Sri Lanka's Marvan Atapattu with his first ball in ODIs, at Bloemfontein in December 2002: only 14 others have achieved this feat (the only other South African was Martin van Jaarsveld) ... Zondeki took 6 for 39 in a Test against Zimbabwe at Centurion in March 2005 ... He took 6 for 37 in a one-day game for South Africa A against Sri Lanka A at Centurion in October 2003 ...

THE FIGURES to 21.9.09   www.cricinfo.com

Batting & Fielding	M	Inns	NO	Runs	HS	Avge	S/R	100	50	4s	6s	Ct	St
Tests	6	5	0	82	59	16.40	36.28	0	1	12	0	1	0
ODIs	13	3	2	4	3*	4.00	80.00	0	0	0	0	3	0
Twenty20 Ints	1	1	0	0	0	0.00	0.00	0	0	0	0	0	0
First-class	73	101	31	645	59	9.21	–	0	1	–	–	22	0

Bowling	M	Balls	Runs	Wkts	BB	Avge	RpO	S/R	5i	10m
Tests	6	780	480	19	6–39	25.26	3.69	41.05	1	0
ODIs	13	558	504	11	2–40	45.81	5.41	50.72	0	0
Twenty20 Ints	1	18	41	1	1–41	41.00	13.66	18.00	0	0
First-class	73	12216	6499	228	6–39	28.50	3.19	53.57	9	1

AFGHANISTAN

Nowroz Mangal

Mohammad Shahzad

Noor Ali

The improbable rise of war-torn Afghanistan as a cricket power was one of the great feelgood stories of 2008 and 2009. Starting in the lowly backwaters of world cricket's fifth division in May 2008, they won in Jersey to progress up the ladder a notch. They topped Division Four, too, in Tanzania – in all they won 12 of their 13 matches in those two tournaments – then emerged from Division Three, in Argentina at the end of January 2009. That put them into the World Cup qualifying series in South Africa, where they finished just one win short of a fairytale appearance in the main event itself in 2011. The decision to reduce the number of associate nations in the World Cup from six in 2007 to four next time ultimately cost Afghanistan a place, as they finished sixth – but that did bring the considerable consolation (and considerable funding) of official one-day international status for the next four years. They celebrated by walloping Scotland in their first ODI, and later in the year shared a short series in the unfamiliar surroundings of the Netherlands. They were also holding their own in the ICC's first-class Intercontinental Cup competition: also in Holland, the Afghan opener Noor Ali became only the fourth man – after Test players in Arthur Morris of Australia, India's Nari Contractor and Aamer Malik of Pakistan – to score two centuries on his first-class debut. Afghanistan's cricketers still have hurdles to overcome – it's difficult to imagine many teams wanting to tour there in the current climate, so home matches will be difficult – but they have coped admirably with everything that has been thrown at them so far.

Afghanistan's ODI records *as at 21.9.09*

Highest total	295-8	v Scotland at Benoni 2008-09
Lowest total	180	v Netherlands at Amstelveen 2009
Most runs	126	Mohammad Shahzad (avge. 63.00)
Highest score	110	Moh'd Shahzad v Netherlands at Amstelveen 2009
Most wickets	6	Hamid Hassan (avge. 23.16)
Best bowling	4-24	Shapoor Zadran v Netherlands at Amstelveen 2009
Most matches	3	(seven different players)
World Cup record	Have not qualified yet	
Overall ODI record	Played 3: Won 2, Lost 1	

AFGHANISTAN

AHMED SHAH Ahmedzi   October 20, 1983, Paktika
LHB, SLA: 1 ODI, 2 runs at 2.00, HS 2; 0 wickets.
Opener who scored 73* against Malaysia in Kuala Lumpur in 2006.

ASGHAR STANIKZAI, Mohammad   February 22, 1987, Kabul
RHB, RFM: 3 ODIs, 62 runs at 20.66, HS 30.
Middle-order batsman who made 102 against Bahrain in July 2008.

DAWLAT AHMADZAI, Khan   September 5, 1984, Loger
RHB, RFM: 1 ODI, did not bat; 1 wicket at 40.00, BB 1-40.
Long-serving fast bowler, and former captain, who first played for Afghanistan in 2001.

HAMID HASSAN   June 1, 1987, Bati Kot, Nangrahar
RHB, RFM: 3 ODIs, 0 runs, HS 0*; 6 wickets at 23.16, BB 3-33.
Took 5-23 against Ireland in World Cup qualifier in South Africa in April 2009.

HASTI GUL, Abid   January 1, 1984, Nangrahar
RHB, RM: 2 ODIs, 23 runs at no average, HS 23*; 3 wickets at 24.33, BB 2-48.
Economical opening bowler who has played for Sebastianites in Sri Lanka.

KARIM KHAN Saadiq   February 18, 1984, Nangrahar
RHB, OB, WK: 1 ODI, 20 runs at 20.00, HS 20.
Opened and kept wicket in Afghanistan's first official ODI, against Scotland in 2009.

KHALIQ DAD Noori   January 1, 1984, Baghlan
RHB, RFM: 1 ODI, 0 runs at 0.00, HS 0; 2 wickets at 12.50, BB 2-25.
Medium-pacer whose brother, Allah Dad, has also played for Afghanistan.

MIRWAIS ASHRAF   June 30, 1988, Kunduz
RHB, RFM: 1 ODI, 17 runs at 17.00, HS 17; 0 wickets.
Medium-pacer who took 4-24 v Netherlands in Intercontinental Cup match in August 2009.

MOHAMMAD NABI Eisakhil   March 7, 1985, Loger
RHB, OB: 3 ODIs, 74 runs at 37.00, HS 58; 0 wickets.
Promising batsman who spent some time on the MCC cricket staff at Lord's.

MOHAMMAD SHAHZAD Mohammadi   July 15, 1991, Nangrahar
RHB, WK: 2 ODIs, 126 runs at 63.00, HS 110, 1x100.
Scored Afghanistan's first ODI hundred. against the Netherlands at Amstelveen in his second match.

NOOR ALI Zadran   July 10, 1988, Khost
RHB, RM: 3 ODIs, 94 runs at 31.33, HS 45.
Made 130 and 100* on first-class debut, for Afghanistan v Zimbabwe A in August 2009.

NOWROZ MANGAL, Khan   November 28, 1984, Kabul
RHB, OB: 3 ODIs, 66 runs at 22.00, HS 32; 4 wickets at 10.75, BB 3-35.
Afghanistan's captain during their astonishing rise. Took 5-24 v Malaysia in 2008.

RAEES AHMADZAI, Khan   September 3, 1984, Loger
RHB, OB: 3 ODIs, 45 runs at 22.50, HS 39.
Scored 78 v Uganda in January 2009: has also played for Sebastianites in Sri Lanka.

SAMIULLAH SHENWARI   December 31, 1987, Nangrahar
RHB, LBG: 3 ODIs, 118 runs at 59.00, HS 52; 2 wickets at 47.00, BB 2-56.
Improving legspinner who took 4-28 v Bermuda in World Cup qualifier in 2009.

SHAPOOR ZADRAN   January 1, 1985, Loger
LHB, LFM: 2 ODIs, 1 run at 1.00, HS 1; 5 wickets at 12.40, BB 4-24.
Left-armer who took 4-24 - including 3 for 1 in 8 balls - on ODI debut v Netherlands in Aug 2009.

IRELAND

Trent Johnston   *Niall O'Brien*   *Alex Cusack*

Cricket in Ireland was once so popular that Oliver Cromwell banned it in 1656. Since then, it has been something of a minority sport, although there have been occasional big days, as in 1969 when the West Indians were skittled for 25 on a boggy pitch at Sion Mills in County Tyrone (rumours that the visitors enjoyed lavish hospitality at a nearby Guinness brewery the night before are thought to be unfounded). Cricket continued as an amateur pastime until the 1990s, when the Irish board left the auspices of the English one and attained independent ICC membership. Ireland became eligible to play in the World Cup, and narrowly missed out on the 1999 tournament, when they lost a playoff to Scotland. They made no mistake for 2007, though, winning the ICC Trophy (handily, it was played in Ireland) to ensure qualification. A change of captain to the Australian-born Trent Johnston ushered in a new, more professional set-up, and Ireland travelled to the Caribbean hopeful of making a mark. No-one, though, was quite prepared for what happened – except maybe Johnston himself, who packed enough for a seven-week stay when most were expecting a quiet return home in a week or two. In their first World Cup match, Ireland tied with Zimbabwe, then went one better on a Sabina Park greentop on St Patrick's Day, hanging on to beat Pakistan and eliminate one of the pre-tournament favourites. Ireland sailed on to the Super Eights, where they beat Bangladesh too. They also did well in the World Twenty20 in England in 2009, and soon after that almost capsized England in a one-dayer. But the better Irish players are already with English counties (Ed Joyce and Eoin Morgan have already played for England, and others are trying to follow suit), and the others struggle to fit in ever-increasing international commitments around a steady job. Irish cricket needs a more professional domestic structure if the impression made by Johnston's merry men is to be anything more than a footnote in cricket history.

Ireland's ODI records as at 21.9.09

Highest total	308-7	v Canada at Nairobi 2006-07
Lowest total	77	v Sri Lanka at St George's 2006-07
Most runs	1150	WTS Porterfield (avge. 33.82)
Highest score	142	KJ O'Brien v Kenya at Nairobi 2006-07
Most wickets	39	WK McCallan (avge. 30.97)
Best bowling	5-14	DT Johnston v Canada at Centurion 2008-09
Most matches	39	WK McCallan (2006-2009)
World Cup record		Reached Super Eight stage in only appearance, 2006-07
Overall ODI record		Played 41: Won 17, Lost 20, Tied 1, No result 3

IRELAND

BOTHA, Andre Cornelius　　　September 12, 1975, Johannesburg, South Africa
LHB, RM: 35 ODIs, 567 runs at 21.00, HS 56; 37 wickets at 24.97, BB 4-19.
Former South African provincial player: made 186 for Ireland v Scotland in August 2007.

BRAY, Jeremy Paul　　　November 30, 1973, Newtown, Sydney, Australia
LHB: 15 ODIs, 401 runs at 28.64, HS 116, 2x100.
Aggressive opener who made 115* against Zimbabwe in the 2007 World Cup.

CONNELL, Peter　　　August 13, 1981, Dannevirke, New Zealand
RHB, RFM: 11 ODIs, 38 runs at 38.00, HS 22*; 12 wickets at 38.00, BB 3-68.
North Down seamer who took 10 for 69 v Holland in Intercontinental Cup at Rotterdam in July 2008.

CUSACK, Alex Richard　　　October 29, 1980, Brisbane, Australia
RHB, RFM: 20 ODIs, 244 runs at 24.40, HS 38; 21 wickets at 21.19, BB 3-15.
Man of the Match on ODI debut for 36* and 3-15 v South Africa at Belfast in June 2007.

JOHNSTON, David Trent　　　April 29, 1974, Wollongong, NSW, Australia
RHB, RFM: 31 ODIs, 405 runs at 22.50, HS 45*; 26 wickets at 36.84, BB 5-14.
Inspirational captain (and innovative chicken dancer) during Ireland's World Cup run.

McCALLAN, William Kyle　　　August 27, 1975, Carrickfergus, Co. Antrim
RHB, OB: 39 ODIs, 361 runs at 20.05, HS 50*; 39 wickets at 30.97, BB 4-30.
Tidy offspinner from Ulster club Waringstown: took 10 wickets at 23.30 in the World Cup.

MOONEY, John Francis　　　February 10, 1982, Dublin
LHB, RM: 13 ODIs, 176 runs at 25.14, HS 72; 5 wickets at 57.40, BB 3-79.
Left-hander with a mean reverse-sweep; his brother Paul played for Ireland too.

O'BRIEN, Kevin Joseph　　　March 4, 1984, Dublin
RHB, RFM: 35 ODIs, 884 runs at 31.57, HS 142, 1×100; 18 wickets at 42.05, BB 3-30.
Allrounder with Dublin's Railway Union club: hit 142 (11 fours, six sixes) v Kenya in Feb 2007.

O'BRIEN, Niall John　　　November 8, 1981, Dublin
LHB, WK: 33 ODIs, 815 runs at 27.16, HS 72; 24 ct, 6 st.
Feisty keeper who has played for Kent and Northants: made 72 in World Cup win over Pakistan.

PORTERFIELD, William Thomas Stuart　　　September 6, 1984, Londonderry
RHB: 37 ODIs, 1150 runs at 33.82, HS 112*, 4×100.
Solid opener: made two ODI hundreds in three days early in 2007; took over as captain in 2008.

RANKIN, William Boyd　　　July 5, 1984, Derry
LHB, RFM: 20 ODIs, 16 runs at 8.00, HS 7*; 28 wickets at 24.75, BB 3-32.
Tall (6ft 8ins) fast bowler who did well at the World Cup and later joined Warwickshire.

STIRLING, Paul Robert　　　September 3, 1990, Belfast
RHB: 6 ODIs, 128 runs at 25.60, HS 84.
Young batsman who hit a matchwinning 84 against Kenya in Dublin in June 2009.

WEST, Regan Morris　　　April 27, 1979, New Plymouth, New Zealand
LHB, SLA: 10 ODIs, 61 runs at 30.50, HS 41; 9 wickets at 31.00, BB 4-26.
Solidly built spinner who took 4-26 against Scotland in August 2009.

WHITE, Andrew Roland　　　July 3, 1980, Newtownards, Co. Down
RHB, OB: 32 ODIs, 421 runs at 18.30, HS 40; 14 wickets at 29.85, BB 2-5.
Offspinner, formerly with Northants, who hit 152* on first-class debut, for Ireland v Holland in 2004.

WILSON, Gary Craig　　　February 5, 1986, Dundonald, Northern Ireland
RHB, WK: 16 ODIs, 290 runs at 19.33, HS 51*; 10 ct, 4 st.
Handy keeper-batsman who is on the Surrey staff; scored 51* v Kenya in Dublin in 2009.

KENYA

Collins Obuya

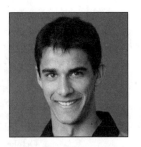
Seren Waters

Steve Tikolo

The British Empire spread cricket to Kenya: the first notable match was played there in 1899, and English-style country clubs still flourish in Nairobi, which can claim one cricket record – six different grounds there have staged official one-day internationals, more than any other city. Strong MCC teams have made several visits to East Africa – one of them, in the early 1960s, unearthed Basharat Hassan, who went on to enjoy a long career with Nottinghamshire. Kenyan players formed the backbone of the East African side in the first World Cup, in 1975, but soon after that they struck out on their own, joining the ICC in their own right in 1981. Kenyan cricket continued to improve quietly until they qualified for the World Cup in 1995-96, where they amazed everyone by upsetting West Indies in a group game. Players reared on hard pitches struggled in early-season England at the 1999 Cup, but the 2003 version was different: it was held in Africa, and some of the matches were played in Kenya. Helped by outside events (England refused to go to Zimbabwe, while New Zealand boycotted Nairobi for security reasons), the Kenyans progressed to the semi-finals. It seemed like the start of a golden era: instead it ushered in a depressing time, marked by player strikes and arguments about administration. Peace broke out in time for the 2007 World Cup, but with several players approaching the veteran stage – many of them come from the same Luo tribe, which is why so many of their surnames begin with O – the results were poor, and by 2009 Ireland had comfortably usurped them as the leading non-Test country. Still, Kenya boast arguably the best batsman outside the Test arena, in their captain Steve Tikolo, while the solidly built allrounder Thomas Odoyo (who played in the 1996 World Cup at 17) was the first bowler from a non-Test nation to take 100 wickets in one-day internationals.

Kenya's ODI records as at 21.9.09

Highest total	347-3	v Bangladesh at Nairobi 1997-98
Lowest total	84	v Australia at Nairobi 2002-03
Most runs	3171	SO Tikolo (avge. 30.78)
Highest score	144	KO Otieno v Bangladesh at Nairobi 1997-98
Most wickets	117	TM Odoyo (avge. 30.27)
Best bowling	5-24	CO Obuya v Sri Lanka at Nairobi 2002-03
Most matches	118	SO Tikolo (1996-2009)
World Cup record		Semi-finalists in 2002-03; first phase 1995-96, 1999, 2006-07
Overall ODI record		Played 120: Won 34, Lost 81, No result 5

KENYA

BHUDIA, Rajesh Lalji   November 22, 1984, Raydhanjar, Gujarat, India
RHB, RM: 5 ODIs, 122 runs at 24.40, HS 47; 3 wickets at 50.33, BB 2-42.
Medium-pacer who was in the 2007 World Cup squad but didn't actually play.

KAMANDE, James Kabatha   December 12, 1978, Muranga
RHB, OB: 66 ODIs, 794 runs at 17.64, HS 74; 36 wickets at 44.19, BB 3-32.
Former medium-pacer who now bowls offspin, after his action was reported to the ICC.

OBANDA, Alex Ouma   December 25, 1987, Nairobi
RHB: 23 ODIs, 687 runs at 38.16, HS 96*.
*Strokeplaying batsman who was stranded four short of a century against Zimbabwe in
Feb 2009.*

OBUYA, Collins Omondi   July 27, 1981, Nairobi
RHB, LB: 70 ODIs, 1064 runs at 22.16, HS 78*; 29 wickets at 50.75, BB 5-24.
Tall legspinner who played a few matches for Warwickshire after doing well at the 2003 World Cup.

OBUYA, David Oluoch   August 14, 1979, Nairobi
RHB, WK: 57 ODIs, 954 runs at 18.00, HS 93; 30 ct, 4 st.
Opener, wicketkeeper, and brother of Collins Obuya and Kennedy Otieno.

ODHIAMBO, Nehemiah Ngoche   August 7, 1983, Nairobi, Kenya
RHB, RFM: 38 ODIs, 332 runs at 14.43, HS 66; 30 wickets at 43.46, BB 3-25.
Fast bowler who took 5-54 on first-class debut, v Canada in 2006: brother of Lameck Onyango.

ODOYO, Thomas Migai   May 12, 1978, Nairobi
RHB, RFM: ODIs 117 (5 for Africa), 2085 runs (24.24), HS 111*; 121 wkts (30.57), BB 4-25.
Hard-hitting allrounder: the first bowler from a non-Test nation to take 100 wickets in ODIs.

ONGONDO, Peter Jimmy Carter   February 10, 1977, Nairobi
RHB, RFM: 75 ODIs (1 for Africa), 372 runs at 9.53, HS 36; 77 wkts at 28.24, BB 5-51.
Handy seamer and useful tailender who once top-scored against West Indies with 36 from No. 11.

ONYANGO, Lameck Ngoche   September 22, 1973, Nairobi
RHB, RM: 22 ODIs, 99 runs at 12.37, HS 34*; 20 wickets at 33.35, BB 3-29.
Seamer and late-order blocker who once went in last in an ODI and didn't bowl.

OTIENO, Elijah Asoyo   January 3, 1988, Nairobi
RHB, RFM: 7 ODIs, 4 runs at 4.00, HS 3; 6 wickets at 38.16, BB 2-29.
Promising young seamer – but with the bat collected five ducks in his first seven first-class innings.

OTIENO, Kennedy Obuya   March 11, 1972, Nairobi
RHB, WK: 90 ODIs, 2016 runs at 23.44, HS 144, 2×100; 43 ct, 14 st.
Veteran of the 1996 World Cup win over West Indies: has made two ODI centuries v Bangladesh.

OUMA, Maurice Akumu   November 8, 1982, Kiambli
RHB, WK: 52 ODIs, 986 runs at 20.54, HS 61; 32 ct, 6 st.
Handy striker who often opens with David Obuya, with whom he vies for the keeper's gloves.

TIKOLO, Stephen Ogonji   June 25, 1971, Nairobi
RHB, OB: 122 ODIs (4 for Africa), 3230 runs at 30.18, HS 111, 3×100; 88 wkts at 32.30, BB 4-41.
Probably the best batsman outside the Test arena: 28 hundreds for Kenya, including two doubles.

VARAIYA, Hiren Ashok   April 9, 1984, Nairobi
RHB, SLA: 42 ODIs, 160 runs at 13.33, HS 34; 46 wickets at 27.06, BB 4-25.
Young spinner who flights the ball well: took a wicket with first ball in an ODI, v Canada in 2006.

WATERS, Seren Robert   April 11, 1990, Nairobi
RHB: 12 ODIs, 261 runs at 21.75, HS 74.
Precocious batsman who scored 74 against South Africa while still a schoolboy.

THE NETHERLANDS

Edgar Schiferli

Alexei Kervezee

Ryan ten Doeschate

Cricket was brought to The Netherlands by British soldiers during the Napoleonic War: by 1881 there was a Dutch team, and two years later a national board, comprising 18 clubs, four of which still exist. A league system has long flourished, and there has been a tradition of foreign players coming over to coach. Dutch cricket received a boost in 1964 when Australia visited after an Ashes tour and lost by three wickets, and more noses were tweaked in 1989, with a win over England A. West Indies (1991) and South Africa (1994) also succumbed – it's safe to say they were more relaxed than they might have been for an official international – and another strongish England side was beaten in 1993. The Netherlands qualified for their first World Cup three years later, and weren't disgraced, and they were there again in 2003, when they beat Namibia. They just scraped in to the 2007 tournament, winning a playoff against the UAE, but again managed a consolation win, this time over Scotland, which made up for being pummelled by South Africa and Australia. Perhaps their biggest moment, though, came in the first match of the World Twenty20 in 2009, when they embarrassed England – at Lord's, too. Standout performers in recent years have included Roland Lefebvre, who played for Somerset and Glamorgan, and Bas Zuiderent, who had a spell with Sussex. A South African-born newcomer has taken the eye of late: Essex's Ryan ten Doeschate hammered four centuries in three ICC Intercontinental Cup games in 2006, and soon shot to the top of the national one-day runscoring and wicket-taking lists. The local players are very keen, but there are not that many of them, fans are thin on the ground, and there's really no chance of a proper first-class competition. The future might not be too bright, but for the Dutch one-day team at least, it's certainly orange.

The Netherlands' ODI records as at 21.9.09

Highest total	315-8	v Bermuda at Rotterdam 2007
Lowest total	80	v West Indies at Dublin 2007
Most runs	1026	RN ten Doeschate (avge. 64.12)
Highest score	134*	KJJ van Noortwijk v Namibia at Bloemfontein 2002-03
Most wickets	44	RN ten Doeschate (avge. 20.86)
Best bowling	4-23	E Schiferli v Kenya at Potchefstroom 2008-09
Most matches	41	B Zuiderent (1996-2009)
World Cup record	Eliminated in first round 1995-96, 2002-03 and 2006-07	
Overall ODI record	Played 45: Won 18, Lost 25, No result 2	

THE NETHERLANDS

BORREN, Peter William   August 21, 1983, Christchurch, New Zealand
RHB, RM: 27 ODIs, 356 runs at 16.18, HS 96; 23 wickets at 37.26, BB 3-54.
Combative allrounder who played for NZ Under-19s: made 105 and 96 v Canada in 2006.

BUKHARI, Mudassar   December 26, 1983, Gujrat, Pakistan
RHB, RFM: 16 ODIs, 207 runs at 20.70, HS 71; 19 wickets at 24.36, BB 3-24.
Primarily a bowler, he scored 71 (after opening) and took 3-24 against Ireland in July 2007.

de GROOTH, Tom Nico   May 14, 1979, The Hague
RHB, OB: 17 ODIs, 326 runs at 25.07, HS 97; 1 wicket at 2.00, BB 1-2.
Made 98 (v Scotland), 196 and 97 (v Bermuda) in successive matches in August 2007.

JONKMAN, Maurits Maarten Alexander   March 20, 1986, The Hague
RHB, RM: 2 ODIs, has not batted; 3 wickets at 19.00, BB 3-22.
Handy medium-pacer whose twin brother Mark played 7 ODIs for the Netherlands.

KERVEZEE, Alexei Nicolaas   September 11, 1989, Walvis Bay, Namibia
RHB, occasional RM: 24 ODIs, 505 runs at 26.57, HS 75; 0 wickets.
Precocious talent: World Cup debut at 17, later made 98 v Canada, and joined Worcestershire in 2007.

MOHAMMAD KASHIF   December 3, 1984, Khanewal, Punjab, Pakistan
RHB, OB: 8 ODIs, 1 run at 0.50, HS 1; 8 wickets at 35.37, BB 3-42.
Offspinner (and fine fielder) who is trying to develop a doosra.

REEKERS, Darron John   May 26, 1973, Christchurch, New Zealand
RHB, RFM: 19 ODIs, 481 runs at 25.31, HS 104, 1×100; 13 wickets at 33.53, BB 3-54.
Has opened the batting and bowling in ODIs, and hit 104 against Ireland in Feb 2007.

SCHIFERLI, Edgar   May 17, 1976, The Hague
RHB, RFM: 27 ODIs, 153 runs at 11.76, HS 41; 31 wickets at 30.12, BB 4-23.
Holland's most experienced fast bowler: missed the 2007 World Cup with a leg injury.

SEELAAR, Pieter Marinus   July 2, 1987, Schiedam
RHB, SLA: 13 ODIs, 9 runs at 4.50, HS 5*; 15 wickets at 27.26, BB 3-22.
Tidy spinner who took 5 for 57 in Intercontinental Cup match against Kenya at Amstelveen in 2008.

SMITS, Jeroen   June 21, 1972, The Hague
RHB, WK: 38 ODIs, 169 runs at 16.90, HS 29*; 41 ct, 7 st.
Steady keeper (and Jamiroquai fan): took over as captain after the 2007 World Cup.

STATHAM, Nickholas Alexander   March 15, 1975, The Hague
RHB, occasional OB: 3 ODIs, 7 runs at 2.33, HS 7.
Reappeared in 2009 six years after becoming Wasim Akram's 500th ODI wicket in 2003 World Cup.

SZWARCZYNSKI, Eric Stefan   February 13, 1983, Vanderbijlpark, South Africa
RHB: 18 ODIs, 493 runs at 30.81, HS 65.
Batsman whose favourite player is Allan Donald: made 65 against Afghanistan in Sept 2009.

ten DOESCHATE, Ryan Neil   June 30, 1980, Port Elizabeth, South Africa
RHB, RFM: 24 ODIs, 1026 runs at 64.12, HS 109*, 2×100; 44 wickets at 20.86, BB 4-31.
Allrounder who reached 1000 ODI runs quicker than anyone bar Viv Richards and Gordon Greenidge.

van BUNGE, Daan Lodewijk Samuel   October 19, 1982, Voorburg
RHB, LB: 32 ODIs, 564 runs at 21.69, HS 80; 11 wickets at 29.18, BB 3-16.
Talented batsman ... but his legspin was hit for six sixes by Herschelle Gibbs at the 2007 World Cup.

ZUIDERENT, Bastiaan   March 3, 1977, Utrecht
RHB: 41 ODIs, 792 runs at 24.00, HS 77*.
Orthodox opener who had a spell with Sussex: has played in all Holland's World Cup matches.

SCOTLAND

| Gavin Hamilton | Fraser Watts | Neil McCallum |

Cricket crept over the border from England in the mid-18th century: soldiers played it near Perth in 1750, although the first recorded match in Scotland was not till 1785. More recently there has long been a strong amateur league system in the country, although – just as in Ireland – international aspirations have always been handicapped by the absence of a proper professional set-up, which has meant that the better players have always migrated south. One of them, the Ayr-born Mike Denness, captained England, while one of the few bowlers to trouble Don Bradman in 1930 was the Scottish legspinner Ian Peebles. More recently, offspinner Peter Such (born in Helensburgh) played for England, while Gavin Hamilton (born in Broxburn) also won an England Test cap after impressing for Scotland at the 1999 World Cup. Unfortunately, Hamilton bagged a pair, and was soon back playing for Scotland: he hit his maiden ODI century in 2008, and is now their captain. At the 2007 World Cup, Hamilton appeared alongside another former England player in Dougie Brown, the combative allrounder who had a long career with Warwickshire and played nine ODIs in 1997-98. Scotland left the auspices of the English board and joined the ICC in 1994, but they failed to win a match – or reach 200 – in any of their World Cup games in 1999 or 2007. They also competed in the English counties' limited-overs league for many years, without managing more than the occasional upset. The main problem lying in the way of Scotland's advancement – apart from the weather – remains the lack of a sound domestic structure which might support first-class cricket; local support is also patchy, despite the sterling efforts of a few diehards. Until this is addressed – if it ever can be – Scotland will continue to suffer from a player drain to English counties.

Scotland's ODI records as at 21.9.09

Highest total	293-8	v Canada at Mombasa 2006-07
Lowest total	68	v West Indies at Leicester 1999
Most runs	1150	GM Hamilton (avge. 35.93)
Highest score	123*	RR Watson v Canada at Mombasa 2006-07
Most wickets	41	JAR Blain (avge. 28.60)
Best bowling	5-22	JAR Blain v Netherlands at Dublin 2008
Most matches	35	GM Hamilton (1999-2009)
World Cup record		Eliminated in first round 1999 and 2006-07
Overall ODI record		Played 40: Won 10, Lost 27, No result 3

SCOTLAND

COETZER, Kyle James   April 14, 1984, Aberdeen
RHB, RM: 4 ODIs, 81 runs at 20.25, HS 44.
Attractive batsman who is on Durham's books, and scored two first-class hundreds for them in 2007.

DRUMMOND, Gordon David   April 21, 1980, Meigle, Perthshire
RHB, RFM: 11 ODIs, 67 runs at 16.75, HS 25*; 10 wickets at 34.20, BB 4-41.
Watsonians fast bowler who took 4-41 against Canada in July 2009.

GOUDIE, Gordon   August 12, 1987, Aberdeen
RHB, RFM: 4 ODIs, 32 runs at 16.00, HS 17*; 8 wickets at 21.12, BB 5-73.
West of Scotland fast bowler who took 5-73 against Australia in 2009.

HAMILTON, Gavin Mark   September 16, 1974, Broxburn, West Lothian
LHB, RFM: 35 ODIs, 1150 runs at 35.93, HS 119, 2×100; 3 wickets at 53.33, BB 2-36.
Played for Yorks & Durham – and once for England, after doing well for Scotland in 1999 World Cup.

HAQ Khan, Rana Majid   February 11, 1983, Paisley
LHB, OB: 23 ODIs, 388 runs at 18.47, HS 71; 28 wickets at 32.46, BB 4-28.
Hard-hitting allrounder, who plays for Ferguslie: took 4-28 v West Indies at Clantarf in 2007.

LYONS, Ross Thomas   December 8, 1984, Greenock
LHB, SLA: 16 ODIs, 86 runs at 28.66, HS 28; 11 wickets at 58.54, BB 2-28.
Promising spinner who dismissed Shahid Afridi in his first ODI.

McCALLUM, Neil Francis Ian   November 22, 1977, Edinburgh
RHB: 33 ODIs, 764 runs at 28.29, HS 121*, 2×100.
PE teacher who made 181 v Holland in 2007, and has also hit two ODI centuries against Ireland.

MacLEOD, Calum Scott   November 15, 1988, Glasgow
RHB, RFM: 4 ODIs, 12 runs at 6.00, HS 10*; 3 wickets at 46.33, BB 2-46.
Fast bowler on Warwickshire's books, whose bowling action has been under scrutiny.

NEL, Johann Dewald   June 6, 1980, Klerksdorp, South Africa
RHB, RFM: 18 ODIs, 20 runs at 10.00, HS 5*; 14 wickets at 44.42, BB 4-25.
Fast bowler who dismissed Inzamam-ul-Haq on his ODI debut, and both Australia's openers in 2009.

PETRIE, Marc John   March 2, 1990, Dundee
LHB, WK: 4 ODIs, 3 runs at 1.50, HS 3; 3 ct, 1 st.
Arbroath wicketkeeper who replaced the long-serving Colin Smith, who retired in 2009.

POONIA, Naveed Singh   May 11, 1986, Govan, Glasgow
RHB: 21 ODIs, 237 runs at 11.28, HS 67.
Stylish batsman on the Warwickshire staff: he has made eight centuries for their 2nd XI.

SHEIKH, Mohammad Qasim   October 30, 1984, Glasgow
LHB, LM: 6 ODIs, 49 runs at 9.80, HS 23.
Captain of the Clydesdale club, he hit 92 for Scotland v Canada in the Intercontinental Cup in 2008.

STANDER, Jan Hendrik   January 4, 1982, Port Elizabeth, South Africa
RHB, RFM: 4 ODIs, 36 runs at 12.00, HS 22*; 6 wickets at 27.66, BB 2-25.
Allrounder who made 64 and took five Intercontinental Cup wickets against Canada in 2009.

WATSON, Ryan Robert   November 12, 1976, Salisbury (now Harare), Zimbabwe
RHB, RM: 34 ODIs, 956 runs at 31.86, HS 123*, 1×100; 12 wickets at 44.00, BB 3-18.
Chunky batsman, at school with SA's Graeme Smith, who hit 123 v Canada in Mombasa in 2006-07.*

WATTS, David Fraser   June 5, 1979, King's Lynn, Norfolk
RHB: 26 ODIs, 572 runs at 22.88, HS 101.
Banker-turned-batsman who scored 171 v Denmark in 2006, and 101 v Canada in July 2009.*

ZIMBABWE

Charles Coventry   *Hamilton Masakadza*   *Tatenda Taibu*

The decline of cricket in Zimbabwe is one of the game's saddest tales – outranked, of course, by the decline of the country itself from prosperous to dangerous. Cricket was first played in what was then Rhodesia in 1891, and for years the national side took part in South Africa's Currie Cup. Several Rhodesians played for South Africa, notably Colin Bland ... and offspinner John Traicos, in 1970: he was still around 22 years later when Zimbabwe were given Test status themselves. That came after years of consistent performances, including a famous World Cup win over Australia in 1983, inspired by Duncan Fletcher, later England's Ashes-winning coach. Zimbabwe were always hampered by a small player-base, but punched above their weight thanks to a nucleus of world-class players including Dave Houghton, the Flower brothers and Heath Streak. Probably their strongest side was assembled for the 1999 World Cup, following the return of Neil Johnson (previously based in South Africa) and Murray Goodwin (Australia). Zimbabwe qualified for the second phase that year, and six of their eight Test wins came between October 1998 and November 2001. And then it all started to go wrong. At the 2003 World Cup, with the political situation at home worsening, Andy Flower and the black fast bowler Henry Olonga sported black armbands bemoaning the "death of democracy" in Zimbabwe: their reward was to be hounded out of the country. A divisive dispute over payments and selection then tore the rest of the side apart. Zimbabwe pulled out of Test cricket in 2005, just ahead of official ICC action. There was a chink of light late in 2007, when ICC's new president Ray Mali claimed that Zimbabwe's young side could top the world rankings in three years, after witnessing some encouraging performances against South Africa. The beleaguered young side has shown some improvement, but there's still a long way to go.

Zimbabwe's ODI records *as at 21.9.09*

Highest total	351-7	v Kenya at Mombasa 2008-09
Lowest total	35	v Sri Lanka at Harare 2003-04
Most runs	6786	A Flower (avge. 35.34)
Highest score	194*	CK Coventry v Bangladesh at Bulawayo 2009
Most wickets	237	HH Streak (avge. 29.81)
Best bowling	6-19	HK Olonga v England at Cape Town 1999-2000
Most matches	219	GW Flower (1992-2004)
World Cup record	Second phase 1999 and 2002-03	
Overall ODI record	Played 355: Won 89, Lost 252, Tied 5, No result 9	

Test records for Zimbabwe can be found in the 2008 Cricinfo Guide

ZIMBABWE

CHIBHABHA, Chamunorwa Justice September 6, 1986, Masvingo
RHB, RM: 0 Tests. 43 ODIs, 943 runs (21.93); 14 wkts (51.35).
Good-looking off-driver, and fine fielder: his sister Julia captains Zimbabwe's women's team.

CHIGUMBURA, Elton March 14, 1986, Kwekwe
RHB, RFM: 6 Tests, 187 runs (15.58), 9 wkts (55.33). 93 ODIs, 1906 runs (24.43), 67 wkts (35.80).
Big-hitting allrounder, and good outfielder, who made his first-class debut before he was 16.

COVENTRY, Charles Kevin March 8, 1983, Kwekwe
RHB, WK: 2 Tests, 88 runs (22.00). 16 ODIs, 495 runs (35.35).
Equalled the ODI record by hammering 194* against Bangladesh at Bulawayo in 2009.

DABENGWA, Keith Mbusi August 17, 1980, Bulawayo
LHB, SLA: 3 Tests, 90 runs (15.00), 5 wkts (49.80). 32 ODIs, 433 runs (19.68), 21 wkts (37.61).
Fitfully brilliant allrounder who scored 161 in 2005 and took 7-1 in a first-class match in 2007.

MASAKADZA, Hamilton August 9, 1983, Harare
RHB, LB: 15 Tests, 785 runs (27.06), 2 wkts (19.50). 73 ODIs, 1712 runs (24.45), 20 wkts (36.05).
Early-flowering batsman who made 119 on Test debut against West Indies in 2001, aged 17.

MATSIKENYERI, Stuart May 3, 1983, Harare
RHB, OB: 8 Tests, 351 runs (23.40), 2 wkts (172.50). 93 ODIs, 1826 runs (21.23), 14 wkts (50.92).
Cheerful, diminutive allrounder who made 150 for Zimbabwe v Bangladesh Board XI in 2005.

MUPARIWA, Tawanda April 16, 1985, Bulawayo
RHB, RFM: 1 Test, 15 runs (15.00), 0 wkts. 35 ODIs, 165 runs (8.68), 55 wkts (26.29).
Fast bowler with a good inswinger, who took 4-46 v Pakistan at Multan in January 2008.

PRICE, Raymond William June 12, 1976, Salisbury (now Harare)
RHB, SLA: 18 Tests, 224 runs (9.73), 69 wkts (39.86). 57 ODIs, 245 runs (11.13), 51 wkts (37.47).
Economical spinner who played for Worcestershire between 2004 and 2007.

RAINSFORD, Edward Charles December 14, 1984, Kadoma
RHB, RFM: 0 Tests. 36 ODIs, 40 runs (4.44), 35 wkts (36.74).
Fast bowler with a good outswinger and yorker: took 6-67 v South Africa A in 2004.

SIBANDA, Vusimuzi October 10, 1983, Highfields, Harare
RHB, RM: 3 Tests, 48 runs (8.00). 79 ODIs, 1677 runs (22.06), 2 wkts (74.00).
Stylish opener who often gets out when set: made 116 in tri-series final v Bermuda in 2006.

TAIBU, Tatenda May 14, 1983, Harare
RHB, WK: 24 Tests, 1273 runs (29.60), 1 wkt (27.00). 107 ODIs, 2045 runs (26.21), 2 wkts (30.50).
Tiny keeper, big-hearted batter: the youngest Test captain at 20, he later fell out with the Board.

TAYLOR, Brendan Ross Murray February 6, 1986, Harare
RHB, OB, WK: 10 Tests, 422 runs (21.10), 0 wkts. 80 ODIs, 2122 runs (29.06), 8 wkts (28.00).
Occasionally brilliant batsman, with a booming cover-drive: has had disciplinary problems.

UTSEYA, Prosper March 26, 1985, Harare
RHB, OB: 1 Test, 45 runs (22.50), 0 wkts. 93 ODIs, 696 runs (13.92), 62 wkts (51.19).
Short offspinner who keeps the runs down: took over as captain in July 2006, when he was 21.

VERMEULEN, Mark Andrew March 2, 1979, Salisbury (now Harare)
RHB, OB: 8 Tests, 414 runs (25.87). 36 ODIs, 707 runs (22.09).
Temperamental but occasionally brilliant batsman who made a Test century against West Indies in 2003.

WILLIAMS, Sean Colin September 26, 1986, Bulawayo
LHB, SLA: 0 Tests. 38 ODIs, 948 runs (29.62), 9 wkts (62.22).
Former national Under-19 captain: scored 70* v West Indies in the 2007 World Cup.

COACHES

MICKEY **ARTHUR**

Full name **John Michael Arthur**
Born **May 17, 1968, Johannesburg, Transvaal**
Country **South Africa**

Mickey Arthur was a dedicated batsman for Free State and Griqualand West, scoring over 6000 first-class runs before turning to coaching. He twice coached Eastern Cape to the finals of South Africa's new Twenty20 competition before being the surprise choice to succeed Ray Jennings at the helm of the national side in May 2005. After a tough baptism – home and away series against Australia – he settled down, and in 2007-08 South Africa won series in Pakistan and India, before coming to England in 2008 and winning the Tests there too, although the wheels fell off in the one-dayers that followed. Then came the big one: victory in Australia in 2008-09. Throughout, Arthur proved a canny and urbane presence at Graeme Smith's shoulder.

TREVOR **BAYLISS**

Full name **Trevor Harley Bayliss**
Born **December 21, 1962, Goulburn, NSW, Australia**
Country **Sri Lanka**

Trevor Bayliss was a strokeplaying middle-order batsman and brilliant cover fielder for New South Wales, and replaced Steve Rixon as their coach in 2004-05. He immediately guided them to the Pura Cup title, and added the one-day cup the following year. In 2007 Bayliss, who never won a Test cap, was named to succeed another Australian, Tom Moody, as Sri Lanka's coach, and although he lost the short Test series in Australia he was then in charge for home victories over England and India, as well as a shared series in the West Indies that included Sri Lanka's first Test win there. For good measure his side won the one-day Asia Cup, too, helped after they unearthed a new spin sensation in Ajantha Mendis, and continued to do well in 2009.

ANDY **FLOWER**

Full name **Andrew Flower**
Born **April 28, 1968, Cape Town, South Africa**
Country **England**

Andy Flower was often a lone beacon of class in an underpowered Zimbabwe side. A compact left-hander strong on the sweep, Flower scored 4,794 Tests runs at 51, and nearly 7,000 in ODIs. On top of this, he usually kept wicket too, and often captained. A deep thinker, Flower was hounded out of Zimbabwe after he and Henry Olonga wore black armbands mourning the "death of democracy" there during the 2003 World Cup. Flower moved to England, where he had several fine seasons for Essex alongside his brother Grant, then joined the England coaching set-up, first as Peter Moores's assistant. When Moores and Kevin Pietersen fell out late in 2008, Flower - who is calm, understated and polite - stepped into the breach, being confirmed as fulltime coach in time for the 2009 Ashes series ... and, like his fellow Zimbabwean Duncan Fletcher, he delighted English fans by overseeing the recapture of the urn.

COACHES

INTIKHAB ALAM

Full name **Intikhab Alam Khan**
Born **December 28, 1941, Hoshiarpur, Punjab, India**
Country **Pakistan**

The jovial "Inti" has been involved in international cricket since he took a wicket with his first ball in a Test, bowling Australia's Colin McDonald at Karachi in December 1959. He went on to captain Pakistan in 17 of his 47 Tests, played for Garry Sobers's Rest of the World side in 1970, entertained The Oval with big hitting and big-turning legspin for Surrey, then had several stints in the volatile position of Pakistan's coach/manager. The most recent of these began in October 2008, when the Australian Geoff Lawson was sacked and Intikhab answered the call once again. Results were mixed – there was some success in one-dayers, but a Test series in Sri Lanka was lost. However, Intikhab's Pakistan did bring some joy to a troubled land when they won the World Twenty20 title in England in June 2009.

GARY **KIRSTEN**

Full name **Gary Kirsten**
Born **November 23, 1967, Cape Town, South Africa**
Country **India**

A gritty left-hander, Gary Kirsten worked out his strengths and played to them superbly in a career that brought him 7289 runs in 101 Tests for South Africa, with 21 centuries. His highest score of 275 stretched over 14½ hours, and remains the second-longest innings in Test history. Kirsten was probably the most organised batsman to play for South Africa since their readmission to international cricket, and this methodical approach helped when he turned to coaching, first as a batting consultant for the Warriors franchise, then as director of his own coaching academy in Cape Town. In December 2007 he signed a two-year deal to succeed Greg Chappell as coach of India, and started with a drawn series against his native South Africa before suffering defeat in Sri Lanka.

ANDY **MOLES**

Full name **Andrew James Moles**
Born **February 12, 1961, Solihull, England**
Country **New Zealand**

Andy Moles had a fine career for Warwickshire, where he was regularly among the leading county runscorers without attracting much interest from the selectors – largely, it was said, because of his size (he was comfortably upholstered even in his county days, and has expanded even more since). Moles was one of the few batsmen to average over 40 in first-class cricket – 40.70, with 29 centuries, four of them doubles – without ever playing a Test. A varied coaching career since, including stints with Kenya, Scotland and the ICC high-performance unit, culminated in 2009 when he succeeded John Bracewell as New Zealand's coach. Moles made a slow start with an admittedly modest side which is overly dependent on captain Daniel Vettori, losing Test series at home to India and away to Sri Lanka, although they remained competitive in the shorter formats.

COACHES

TIM **NIELSEN**

Full name **Timothy John Nielsen**
Born **May 5, 1968, Forest Gate, London, England**
Country **Australia**

Tim Nielsen had a hard act to follow, replacing John Buchanan after his incredibly
successful stint as Australia's coach, which ended in 2007 after two World Cup titles
and countless Test victories. Nielsen, a talented wicketkeeper-batsman for South Australia whose
international hopes were stymied by the perpetual presence under the Baggy Green of Ian Healy, had
been around for part of the Buchanan era as the assistant coach and computer analyst, although he
left to take charge of the national Centre of Excellence in Brisbane in 2005. "Working with 'Buck' was
great," said Nielsen. "He's almost a mentor for me and we bounced ideas off each other." Nielsen's
arrival coincided with the retirements of several senior players, and his rebuilt side lost to India and
South Africa before surrendering the Ashes in England in 2009.

JAMIE **SIDDONS**

Full name **James Darren Siddons**
Born **April 25, 1964, Robinvale, Victoria, Australia**
Country **Bangladesh**

A stylish, attacking batsman and a superb fielder, Jamie Siddons scored more than
10,000 runs in the Sheffield Shield (later Pura Cup), a record when he retired in
1999-2000. But he never played a Test, at a time of plenty for Australian batting, and made a solitary
one-day international appearance in Pakistan in 1988-89. A severe stomach bug he picked up on
that tour didn't help his Test prospects, and nor did a fractured cheekbone, courtesy of Merv Hughes,
in 1991-92: "It ruined my chances of playing for Australia," said Siddons. After retiring he coached
at Australia's Centre of Excellence, then in October 2007 accepted an offer to coach Bangladesh. The
size of his task, if he didn't realise it before, was hammered home when they lost nine of his first
ten Tests in charge, before beating a weakened West Indies in July 2009.

DAVID **WILLIAMS**

Full name **David Williams**
Born **November 4, 1963, Penal, Trinidad**
Country **West Indies**

The diminutive David Williams had the thankless task of following Jeff Dujon as West
Indies' wicketkeeper. Williams played 11 Tests and 36 ODIs but, not helped by his lack
of inches, never quite scored enough runs. There were seven ducks in his 18 Test innings, although his
fighting 65 was instrumental in overhauling a ticklish target of 282 to beat England at Port-of-Spain in
1997-98. After five years coaching Trinidad & Tobago, Williams joined the regional side's support staff,
and was still fit enough, at 45, to field as a substitute against England in the Caribbean early in 2009.
Williams was appointed as West Indies' temporary coach when the Australian John Dyson was released
late in 2009. Williams's first task was to guide a makeshift side, torn apart by a damaging dispute about
sponsorship and contracts, through the Champions Trophy in South Africa.

UMPIRES AND REFEREES

ALEEM DAR

Full name	**Aleem Sarwar Dar**	*Tests*	**57 since 2003-04**
Born	**June 6, 1968, Jhang, Punjab**	*ODIs*	**116 since 1999-2000**
Country	**Pakistan**	*T20Is*	**6 since 2009**

Aleem Dar played 17 first-class matches as an offspinning allrounder, but never surpassed the 39 he scored in his first innings, for Railways in February 1987. He took up umpiring in 1998-99, and stood in his first ODI the following season. He officiated at the 2003 World Cup, and a year later was the first Pakistani to join the ICC's elite panel. Calm and unobtrusive, he soon established a good reputation, and it was no surprise when he was chosen to stand in the 2007 World Cup final. What was a surprise was his part in the chaos in the dark at the end, for which all the officials were excluded from the World Twenty20 championships later in the year. Unlike most of his colleagues, he continues to play, and made 82 in a club game the day after umpiring a Test in Mumbai in November 2004.

ASAD RAUF

Full name	**Asad Rauf**	*Tests*	**26 since 2004-05**
Born	**May 12, 1956, Lahore, Punjab**	*ODIs*	**65 since 1999-2000**
Country	**Pakistan**	*T20Is*	**11 since 2007-08**

Asad Rauf was a right-hand batsman who enjoyed a solid if unspectacular first-class career in Pakistan in the 1980s, four times making more than 600 runs in a season and scoring three centuries, the highest 130 for Railways against National Bank in November 1981. He umpired his first first-class match in 1998-99, and stood in his first ODI early in 2000. It took a bit longer to crack the Test scene, but he advanced rapidly once he did, joining the ICC's elite panel in April 2006. A former offspinner himself, he is more prepared than some to give spinners lbws when batsmen prop forward hiding bat behind pad.

MARK **BENSON**

Full name	**Mark Richard Benson**	*Tests*	**26 since 2004-05**
Born	**July 6, 1958, Shoreham-by-Sea, Sussex**	*ODIs*	**72 since 2004**
Country	**England**	*T20Is*	**19 since 2007-08**

A gritty left-hander, Mark Benson won his only Test cap against India in June 1986, and played his solitary ODI a week later. He played on for almost a decade without catching the selectors' eyes again, making 18,387 runs, with 48 hundreds, the highest 257 against Hampshire on his first day as Kent's captain in 1991. He became a fulltime umpire in 2000, and his star rose rapidly: he was the TV official for an ODI the following season. He stood in an ODI for the first time in 2004, and joined the elite panel in April 2006. Later that year he had to have minor heart surgery after a turn during a Test in South Africa, but returned in time for the 2007 World Cup, in which six of his eight matches involved the South Africans.

UMPIRES AND REFEREES

UMPIRE

BILLY **BOWDEN**

Full name	**Brent Fraser Bowden**	*Tests*	**56 since 1999-2000**
Born	**April 11, 1963, Henderson, Auckland**	*ODIs*	**132 since 1994-95**
Country	**New Zealand**	*T20Is*	**11 since 2004-05**

Some eccentrics are born. Others thrust eccentricity upon themselves. Brent "Billy" Bowden shot to fame with a zany array of embellished signals and a preposterous eye for showmanship. Bowden turned to umpiring after the onset of arthritis in his early twenties, and earned a reputation for giving batsmen out with a curiously bent finger. The most celebrated of his antics is the hop-on-one-leg-and-reach-for-Jesus signal for six. For all the embellishments, his decision-making is usually spot-on, although in 2007 he was suspended from standing in the inaugural World Twenty20 championship following his role (as fourth umpire) in the farcical conclusion of the World Cup final in Barbados.

REFEREE

CHRIS **BROAD**

Full name	**Brian Christopher Broad**	*Tests*	**35 since 2003-04**
Born	**Sept 29, 1957, Knowle, Somerset**	*ODIs*	**155 since 2003-04**
Country	**England**	*T20Is*	**37 since 2005-06**

It was a classic case of poacher turned gamekeeper when Chris Broad became a match referee: he had several jousts with authority during a largely successful 25-Test career in the 1980s, refusing to walk after being given out in a Test in Pakistan, and smashing down the stumps after being bowled for 139 in the Bicentennial Test at Sydney in 1987-88. A tall, angular left-hander, Broad did well in Australia, scoring three more Test hundreds there in the 1986-87 Ashes series. After a back injury hastened his retirement, he tried his hand at TV commentary, then in 2003 became a match referee keen on enforcing the Code of Conduct. In 2009 he was caught up in the terrorist attack on the Sri Lankan team coach in Lahore, and showed immense bravery in shielding an injured colleague. His son, Stuart, made his England debut in 2006.

REFEREE

JEFF **CROWE**

Full name	**Jeffrey John Crowe**	*Tests*	**35 since 2004-05**
Born	**September 14, 1958, Auckland**	*ODIs*	**107 since 2003-04**
Country	**New Zealand**	*T20Is*	**13 since 2005**

Jeff Crowe might have played for Australia – he had several successful Sheffield Shield seasons in Adelaide – but he eventually returned to New Zealand, winning 39 Test caps, six as captain. Although he was often overshadowed by his younger brother Martin, Jeff managed three Test centuries of his own. After retirement he had a spell as New Zealand's manager, before becoming a referee in 2003. He was in charge for the 2007 World Cup final, where he presided over the embarrassing finale, which led to him and the umpires being suspended from the inaugural World Twenty20 championship later in the year, but he was back for England's series in Sri Lanka a couple of months later, and oversaw part of the 2009 Ashes series in England.

UMPIRES AND REFEREES

STEVE **DAVIS**

Full name	**Stephen James Davis**	*Tests*	**19 since 1997-98**
Born	**April 9, 1952, London, England**	*ODIs*	**91 since 1992-93**
Country	**Australia**	*T20Is*	**8 since 2007-08**

Steve Davis played club cricket for the Adelaide club West Torrens before turning to umpiring. He had a rapid rise: appointed to the Australian first-class list in 1990-91, he joined the national panel two years later and stood in his first ODI the same season. Test cricket took a little longer, but in 1997-98 he made his debut at Hobart, when New Zealand's last pair hung on to deny Australia victory. Since then he has been a familiar face on the international scene. He stood in three matches in the 2007 World Cup, then officiated in the final two Tests in his native England in 2008, against South Africa, shortly after being elevated to the elite panel. He was one of the umpires in Lahore early the following year and was lucky to survive the terrorist attack on the Sri Lankan team coach.

ASOKA **DE SILVA**

Full name	**Ellawalakankanamge Asoka Ranjit de Silva**	*Tests*	**41 since 2000**
		ODIs	**92 since 1999-2000**
Born	**March 28, 1956, Kalutara**	*T20Is*	**5 since 2009**
Country	**Sri Lanka**		

Asoka de Silva played 10 Tests and 28 one-day internationals for Sri Lanka between 1985 and 1992 as a legspinner, although he found it hard to replicate his good domestic form on the international stage. He took up umpiring after retiring from first-class cricket in 1996-97, and soon became Sri Lanka's best-regarded official. He first stood in an ODI against Pakistan at Galle in August 1999, and umpired a Test the following year (Aravinda de Silva and Sanath Jayasuriya, who were both in de Silva's last Test as a player, were still playing for his umpiring debut). He had a spell on the ICC's elite panel before being dropped from it in 2004. But he was back for the 2007 World Cup – he also officiated in the 2003 tournament – was restored to the elite panel in the middle of 2008, and stood in the World Twenty20 in England the following year. No Sri Lankan has umpired in more Tests or ODIs.

BILLY **DOCTROVE**

Full name	**Billy Raymond Doctrove**	*Tests*	**25 since 1999-2000**
Born	**July 3, 1955, Marigot, Dominica**	*ODIs*	**89 since 1997-98**
Country	**West Indies**	*T20Is*	**10 since 2007-08**

Billy Doctrove played club cricket in Dominica for a number of years, but his first love was football, particularly Liverpool, which explains his odd nickname "Toshack". In 1995 he became Dominica's first FIFA referee, and officiated in a number of internationals in the Caribbean, including a World Cup qualifier between Guyana and Grenada. In 1997 he quit football to concentrate on cricket umpiring, and stood in his first Test in 2000. He joined the international panel in 2004 and the elite one in 2006, but his first forays at the highest level were uninspiring, and he found himself embroiled in the Pakistan ball-tampering furore at The Oval in 2006, as the "other umpire" to Darrell Hair. He grew in stature, though, and stood in the first two Tests of the 2009 Ashes series.

UMPIRES AND REFEREES

IAN **GOULD**

Full name	**Ian James Gould**
Born	**August 19, 1957, Taplow,**
	Buckinghamshire
Country	**England**

Tests **6 since 2008-09**
ODIs **33 since 2006**
T20Is **7 since 2006**

Ian "Gunner" Gould was a combative wicketkeeper/batsman who scored nearly 9000 runs and made more than 700 dismissals in first-class cricket. He started with Middlesex, then moved to Sussex, who he captained to the NatWest Trophy in 1986 (famously announcing afterwards "Watch out Soho!"). Although he never won a Test cap, he did appear in 18 ODIs, all of them in 1983, including that year's World Cup in England. "Gould was all gloves, pads, hair and sunhat," John Woodcock once observed. "He was a cricketer who had been turned into a wicketkeeper." A genial and popular character, he joined the English first-class umpires' panel in 2002, was promoted to the international panel in April 2006, and joined the elite panel three years later.

DARYL **HARPER**

Full name	**Daryl John Harper**
Born	**October 23, 1951, Adelaide**
Country	**Australia**

Tests **85 since 1998-99**
ODIs **158 since 1993-94**
T20Is **10 since 2007-08**

Daryl Harper played club cricket in Adelaide for many years before turning to umpiring. He stood in his first first-class match in 1987-88, and joined Australia's international panel six years later. Quiet and undemonstrative, he was Australia's first representative on the ICC's international panel when it was set up in 2002, being chosen ahead of Darrell Hair and Simon Taufel, and is one of only two survivors (with Rudi Koertzen) from that original intake. He stood (along with his compatriot Simon Taufel) in the World Twenty20 final at Lord's in 2009. He likes most sports, particularly Aussie Rules football and basketball, and writes an entertaining online blog about his travels at www.cricketump.com.

TONY **HILL**

Full name	**Anthony Lloyd Hill**
Born	**June 26, 1951, Auckland**
Country	**New Zealand**

Tests **11 since 2001-02**
ODIs **71 since 1997-98**
T20Is **13 since 2004-05**

Tony Hill came into umpiring without any background in first-class cricket, but soon established himself as a competent and reliable official, being appointed to the ICC's international panel in 1998 – he stood in an ODI against Zimbabwe that March – and to the full elite panel in 2009, although he had umpired the occasional Test since 2001-02. Hill was one of the umpires for the inaugural Twenty20 international, Australia's victory over New Zealand at Auckland in 2004-05, and stood in both the first two World Twenty20 events. He also officiated in three matches at the 2007 World Cup. A keen golfer, he is a regional training officer and mentor for umpires in the Northern Districts, and runs an online question-and-answer forum for umpires of all levels.

UMPIRES AND REFEREES

ALAN **HURST**

Full name	**Alan George Hurst**	*Tests*	**33 since 2004-05**
Born	**July 15, 1950, Altona, Melbourne**	*ODIs*	**75 since 2004-05**
Country	**Australia**	*T20Is*	**11 since 2007-08**

A strapping fast bowler, Alan Hurst won all but one of his dozen Test caps during the World Series Cricket era, after Australia's leading players had been poached by Kerry Packer. He nonetheless took 25 wickets in the 1978-79 Ashes series, which Australia lost 5-1, before the return of Lillee and Co., and a serious back injury, put paid to his future prospects. He was also a notably bad batsman, collecting ducks in exactly half his 20 Test innings. After a spell as a teacher he joined the ICC's panel of referees in 2004. His mettle was tested in Antigua early in 2009 when poor drainage at the new Sir Vivian Richards Stadium meant a rapid move to the old Recreation Ground.

RUDI **KOERTZEN**

Full name	**Rudolf Eric Koertzen**	*Tests*	**101 since 1992-93**
Born	**March 26, 1949, Knysna, Cape Province**	*ODIs*	**201 since 1992-93**
Country	**South Africa**	*T20Is*	**8 since 2006-07**

Rudi Koertzen is a modern umpire in the traditional mould, a curious blend of old and new – his flat white cap is usually offset by a pair of wraparound shades, while his trademark is a dalek-like super-slo-mo raise of the fatal finger to exterminate a batsman's innings. A lifelong cricket fan, he played league cricket while working as a railway clerk, but turned to umpiring in 1981. He first stood in a Test in 1992-93, in South Africa's first home series after readmission, and has been a fixture ever since: he has now umpired more ODIs than anyone else, and in 2009 became the second (after Steve Bucknor) to stand in 100 Tests. An original member of the elite panel, he leaves little to chance, putting in regular sessions in the gym as well as long hours in front of the TV studying the techniques – and previous dismissals – of the batsmen at his mercy. He was one of the support officials for the 2007 World Cup final, but his lead role in the farcical finale cost him a place at the inaugural World Twenty20 championship later in the year.

RANJAN **MADUGALLE**

Full name	**Ranjan Serenath Madugalle**	*Tests*	**112 since 1993-94**
Born	**April 22, 1959, Kandy**	*ODIs*	**236 since 1993-94**
Country	**Sri Lanka**	*T20Is*	**27 since 2006-07**

A stylish right-hander, Ranjan Madugalle won 21 Test caps, the first of them in Sri Lanka's inaugural Test, against England in 1981-82, when he top-scored with 65 in the first innings. He also made 103 against India in Colombo in 1985, and captained Sri Lanka twice. Not long after retiring, and trying his hand at marketing, he became one of the first match refs, and was appointed the ICC's chief referee in 2001. His easy-going exterior and charming personality are a mask for someone who has a reputation as a strict disciplinarian.

UMPIRES AND REFEREES

ROSHAN **MAHANAMA**

Full name **Roshan Siriwardene Mahanama**
Born **May 31, 1966, Colombo**
Country **Sri Lanka**

Tests **24 since 2003-04**
ODIs **127 since 2003-04**
T20Is **5 since 2007-08**

Roshan Mahanama's playing career had two major highlights: he was part of the winning team in the 1996 World Cup, and the following year made 225 (the highest score in his 52 Tests) as he and Sanath Jayasuriya put on 576, then a record Test partnership, as Sri Lanka ran up 952 for 6 (another record) against India in Colombo. An attacking right-hander who made four Test centuries in all (three in nine months in 1992-93), he was also a fine fielder. He was jettisoned after the 1999 World Cup and quit not long afterwards, blaming the selectors for their shabby treatment of him in a book he called *Retired Hurt*. He joined the ICC's referees panel in 2003.

ANDY **PYCROFT**

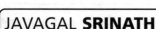

Full name **Andrew John Pycroft**
Born **June 6, 1956, Salisbury (now Harare)**
Country **Zimbabwe**

Tests **6 since 2009**
ODIs **2 since 2009**
T20Is **1 since 2009**

A fine batsman, especially strong off the back foot, Andy Pycroft was a Zimbabwe regular throughout the 1980s, although he was slightly past his peak when they gained Test status in 1992-93. Still, he played in their first three Tests, scoring 60 against New Zealand at Harare in the last of them. The first and last of his 20 ODIs produced famous wins: over Australia in the 1983 World Cup and England in the 1991-92 one. After retiring from playing he was successively a Zimbabwean selector, team manager, and coach. He also found time to fit in the occasional commentary. Outside cricket he was an attorney-at-law for 17 years, which stood him in good stead when he joined the ICC's referees' panel. His first Test as a referee was at Lord's – England v West Indies in May 2009 – and two months later he oversaw Bangladesh's victory over a makeshift West Indian side in the Caribbean.

JAVAGAL **SRINATH**

Full name **Javagal Srinath**
Born **August 31, 1969, Mysore, Karnataka**
Country **India**

Tests **13 since 2006**
ODIs **64 since 2006-07**
T20Is **8 since 2006-07**

Arguably the fastest bowler India has ever produced, Javagal Srinath took 236 wickets in Tests, and 315 more in ODIs. He was tall, and usually slanted the ball in. Unusually for a quick bowler, he did better in India than overseas, his bowling average of 26 at home being four runs lower than his overall one. He went out at the top: his last international match was the 2003 World Cup final. Sadly, there was no fairytale farewell – Srinath was caned (0 for 87) as Australia ran out easy winners. He was not long away from the international arena, though: after a spell as a commentator he joined the referees' panel in 2006. "I'll have to concentrate more than I did during my playing days," he observed.

UMPIRES AND REFEREES

SIMON **TAUFEL**

Full name **Simon James Arnold Taufel**   *Tests* **59 since 2000-01**
Born **Jan 21, 1971, St Leonards, Sydney**   *ODIs* **139 since 1999-2000**
Country **Australia**   *T20Is* **16 since 2007-08**

Simon Taufel came young to umpiring: he was only 24 when he stood in his
first Sheffield Shield match, and still under 30 – and younger than some of
the players – when he made his Test debut on Boxing Day 2000. He started after being forced
to retire from Sydney club cricket with a back injury. Calm and collected on the field, he
leaves little to chance, regularly running laps of the ground to keep fit and often standing in
the practice nets to familiarise himself with players' techniques. And it has paid off: he joined
the ICC's elite panel in 2003, and won the award as the world's leading umpire (voted on by
the Test captains and referees) five times running from 2004. He stood in the World
Twenty20 final at Lord's in 2009.

*As well as its "elite" panel of umpires, the ICC also has an "international" panel, who
fill in when gaps arise in the rota. This reserve list includes:*

Barbour, Kevan Christopher (Zimbabwe)   b. October 23, 1949, Bulawayo
Has stood in 4 Tests and 46 ODIs.

Baxter, Gary Arthur Vincent (New Zealand)   b. March 5, 1953, Christchurch
Has stood in 27 ODIs and 5 Twenty20 internationals.

Duncan, Clyde Rory (West Indies)   b. January 7, 1954, Vreed-En-Hoop, Guyana
Has stood in 2 Tests, 18 ODIs and 3 Twenty20 internationals.

Enamul Haque (Bangladesh)   b. February 27, 1966, Comilla, Chittagong
Played 10 Tests and 29 ODIs: has stood in 18 ODIs and 1 Twenty20 international.

Erasmus, Marais (South Africa)   b. February 27, 1964, George, Cape Province
Has stood in 10 ODIs and 6 Twenty20 internationals.

Jerling, Brian George (South Africa)   b. August 13, 1958, Port Elizabeth, Cape Province
Has stood in 4 Tests, 80 ODIs and 8 Twenty20 internationals.

Llong, Nigel James (England)   b. February 11, 1969, Ashford, Kent
Has stood in 6 Tests, 32 ODIs and 12 Twenty20 internationals.

Malcolm, Norman Alexander (West Indies)   b. March 19, 1955, Manchester, Jamaica
Has stood in 7 ODIs and 2 Twenty20 internationals.

Nadeem Ghauri, Mohammad (Pakistan)   b. October 12, 1962, Lahore, Punjab
Played 1 Test and 6 ODIs: has stood in 5 Tests, 41 ODIs and 1 Twenty20 international.

Nadir Shah (Bangladesh)   b. February 7, 1964, Dacca (now Dhaka)
Has stood in 23 ODIs and 1 Twenty20 international.

Oxenford, Bruce Nicholas James (Australia)   b. March 5, 1960, Southport, Queensland
Has stood in 5 ODIs and 4 Twenty20 internationals.

Saheba, Amiesh Maheshbhai (India)   b. November 15, 1959, Ahmedabad, Gujarat
Has stood in 2 Tests, 34 ODIs and 3 Twenty20 internationals.

Silva, Mangamuni Gamini (Sri Lanka)   b. December 19, 1960, Colombo
Has stood in 3 Tests, 21 ODIs and 1 Twenty20 international.

Tarapore, Shavir Keki (India)   b. December 26, 1957, Calcutta (now Kolkata)
Has stood in 3 ODIs.

Tiffin, Russell Blair (Zimbabwe)   b. June 4, 1959, Salisbury (now Harare)
Has stood in 44 Tests and 111 ODIs.

Tucker, Rodney James (Australia)   b. August 28, 1964, Auburn, Sydney
Has stood in 5 ODIs and 4 Twenty20 internationals.

Wijewardene, Tyron Hirantha (Sri Lanka)   b. August 29, 1961, Maradana
Has stood in 4 Tests, 48 ODIs and 2 Twenty20 internationals.

Zameer Haider (Pakistan)   b. September 30, 1962, Lahore
Has stood in 7 ODIs and 2 Twenty20 internationals.

OVERALL RECORDS
Test Matches

Most appearances

168	SR Waugh A
159	SR Tendulkar I
156	AR Border A
145	SK Warne A
136	RT Ponting A
135	R Dravid I*
133	AJ Stewart E
132	A Kumble I
132	CA Walsh WI
131	JH Kallis SA*
131	Kapil Dev I
131	BC Lara WI*

The records for Dravid, Kallis and Lara include one Test for the World XI

Most runs

		Avge
12773	SR Tendulkar I	54.58
11953	BC Lara WI*	52.88
11345	RT Ponting A	55.88
11174	AR Border A	50.56
10927	SR Waugh A	51.06
10823	R Dravid I*	52.53
10277	JH Kallis SA*	54.66
10122	SM Gavaskar I	51.12
8900	GA Gooch E	42.58
8832	Javed Miandad P	52.57

*The records for Dravid, Kallis and Lara include one Test for the World XI

Most wickets

		Avge
783	M Muralitharan SL*	22.21
708	SK Warne A	25.41
619	A Kumble I	29.65
563	GD McGrath A	21.64
519	CA Walsh WI	24.44
434	Kapil Dev I	29.64
431	RJ Hadlee NZ	22.29
421	SM Pollock SA	23.11
414	Wasim Akram P	23.62
405	CEL Ambrose WI	20.99

*Muralitharan's record includes one Test for the World XI

Highest scores

400*	BC Lara	WI v Eng at St John's	2003-04
380	ML Hayden	Aust v Zim at Perth	2003-04
375	BC Lara	WI v Eng at St John's	1993-94
374	DPMD Jayawardene	SL v SA at Colombo	2006
365*	GS Sobers	WI v Pak at Kingston	1957-58
364	L Hutton	Eng v Aust at The Oval	1938
340	ST Jayasuriya	SL v India at Colombo	1997-98
337	Hanif Mohammad	Pak v WI at Bridgetown	1957-58
336*	WR Hammond	Eng v NZ at Auckland	1932-33
334*	MA Taylor	Aust v Pak at Peshawar	1998-99
334	DG Bradman	Aust v Eng at Leeds	1930

In all 23 scores of 300 or more have been made in Tests

Best innings bowling

10-53	JC Laker	Eng v Aust at Manchester	1956
10-74	A Kumble	India v Pak at Delhi	1998-99
9-28	GA Lohmann	Eng v SA at Jo'burg	1895-96
9-37	JC Laker	Eng v Aust at Manchester	1956
9-51	M Muralitharan	SL v Zim at Kandy	2001-02
9-52	RJ Hadlee	NZ v Aust at Brisbane	1985-86
9-56	Abdul Qadir	Pak v Eng at Lahore	1987-88
9-57	DE Malcolm	Eng v SA at The Oval	1994
9-65	M Muralitharan	SL v Eng at The Oval	1998
9-69	JM Patel	India v Aust at Kanpur	1959-60

There have been seven further instances of a bowler taking nine wickets in an innings

Record wicket partnerships

1st	415	ND McKenzie (226) and GC Smith (232)	South Africa v Bangladesh at Chittagong	2007-08
2nd	576	ST Jayasuriya (340) and RS Mahanama (225)	Sri Lanka v India at Colombo	1997-98
3rd	624	KC Sangakkara (287) and DPMD Jayawardene (374)	Sri Lanka v South Africa at Colombo	2006
4th	437	DPMD Jayawardene (240) and TT Samaraweera (231)	Sri Lanka v Pakistan at Karachi	2008-09
5th	405	SG Barnes (234) and DG Bradman (234)	Australia v England at Sydney	1946-47
6th	346	JHW Fingleton (136) and DG Bradman (270)	Australia v England at Melbourne	1936-37
7th	347	DS Atkinson (219) and CC Depeiaza (122)	West Indies v Australia at Bridgetown	1954-55
8th	313	Wasim Akram (257*) and Saqlain Mushtaq (79)	Pakistan v Zimbabwe at Sheikhupura	1996-97
9th	195	MV Boucher (78) and PL Symcox (108)	South Africa v Pakistan at Johannesburg	1997-98
10th	151	BF Hastings (110) and RO Collinge (68*)	New Zealand v Pakistan at Auckland	1972-73
	151	Azhar Mahmood (128*) and Mushtaq Ahmed (59)	Pakistan v South Africa at Rawalpindi	1997-98

Figures to 21.9.09. Updated records can be found at **www.cricinfo.com/ci/engine/records**

Test Matches **OVERALL RECORDS**

Most catches

Fielders

184	R Dravid *I/World*	
181	ME Waugh *A*	
171	SP Fleming *NZ*	
164	BC Lara *WI/World*	
159	RT Ponting *A*	

Most dismissals

Wicketkeepers		*Ct/St*
475	MV Boucher	
	SA/World	453/22
416	AC Gilchrist *A*	379/37
395	IA Healy *A*	366/29
355	RW Marsh *A*	343/12
270	PJL Dujon *WI*	265/5

Highest team totals

952-6d	**Sri Lanka** v India at Colombo 1997-98
903-7d	**Eng** v Australia at The Oval 1938
849	**Eng** v WI at Kingston 1929-30
790-3d	**WI** v Pakistan at Kingston 1957-58
765-6d	**Pak** v Sri Lanka at Karachi 2008-09
758-8d	**Aust** v WI at Kingston 1954-55
756-5d	**Sri Lanka** v SA at Colombo 2006
751-5d	**WI** v England at St John's 2003-04
749-9d	**WI** v England at Bridgetown 2008-09
747	**WI** v SA at St John's 2004-05

There have been six further totals of more than 700, three by Australia, and one by India, Pakistan and Sri Lanka

Lowest team totals

Completed innings

26	**NZ** v Eng at Auckland 1954-55
30	**SA** v Eng at Pt Elizabeth 1895-96
30	**SA** v Eng at Birmingham 1924
35	**SA** v Eng at Cape Town 1898-99
36	**Aust** v Eng at B'ham 1902
36	**SA** v Aust at M'bourne 1931-32
42	**Aust** v Eng at Sydney 1887-88
42	**NZ** v Aust at W'ton 1945-46
42*	**India** v England at Lord's 1974
43	**SA** v Eng at Cape Town 1888-89

* One batsmen absent hurt. There have been seven further totals of less than 50, the most recent West Indies' 47 v England at Kingston in 2003-04

Best match bowling

19-90	JC Laker	Eng v Aust at Manchester	1956
17-159	SF Barnes	Eng v SA at Jo'burg	1913-14
16-136	ND Hirwani	India v WI at Madras	1987-88
16-137	RAL Massie	Aust v England at Lord's	1972
16-220	M Muralitharan	SL v England at The Oval	1998
15-28	J Briggs	Eng v SA at Cape Town	1888-89
15-45	GA Lohmann	Eng v SA at Pt Elizabeth	1895-96
15-99	C Blythe	Eng v SA at Leeds	1907
15-104	H Verity	England v Aust at Lord's	1934
15-123	RJ Hadlee	NZ v Aust at Brisbane	1985-86

Hirwani and Massie were making their Test debuts. W Rhodes (15-124) and Harbhajan Singh (15-217) also took 15 wickets in a match

Most centuries

		Tests
42	SR Tendulkar *India*	159
38	RT Ponting *Australia*	136
34	SM Gavaskar *India*	125
34	BC Lara *West Indies/World XI*	131
32	SR Waugh *Australia*	168
31	JH Kallis *South Africa/World XI*	131
30	ML Hayden *Australia*	94
29	DG Bradman *Australia*	52
27	AR Border *Australia*	156
26	R Dravid *India/World XI*	134
26	DPMD Jayawardene *Sri Lanka*	107
26	GS Sobers *West Indies*	93

Test match results

	Played	Won	Lost	Drawn	Tied	% win
Australia	713	332	186	193	2	46.56
Bangladesh	61	3	52	6	0	4.91
England	891	310	258	323	0	34.79
India	430	99	136	194	1	23.02
New Zealand	353	66	142	145	0	18.69
Pakistan	340	103	91	146	0	30.29
South Africa	344	120	121	103	0	34.88
Sri Lanka	189	60	67	62	0	31.74
West Indies	459	152	150	156	1	33.11
Zimbabwe	83	8	49	26	0	9.63
World XI	1	0	1	0	0	0.00
TOTAL	**1932**	**1253**	**1253**	**677**	**2**	

OVERALL RECORDS *One-day Internationals*

Most appearances

438	ST Jayasuriya	SL/Asia
428	SR Tendulkar	I
378	Inzamam-ul-Haq	P/Asia
356	Wasim Akram	P
336	R Dravid	I/Asia/World
334	M Azharuddin	I
332	M Muralitharan	
		SL/Asia/World
325	SR Waugh	A
322	WPUJC Vaas	SL/Asia
319	RT Ponting	A/World

A further 22 men have played in 250 or more ODIs

Most runs

		Avge
16895	SR Tendulkar	I	44.57
13343	ST Jayasuriya	SL/Asia	32.70
11756	RT Ponting	A/World	42.74
11739	Inzamam-ul-Haq	P/Asia	39.52
11363	SC Ganguly	I/Asia	41.02
10685	R Dravid	I/Asia/World	39.42
10405	BC Lara	WI/World	40.48
10239	JH Kallis	SA/Af/World	45.30
9619	AC Gilchrist	A/World	35.89
9378	M Azharuddin	I	36.92

Mohammad Yousuf (9295) and PA de Silva (9284) have also reached 9000 runs in ODIs

Most wickets

		Avge
511	M Muralitharan	SL/World	22.77
502	Wasim Akram	P	23.52
416	Waqar Younis	P	23.84
400	WPUJC Vaas	SL/Asia	27.53
393	SM Pollock	SA/Af/World	24.50
381	GD McGrath	A/World	22.02
337	A Kumble	I/Asia	30.89
319	ST Jayasuriya	SL/Asia	36.57
317	B Lee	A	22.92
315	J Srinath	I	28.08

Eight other bowlers have passed 250 wickets in ODIs, and 12 more have reached 200

Highest scores

194*	CK Coventry	Zim v Bangladesh at Bulawayo	2008-09
194	Saeed Anwar	Pakistan v India at Chennai	1996-97
189*	IVA Richards	W Indies v England at Manchester	1984
189	ST Jayasuriya	Sri Lanka v India at Sharjah	2000-01
188*	G Kirsten	SA v UAE at Rawalpindi	1995-96
186*	SR Tendulkar	India v NZ at Hyderabad	1999-2000
183*	MS Dhoni	India v Sri Lanka at Jaipur	2005-06
183	SC Ganguly	India v Sri Lanka at Taunton	1999
181*	ML Hayden	Aust v N Zealand at Hamilton	2006-07
181	IVA Richards	WI v Sri Lanka at Karachi	1987-88

SR Tendulkar has scored 44 ODI centuries, ST Jayasuriya 28, RT Ponting 27, SC Ganguly 22, HH Gibbs 21 and Saeed Anwar 20

Best innings bowling

8-19	WPUJC Vaas	SL v Zimbabwe at Colombo	2001-02
7-15	GD McGrath	Aust v Namibia at P'stroom	2002-03
7-20	AJ Bichel	Aust v Eng at Port Elizabeth	2002-03
7-30	M Muralitharan	Sri Lanka v India at Sharjah	2000-01
7-36	Waqar Younis	Pakistan v England at Leeds	2001
7-37	Aqib Javed	Pakistan v India at Sharjah	1991-92
7-51	WW Davis	West Indies v Australia at Leeds	1983
6-12	A Kumble	India v West Indies at Calcutta	1993-94
6-13	BAW Mendis	Sri Lanka v India at Karachi	2008
6-14	GJ Gilmour	Australia v England at Leeds	1975
6-14	Imran Khan	Pakistan v India at Sharjah	1984-85
6-14	MF Maharoof	Sri Lanka v W Indies at Mumbai	2006-07

Waqar Younis took five in an innings 13 times and Muralitharan 10

Record wicket partnerships

1st	286	WU Tharanga (109) and ST Jayasuriya (152)	Sri Lanka v England at Leeds	2006
2nd	331	SR Tendulkar (186*) and R Dravid (153)	India v New Zealand at Hyderabad	1999-2000
3rd	237*	R Dravid (104*) and SR Tendulkar (140*)	India v Kenya at Bristol	1999
4th	275*	M Azharuddin (153*) and A Jadeja (116*)	India v Zimbabwe at Cuttack	1997-98
5th	223	M Azharuddin (111*) and A Jadeja (119)	India v Sri Lanka at Colombo	1997-98
6th	218	DPMD Jayawardene (107) and MS Dhoni (139*)	Asia XI v Africa XI at Chennai	2007
7th	130	A Flower (142*) and HH Streak (56)	Zimbabwe v England at Harare	2001-02
8th	138*	JM Kemp (110*) and AJ Hall (56*)	South Africa v India at Cape Town	2006-07
9th	126*	Kapil Dev (175*) and SMH Kirmani (24*)	India v Zimbabwe at Tunbridge Wells	1983
10th	106*	IVA Richards (189*) and MA Holding (12*)	West Indies v England at Manchester	1984

Figures to 21.9.09. Updated records can be found at **www.cricinfo.com/ci/engine/records**

Most catches

Fielders

162	DPMD Jayawardene *SL/Asia*	
156	M Azharuddin *I*	
138	RT Ponting *A/World*	
133	SP Fleming *NZ/World*	
129	SR Tendulkar *I*	

Most dismissals

Wicketkeepers   *Ct/St*

472	AC Gilchrist *A/World*	417/55
406	MV Boucher *SA/Africa*	385/21
287	Moin Khan *P*	214/73
287	KC Sangakkara *SL*	223/64
233	IA Healy *A*	194/39

Most sixes

270	ST Jayasuriya *SL/Asia*
250	Shahid Afridi *Pak/Asia/World*
190	SC Ganguly *I/Asia*
177	SR Tendulkar *I*
153	CL Cairns *NZ/World*
151	CH Gayle *WI/World*
149	AC Gilchrist *A/World*
144	Inzamam-ul-Haq *P/Asia*
141	RT Ponting *A/World*
133	BC Lara *WI/World*

Ten other men have hit 100 sixes

Highest team totals

443-9	SL v N'lands at Amstelveen	2006
438-9	SA v Aust at Johannesburg	2005-06
434-4	Australia v SA at Jo'burg	2005-06
418-5	SA v Zim at P'stroom	2006-07
413-5	Ind v Bermuda at P-o-Spain	2006-07
402-2	NZ v Ireland at Aberdeen	2008
398-5	SL v Kenya at Kandy	1995-96
397-5	NZ v Zimbabwe at Bulawayo	2005-06
392-6	SA v Pakistan at Centurion	2006-07
392-4	India v NZ at Christchurch	2008-09

NZ's 397-5 was made in 44 overs, all the other totals in 50 except SA's 438-9, when the winning run came off the fifth ball of the 50th over

Best strike rate

Runs per 100 balls   *Runs*

110.99	Shahid Afridi *P/Asia/World*	5715
101.85	V Sehwag *I/Asia/World*	6592
99.43	IDS Smith *NZ*	1055
96.94	AC Gilchrist *A/World*	9619
96.66	RL Powell *WI*	2085
95.07	Kapil Dev *I*	3783
92.44	A Symonds *A*	5088
91.26	ST Jayasuriya *SL/Asia*	13343
90.25	MS Dhoni *I/Asia*	4666
90.20	IVA Richards *WI*	6721

Qualification: 1000 runs

Lowest team totals

Completed innings

35	Zim v SL at Harare	2003-04
36	Canada v SL at Paarl	2002-03
38	Zim v SL at Colombo	2001-02
43	Pak v WI at Cape Town	1992-93
45	Can v Eng at Manchester	1979
45	Nam v Aust at P'stroom	2002-03
54	India v SL at Sharjah	2000-01
54	WI v SA at Cape Town	2003-04
55	SL v WI at Sharjah	1986-87
63	India v Aust at Sydney	1980-81

The lowest total successfully defended in a non-rain-affected ODI is 125, by India v Pakistan (87) at Sharjah in 1984-85

Most economical bowlers

Runs per over   *Wkts*

3.09	J Garner *WI*	146
3.28	RGD Willis *E*	80
3.30	RJ Hadlee *NZ*	158
3.32	MA Holding *WI*	142
3.37	SP Davis *A*	44
3.40	AME Roberts *WI*	87
3.48	CEL Ambrose *WI*	225
3.53	MD Marshall *WI*	157
3.54	ARC Fraser *E*	47
3.55	MR Whitney *A*	46

Qualification: 2000 balls bowled

One-day international results

	Played	Won	Lost	Tied	No result	% win
Australia	715	440	245	8	22	64.06
Bangladesh	206	51	153	0	2	25.00
England	518	247	248	5	18	49.90
India	718	348	335	3	32	50.94
Kenya	120	34	81	0	5	29.56
New Zealand	568	245	288	5	30	46.00
Pakistan	703	379	303	6	15	55.52
South Africa	423	263	143	5	12	64.59
Sri Lanka	585	271	289	3	22	48.40
West Indies	617	329	261	5	22	55.71
Zimbabwe	355	89	252	5	9	26.44
Others (see below)	256	73	171	1	11	28.51
TOTAL	2892	2769	2769	23	100	

Others: Afghanistan (P3, W2, L1), Africa XI (P6, W1, L4, NR1), Asia XI (P7, W4, L2, NR1), Bermuda (P35, W7, L28), Canada (P49, W12, L36, NR1), East Africa (P3, L3), Hong Kong (P4, L4), Ireland (P41, W17, L20, T1, NR3), Namibia (P6, L6), Netherlands (P45, W18, L25, NR2), Scotland (P40, W10, L27, NR3), UAE (P11, W1, L10), USA (P2, L2), World XI (P4, W1, L3).

OVERALL RECORDS *Twenty20 Internationals*

Most appearances

28	BB McCullum *NZ*
25	Kamran Akmal *P*
25	Shoaib Malik *P*
24	Shahid Afridi *P*
23	Misbah-ul-Haq *P*
22	Younis Khan *P*
22	JA Morkel *SA*
22	LRPL Taylor *NZ*
21	PD Collingwood *E*
21	AB de Villiers *SA*
21	TM Dilshan *SL*
21	ST Jayasuriya *SL*
21	DPMD Jayawardene *SL*
21	Umar Gul *P*

Most runs

		Avge
747	BB McCullum *NZ*	31.12
572	TM Dilshan *SL*	33.64
549	ST Jayasuriya *SL*	27.45
541	Shoaib Malik *P*	30.05
529	KP Pietersen *E*	29.38
513	GC Smith *SA*	32.06
509	Misbah-ul-Haq *P*	46.27
476	G Gambhir *I*	29.75
454	CH Gayle *WI*	41.27
450	LRPL Taylor *NZ*	23.68

The highest batting average for anyone who has played more than 5 matches is 51.33, by ML Hayden of Australia

Most wickets

		Avge
37	Umar Gul *P*	11.08
34	Shahid Afridi *P*	15.73
27	DL Vettori *NZ*	14.44
25	BAW Mendis *SL*	9.76
23	SL Malinga *SL*	19.26
22	SCJ Broad *E*	23.54
20	DW Steyn *SA*	14.50
19	Abdur Razzaq *B*	13.57
19	NW Bracken *A*	23.05
17	JE Taylor *WI*	20.23
17	B Lee *A*	26.70
17	JM Anderson *E*	29.41

Six further bowlers have taken 16 wkts

Highest Scores

117	CH Gayle	WI v SA at Johannesburg	2007-08
98*	RT Ponting	Australia v NZ at Auckland	2004-05
96*	TM Dilshan	Sri Lanka v WI at The Oval	2009
96	DR Martyn	Australia v SA at Brisbane	2005-06
90*	HH Gibbs	SA v WI at Johannesburg	2007-08
89*	GC Smith	SA v Australia at Johannesburg	2005-06
89*	JM Kemp	SA v New Zealand at Durban	2007-08
89	DA Warner	Australia v SA at Melbourne	2008-09
88*	DJ Hussey	Australia v SA at Johannesburg	2008-09
88	ST Jayasuriya	Sri Lanka v Kenya at Johannesburg	2007-08
88	CH Gayle	WI v Australia at The Oval	2009

Ponting's innings, in the very first such international, is the highest score on T20I debut

Best innings bowling

5-6	Umar Gul	Pakistan v NZ at The Oval	2009
4-7	MR Gillespie	NZ v Kenya at Durban	2007-08
4-8	Umar Gul	Pak v Australia at Dubai	2009-09
4-9	DW Steyn	SA v WI at Port Elizabeth	2007-08
4-11	Shahid Afridi	Pak v Netherlands at Lord's	2009
4-13	RP Singh	India v SA at Durban	2007-08
4-13	WD Parnell	SA v WI at The Oval	2009
4-13	Umar Gul	Pakistan v SL at King City	2008-09
4-15	BAW Mendis	SL v Zimbabwe at King City	2008-09
4-16	Abdur Razzak	B'desh v SA at Jo'burg	2008-09

There have been 21 further instances of a bowler taking 4 wickets in an innings

Record wicket partnerships

1st	145	CH Gayle (117) and DS Smith (35)	WI v South Africa at Johannesburg	2007-08
2nd	111	GC Smith (89*) and HH Gibbs (56)	SA v Australia at Johannesburg	2005-06
3rd	120*	HH Gibbs (90*) and JM Kemp (46*)	SA v West indies at Johannesburg	2007-08
4th	101	Younis Khan (51) and Shoaib Malik (57)	Pakistan v Sri Lanka at Johannesburg	2007-08
5th	119*	Shoaib Malik (52*) and Misbah-ul-Haq (66*)	Pakistan v Australia at Johannesburg	2007-08
6th	77*	RT Ponting (98*) and MEK Hussey (31*)	Australia v New Zealand at Auckland	2004-05
7th	91	PD Collingwood (79) and MH Yardy (23*)	England v West Indies at The Oval	2007
8th	61	SK Raina (61*) and Harbhajan Singh (21)	India v New Zealand at Christchurch	2008-09
9th	44	SL Malinga (27) and CRD Fernando (21)	Sri Lanka v New Zealand at Auckland	2006-07
10th	28	JDP Oram (66*) and JS Patel (4)	New Zealand v Australia at Perth	2007-08

Figures to 21.9.09. Updated records can be found at www.cricinfo.com/ci/engine/records

234

Twenty20 Internationals **OVERALL RECORDS**

Most catches

Fielders

18	LRPL Taylor	*NZ*
16	AB de Villiers	*SA*
11	JP Duminy	*SA*
11	Younis Khan	*P*
10	MEK Hussey	*A*
10	JA Morkel	*SA*

Most dismissals

Wicketkeepers   *Ct/St*

26	Kamran Akmal	*P*	17/4
17	AC Gilchrist	*A*	17/0
16	BB McCullum	*NZ*	13/3
16	KC Sangakkara	*SL*	9/7
14	MV Boucher	*SA*	13/1

Highest team totals

260-6	Sri Lanka v Kenya at Jo'burg	2007-08
221-5	Aust v England at Sydney	2006-07
218-4	India v England at Durban	2007-08
214-5	Australia v NZ at Auckland	2004-05
211-5	SA v Scotland at The Oval	2009
209-3	Australia v SA at Brisbane	2005-06
208-2	SA v WI at Jo'burg	2007-08
208-8	WI v England at The Oval	2007
205-6	West Indies v SA at Jo'burg	2007-08
203-5	Pakistan v B'desh at Karachi	2007-08

The only other scores of 200 or more are SA's 201-5 v Australia at Jo'burg in 2005-06 and England's 200-6 v India at Durban in 2007-08

Lowest team totals

Completed innings

67	Kenya v Ireland at Belfast	2008
70	Bermuda v Can at Belfast	2008
73	Kenya v NZ at Durban	2007-08
74	India v Aus at M'bourne	2007-08
75	Can v Zim at King City	2008-09
79	Aust v Eng at Southampton	2005
81	Scotland v SA at The Oval	2009
83	B'desh v SL at Jo'burg	2007-08
88	Kenya v SL at Jo'burg	2007-08
91	Canada v Kenya at Belfast	2008

There have been five other totals of less than 100

Most sixes

30	Yuvraj Singh	*I*
27	BB McCullum	*NZ*
24	CH Gayle	*WI*
22	ST Jayasuriya	*SL*
22	LRPL Taylor	*NZ*
20	JA Morkel	*SA*
19	Misbah-ul-Haq	*P*
18	JDP Oram	*NZ*
16	SB Styris	*NZ*
15	PD Collingwood	*E*

Yuvraj's sixes included 6 in one over

Best strike rate

Runs per 100 balls   *Runs*

169.34	A Symonds	*A*	337
160.85	Yuvraj Singh	*I*	415
159.82	CD McMillan	*NZ*	187
150.00	CL White	*A*	207
148.76	Imran Nazir	*P*	241
148.36	CH Gayle	*WI*	454
147.71	Shahid Afridi	*P*	421
146.53	KP Pietersen	*E*	529
144.80	V Sehwag	*I*	223
143.92	ML Hayden	*A*	308

Qualification: 100 balls faced

Meanest bowlers

Runs per over   *Wkts*

4.88	TM Odoyo	*Kenya*	6
5.29	P Utseya	*Zim*	9
5.30	BAW Mendis	*SL*	25
5.38	Umar Gul	*P*	37
5.40	JAR Blain	*Scot*	6
5.49	DL Vettori	*NZ*	27
5.53	S Dhaniram	*Canada*	5
5.58	Saeed Ajmal	*P*	16
5.72	Shahid Afridi	*P*	34
5.81	WPUJC Vaas	*SL*	6

Qualification: 120 balls bowled

Twenty20 international results

	Played	Won	Lost	Tied	No Result	% win
Australia	24	11	12	0	1	47.82
Bangladesh	13	3	10	0	0	23.07
England	21	8	12	0	1	40.00
India	18	9	7	1	1	55.88
New Zealand	28	12	14	2	0	46.42
Pakistan	25	19	5	1	0	78.00
South Africa	24	16	8	0	0	66.66
Sri Lanka	23	14	9	0	0	60.86
West Indies	18	8	8	2	0	50.00
Others (see below)	48	14	29	2	3	29.16
TOTAL	121	114	114	4	3	

Other teams: Bermuda (P3, L3), Canada (P7, W2, L4, T1), Ireland (P9, W4, L4, NR1), Kenya (P8, W1, L7), Netherlands (P6, W3, L2, NR1), Scotland (P8, W2, L5, NR1), Zimbabwe (P7, W2, L4, T1).

AUSTRALIA *Test Match Records*

Most appearances

168	SR Waugh
156	AR Border
145	SK Warne
136	RT Ponting
128	ME Waugh
124	GD McGrath
119	IA Healy
107	DC Boon
105	JL Langer
104	MA Taylor

ML Hayden (103) also won more than 100 caps

Most runs

		Avge
11345	RT Ponting	55.88
11174	AR Border	50.56
10927	SR Waugh	51.06
8625	ML Hayden	50.73
8029	ME Waugh	41.81
7696	JL Langer	45.27
7525	MA Taylor	43.49
7422	DC Boon	43.65
7110	GS Chappell	53.86
6996	DG Bradman	99.94

RN Harvey (6149) also reached 6000 Test runs

Most wickets

		Avge
708	SK Warne	25.41
563	GD McGrath	21.64
355	DK Lillee	23.92
310	B Lee	30.81
291	CJ McDermott	28.63
259	JN Gillespie	26.13
248	R Benaud	27.03
246	GD McKenzie	29.78
228	RR Lindwall	23.03
216	CV Grimmett	24.21

MG Hughes (212), SCG MacGill (208) & JR Thomson (200) also reached 200

Highest scores

380	ML Hayden	v Zimbabwe at Perth	2003-04
334*	MA Taylor	v Pakistan at Peshawar	1998-99
334	DG Bradman	v England at Leeds	1930
311	RB Simpson	v England at Manchester	1964
307	RM Cowper	v England at Melbourne	1965-66
304	DG Bradman	v England at Leeds	1934
299*	DG Bradman	v South Africa at Adelaide	1931-32
270	DG Bradman	v England at Melbourne	1936-37
268	GN Yallop	v Pakistan at Melbourne	1983-84
266	WH Ponsford	v England at The Oval	1934

At the time of his retirement in 1948 DG Bradman had made eight of Australia's highest ten Test scores

Best innings bowling

9-121	AA Mailey	v England at Melbourne	1920-21
8-24	GD McGrath	v Pakistan at Perth	2004-05
8-31	FJ Laver	v England at Manchester	1909
8-38	GD McGrath	v England at Lord's	1997
8-43	AE Trott	v England at Adelaide	1894-95
8-53	RAL Massie	v England at Lord's	1972
8-59	AA Mallett	v Pakistan at Adelaide	1972-73
8-61	MG Johnson	v South Africa at Perth	2008-09
8-65	H Trumble	v England at The Oval	1902
8-71	GD McKenzie	v West Indies at Melbourne	1968-69
8-71	SK Warne	v England at Brisbane	1994-95

Trott and Massie were making their Test debuts.

Record wicket partnerships

1st	382	WM Lawry (210) and RB Simpson (205)	v West Indies at Bridgetown	1964-65
2nd	451	WH Ponsford (266) and DG Bradman (244)	v England at The Oval	1934
3rd	315	RT Ponting (206) and DS Lehmann (160)	v West Indies at Port-of-Spain	2002-03
4th	388	WH Ponsford (181) and DG Bradman (304)	v England at Leeds	1934
5th	405	SG Barnes (234) and DG Bradman (234)	v England at Sydney	1946-47
6th	346	JHW Fingleton (136) and DG Bradman (270)	v England at Melbourne	1936-37
7th	217	KD Walters (250) and GJ Gilmour (101)	v New Zealand at Christchurch	1976-77
8th	243	MJ Hartigan (116) and C Hill (160)	v England at Adelaide	1907-08
9th	154	SE Gregory (201) and JM Blackham (74)	v England at Sydney	1894-95
10th	127	JM Taylor (108) and AA Mailey (46*)	v England at Sydney	1924-25

Figures to 21.9.09. Updated records can be found at www.cricinfo.com/ci/engine/records

Test Match Records — AUSTRALIA

Most catches

Fielders

181	ME Waugh	
159	RT Ponting	
157	MA Taylor	
156	AR Border	
128	ML Hayden	

Most dismissals

	Wicketkeepers	*Ct/St*
416	AC Gilchrist	379/37
395	IA Healy	366/29
355	RW Marsh	343/12
187	ATW Grout	163/24
130	WAS Oldfield	78/52

Highest team totals

758-8d	v West Indies at Kingston	1954-55
735-6d	v Zimbabwe at Perth	2003-04
729-6d	v England at Lord's	1930
701	v England at The Oval	1934
695	v England at The Oval	1930
674-6d	v England at Cardiff	2009
674	v India at Adelaide	1947-48
668	v West Indies at Bridgetown	1954-55
659-8d	v England at Sydney	1946-47
656-8d	v England at Manchester	1964

Australia have reached 600 on 29 occasions, 16 of them against England

Lowest team totals

Completed innings

36	v England at Birmingham	1902
42	v England at Sydney	1887-88
44	v England at The Oval	1896
53	v England at Lord's	1896
58*	v England at Brisbane	1936-37
60	v England at Lord's	1888
63	v England at The Oval	1882
65	v England at The Oval	1912
66*	v England at Brisbane	1928-29
68	v England at The Oval	1886

**One or more batsmen absent.
Australia's lowest total against anyone other than England is 75, v South Africa at Durban in 1949-50*

Best match bowling

16-137	RAL Massie	v England at Lord's	1972
14-90	FR Spofforth	v England at The Oval	1882
14-199	CV Grimmett	v South Africa at Adelaide	1931-32
13-77	MA Noble	v England at Melbourne	1901-02
13-110	FR Spofforth	v England at Melbourne	1878-79
13-148	BA Reid	v England at Melbourne	1990-91
13-173	CV Grimmett	v South Africa at Durban	1935-36
13-217	MG Hughes	v West Indies at Perth	1988-89
13-236	AA Mailey	v England at Melbourne	1920-21
12-87	CTB Turner	v England at Sydney	1887-88

Massie was playing in his first Test, Grimmett (1935-36) in his last – he took 10 or more wickets in each of his last three

Hat-tricks

FR Spofforth	v England at Melbourne	1878-79
H Trumble	v England at Melbourne	1901-02
H Trumble	v England at Melbourne	1903-04
TJ Matthews	v South Africa at Manchester	1912
TJ Matthews	v South Africa at Manchester	1912
LF Kline	v South Africa at Cape Town	1957-58
MG Hughes	v West Indies at Perth	1988-89
DW Fleming	v Pakistan at Rawalpindi	1994-95
SK Warne	v England at Melbourne	1994-95
GD McGrath	v West Indies at Perth	2000-01

Fleming was playing in his first Test, Trumble (1903-04) in his last. Matthews, a legspinner, uniquely took a hat-trick in both innings of the same Test

Australia's Test match results

	Played	Won	Lost	Drawn	Tied	% win
v Bangladesh	4	4	0	0	0	100.00
v England	321	132	99	90	0	41.12
v India	76	34	18	23	1	44.73
v New Zealand	48	24	7	17	0	50.00
v Pakistan	52	24	11	17	0	46.15
v South Africa	83	47	18	18	0	56.62
v Sri Lanka	20	13	1	6	0	65.00
v West Indies	105	50	32	22	1	47.61
v Zimbabwe	3	3	0	0	0	100.00
v World XI	1	1	0	0	0	100.00
TOTAL	713	332	186	193	2	46.56

Figures to 21.9.09. Updated records can be found at **www.cricinfo.com/ci/engine/records**

AUSTRALIA
One-day International Records

Most appearances

325	SR Waugh	
318	RT Ponting	
286	AC Gilchrist	
273	AR Border	
249	GD McGrath	
244	ME Waugh	
232	MG Bevan	
208	DR Martyn	
198	A Symonds	
193	SK Warne	

A total of 23 Australians have played in more than 100 ODIs

Most runs

		Avge
11641	RT Ponting	42.48
9595	AC Gilchrist	35.93
8500	ME Waugh	39.35
7569	SR Waugh	32.90
6912	MG Bevan	53.58
6524	AR Border	30.62
6131	ML Hayden	44.10
6068	DM Jones	44.61
5964	DC Boon	37.04
5346	DR Martyn	40.80

A Symonds (5088), MJ Clarke (4945) and GR Marsh (4357) also reached 4000 runs

Most wickets

		Avge
380	GD McGrath	21.98
317	B Lee	22.92
291	SK Warne	25.82
203	CJ McDermott	24.71
195	SR Waugh	34.67
174	NW Bracken	24.36
156	GB Hogg	26.84
142	JN Gillespie	25.42
134	DW Fleming	25.38
133	A Symonds	37.25

SP O'Donnell (108), PR Reiffel (106) and DK Lillee (103) also reached 100 wickets

Highest scores

181*	ML Hayden	v New Zealand at Hamilton	2006-07
173	ME Waugh	v West Indies at Melbourne	2000-01
172	AC Gilchrist	v Zimbabwe at Hobart	2003-04
164	RT Ponting	v South Africa at Johannesburg	2005-06
158	ML Hayden	v West Indies at North Sound	2006-07
156	A Symonds	v New Zealand at Wellington	2005-06
154	AC Gilchrist	v Sri Lanka at Melbourne	1998-99
151	A Symonds	v Sri Lanka at Sydney	2005-06
149	AC Gilchrist	v Sri Lanka at Bridgetown	2006-07
146	ML Hayden	v Pakistan at Nairobi	2002-03

Gilchrist's 149 against Sri Lanka is the highest score in a World Cup final

Best innings bowling

7-15	GD McGrath	v Namibia at Potchefstroom	2002-03
7-20	AJ Bichel	v England at Port Elizabeth	2002-03
6-14	GJ Gilmour	v England at Leeds	1975
6-39	KH MacLeay	v India at Nottingham	1983
5-13	SP O'Donnell	v New Zealand at Christchurch	1989-90
5-14	GD McGrath	v West Indies at Manchester	1999
5-15	GS Chappell	v India at Sydney	1980-81
5-16	CG Rackemann	v Pakistan at Adelaide	1983-84
5-17	TM Alderman	v New Zealand at Wellington	1981-82
5-18	GJ Cosier	v England at Birmingham	1977
5-18	A Symonds	v Bangladesh at Manchester	2005

DK Lillee took 5-34 against Pakistan at Leeds in the 1975 World Cup, the first five-wicket haul in ODIs

Record wicket partnerships

1st	212	GR Marsh (104) and DC Boon (111)	v India at Jaipur	1986-87
2nd	225	AC Gilchrist (124) and RT Ponting (119)	v England at Melbourne	2002-03
3rd	234*	RT Ponting (140*) and DR Martyn (88*)	v India at Johannesburg	2002-03
4th	237	RT Ponting (124) and A Symonds (151)	v Sri Lanka at Sydney	2005-06
5th	220	A Symonds (156) and MJ Clarke (82*)	v New Zealand at Wellington	2005-06
6th	165	MEK Hussey (109*) and BJ Haddin (70)	v West Indies at Kuala Lumpur	2006-07
7th	123	MEK Hussey (73) and B Lee (57)	v South Africa at Brisbane	2005-06
8th	119	PR Reiffel (58) and SK Warne (55)	v South Africa at Port Elizabeth	1993-94
9th	77	MG Bevan (59*) and SK Warne (29)	v West Indies at Port-of-Spain	1998-99
10th	63	SR Watson (35*) and AJ Bichel (28)	v Sri Lanka at Sydney	2002-03

Figures to 21.9.09. Updated records can be found at www.cricinfo.com/ci/engine/records

One-day International Records — **AUSTRALIA**

Most catches

Fielders

137	RT Ponting
127	AR Border
111	SR Waugh
108	ME Waugh
82	A Symonds

Most dismissals

	Wicketkeepers	*Ct/St*
470	AC Gilchrist	416/54
233	IA Healy	194/39
124	RW Marsh	120/4
64	BJ Haddin	59/5
49	WB Phillips	42/7

Highest team totals

434-4	v South Africa at Johannesburg	2005-06
377-6	v South Africa at Basseterre	2006-07
368-5	v Sri Lanka at Sydney	2005-06
359-2†	v India at Johannesburg	2002-03
359-5	v India at Sydney	2003-04
358-5	v Netherlands at Basseterre	2006-07
349-6	v New Zealand at St George's	2006-07
348-6	v New Zealand at C'church	1999-2000
347-2	v India at Bangalore	2003-04
347-5	v New Zealand at Napier	2004-05

† In World Cup final. All scores made in 50 overs

Lowest team totals

Completed innings

70	v England at Birmingham	1977
70	v New Zealand at Adelaide	1985-86
91	v West Indies at Perth	1986-87
93	v S Africa at Cape Town	2005-06
101	v England at Melbourne	1978-79
101	v India at Perth	1991-92
107	v W Indies at Melbourne	1981-82
109	v England at Sydney	1982-83
120	v Pakistan at Hobart	1996-97
124	v New Zealand at Sydney	1982-83

Australia scored 101-9 in a 30-overs match against West Indies at Sydney in 1992-93 – and won

Most sixes

148	AC Gilchrist
138	RT Ponting
103	A Symonds
87	ML Hayden
68	SR Waugh
64	DM Jones
57	ME Waugh
51	MEK Hussey
43	AR Border
37	BJ Haddin

Gilchrist (1) and Ponting (3) also hit sixes for the World XI

Best strike rate

Runs per 100 balls		*Runs*
96.89	AC Gilchrist	9595
92.44	A Symonds	5504
90.12	JR Hopes	958
89.86	CL White	594
88.46	DJ Hussey	598
88.16	IJ Harvey	715
87.82	CJ Ferguson	570
87.51	BJ Hodge	516
86.36	MEK Hussey	3162
85.71	WB Phillips	852

Qualification: 500 runs

Most economical bowlers

Runs per over		*Wkts*
3.37	SP Davis	44
3.55	MR Whitney	46
3.58	DK Lillee	103
3.65	GF Lawson	88
3.65	TM Alderman	88
3.87	GD McGrath	380
3.92	PR Reiffel	106
3.94	CG Rackemann	82
3.94	RM Hogg	85
4.03	CJ McDermott	203

Qualification: 2000 balls bowled

Australia's one-day international results

	Played	Won	Lost	Tied	No Result	% win
v Bangladesh	16	15	1	0	0	93.75
v England	100	58	38	2	2	60.20
v India	96	57	32	0	7	64.04
v New Zealand	117	80	32	0	5	71.42
v Pakistan	79	46	29	1	3	61.18
v South Africa	77	39	35	3	0	52.59
v Sri Lanka	68	46	20	0	2	69.69
v West Indies	119	58	57	2	2	50.42
v Zimbabwe	27	25	1	0	1	96.15
v others *(see below)*	16	16	0	0	0	100.00
TOTAL	**715**	**440**	**245**	**8**	**22**	**64.06**

Other teams: Canada (P1, W1), Ireland (P1, W1), Kenya (P4, W4), Namibia (P1, W1), Netherlands (P2, W2), Scotland (P3, W3), USA (P1, W1), World XI (P3, W3).

BANGLADESH *Test Match Records*

Most appearances

50	Habibul Bashar
50	Mohammad Ashraful
44	Khaled Mashud
40	Javed Omar
36	Mashrafe Mortaza
33	Mohammad Rafique
24	Rajin Saleh
23	Shahadat Hossain
21	Tapash Baisya
17	Alok Kapali
17	Hannan Sarkar
17	Manjural Islam

Habibul Bashar missed only two of Bangladesh's first 52 Tests

Most runs

		Avge
3026	Habibul Bashar	30.87
2149	Mohammad Ashraful	23.10
1720	Javed Omar	22.05
1409	Khaled Mashud	19.04
1141	Rajin Saleh	25.93
1059	Mohammad Rafique	18.57
810	Shahriar Nafees	27.00
797	Mashrafe Mortaza	12.85
715	Shakib Al Hasan	29.79
683	Al Sahariar	22.76

Habibul Bashar reached 2000 runs for Bangladesh before anyone else had made 1000

Most wickets

		Avge
100	Mohammad Rafique	40.76
78	Mashrafe Mortaza	41.52
53	Shahadat Hossain	43.69
48	Shakib Al Hasan	28.27
41	Enamul Haque jnr	39.24
36	Tapash Baisya	59.36
28	Manjural Islam	57.32
19	Mohammad Ashraful	58.63
18	Enamul Haque snr	57.05
14	Mohammad Sharif	79.00
14	Talha Jubair	55.07

Mohammad Rafique completed the 1000-run 100-wicket double in his last Test

Highest scores

158*	Moh'd Ashraful	v India at Chittagong	2004-05
145†	Aminul Islam	v India at Dhaka	2000-01
138	Shahriar Nafees	v Australia at Fatullah	2005-06
136	Moh'd Ashraful	v Sri Lanka at Chittagong	2005-06
129*	Moh'd Ashraful	v Sri Lanka at Colombo	2007
128	Tamim Iqbal	v West Indies at Kingstown	2009
121	Nafees Iqbal	v Zimbabwe at Dhaka	2004-05
119	Javed Omar	v Pakistan at Peshawar	2003-04
114†	Moh'd Ashraful	v Sri Lanka at Colombo	2001-02
113	Habibul Bashar	v West Indies at Gros Islet	2004

† On debut. There have only been five other centuries for Bangladesh, two by Habibul Bashar and one each by Khaled Mashud, Mohammad Ashraful and Mohammad Rafique

Best innings bowling

7-36	Shakib Al Hasan	v NZ at Chittagong	2008-09
7-95	Enamul Haque jnr	v Zimbabwe at Dhaka	2004-05
6-27	Shahadat Hossain	v South Africa at Dhaka	2007-08
6-45	Enamul Haque jnr	v Zim at Chittagong	2004-05
6-77	Moh'd Rafique	v South Africa at Dhaka	2002-03
6-81	Manjural Islam	v Zim at Bulawayo	2000-01
6-99	Shakib Al Hasan	v SA at Centurion	2008-09
6-122	Moh'd Rafique	v New Zealand at Dhaka	2004-05
6-132	Naimur Rahman	v India at Dhaka	2000-01
5-36	Moh'd Rafique	v Pakistan at Multan	2003-04

Other five-wicket hauls have been recorded by Mohammad Rafique (4), Shakib Al Hasan (3), Enamul Haque jnr, Mahmudullah, and Shahadat Hossain

Record wicket partnerships

1st	161	Tamim Iqbal (84) and Junaid Siddique (74)	v New Zealand at Dunedin	2007-08
2nd	187	Shahriar Nafees (138) and Habibul Bashar (76)	v Australia at Fatullah	2005-06
3rd	130	Javed Omar (119) and Mohammad Ashraful (77)	v Pakistan at Peshawar	2003-04
4th	120	Habibul Bashar (77) and Manjural Islam Rana (35)	v West Indies at Kingstown	2004
5th	144	Mehrab Hossain jnr (83) and Mushfiqur Rahim (79)	v New Zealand at Chittagong	2008-09
6th	191	Mohammad Ashraful (129*) and Mushfiqur Rahim (80)	v Sri Lanka at Colombo	2007
7th	111	Shakib Al Hasan (96) and Mushfiqur Rahim (61)	v Sri Lanka at Mirpur	2008-09
8th	87	Mohammad Ashraful (81) and Mohammad Rafique (111)	v West Indies at Gros Islet	2004
9th	77	Mashrafe Mortaza (79) and Shahadat Hossain (31)	v India at Chittagong	2006-07
10th	69	Mohammad Rafique (65) and Shahadat Hossain (3*)	v Australia at Chittagong	2005-06

Figures to 21.9.09. Updated records can be found at **www.cricinfo.com/ci/engine/records**

Test Match Records   **BANGLADESH**

Most catches

Fielders

22	Habibul Bashar	
22	Mohammad Ashraful	
14	Rajin Saleh	
11	Shahriar Nafees	
10	Al Sahariar	
10	Javed Omar	

Most dismissals

Wicketkeepers		*Ct/St*
87	Khaled Mashud	78/9
22	Mushfiqur Rahim	20/2
4	Mohammad Salim	3/1
2	Mehrab Hossain	2/0

Highest team totals

488	v Zimbabwe at Chittagong	2004-05
427	v Australia at Fatullah	2005-06
416	v West Indies at Gros Islet	2004
413	v Sri Lanka at Mirpur	2008-09
400	v India at Dhaka	2000-01
361	v Pakistan at Peshawar	2003-04
345	v West Indies at Kingstown	2009
333	v India at Chittagong	2004-05
331	v Zimbabwe at Harare	2003-04
328	v Sri Lanka at Colombo	2001-02

The 400 against India came in Bangladesh's inaugural Test

Lowest team totals

Completed innings

62	v Sri Lanka at Colombo	2007
86	v Sri Lanka at Colombo	2005-06
87	v West Indies at Dhaka	2002-03
89	v Sri Lanka at Colombo	2007
90	v Sri Lanka at Colombo	2001-02
91	v India at Dhaka	2000-01
96	v Pakistan at Peshawar	2003-04
97	v Australia at Darwin	2003
102	v South Africa at Dhaka	2002-03
104	v Eng at Chester-le-Street	2005

The lowest all-out total by the opposition is 154, by Zimbabwe at Chittagong in 2004-05 (Bangladesh's first Test victory)

Best match bowling

12-200	Enamul Haque jr	v Zimbabwe at Dhaka	2004-05
9-97	Shahadat Hossain	v South Africa at Dhaka	2007-08
9-115	Shakib Al Hasan	v NZ at Chittagong	2008-09
9-160	Moh'd Rafique	v Australia at Fatullah	2005-06
8-110	Mahmudullah	v W Indies at Kingstown	2009
8-129	Shakib Al Hasan	v W Indies at St George's	2009
7-105	Khaled Mahmud	v Pakistan at Multan	2003-04
7-116	Moh'd Rafique	v Pakistan at Multan	2003-04
6-77	Moh'd Rafique	v South Africa at Dhaka	2002-03
6-81	Manjural Islam	v Zimbabwe at Bulawayo	2000-01

Khaled Mahmud took only six other wickets in 11 more Tests

Hat-tricks

Alok Kapali	v Pakistan at Peshawar	2003-04

Alok Kapali's figures were 2.1-1-3-3; he ended Pakistan's innings by dismissing Shabbir Ahmed, Danish Kaneria and Umar Gul. He took only three other Test wickets.

Two bowlers have taken hat-tricks against Bangladesh: AM Blignaut for Zimbabwe at Harare in 2003-04, and JEC Franklin for New Zealand at Dhaka in 2004-05.

Shahadat Hossain took an ODI hat-trick for Bangladesh against Zimbabwe at Harare in 2006

Bangladesh's Test match results

	Played	Won	Lost	Drawn	Tied	% win
v Australia	4	0	4	0	0	0.00
v England	4	0	4	0	0	0.00
v India	5	0	4	1	0	0.00
v New Zealand	8	0	7	1	0	0.00
v Pakistan	6	0	6	0	0	0.00
v South Africa	8	0	8	0	0	0.00
v Sri Lanka	12	0	12	0	0	0.00
v West Indies	6	2	3	1	0	33.33
v Zimbabwe	8	1	4	3	0	12.50
TOTAL	61	3	52	6	0	4.91

Figures to 21.9.09. Updated records can be found at **www.cricinfo.com/ci/engine/records**

BANGLADESH One-day International Records

Most appearances

145	Mohammad Ashraful	
126	Khaled Mashud	
123	Mohammad Rafique	
111	Habibul Bashar	
101	Mashrafe Mortaza	
84	Abdur Razzak	
80	Aftab Ahmed	
77	Khaled Mahmud	
70	Shakib Al Hasan	
65	Alok Kapali	

Habibul Bashar captained in 69 ODIs, Mohammad Ashraful in 38, Khaled Mashud in 30

Most runs

		Avge
3049	Moh'd Ashraful	24.19
2168	Habibul Bashar	21.68
1904	Shakib Al Hasan	34.61
1874	Aftab Ahmed	25.32
1857	Shahriar Nafees	33.76
1818	Khaled Mashud	21.90
1729	Tamim Iqbal	28.34
1312	Javed Omar	23.85
1190	Moh'd Rafique	13.52
1170	Alok Kapali	19.83

Mashrafe Mortaza (1032) and Rajin Saleh (1005) also passed 1000 runs

Most wickets

		Avge
134	Mashrafe Mortaza	29.23
119	Mohammad Rafique	38.75
118	Abdur Razzak	27.61
76	Shakib Al Hasan	31.28
67	Khaled Mahmud	42.76
59	Syed Rasel	30.16
59	Tapash Baisya	41.55
41	Shahadat Hossain	41.24
31	Nazmul Hossain	33.32
29	Hasibul Hossain	46.13

Mohammad Rafique completed the 1000-run/100-wicket double in ODIs as well as Tests

Highest scores

154	Tamim Iqbal	v Zimbabwe at Bulawayo	2009
134*	Shakib Al Hasan	v Canada at St John's	2006-07
129	Tamim Iqbal	v Ireland at Dhaka	2007-08
123*	Shahriar Nafees	v Zimbabwe at Jaipur	2006
118*	Shahriar Nafees	v Zimbabwe at Harare	2006-07
115	Alok Kapali	v India at Karachi	2008
109	Moh'd Ashraful	v UAE at Lahore	2008
108*	Rajin Saleh	v Kenya at Fatullah	2005-06
108	Shakib Al Hasan	v Pakistan at Multan	2007-08
105*	Shahriar Nafees	v Zimbabwe at Khulna	2006-07

Five other centuries have been scored for Bangladesh, by Mehrab Hossain, Mohammad Ashraful (2), Shahriar Nafees and Shakib Al Hasan

Best bowling figures

6-26	Mashrafe Mortaza	v Kenya at Nairobi	2006
5-31	Aftab Ahmed	v NZ at Dhaka	2004-05
5-33	Abdur Razzak	v Zimbabwe at Bogra	2006-07
5-42	Farhad Reza	v Ireland at Dhaka	2007-08
5-47	Moh'd Rafique	v Kenya at Fatullah	2005-06
4-16	Tapash Baisya	v West Indies at Kingstown	2004
4-16	Rajin Saleh	v Zimbabwe at Harare	2006
4-19	Khaled Mahmud	v Zimbabwe at Harare	2003-04
4-22	Syed Rasel	v Kenya at Nairobi	2006
4-23	Abdur Razzak	v Scotland at Dhaka	2006-07

Aftab Ahmed took only seven more wickets in 79 other matches

Record wicket partnerships

1st	170	Shahriar Hossain (68) and Mehrab Hossain (101)	v Zimbabwe at Dhaka	1998-99
2nd	150	Mohammad Rafique (72) and Aftab Ahmed (81*)	v Zimbabwe at Dhaka	2004-05
3rd	141	Mohammad Ashraful (109) and Raqibul Hassan (83)	v United Arab Emirates at Lahore	2008
4th	175*	Rajin Saleh (108*) and Habibul Bashar (64*)	v Kenya at Fatullah	2005-06
5th	119	Shakib Al Hasan (52) and Raqibul Hassan (63)	v South Africa at Dhaka	2007-08
6th	123*	Al Sahariar (62*) and Khaled Mashud (53*)	v West Indies at Dhaka	1999-2000
7th	89	Alok Kapali (55) and Khaled Mashud (39)	v Kenya at Fatullah	2005-06
8th	70*	Khaled Mashud (35*) and Mohammad Rafique (41*)	v New Zealand at Kimberley	2002-03
9th	97	Shakib Al Hasan (108) and Mashrafe Mortaza (38)	v Pakistan at Multan	2007-08
10th	54*	Khaled Mashud (39*) and Tapash Baisya (22*)	v Sri Lanka at Colombo	2005-06

Figures to 21.9.09. Updated records can be found at **www.cricinfo.com/ci/engine/records**

One-day International Records **BANGLADESH**

Most catches

Fielders

32	Mashrafe Mortaza
29	Mohammad Ashraful
28	Mohammad Rafique
27	Aftab Ahmed
26	Habibul Bashar

Most dismissals

	Wicketkeepers	*Ct/St*
126	Khaled Mashud	91/35
42	Mushfiqur Rahim	33/9
13	Dhiman Ghosh	9/4

Highest team totals

320-8	v Zimbabwe at Bulawayo	2009
313-6	v Zimbabwe at Bulawayo	2009
301-7	v Kenya at Bogra	2005-06
300-8	v UAE at Lahore	2008
293-7	v Ireland at Dhaka	2007-08
285-7	v Pakistan at Lahore	2007-08
283-6	v India at Karachi	2008
278-5	v Canada at St John's	2006-07
278-6	v Scotland at Dhaka	2006-07
276-7	v West Indies at Roseau	2009

Bangladesh passed 300 for the first time in their 119th one-day international

Lowest team totals

Completed innings

74	v Australia at Darwin	2008
76	v Sri Lanka at Colombo	2002
76	v India at Dhaka	2002-03
77	v NZ at Colombo	2002-03
86	v NZ at Chittagong	2004-05
87*	v Pakistan at Dhaka	1999-2000
92	v Zimbabwe at Nairobi	1997-98
93	v S Africa at Birmingham	2004
93	v NZ at Queenstown	2007-08
94	v Pakistan at Moratuwa	1985-86

* One batsman absent hurt

Most sixes

49	Aftab Ahmed
36	Mashrafe Mortaza
29	Mohammad Rafique
26	Mohammad Ashraful
21	Tamim Iqbal
14	Shakib Al Hasan
13	Abdur Razzak
10	Alok Kapali
10	Habibul Bashar
8	Farhad Reza

Best strike rate

Runs per 100 balls		*Runs*
85.00	Mashrafe Mortaza	1032
83.54	Aftab Ahmed	1874
74.90	Shakib Al Hasan	1904
72.28	Tamim Iqbal	1729
72.14	Mohammad Ashraful	3049
71.81	Mohammad Rafique	1190
69.68	Shahriar Nafees	1857
68.78	Alok Kapali	1170
67.83	Khaled Mahmud	991
66.45	Mahmudullah	519

Qualification: 500 runs

Most economical bowlers

Runs per over		*Wkts*
4.08	Shakib Al Hasan	76
4.39	Mohammad Rafique	119
4.42	Mushfiqur Rahman	19
4.43	Abdur Razzak	118
4.46	Syed Rasel	59
4.53	Mashrafe Mortaza	134
4.84	Manjural Islam	24
4.95	Naimur Rahman	10
5.07	Khaled Mahmud	67
5.11	Mahmudullah	18

Qualification: 1000 balls bowled

Bangladesh's one-day international results

	Played	Won	Lost	Tied	No Result	% win
v Australia	16	1	15	0	0	6.25
v England	8	0	8	0	0	0.00
v India	19	2	17	0	0	10.52
v New Zealand	14	1	13	0	0	7.14
v Pakistan	25	1	24	0	0	4.00
v South Africa	13	1	12	0	0	7.69
v Sri Lanka	26	2	24	0	0	7.69
v West Indies	16	3	11	0	2	21.42
v Zimbabwe	42	21	21	0	0	50.00
v others (see below)	27	19	8	0	0	70.37
TOTAL	**206**	**51**	**153**	**0**	**2**	**25.00**

Other teams: Bermuda (P2, W2), Canada (P2, W1, L1), Hong Kong (P1, W1), Ireland (P4, W3, L1), Kenya (P14, W8, L6), Scotland (P3, W3), UAE (P1, W1).

ENGLAND
Test Match Records

Most appearances

133	AJ Stewart	
118	GA Gooch	
117	DI Gower	
115	MA Atherton	
114	MC Cowdrey	
108	G Boycott	
102	IT Botham	
100	GP Thorpe	
96	N Hussain	
95	APE Knott	

Cowdrey was the first man to reach 100 Tests, in 1968

Most runs

		Avge
8900	GA Gooch	42.58
8463	AJ Stewart	39.54
8231	DI Gower	44.25
8114	G Boycott	47.72
7728	MA Atherton	37.69
7624	MC Cowdrey	44.06
7249	WR Hammond	58.45
6971	L Hutton	56.67
6806	KF Barrington	58.67
6744	GP Thorpe	44.66

ME Trescothick (5825), DCS Compton (5807), N Hussain (5764) and MP Vaughan (5719) also passed 5500 runs

Most wickets

		Avge
383	IT Botham	28.40
325	RGD Willis	25.20
307	FS Trueman	21.57
297	DL Underwood	25.83
252	JB Statham	24.84
248	MJ Hoggard	30.50
236	AV Bedser	24.89
234	AR Caddick	29.91
229	D Gough	28.39
222	SJ Harmison	31.94

A Flintoff (219) and JA Snow (202) have also taken more than 200 wickets

Highest scores

364	L Hutton	v Australia at The Oval	1938
336*	WR Hammond	v New Zealand at Auckland	1932-33
333	GA Gooch	v India at Lord's	1990
325	A Sandham	v West Indies at Kingston	1929-30
310*	JH Edrich	v New Zealand at Leeds	1965
287	RE Foster	v Australia at Sydney	1903-04
285*	PBH May	v West Indies at Birmingham	1957
278	DCS Compton	v Pakistan at Nottingham	1954
262*	DL Amiss	v West Indies at Kingston	1973-74
258	TW Graveney	v West Indies at Nottingham	1957

Foster was playing in his first Test, Sandham in his last

Best innings bowling

10-53	JC Laker	v Australia at Manchester	1956
9-28	GA Lohmann	v South Africa at Johannesburg	1895-96
9-37	JC Laker	v Australia at Manchester	1956
9-57	DE Malcolm	v South Africa at The Oval	1994
9-103	SF Barnes	v S Africa at Johannesburg	1913-14
8-7	GA Lohmann	v S Africa at Port Elizabeth	1895-96
8-11	J Briggs	v South Africa at Cape Town	1888-89
8-29	SF Barnes	v South Africa at The Oval	1912
8-31	FS Trueman	v India at Manchester	1952
8-34	IT Botham	v Pakistan at Lord's	1978

Botham also scored 108 in England's innings victory

Record wicket partnerships

1st	359	L Hutton (158) and C Washbrook (195)	v South Africa at Johannesburg	1948-49
2nd	382	L Hutton (364) and M Leyland (187)	v Australia at The Oval	1938
3rd	370	WJ Edrich (189) and DCS Compton (208)	v South Africa at Lord's	1947
4th	411	PBH May (285*) and MC Cowdrey (154)	v West Indies at Birmingham	1957
5th	254	KWR Fletcher (113) and AW Greig (148)	v India at Bombay	1972-73
6th	281	GP Thorpe (200*) and A Flintoff (137)	v New Zealand at Christchurch	2001-02
7th	197	MJK Smith (96) and JM Parks (101*)	v West Indies at Port-of-Spain	1959-60
8th	246	LEG Ames (137) and GOB Allen (122)	v New Zealand at Lord's	1931
9th	163*	MC Cowdrey (128*) and AC Smith (69*)	v New Zealand at Wellington	1962-63
10th	130	RE Foster (287) and W Rhodes (40*)	v Australia at Sydney	1903-04

Figures to 21.9.09. Updated records can be found at **www.cricinfo.com/ci/engine/records**

Test Match Records

ENGLAND

Most catches

Fielders

120	IT Botham	
120	MC Cowdrey	
110	WR Hammond	
105	GP Thorpe	
103	GA Gooch	

Most dismissals

Wicketkeepers   *Ct/St*

269	APE Knott	250/19
241	AJ Stewart	227/14
219	TG Evans	173/46
174	RW Taylor	167/7
165	RC Russell	153/12

Highest team totals

903-7d	v Australia at The Oval	1938
849	v West Indies at Kingston	1929-30
658-8d	v Australia at Nottingham	1938
654-5	v South Africa at Durban	1938-39
653-4d	v India at Lord's	1990
652-7d	v India at Madras	1984-85
636	v Australia at Sydney	1928-29
633-5d	v India at Birmingham	1979
629	v India at Lord's	1974
627-9d	v Australia at Manchester	1934

England have made six other totals of 600 or more

Lowest team totals

Completed innings

45	v Australia at Sydney	1886-87
46	v WI at Port-of-Spain	1993-94
51	v WI at Kingston	2008-09
52	v Australia at The Oval	1948
53	v Australia at Lord's	1888
61	v Aust at Melbourne	1901-02
61	v Aust at Melbourne	1903-04
62	v Australia at Lord's	1888
64	v NZ at Wellington	1977-78
65*	v Australia at Sydney	1894-95

One batsman absent

Best match bowling

19-90	JC Laker	v Australia at Manchester	1956
17-159	SF Barnes	v S Africa at Johannesburg	1913-14
15-28	J Briggs	v S Africa at Cape Town	1888-89
15-45	GA Lohmann	v S Africa at Port Elizabeth	1895-96
15-99	C Blythe	v South Africa at Leeds	1907
15-104	H Verity	v Australia at Lord's	1934
15-124	W Rhodes	v Australia at Melbourne	1903-04
14-99	AV Bedser	v Australia at Nottingham	1953
14-102	W Bates	v Australia at Melbourne	1882-83
14-144	SF Barnes	v South Africa at Durban	1913-14

Barnes took ten or more wickets in a match a record seven times for England

Hat-tricks

W Bates	v Australia at Melbourne	1882-83
J Briggs	v Australia at Sydney	1891-92
GA Lohmann	v S Africa at Port Elizabeth	1895-96
JT Hearne	v Australia at Leeds	1899
MJC Allom	v New Zealand at Christchurch	1929-30
TWJ Goddard	v S Africa at Johannesburg	1938-39
PJ Loader	v West Indies at Leeds	1957
DG Cork	v West Indies at Manchester	1995
D Gough	v Australia at Sydney	1998-99
MJ Hoggard	v West Indies at Bridgetown	2003-04
RJ Sidebottom	v New Zealand at Hamilton	2007-08

Allom was playing in his first match

England's Test match results

	Played	Won	Lost	Drawn	Tied	% win
v Australia	321	99	132	90	0	30.84
v Bangladesh	4	4	0	0	0	100.00
v India	99	34	19	46	0	34.34
v New Zealand	94	45	8	41	0	47.87
v Pakistan	67	19	12	36	0	28.35
v South Africa	134	55	28	51	0	41.04
v Sri Lanka	21	8	6	7	0	38.09
v West Indies	145	43	53	49	0	29.65
v Zimbabwe	6	3	0	3	0	50.00
TOTAL	**891**	**310**	**258**	**323**	**0**	**34.79**

Figures to 21.9.09. Updated records can be found at **www.cricinfo.com/ci/engine/records**

ENGLAND

Most appearances

170	AJ Stewart	
166	PD Collingwood	
158	D Gough	
138	A Flintoff	
125	GA Gooch	
123	ME Trescothick	
122	AJ Lamb	
120	GA Hick	
116	IT Botham	
114	DI Gower	

JM Anderson (113), PAJ DeFreitas (103) and NV Knight (100) also played 100 ODIs

Most runs

		Avge
4677	AJ Stewart	31.60
4335	ME Trescothick	37.37
4290	GA Gooch	36.98
4083	PD Collingwood	34.60
4010	AJ Lamb	39.31
3846	GA Hick	37.33
3637	NV Knight	40.41
3293	A Flintoff	31.97
3170	DI Gower	30.77
3109	KP Pietersen	47.83

Eight other batsmen have scored 2000 runs in ODIs for England

Most wickets

		Avge
234	D Gough	26.29
168	A Flintoff	23.61
146	JM Anderson	30.95
145	IT Botham	28.54
115	PAJ DeFreitas	32.82
96	PD Collingwood	37.43
80	RGD Willis	24.60
78	SCJ Broad	28.01
76	JE Emburey	30.86
76	SJ Harmison	32.64

Eight further bowlers have taken 50 wickets in ODIs for England

Highest scores

167*	RA Smith	v Australia at Birmingham	1993
158	DI Gower	v New Zealand at Brisbane	1982-83
152	AJ Strauss	v Bangladesh at Nottingham	2005
142*	CWJ Athey	v New Zealand at Manchester	1986
142	GA Gooch	v Pakistan at Karachi	1987-88
137	DL Amiss	v India at Lord's	1975
137	ME Trescothick	v Pakistan at Lord's	2001
136	GA Gooch	v Australia at Lord's	1989
131	KWR Fletcher	v New Zealand at Nottingham	1975
130	DI Gower	v Sri Lanka at Taunton	1983
130	ME Trescothick	v West Indies at Gros Islet	2003-04

Trescothick has scored 12 centuries in ODIs, Gooch 8, Gower and KP Pietersen 7, GA Hick and NV Knight 5

Best innings bowling

6-31	PD Collingwood	v B'desh at Nottingham	2005
5-15	MA Ealham	v Zim at Kimberley	1999-2000
5-19	A Flintoff	v WI at Gros Islet	2008-09
5-20	VJ Marks	v NZ at Wellington	1983-84
5-21	C White	v Zim at Bulawayo	1999-2000
5-23	SCJ Broad	v S Africa at Nottingham	2008
5-26	RC Irani	v India at The Oval	2002
5-28	GP Swann	v Aust at Chester-le-Street	2009
5-31	M Hendrick	v Australia at The Oval	1980
5-32	MA Ealham	v Sri Lanka at Perth	1998-99

Collingwood also scored 112* in the same match.
All Ealham's 5 wickets at Kimberley were lbw, an ODI record

Record wicket partnerships

1st	200	ME Trescothick (114*) and VS Solanki (106)	v South Africa at The Oval	2003
2nd	202	GA Gooch (117*) and DI Gower (102)	v Australia at Lord's	1985
3rd	213	GA Hick (86*) and NH Fairbrother (113)	v West Indies at Lord's	1991
4th	226	AJ Strauss (100) and A Flintoff (123)	v West Indies at Lord's	2004
5th	174	A Flintoff (99) and PD Collingwood (79*)	v India at The Oval	2004
6th	150	MP Vaughan (90*) and GO Jones (80)	v Zimbabwe at Bulawayo	2004-05
7th	110	PD Collingwood (100) and C White (48)	v Sri Lanka at Perth	2002-03
8th	99*	RS Bopara (43*) and SCJ Broad (45*)	v India at Manchester	2007
9th	100	LE Plunkett (56) and VS Solanki (39*)	v Pakistan at Lahore	2005-06
10th	50*	D Gough (46*) and SJ Harmison (11*)	v Australia at Chester-le-Street	2005

Figures to 21.9.09. Updated records can be found at **www.cricinfo.com/ci/engine/records**

One-day International Records — ENGLAND

Most catches

Fielders

96	PD Collingwood	
64	GA Hick	
46	A Flintoff	
45	GA Gooch	
45	ME Trescothick	

Most dismissals

Wicketkeepers		*Ct/St*
163	AJ Stewart	148/15
72	GO Jones	68/4
53	MJ Prior	49/4
47	RC Russell	41/6
43	CMW Read	41/2

Highest team totals

391-4	v Bangladesh at Nottingham	2005
363-7	v Pakistan at Nottingham	1992
340-6	v New Zealand at Napier	2007-08
334-4	v India at Lord's	1975
333-9	v Sri Lanka at Taunton	1983
328-7	v West Indies at Birmingham	2009
327-4	v Pakistan at Lahore	2005-06
325-5	v India at Lord's	2002
322-6	v New Zealand at The Oval	1983
321-7	v Sri Lanka at Leeds	2006

England have reached 300 on 12 other occasions

Lowest team totals

Completed innings

86	v Australia at Manchester	2001
88	v SL at Dambulla	2003-04
89	v NZ at Wellington	2001-02
93	v Australia at Leeds	1975
94	v Aust at Melbourne	1978-79
101	v NZ at Chester-le-Street	2004
103	v SA at The Oval	1999
104	v SL at Colombo	2007-08
107	v Zim at Cape Town	1999-2000
110	v Aust at Melbourne	1998-99
110	v Aust at Adelaide	2006-07

The lowest totals against England are 45 by Canada (1979), and 70 by Australia (1977)

Most sixes

92	A Flintoff*	
57	KP Pietersen*	
51	PD Collingwood	
44	IT Botham	
41	GA Hick	
41	ME Trescothick	
30	AJ Lamb	
26	AJ Stewart	
22	DI Gower	
22	RA Smith	

*Also hit one six for the World XI

Best strike rate

Runs per 100 balls		*Runs*
89.14	A Flintoff	3293
87.60	KP Pietersen	3109
85.21	ME Trescothick	4335
83.83	PAJ DeFreitas	690
79.10	IT Botham	2113
78.33	OA Shah	1689
78.21	GO Jones	815
76.87	AJ Strauss	2766
76.16	PD Collingwood	4083
75.54	AJ Lamb	4010

Qualification: 500 runs

Most economical bowlers

Runs per over		*Wkts*
3.28	RGD Willis	80
3.54	ARC Fraser	47
3.79	GR Dilley	48
3.84	AD Mullally	63
3.96	IT Botham	145
3.96	PAJ DeFreitas	115
4.01	AR Caddick	69
4.08	MA Ealham	67
4.10	JE Emburey	76
4.17	GC Small	58

Qualification: 2000 balls bowled

England's one-day international results

	Played	Won	Lost	Tied	No result	% win
v Australia	100	38	58	2	2	39.79
v Bangladesh	8	8	0	0	0	100.00
v India	70	30	38	0	2	44.11
v New Zealand	69	29	34	2	4	46.15
v Pakistan	63	35	26	0	2	57.37
v South Africa	40	15	22	1	2	40.78
v Sri Lanka	43	22	21	0	0	51.16
v West Indies	82	37	41	0	4	47.43
v Zimbabwe	30	21	8	0	1	72.41
v others (see below)	13	12	0	0	1	92.30
TOTAL	**518**	**247**	**248**	**5**	**18**	**49.90**

Other teams: Canada (P2, W2), East Africa (P1, W1), Ireland (P3, W3), Kenya (P2, W2), Namibia (P1, W1), Netherlands (P2, W2), Scotland (P1, NR1), United Arab Emirates (P1, W1).

INDIA

Test Match Records

Most appearances

159	SR Tendulkar	
133	R Dravid	
132	A Kumble	
131	Kapil Dev	
125	SM Gavaskar	
116	DB Vengsarkar	
113	SC Ganguly	
105	VVS Laxman	
99	M Azharuddin	
91	GR Viswanath	

Gavaskar played 106 consecutive matches between 1974-75 and 1986-87

Most runs

		Avge
12773	SR Tendulkar	54.58
10800	R Dravid	52.94
10122	SM Gavaskar	51.12
7212	SC Ganguly	42.17
6868	DB Vengsarkar	42.13
6741	VVS Laxman	45.24
6215	M Azharuddin	45.03
6080	GR Viswanath	41.74
5674	V Sehwag	50.21
5248	Kapil Dev	31.05

Tendulkar has scored 42 centuries, Gavaskar 34, Dravid 26, Azharuddin 22

Most wickets

		Avge
619	A Kumble	29.65
434	Kapil Dev	29.64
330	Harbhajan Singh	30.42
266	BS Bedi	29.74
242	BS Chandrasekhar	29.74
236	J Srinath	30.49
210	Z Khan	33.84
189	EAS Prasanna	30.38
162	MH Mankad	32.32
156	S Venkataraghavan	36.11

In all 16 Indians have reached 100 wickets

Highest scores

319	V Sehwag	v South Africa at Chennai	2007-08
309	V Sehwag	v Pakistan at Multan	2003-04
281	VVS Laxman	v Australia at Kolkata	2000-01
270	R Dravid	v Pakistan at Rawalpindi	2003-04
254	V Sehwag	v Pakistan at Lahore	2005-06
248*	SR Tendulkar	v Bangladesh at Dhaka	2004-05
241*	SR Tendulkar	v Australia at Sydney	2003-04
239	SC Ganguly	v Pakistan at Bangalore	2007-08
236*	SM Gavaskar	v West Indies at Madras	1983-84
233	R Dravid	v Australia at Adelaide	2003-04

Dravid and Sehwag have scored five double-centuries, Gavaskar and Tendulkar four

Best innings bowling

10-74	A Kumble	v Pakistan at Delhi	1998-99
9-69	JM Patel	v Australia at Kanpur	1959-60
9-83	Kapil Dev	v WI at Ahmedabad	1983-84
9-102	SP Gupte	v W Indies at Kanpur	1958-59
8-52	MH Mankad	v Pakistan at Delhi	1952-53
8-55	MH Mankad	v England at Madras	1951-52
8-61	ND Hirwani	v W Indies at Madras	1987-88
8-72	S Venkataraghavan	v N Zealand at Delhi	1964-65
8-75	ND Hirwani	v W Indies at Madras	1987-88
8-76	EAS Prasanna	v NZ at Auckland	1975-76

Hirwani's two performances were in the same match, his Test debut

Record wicket partnerships

1st	413	MH Mankad (231) and P Roy (173)	v New Zealand at Madras	1955-56
2nd	344*	SM Gavaskar (182*) and DB Vengsarkar (157*)	v West Indies at Calcutta	1978-79
3rd	336	V Sehwag (309) and SR Tendulkar (194*)	v Pakistan at Multan	2003-04
4th	353	SR Tendulkar (241*) and VVS Laxman (178)	v Australia at Sydney	2003-04
5th	376	VVS Laxman (281) and R Dravid (180)	v Australia at Calcutta	2000-01
6th	298*	DB Vengsarkar (164*) and RJ Shastri (121*)	v Australia at Bombay	1986-87
7th	235	RJ Shastri (142) and SMH Kirmani (102)	v England at Bombay	1984-85
8th	161	M Azharuddin (109) and A Kumble (88)	v South Africa at Calcutta	1996-97
9th	149	PG Joshi (52*) and RB Desai (85)	v Pakistan at Bombay	1960-61
10th	133	SR Tendulkar (248*) and Z Khan (75)	v Bangladesh at Dhaka	2004-05

Figures to 21.9.09. Updated records can be found at **www.cricinfo.com/ci/engine/records**

Test Match Records

INDIA

Most catches

Fielders

183	R Dravid	
111	VVS Laxman	
108	SM Gavaskar	
105	M Azharuddin	
102	SR Tendulkar	

Most dismissals

	Wicketkeepers	*Ct/St*
198	SMH Kirmani	160/38
130	KS More	110/20
110	MS Dhoni	92/18
107	NR Mongia	99/8
82	FM Engineer	66/16

Highest team totals

705-7d	v Australia at Sydney	2003-04
676-7	v Sri Lanka at Kanpur	1986-87
675-5d	v Pakistan at Multan	2003-04
664	v England at The Oval	2007
657-7d	v Australia at Kolkata	2000-01
644-7d	v West Indies at Kanpur	1978-79
633-5d	v Australia at Kolkata	1997-98
628-8d	v England at Leeds	2002
627	v South Africa at Chennai	2007-08
626	v Pakistan at Bangalore	2007-08

India have reached 600 on eight other occasions

Lowest team totals

Completed innings

42*	v England at Lord's	1974
58	v Australia at Brisbane	1947-48
58	v England at Manchester	1952
66	v S Africa at Durban	1996-97
67	v Aust at Melbourne	1947-48
75	v West Indies at Delhi	1987-88
76	v SA at Ahmedabad	2007-08
81*	v NZ at Wellington	1975-76
81	v W Indies at Bridgetown	1996-97
82	v England at Manchester	1952

*One or more batsmen absent

Best match bowling

16-136	ND Hirwani	v West Indies at Madras	1987-88
15-217	Harbhajan Singh	v Australia at Chennai	2000-01
14-124	JM Patel	v Australia at Kanpur	1959-60
14-149	A Kumble	v Pakistan at Delhi	1998-99
13-131	MH Mankad	v Pakistan at Delhi	1952-53
13-132	J Srinath	v Pakistan at Calcutta	1998-99
13-181	A Kumble	v Australia at Chennai	2004-05
13-196	Harbhajan Singh	v Australia at Kolkata	2000-01
12-104	BS Chandrasekhar	v Australia at Melbourne	1977-78
12-108	MH Mankad	v England at Madras	1951-52

Hirwani's feat was on his Test debut

Hat-tricks

Harbhajan Singh	v Australia at Kolkata	2000-01

The wickets of RT Ponting, AC Gilchrist and SK Warne, as India fought back to win after following on.

IK Pathan	v Pakistan at Karachi	2005-06

Salman Butt, Younis Khan and Mohammad Yousuf with the fourth, fifth and sixth balls of the match – Pakistan still won the match by 341 runs.

India have never conceded a hat-trick in a Test match

India's Test match results

	Played	Won	Lost	Drawn	Tied	% win
v Australia	76	18	34	23	1	23.68
v Bangladesh	5	4	0	1	0	80.00
v England	99	19	34	46	0	19.19
v New Zealand	47	15	9	23	0	31.91
v Pakistan	59	9	12	38	0	15.25
v South Africa	22	5	10	7	0	22.72
v Sri Lanka	29	11	5	13	0	37.93
v West Indies	82	11	30	41	0	13.41
v Zimbabwe	11	7	2	2	0	63.63
TOTAL	**430**	**99**	**136**	**194**	**1**	**23.02**

Figures to 21.9.09. Updated records can be found at **www.cricinfo.com/ci/engine/records**

INDIA
One-day International Records

Most appearances

428	SR Tendulkar
334	M Azharuddin
332	R Dravid
308	SC Ganguly
269	A Kumble
229	J Srinath
225	Kapil Dev
214	Yuvraj Singh
196	A Jadeja
195	V Sehwag

Robin Singh played 136 ODIs for India – but only one Test match

Most runs

		Avge
16895	SR Tendulkar	44.57
11221	SC Ganguly	40.95
10564	R Dravid	39.41
9378	M Azharuddin	36.92
7006	Yuvraj Singh	37.66
6314	V Sehwag	34.69
5359	A Jadeja	37.47
4492	MS Dhoni	49.36
4413	NS Sidhu	37.08
4091	K Srikkanth	29.01

Kapil Dev (3783), DB Vengsarkar (3508), RJ Shastri (3108) and SM Gavaskar (3092) also reached 3000 runs

Most wickets

		Avge
334	A Kumble	30.83
315	J Srinath	28.08
288	AB Agarkar	27.85
253	Kapil Dev	27.45
212	Harbhajan Singh	32.90
212	Z Khan	30.03
196	BKV Prasad	32.30
157	M Prabhakar	28.87
154	SR Tendulkar	44.19
152	IK Pathan	29.91

RJ Shastri (129), SC Ganguly (100) and A Nehra (100) also reached 100 wickets

Highest scores

186*	SR Tendulkar	v N Zealand at Hyderabad	1999-2000
183*	MS Dhoni	v Sri Lanka at Jaipur	2005-06
183	SC Ganguly	v Sri Lanka at Taunton	1999
175*	Kapil Dev	v Zimbabwe at Tunbridge Wells	1983
163*	SR Tendulkar	v NZ at Christchurch	2008-09
159*	D Mongia	v Zimbabwe at Guwahati	2001-02
153*	M Azharuddin	v Zimbabwe at Cuttack	1997-98
153*	SC Ganguly	v New Zealand at Gwalior	1999-2000
153	R Dravid	v N Zealand at Hyderabad	1999-2000
152	SR Tendulkar	v Nam at Pietermaritzburg	2002-03

Tendulkar has scored 44 centuries (the ODI record), Ganguly 22, Dravid and Yuvraj Singh 12, and V Sehwag 11

Best bowling figures

6-12	A Kumble	v West Indies at Calcutta	1993-94
6-23	A Nehra	v England at Durban	2002-03
6-27	M Kartik	v Australia at Mumbai	2007-08
6-42	AB Agarkar	v Australia at Melbourne	2003-04
6-55	S Sreesanth	v England at Indore	2005-06
6-59	A Nehra	v Sri Lanka at Colombo	2005
5-6	SB Joshi	v South Africa at Nairobi	1999-2000
5-15	RJ Shastri	v Australia at Perth	1991-92
5-16	SC Ganguly	v Pakistan at Toronto	1997-98
5-21	Arshad Ayub	v Pakistan at Dhaka	1988-89
5-21	N Chopra	v West Indies at Toronto	1999-2000

Agarkar took four wickets in an ODI innings 12 times

Record wicket partnerships

1st	258	SC Ganguly (111) and SR Tendulkar (146)	v Kenya at Paarl	2001-02
2nd	331	SR Tendulkar (186*) and R Dravid (153)	v New Zealand at Hyderabad	1999-2000
3rd	237*	R Dravid (104*) and SR Tendulkar (140*)	v Kenya at Bristol	1999
4th	275*	M Azharuddin (153*) and A Jadeja (116*)	v Zimbabwe at Cuttack	1997-98
5th	223	M Azharuddin (111*) and A Jadeja (119)	v Sri Lanka at Colombo	1997-98
6th	158	Yuvraj Singh (120) and MS Dhoni (67*)	v Zimbabwe at Harare	2005-06
7th	102	HK Badani (60*) and AB Agarkar (53)	v Australia at Melbourne	2003-04
8th	82*	Kapil Dev (72*) and KS More (42*)	v New Zealand at Bangalore	1987-88
9th	126*	Kapil Dev (175*) and SMH Kirmani (24*)	v Zimbabwe at Tunbridge Wells	1983
10th	64	Harbhajan Singh (41*) and L Balaji (18)	v England at The Oval	2004

*Figures to 21.9.09. Updated records can be found at **www.cricinfo.com/ci/engine/records***

One-day International Records

INDIA

Most catches

Fielders

156	M Azharuddin	
129	SR Tendulkar	
121	R Dravid	
99	SC Ganguly	
85	A Kumble	

Most dismissals

Wicketkeepers		*Ct/St*
180	MS Dhoni	137/43
154	NR Mongia	110/44
90	KS More	63/27
86	R Dravid	72/14

Highest team totals

413-5	v Bermuda at Port-of-Spain	2006-07
392-4	v N Zealand at Christchurch	2008-09
387-5	v England at Rajkot	2008-09
376-2	v N Zealand at Hyderabad	1999-2000
374-4	v Hong Kong at Karachi	2008
373-6	v Sri Lanka at Taunton	1999
363-5	v Sri Lanka at Colombo	2008-09
356-9	v Pakistan at Visakhapatnam	2004-05
353-5	v New Zealand at Hyderabad	2003-04
351-3	v Kenya at Paarl	2001-02

All scored in 50 overs

Lowest team totals

Completed innings

54	v Sri Lanka at Sharjah	2000-01
63	v Australia at Sydney	1980-81
78	v Sri Lanka at Kanpur	1986-87
79	v Pakistan at Sialkot	1978-79
91	v South Africa at Durban	2006-07
100	v WI at Ahmedabad	1993-94
100	v Australia at Sydney	1999-2000
103	v Sri Lanka at Colombo	2008-09
108	v N Zealand at Auckland	2002-03
108	v NZ at Christchurch	2002-03

The lowest score against India is Zimbabwe's 65 at Harare in 2005-06

Most sixes

189	SC Ganguly	
177	SR Tendulkar	
128	Yuvraj Singh	
102	V Sehwag	
95	MS Dhoni	
85	A Jadeja	
77	M Azharuddin	
67	Kapil Dev	
44	NS Sidhu	
42	R Dravid	

Dhoni hit 10 sixes in one innings

Best strike rate

Runs per 100 balls		*Runs*
101.87	V Sehwag	6314
95.07	Kapil Dev	3783
91.92	RV Uthappa	786
89.43	SB Joshi	584
89.28	MS Dhoni	4492
89.18	Yuvraj Singh	7006
86.05	SK Raina	1611
85.77	SR Tendulkar	16895
83.92	G Gambhir	2594
82.17	SM Patil	1005

Qualification: 500 runs

Most economical bowlers

Runs per over		*Wkts*
3.71	Kapil Dev	253
3.95	Maninder Singh	66
4.05	Madan Lal	73
4.21	RJ Shastri	129
4.24	Harbhajan Singh	212
4.27	M Prabhakar	157
4.29	A Kumble	334
4.33	M Amarnath	46
4.36	SLV Raju	63
4.44	SB Joshi	69
4.44	J Srinath	315

Qualification: 2000 balls bowled

India's one-day international results

	Played	Won	Lost	Tied	No result	% win
v Australia	96	32	57	0	7	35.95
v Bangladesh	19	17	2	0	0	89.47
v England	70	38	30	0	2	55.88
v New Zealand	81	40	36	0	5	52.63
v Pakistan	117	45	68	0	4	39.82
v South Africa	57	20	35	0	2	36.36
v Sri Lanka	113	60	43	0	10	58.25
v West Indies	94	37	54	1	2	40.76
v Zimbabwe	49	39	8	2	0	81.63
v others (see below)	22	20	2	0	0	90.90
TOTAL	718	348	335	3	32	50.94

Other teams: Bermuda (P1, W1), East Africa (P1, W1), Hong Kong (P1, W1), Ireland (P1, W1), Kenya (P13, W11, L2), Namibia (P1, W1), Netherlands (P1, W1), Scotland (P1, W1), United Arab Emirates (P2, W2).

NEW ZEALAND *Test Match Records*

Most appearances

111	SP Fleming	
93	DL Vettori	
86	RJ Hadlee	
82	JG Wright	
81	NJ Astle	
78	AC Parore	
77	MD Crowe	
63	IDS Smith	
62	CL Cairns	
61	BE Congdon	

Vettori also played one Test for the World XI against Australia in October 2005

Most runs

		Avge
7172	SP Fleming	40.06
5444	MD Crowe	45.36
5334	JG Wright	37.82
4702	NJ Astle	37.02
3484	DL Vettori	29.77
3448	BE Congdon	32.22
3428	JR Reid	33.28
3320	CL Cairns	33.53
3124	RJ Hadlee	27.16
3116	CD McMillan	38.46

Crowe scored 17 Test centuries, Wright 12 and Astle 11

Most wickets

		Avge
431	RJ Hadlee	22.29
302	DL Vettori	33.26
218	CL Cairns	29.40
165	CS Martin	33.78
160	DK Morrison	34.68
130	BL Cairns	32.92
123	EJ Chatfield	32.17
116	RO Collinge	29.25
111	BR Taylor	26.60
102	JG Bracewell	35.81

RC Motz (100) also took 100 Test wickets. Vettori also took one wicket for the World XI

Highest scores

299	MD Crowe	v Sri Lanka at Wellington	1990-91
274*	SP Fleming	v Sri Lanka at Colombo	2002-03
267*	BA Young	v Sri Lanka at Dunedin	1996-97
262	SP Fleming	v South Africa at Cape Town	2005-06
259	GM Turner	v West Indies at Georgetown	1971-72
239	GT Dowling	v India at Christchurch	1967-68
230*	B Sutcliffe	v India at Delhi	1955-56
224	L Vincent	v Sri Lanka at Wellington	2004-05
223*	GM Turner	v West Indies at Kingston	1971-72
222	NJ Astle	v England at Christchurch	2001-02

There have been five other double-centuries, two by MS Sinclair and one each by MP Donnelly, SP Fleming and JD Ryder

Best innings bowling

9-52	RJ Hadlee	v Australia at Brisbane	1985-86
7-23	RJ Hadlee	v India at Wellington	1975-76
7-27	CL Cairns	v West Indies at Hamilton	1999-2000
7-52	C Pringle	v Pakistan at Faisalabad	1990-91
7-53	CL Cairns	v Bangladesh at Hamilton	2001-02
7-65	SB Doull	v India at Wellington	1998-99
7-74	BR Taylor	v West Indies at Bridgetown	1971-72
7-74	BL Cairns	v England at Leeds	1983
7-87	SL Boock	v Pakistan at Hyderabad	1984-85
7-87	DL Vettori	v Australia at Auckland	1999-2000

Hadlee took five or more wickets in an innings 36 times: the next-best for New Zealand is 18, by DL Vettori

Record wicket partnerships

1st	387	GM Turner (259) and TW Jarvis (182)	v West Indies at Georgetown	1971-72
2nd	241	JG Wright (116) and AH Jones (143)	v England at Wellington	1991-92
3rd	467	AH Jones (186) and MD Crowe (299)	v Sri Lanka at Wellington	1990-91
4th	271	LRPL Taylor (151) and JD Ryder (201)	v India at Napier	2008-09
5th	222	NJ Astle (141) and CD McMillan (142)	v Zimbabwe at Wellington	2000-01
6th	246*	JJ Crowe (120*) and RJ Hadlee (151*)	v Sri Lanka at Colombo	1986-87
7th	225	CL Cairns (158) and JDP Oram (90)	v South Africa at Auckland	2003-04
8th	256	SP Fleming (262) and JEC Franklin (122*)	v South Africa at Cape Town	2005-06
9th	136	IDS Smith (173) and MC Snedden (22)	v India at Auckland	1989-90
10th	151	BF Hastings (110) and RO Collinge (68*)	v Pakistan at Auckland	1972-73

*Figures to 21.9.09. Updated records can be found at **www.cricinfo.com/ci/engine/records***

Test Match Records **NEW ZEALAND**

Most catches

Fielders

171	SP Fleming
71	MD Crowe
70	NJ Astle
64	JV Coney
54	BA Young

Most dismissals

Wicketkeepers   *Ct/St*

201	AC Parore	194/7
176	IDS Smith	168/8
147	BB McCullum	138/9
96	KJ Wadsworth	92/4
59	WK Lees	52/7

Highest team totals

671-4	v Sri Lanka at Wellington	1990-91
630-6d	v India at Chandigarh	2003-04
619-9d	v India at Napier	2008-09
595	v South Africa at Auckland	2003-04
593-8d	v South Africa at Cape Town	2005-06
586-7d	v Sri Lanka at Dunedin	1996-97
563	v Pakistan at Hamilton	2003-04
561	v Sri Lanka at Napier	2004-05
553-7d	v Australia at Brisbane	1985-86
551-9d	v England at Lord's	1973

671-4 is the record score in any team's second innings in a Test match

Lowest team totals

Completed innings

26	v England at Auckland	1954-55
42	v Australia at Wellington	1945-46
47	v England at Lord's	1958
54	v Australia at Wellington	1945-46
65	v England at Christchurch	1970-71
67	v England at Leeds	1958
67	v England at Lord's	1978
70	v Pakistan at Dacca	1955-56
73	v Pakistan at Lahore	2001-02
74	v W Indies at Dunedin	1955-56
74	v England at Lord's	1958

26 is the lowest total by any team in a Test match

Best match bowling

15-123	RJ Hadlee	v Australia at Brisbane	1985-86
12-149	DL Vettori	v Australia at Auckland	1999-2000
12-170	DL Vettori	v Bangladesh at Chittagong	2004-05
11-58	RJ Hadlee	v India at Wellington	1975-76
11-102	RJ Hadlee	v West Indies at Dunedin	1979-80
11-152	C Pringle	v Pakistan at Faisalabad	1990-91
11-155	RJ Hadlee	v Australia at Perth	1985-86
11-169	DJ Nash	v England at Lord's	1994
11-180	CS Martin	v South Africa at Auckland	2003-04
10-88	RJ Hadlee	v India at Bombay	1988-89

Hadlee took 33 wickets at 12.15 in the three-Test series in Australia in 1985-86

Hat-tricks

PJ Petherick	v Pakistan at Lahore	1976-77
JEC Franklin	v Bangladesh at Dhaka	2004-05

*Petherick's hat-trick was on Test debut: he dismissed Javed Miandad (who had made 163 on **his** debut), Wasim Raja and Intikhab Alam. Petherick won only five more Test caps.*

Franklin is one of only five men to have scored a century and taken a hat-trick in Tests: the others are J Briggs of England, Abdul Razzaq and Wasim Akram of Pakistan, and IK Pathan of India

New Zealand's Test match results

	Played	Won	Lost	Drawn	Tied	% win
v Australia	48	7	24	17	0	14.58
v Bangladesh	8	7	0	1	0	87.50
v England	94	8	45	41	0	8.51
v India	47	9	15	23	0	19.14
v Pakistan	45	6	21	18	0	13.33
v South Africa	35	4	20	11	0	11.42
v Sri Lanka	26	9	7	10	0	34.61
v West Indies	37	9	10	18	0	24.32
v Zimbabwe	13	7	0	6	0	53.84
TOTAL	**353**	**66**	**142**	**145**	**0**	**18.69**

Figures to 21.9.09. Updated records can be found at **www.cricinfo.com/ci/engine/records**

NEW ZEALAND One-day International Records

Most appearances

279	SP Fleming
250	CZ Harris
237	DL Vettori
223	NJ Astle
214	CL Cairns
197	CD McMillan
179	AC Parore
157	SB Styris
155	BB McCullum
149	JG Wright

Fleming (1), Cairns (1) and Vettori (4) also played in official ODIs for the World XI

Most runs

		Avge
8007	SP Fleming	32.41
7090	NJ Astle	34.92
4881	CL Cairns	29.22
4707	CD McMillan	28.18
4704	MD Crowe	38.55
4379	CZ Harris	29.00
3891	JG Wright	26.46
3715	SB Styris	32.58
3314	AC Parore	25.68
3143	KR Rutherford	29.65

Astle scored 16 centuries: Fleming is next with eight. Fleming also scored 30 runs and Cairns 69 for the World XI

Most wickets

		Avge
236	DL Vettori	32.64
203	CZ Harris	37.50
200	CL Cairns	32.78
158	RJ Hadlee	21.56
150	KD Mills	26.40
140	EJ Chatfield	25.84
132	JDP Oram	30.99
128	SE Bond	19.44
126	DK Morrison	27.53
122	SB Styris	34.49

MC Snedden (114), GR Larsen (113) and C Pringle (103) also took 100 wickets. Vettori also took 8 wickets, and Cairns 1, for the World XI

Highest scores

172	L Vincent	v Zimbabwe at Bulawayo	2005-06
171*	GM Turner	v East Africa at Birmingham	1975
166	BB McCullum	v Ireland at Aberdeen	2008
161	JAH Marshall	v Ireland at Aberdeen	2008
145*	NJ Astle	v USA at The Oval	2004
141	SB Styris	v Sri Lanka at Bloemfontein	2002-03
140	GM Turner	v Sri Lanka at Auckland	1982-83
141	SB Styris	v Sri Lanka at Bloemfontein	2002-03
139	JM How	v England at Napier	2007-08
130	CZ Harris	v Australia at Madras	1995-96

Turner's 171 was the highest score in the first World Cup*

Best bowling figures

6-19	SE Bond	v India at Bulawayo	2005-06
6-23	SE Bond	v Australia at Port Elizabeth	2002-03
6-25	SB Styris	v West Indies at Port-of-Spain	2001-02
5-7	DL Vettori	v Bangladesh at Queenstown	2007-08
5-22	MN Hart	v West Indies at Margao	1994-95
5-22	AR Adams	v India at Queenstown	2002-03
5-23	RO Collinge	v India at Christchurch	1975-76
5-23	SE Bond	v Australia at Wellington	2006-07
5-25	RJ Hadlee	v Sri Lanka at Bristol	1983
5-25	SE Bond	v Australia at Adelaide	2001-02
5-25	KD Mills	v South Africa at Durban	2007-08

In all Hadlee took five wickets in an ODI on five occasions

Record wicket partnerships

1st	274	JAH Marshall (161) and BB McCullum (166)	v Ireland at Aberdeen	2008
2nd	156	L Vincent (102) and NJ Astle (81)	v West Indies at Napier	2005-06
3rd	181	AC Parore (96) and KR Rutherford (108)	v India at Baroda	1994-95
4th	168	LK Germon (89) and CZ Harris (130)	v Australia at Chennai	1995-96
5th	148	RG Twose (80*) and CL Cairns (60)	v Australia at Cardiff	1999
6th	165	CD McMillan (117) and BB McCullum (86*)	v Australia at Hamilton	2006-07
7th	115	AC Parore (78) and LK Germon (52)	v Pakistan at Sharjah	1996-97
8th	79	SB Styris (63) and DL Vettori (47)	v Zimbabwe at Harare	2005-06
9th	83	KD Mills (54) and TG Southee (32)	v India at Christchurch	2008-09
10th	65	MC Snedden (40) and EJ Chatfield (19*)	v Sri Lanka at Derby	1983

Figures to 21.9.09. Updated records can be found at www.cricinfo.com/ci/engine/records

Most catches

Fielders

132	SP Fleming	
96	CZ Harris	
83	NJ Astle	
66	CL Cairns	
66	MD Crowe	

Most dismissals

Wicketkeepers		*Ct/St*
174	BB McCullum	161/13
136	AC Parore	111/25
85	IDS Smith	80/5
37	TE Blain	36/1
30	LK Germon	21/9
30	WK Lees	28/2

Highest team totals

402-2	v Ireland at Aberdeen	2008
397-5	v Zimbabwe at Bulawayo	2005-06
363-5	v Canada at St Lucia	2006-07
350-9	v Australia at Hamilton	2006-07
349-9	v India at Rajkot	1999-2000
348-8	v India at Nagpur	1995-96
347-4	v USA at The Oval	2004
340-5	v Australia at Auckland	2006-07
340-7	v England at Napier	2007-08
338-4	v Bangladesh at Sharjah	1989-90

The 397-5 came from 44 overs; all the others were from 50, except 350-9 (49.3), and 340-5 (48.4)

Lowest team totals

Completed innings

64	v Pakistan at Sharjah	1985-86
73	v Sri Lanka at Auckland	2006-07
74	v Aust at Wellington	1981-82
74	v Pakistan at Sharjah	1989-90
94	v Aust at Christchurch	1989-90
97	v Aust at Faridabad	2003-04
105	v Aust at Auckland	2005-06
108	v Pakistan at Wellington	1992-93
110	v Pakistan at Auckland	1993-94
112	v Aust at Port Elizabeth	2002-03

The lowest score against New Zealand is 70, by Australia at Adelaide in 1985-86

Most sixes

151	CL Cairns	
86	NJ Astle	
85	BB McCullum	
84	CD McMillan	
64	JDP Oram	
63	SP Fleming	
59	SB Styris	
43	CZ Harris	
41	BL Cairns	
39	LRPL Taylor	

CL Cairns also hit 2 for the World XI

Best strike rate

Runs per 100 balls		*Runs*
104.88	BL Cairns	987
99.43	IDS Smith	1055
90.53	JD Ryder	555
87.99	BB McCullum	3004
83.76	CL Cairns	4881
83.39	LRPL Taylor	1179
82.92	JDP Oram	2050
78.89	SB Styris	3715
78.84	DL Vettori	1480
77.87	CM Spearman	936

Qualification: 500 runs

Most economical bowlers

Runs per over		*Wkts*
3.30	RJ Hadlee	158
3.57	EJ Chatfield	140
3.76	GR Larsen	113
4.06	BL Cairns	89
4.14	W Watson	74
4.16	DL Vettori	236
4.17	DN Patel	45
4.17	JV Coney	54
4.18	SE Bond	128
4.28	CZ Harris	203

Qualification: 2000 balls bowled

New Zealand's one-day international results

	Played	Won	Lost	Tied	No result	% win
v Australia	117	32	80	0	5	28.57
v Bangladesh	14	13	1	0	0	92.85
v England	69	34	29	2	4	53.84
v India	81	36	40	0	5	47.36
v Pakistan	78	29	47	1	1	38.31
v South Africa	50	17	29	0	4	36.95
v Sri Lanka	69	34	31	1	3	52.27
v West Indies	51	20	24	0	7	45.45
v Zimbabwe	28	19	7	1	1	72.22
v others (see below)	11	11	0	0	0	100.00
TOTAL	**568**	**245**	**288**	**5**	**30**	**46.00**

Other teams: Canada (P2, W2), East Africa (P1, W1), Ireland (P2, W2), Kenya (P1, W1), Netherlands (P1, W1), Scotland (P2, W2), United Arab Emirates (P1, W1), United States of America (P1, W1).

PAKISTAN
Test Match Records

Most appearances

124	Javed Miandad	
119	Inzamam-ul-Haq	
104	Wasim Akram	
103	Salim Malik	
88	Imran Khan	
87	Waqar Younis	
82	Mohammad Yousuf	
81	Wasim Bari	
78	Zaheer Abbas	
76	Mudassar Nazar	

Inzamam-ul-Haq also played one Test for the World XI

Most runs

		Avge
8832	Javed Miandad	52.57
8829	Inzamam-ul-Haq	50.16
7023	Mohammad Yousuf	54.86
5768	Salim Malik	43.69
5260	Younis Khan	50.09
5062	Zaheer Abbas	44.79
4114	Mudassar Nazar	38.09
4052	Saeed Anwar	45.52
3931	Majid Khan	38.92
3915	Hanif Mohammad	43.98

Mohammad Yousuf was known as Yousuf Youhana until September 2005

Most wickets

		Avge
414	Wasim Akram	23.62
373	Waqar Younis	23.56
362	Imran Khan	22.81
236	Abdul Qadir	32.80
232	Danish Kaneria	34.57
208	Saqlain Mushtaq	29.83
185	Mushtaq Ahmed	32.97
178	Shoaib Akhtar	25.69
177	Sarfraz Nawaz	32.75
171	Iqbal Qasim	28.11

Fazal Mahmood (139), Intikhab Alam (125) and Abdul Razzaq (100) also took 100 wkts

Highest scores

337	Hanif Mohammad	v WI at Bridgetown	1957-58
329	Inzamam-ul-Haq	v NZ at Lahore	2001-02
313	Younis Khan	v Sri Lanka at Karachi	2008-09
280*	Javed Miandad	v India at Hyderabad	1982-83
274	Zaheer Abbas	v Eng at Birmingham	1971
271	Javed Miandad	v NZ at Auckland	1988-89
267	Younis Khan	v India at Bangalore	2004-05
260	Javed Miandad	v England at The Oval	1987
257*	Wasim Akram	v Zim at Sheikhupura	1996-97
240	Zaheer Abbas	v England at The Oval	1974

Wasim Akram's innings included 12 sixes, a record for any Test innings

Best innings bowling

9-56	Abdul Qadir	v England at Lahore	1987-88
9-86	Sarfraz Nawaz	v Australia at Melbourne	1978-79
8-58	Imran Khan	v Sri Lanka at Lahore	1981-82
8-60	Imran Khan	v India at Karachi	1982-83
8-69	Sikander Bakht	v India at Delhi	1979-80
8-164	Saqlain Mushtaq	v England at Lahore	2000-01
7-40	Imran Khan	v England at Leeds	1987
7-42	Fazal Mahmood	v India at Lucknow	1952-53
7-49	Iqbal Qasim	v Australia at Karachi	1979-80
7-52	Intikhab Alam	v NZ at Dunedin	1972-73
7-52	Imran Khan	v Eng at Birmingham	1982

Wasim Akram took five or more wickets in a Test innings on 25 occasions, Imran Khan 23, Waqar Younis 22

Record wicket partnerships

1st	298	Aamer Sohail (160) and Ijaz Ahmed (151)	v West Indies at Karachi	1997-98
2nd	291	Zaheer Abbas (274) and Mushtaq Mohammad (100)	v England at Birmingham	1971
3rd	451	Mudassar Nazar (231) and Javed Miandad (280*)	v India at Hyderabad	1982-83
4th	350	Mushtaq Mohammad (201) and Asif Iqbal (175)	v New Zealand at Dunedin	1972-73
5th	281	Javed Miandad (163) and Asif Iqbal (166)	v New Zealand at Lahore	1976-77
6th	269	Mohammad Yousuf (223) and Kamran Akmal (154)	v England at Lahore	2005-06
7th	308	Waqar Hasan (189) and Imtiaz Ahmed (209)	v New Zealand at Lahore	1955-56
8th	313	Wasim Akram (257*) and Saqlain Mushtaq (79)	v Zimbabwe at Sheikhupura	1996-97
9th	190	Asif Iqbal (146) and Intikhab Alam (51)	v England at The Oval	1967
10th	151	Azhar Mahmood (128*) and Mushtaq Ahmed (59)	v South Africa at Rawalpindi	1997-98

Figures to 21.9.09. Updated records can be found at www.cricinfo.com/ci/engine/records

Test Match Records

PAKISTAN

Most catches

Fielders

93	Javed Miandad	
81	Inzamam-ul-Haq	
67	Younis Khan	
66	Majid Khan	
65	Salim Malik	

Most dismissals

Wicketkeepers   *Ct/St*

228	Wasim Bari	201/27
162	Kamran Akmal	142/20
147	Moin Khan	127/20
130	Rashid Latif	119/11
104	Salim Yousuf	91/13

Highest team totals

765-6d	v Sri Lanka at Karachi	2008-09
708	v England at The Oval	1987
699-5	v India at Lahore	1989-90
679-7d	v India at Lahore	2005-06
674-6	v India at Faisalabad	1984-85
657-8d	v West Indies at Bridgetown	1957-58
652	v India at Faisalabad	1982-83
643	v New Zealand at Lahore	2001-02
636-8d	v England at Lahore	2005-06
624	v Australia at Adelaide	1983-84

Pakistan have made four other scores of 600 or more, and one of 599-7d

Lowest team totals

Completed innings

53*	v Australia at Sharjah	2002-03
59	v Australia at Sharjah	2002-03
62	v Australia at Perth	1981-82
72	v Australia at Perth	2004-05
77*	v West Indies at Lahore	1986-87
87	v England at Lord's	1954
90	v England at Manchester	1954
90	v Sri Lanka at Colombo	2009
92	v S Africa at Faisalabad	1997-98
97*	v Australia at Brisbane	1995-96

* One batsman retired hurt or absent hurt. The lowest two totals came in the same game in 2002-03

Best match bowling

14-116	Imran Khan	v Sri Lanka at Lahore	1981-82
13-101	Abdul Qadir	v England at Lahore	1987-88
13-114	Fazal Mahmood	v Australia at Karachi	1956-57
13-135	Waqar Younis	v Zimbabwe at Karachi	1993-94
12-94	Fazal Mahmood	v India at Lucknow	1952-53
12-94	Danish Kaneria	v Bangladesh at Multan	2001-02
12-99	Fazal Mahmood	v England at The Oval	1954
12-100	Fazal Mahmood	v West Indies at Dacca	1958-59
12-130	Waqar Younis	v NZ at Faisalabad	1990-91
12-165	Imran Khan	v Australia at Sydney	1976-77

Imran Khan took ten or more wickets in a match six times, Abdul Qadir, Waqar Younis and Wasim Akram five each

Hat-tricks

Wasim Akram	v Sri Lanka at Lahore	1998-99
Wasim Akram	v Sri Lanka at Dhaka	1998-99
Abdul Razzaq	v Sri Lanka at Galle	1999-2000
Mohammad Sami	v Sri Lanka at Lahore	2001-02

Wasim Akram's hat-tricks came in successive matches: he also took Pakistan's first two hat-tricks in one-day internationals.

RS Kaluwitharana was the first victim in both Wasim Akram's first hat-trick and in Abdul Razzaq's

Pakistan's Test match results

	Played	Won	Lost	Drawn	Tied	% win
v Australia	52	11	24	17	0	21.15
v Bangladesh	6	6	0	0	0	100.00
v England	67	12	19	36	0	17.91
v India	59	12	9	38	0	20.33
v New Zealand	45	21	6	18	0	46.66
v South Africa	16	3	8	5	0	18.75
v Sri Lanka	37	15	9	13	0	40.54
v West Indies	44	15	14	15	0	34.09
v Zimbabwe	14	8	2	4	0	57.14
TOTAL	340	103	91	146	0	30.29

Figures to 21.9.09. Updated records can be found at **www.cricinfo.com/ci/engine/records**

PAKISTAN
One-day International Records

Most appearances

375	Inzamam-ul-Haq	
356	Wasim Akram	
283	Salim Malik	
276	Shahid Afridi	
265	Mohammad Yousuf	
262	Waqar Younis	
250	Ijaz Ahmed	
247	Saeed Anwar	
233	Javed Miandad	
230	Abdul Razzaq	

Moin Khan (219) also played in more than 200 ODIs

Most runs

		Avge
11701	Inzamam-ul-Haq	39.53
9129	Mohammad Yousuf	43.26
8824	Saeed Anwar	39.21
7381	Javed Miandad	41.70
7170	Salim Malik	32.88
6564	Ijaz Ahmed	32.33
5841	Rameez Raja	32.09
5678	Shahid Afridi	23.56
5623	Younis Khan	33.87
4858	Shoaib Malik	34.70

Aamer Sohail (4780) and Abdul Razzaq (4480) also passed 4000 runs

Most wickets

		Avge
502	Wasim Akram	23.52
416	Waqar Younis	23.84
288	Saqlain Mushtaq	21.78
257	Shahid Afridi	34.75
249	Abdul Razzaq	30.82
217	Shoaib Akhtar	23.52
182	Aqib Javed	31.43
182	Imran Khan	26.61
161	Mushtaq Ahmed	33.29
132	Abdul Qadir	26.16

Shoaib Malik (124), Azhar Mahmood (123), Moh'd Sami (118), Mudassar Nazar (111) and Naved-ul-Hasan (100) also took 100

Highest scores

194	Saeed Anwar	v India at Chennai	1996-97
160	Imran Nazir	v Zimbabwe at Kingston	2006-07
144	Younis Khan	v Hong Kong at Colombo	2004
143	Shoaib Malik	v India at Colombo	2004
141*	Mohammad Yousuf	v Zim at Bulawayo	2002-03
140	Saeed Anwar	v India at Dhaka	1997-98
139*	Ijaz Ahmed	v India at Lahore	1997-98
137*	Inzamam-ul-Haq	v N Zealand at Sharjah	1993-94
137	Ijaz Ahmed	v England at Sharjah	1998-99
136	Salman Butt	v Bangladesh at Karachi	2007-08

Saeed Anwar scored 20 centuries, Mohammad Yousuf 15, Ijaz Ahmed and Inzamam-ul-Haq 10

Best innings bowling

7-36	Waqar Younis	v England at Leeds	2001
7-37	Aqib Javed	v India at Sharjah	1991-92
6-14	Imran Khan	v India at Sharjah	1984-85
6-16	Shoaib Akhtar	v New Zealand at Karachi	2001-02
6-18	Azhar Mahmood	v W Indies at Sharjah	1999-2000
6-26	Waqar Younis	v Sri Lanka at Sharjah	1989-90
6-27	Naved-ul-Hasan	v India at Jamshedpur	2004-05
6-30	Waqar Younis	v N Zealand at Auckland	1993-94
6-35	Abdul Razzaq	v Bangladesh at Dhaka	2001-02
6-38	Shahid Afridi	v Australia at Dubai	2008-09

Waqar Younis took five or more wickets in an innings 13 times (the ODI record), Saqlain Mushtaq and Wasim Akram 6

Record wicket partnerships

1st	204	Saeed Anwar (110) and Rameez Raja (109*)	v Sri Lanka at Sharjah	1992-93
2nd	263	Aamer Sohail (134) and Inzamam-ul-Haq (137*)	v New Zealand at Sharjah	1993-94
3rd	230	Saeed Anwar (140) and Ijaz Ahmed (117)	v India at Dhaka	1997-98
4th	198*	Kamran Akmal (116*) and Misbah-ul-Haq (76*)	v Australia at Abu Dhabi	2008-09
5th	176	Younis Khan (89) and Umar Akmal (102*)	v Sri Lanka at Colombo	2009
6th	144	Imran Khan (102*) and Shahid Mahboob (77)	v Sri Lanka at Leeds	1983
7th	124	Mohammad Yousuf (91*) and Rashid Latif (66)	v Australia at Cardiff	2001
8th	100	Fawad Alam (63*) and Sohail Tanvir (59)	v Hong Kong at Karachi	2008
9th	73	Shoaib Malik (52*) and Mohammad Sami (46)	v South Africa at Centurion	2006-07
10th	72	Abdul Razzaq (46*) and Waqar Younis (33)	v South Africa at Durban	1997-98

Figures to 21.9.09. Updated records can be found at www.cricinfo.com/ci/engine/records

One-day International Records

PAKISTAN

Most catches

Fielders

113	Inzamam-ul-Haq
96	Shahid Afridi
96	Younis Khan
90	Ijaz Ahmed
88	Wasim Akram

Most dismissals

Wicketkeepers   *Ct/St*

287	Moin Khan	214/73
220	Rashid Latif	182/38
125	Kamran Akmal	108/17
103	Salim Yousuf	81/22
62	Wasim Bari	52/10

Highest team totals

371-9	v Sri Lanka at Nairobi	1996-97
353-6	v England at Karachi	2005-06
351-4	v South Africa at Durban	2006-07
349	v Zimbabwe at Kingston	2006-07
347-5	v Zimbabwe at at Karachi	2007-08
344-5	v Zimbabwe at Bulawayo	2002-03
344-8	v India at Karachi	2003-04
343-5	v Hong Kong at Colombo	2004
338-5	v Sri Lanka at Swansea	1983
335-6	v South Africa at Port Elizabeth	2002-03

Pakistan have reached 300 on 40 further occasions

Lowest team totals

Completed innings

43	v W Indies at Cape Town	1992-93
71	v W Indies at Brisbane	1992-93
74	v England at Adelaide	1991-92
75	v Sri Lanka at Lahore	2008-09
81	v West Indies at Sydney	1992-93
85	v England at Manchester	1978
87	v India at Sharjah	1984-85
89	v S Africa at Mohali	2006-07
107	v S Africa at Cape Town	2006-07
108	v Australia at Nairobi	2002-03

Against India in 1984-85 Pakistan were chasing only 126 to win

Most sixes

248	Shahid Afridi
143	Inzamam-ul-Haq
121	Wasim Akram
105	Abdul Razzaq
97	Saeed Anwar
87	Ijaz Ahmed
84	Mohammad Yousuf
61	Moin Khan
57	Shoaib Malik
50	Younis Khan

Afridi hit 2 other sixes in official ODIs

Best strike rate

Runs per 100 balls   *Runs*

110.87	Shahid Afridi	5678
89.60	Manzoor Elahi	741
88.33	Wasim Akram	3717
84.90	Kamran Akmal	2053
84.80	Zaheer Abbas	2572
82.00	Misbah-ul-Haq	1476
81.30	Moin Khan	3266
80.93	Imran Nazir	1842
80.67	Saeed Anwar	8824
80.30	Ijaz Ahmed	6564

Qualification: 500 runs

Most economical bowlers

Runs per over   *Wkts*

3.63	Sarfraz Nawaz	63
3.71	Akram Raza	38
3.89	Imran Khan	182
3.89	Wasim Akram	502
4.06	Abdul Qadir	132
4.14	Arshad Khan	56
4.14	Tauseef Ahmed	55
4.24	Mudassar Nazar	111
4.26	Mushtaq Ahmed	161
4.28	Aqib Javed	182

Qualification: 2000 balls bowled

Pakistan's one-day international results

	Played	Won	Lost	Tied	No result	% win
v Australia	79	29	46	1	3	38.81
v Bangladesh	25	24	1	0	0	96.00
v England	63	26	35	0	2	42.62
v India	117	68	45	0	4	60.17
v New Zealand	78	47	29	1	1	61.68
v South Africa	52	16	35	0	1	31.37
v Sri Lanka	119	70	45	1	3	60.77
v West Indies	113	47	64	2	0	42.47
v Zimbabwe	40	36	2	1	1	93.58
v others (see below)	17	16	1	0	0	94.11
TOTAL	**703**	**379**	**303**	**6**	**15**	**55.52**

Other teams: Canada (P1, W1), Hong Kong (P2, W2), Ireland (P1, L1), Kenya (P5, W5), Namibia (P1, W1), Netherlands (P3, W3), Scotland (P2, W2), United Arab Emirates (P2, W2).

SOUTH AFRICA *Test Match Records*

Most appearances

130	JH Kallis	
125	MV Boucher	
108	SM Pollock	
101	G Kirsten	
99	M Ntini	
90	HH Gibbs	
76	GC Smith	
72	AA Donald	
70	DJ Cullinan	
68	WJ Cronje	

Kallis, Boucher and Smith all also played one Test for the World XI against Australia

Most runs

		Avge
10194	JH Kallis	54.51
7289	G Kirsten	45.27
6330	GC Smith	51.04
6167	HH Gibbs	41.95
4671	MV Boucher	30.13
4554	DJ Cullinan	44.21
3781	SM Pollock	32.31
3714	WJ Cronje	36.41
3558	AB de Villiers	43.92
3471	B Mitchell	48.88

Kallis (83 runs), Smith (12) and Boucher (17) also played one Test for the World XI against Australia

Most wickets

		Avge
421	SM Pollock	23.11
388	M Ntini	28.37
330	AA Donald	22.25
257	JH Kallis	31.06
170	DW Steyn	23.70
170	HJ Tayfield	25.91
134	PR Adams	32.87
123	TL Goddard	26.22
123	A Nel	31.86
116	PM Pollock	24.18

NAT Adcock (104) and N Boje (100) also took 100 wickets. Kallis also took one wicket for the World XI

Highest scores

277	GC Smith	v England at Birmingham	2003
275*	DJ Cullinan	v New Zealand at Auckland	1998-99
275	G Kirsten	v England at Durban	1999-2000
274	RG Pollock	v Australia at Durban	1969-70
259	GC Smith	v England at Lord's	2003
255*	DJ McGlew	v New Zealand at Wellington	1952-53
236	EAB Rowan	v England at Leeds	1951
232	GC Smith	v Bangladesh at Chittagong	2007-08
231	AD Nourse	v Australia at Johannesburg	1935-36
228	HH Gibbs	v Pakistan at Cape Town	2002-03

Smith's 277 and 259 were in consecutive matches

Best innings bowling

9-113	HJ Tayfield	v England at Johannesburg	1956-57
8-53	GB Lawrence	v N Zealand at Johannesburg	1961-62
8-64	L Klusener	v India at Calcutta	1996-97
8-69	HJ Tayfield	v England at Durban	1956-57
8-70	SJ Snooke	v England at Johannesburg	1905-06
8-71	AA Donald	v Zimbabwe at Harare	1995-96
7-23	HJ Tayfield	v Australia at Durban	1949-50
7-29	GF Bissett	v England at Durban	1927-28
7-37	M Ntini	v W Indies at Port-of-Spain	2004-05
7-63	AE Hall	v England at Cape Town	1922-23

Klusener and Hall were making their Test debuts

Record wicket partnerships

1st	415	ND McKenzie (226) and GC Smith (232)	v Bangladesh at Chittagong	2007-08
2nd	315*	HH Gibbs (211*) and JH Kallis (148*)	v New Zealand at Christchurch	1998-99
3rd	429*	JA Rudolph (222*) and HH Dippenaar (177*)	v Bangladesh at Chittagong	2002-03
4th	249	JH Kallis (177) and G Kirsten (137)	v West Indies at Durban	2003-04
5th	267	JH Kallis (147) and AG Prince (131)	v West Indies at St John's	2004-05
6th	271	AG Prince (162*) and MV Boucher (117)	v Bangladesh at Centurion	2008-09
7th	246	DJ McGlew (255*) and ARA Murray (109)	v New Zealand at Wellington	1952-53
8th	150	ND McKenzie (103) and SM Pollock (111)	v Sri Lanka at Centurion	2000-01
	150	G Kirsten (130) and M Zondeki (59)	v England at Leeds	2003
9th	195	MV Boucher (78) and PL Symcox (108)	v Pakistan at Johannesburg	1997-98
10th	103	HG Owen-Smith (129) and AJ Bell (26*)	v England at Leeds	1929

Figures to 21.9.09. Updated records can be found at **www.cricinfo.com/ci/engine/records**

Test Match Records   SOUTH AFRICA

Most catches

Fielders
143	JH Kallis
101	GC Smith
94	HH Gibbs
83	G Kirsten
72	SM Pollock

Most dismissals

	Wicketkeepers	Ct/St
473	MV Boucher	451/22
152	DJ Richardson	150/2
141	JHB Waite	124/17
56	DT Lindsay	54/2
51	HB Cameron	39/12

Highest team totals

682-6d	v England at Lord's	2003
658-9d	v West Indies at Durban	2003-04
651	v Australia at Cape Town	2008-09
622-9d	v Australia at Durban	1969-70
621-5d	v New Zealand at Auckland	1998-99
620-7d	v Pakistan at Cape Town	2002-03
620	v Australia at Johannesburg	1966-67
604-6d	v West Indies at Centurion	2003-04
600-3d	v Zimbabwe at Harare	2001-02
595	v Australia at Adelaide	1963-64

The 620 was scored in the second innings of the match

Lowest team totals

	Completed innings	
30	v Eng at Port Elizabeth	1895-96
30	v Eng at Birmingham	1924
35	v Eng at Cape Town	1898-99
36	v Aust at Melbourne	1931-32
43	v Eng at Cape Town	1888-89
45	v Aust at Melbourne	1931-32
47	v Eng at Cape Town	1888-89
58	v England at Lord's	1912
72	v Eng at Johannesburg	1956-57
72	v Eng at Cape Town	1956-57

South Africa's lowest total since their return to Test cricket in 1991-92 is 84 against India at Johannesburg in 2006-07

Best match bowling

13-132	M Ntini	v W Indies at Port-of-Spain	2004-05
13-165	HJ Tayfield	v Australia at Melbourne	1952-53
13-192	HJ Tayfield	v England at Johannesburg	1956-57
12-127	SJ Snooke	v England at Johannesburg	1905-06
12-139	AA Donald	v India at Port Elizabeth	1992-93
12-181	AEE Vogler	v England at Johannesburg	1909-10
11-112	AE Hall	v England at Cape Town	1922-23
11-113	AA Donald	v Zimbabwe at Harare	1995-96
11-127	AA Donald	v England at Jo'burg	1999-2000
11-150	EP Nupen	v England at Jo'burg	1930-31

Hall was making his Test debut. His performance, and Vogler's, were at the old Wanderers ground in Johannesburg

Hat-tricks

GM Griffin	v England at Lord's	1960

Griffin achieved the feat in his second and final Test (he was no-balled for throwing in the same match).

GA Lohmann (for England at Port Elizabeth in 1895-96), TJ Matthews (twice in the same match for Australia at Manchester in 1912) and TWJ Goddard (for England at Johannesburg in 1938-39) have taken Test hat-tricks against South Africa

South Africa's Test match results

	Played	Won	Lost	Drawn	Tied	% win
v Australia	83	18	47	18	0	21.68
v Bangladesh	8	8	0	0	0	100.00
v England	134	28	55	51	0	20.89
v India	22	10	5	7	0	45.45
v New Zealand	35	20	4	11	0	57.14
v Pakistan	16	8	3	5	0	50.00
v Sri Lanka	17	8	4	5	0	47.05
v West Indies	22	14	3	5	0	63.63
v Zimbabwe	7	6	0	1	0	85.71
TOTAL	344	120	121	103	0	34.88

Figures to 21.9.09. Updated records can be found at **www.cricinfo.com/ci/engine/records**

SOUTH AFRICA One-day International Records

Most appearances

294	SM Pollock
286	JH Kallis
275	MV Boucher
245	JN Rhodes
244	HH Gibbs
188	WJ Cronje
185	G Kirsten
172	M Ntini
171	L Klusener
164	AA Donald

Pollock (9), Kallis (5), Boucher (5) and Ntini (1) also appeared in official ODIs for composite teams

Most runs

		Avge
10210	JH Kallis	46.19
8038	HH Gibbs	36.37
6798	G Kirsten	40.95
5935	JN Rhodes	35.11
5565	WJ Cronje	38.64
5251	GC Smith	40.70
4300	MV Boucher	29.05
3860	DJ Cullinan	32.99
3576	L Klusener	41.10
3300	HH Dippenaar	44.00

Kallis (29 runs), Smith (0), Boucher (163) and Dippenaar (91) also appeared in official ODIs for composite teams

Most wickets

		Avge
387	SM Pollock	24.31
272	AA Donald	21.78
265	M Ntini	24.53
243	JH Kallis	31.97
192	L Klusener	29.95
114	WJ Cronje	34.78
106	A Nel	27.68
95	N Boje	35.27
95	PS de Villiers	27.74
95	AJ Hall	26.47

Pollock (6 wickets), Ntini (1), Kallis (4) and Boje (1) also appeared in official ODIs for composite teams

Highest scores

188*	G Kirsten	v UAE at Rawalpindi	1995-96
175	HH Gibbs	v Australia at Johannesburg	2005-06
169*	DJ Callaghan	v N Zealand at Verwoerdburg	1994-95
161	AC Hudson	v Netherlands at Rawalpindi	1995-96
153	HH Gibbs	v B'desh at Potchefstroom	2002-03
147*	MV Boucher	v Zimbabwe at Potchefstroom	2006-07
146	AB de Villiers	v West Indies at St George's	2006-07
143	HH Gibbs	v N Zealand at Johannesburg	2002-03
140	HM Amla	v Bangladesh at Benoni	2008-09
139	JH Kallis	v W Indies at Johannesburg	2003-04

Gibbs has scored 21 one-day hundreds, Kallis 16 and Kirsten 13

Best bowling figures

6-22	M Ntini	v Australia at Cape Town	2005-06
6-23	AA Donald	v Kenya at Nairobi	1996-97
6-35	SM Pollock	v W Indies at East London	1998-99
6-49	L Klusener	v Sri Lanka at Lahore	1997-98
5-18	AJ Hall	v England at Bridgetown	2006-07
5-20	SM Pollock	v Eng at Johannesburg	1999-2000
5-21	L Klusener	v Kenya at Amstelveen	1999
5-21	N Boje	v Australia at Cape Town	2001-02
5-21	M Ntini	v Pakistan at Mohali	2006-07
5-23	SM Pollock	v Pakistan at Johannesburg	2006-07

Klusener has taken five wickets in an ODI innings six times, Pollock five and Ntini four

Record wicket partnerships

1st	235	G Kirsten (115) and HH Gibbs (111)	v India at Kochi	1999-2000
2nd	209	G Kirsten (124) and ND McKenzie (131*)	v Kenya at Cape Town	2001-02
3rd	186	JA Morkel (97) and AB de Villiers (107)	v Zimbabwe at Harare	2007
4th	232	DJ Cullinan (124) and JN Rhodes (121)	v Pakistan at Nairobi	1996-97
5th	183*	JH Kallis (109*) and JN Rhodes (94*)	v Pakistan at Durban	1997-98
6th	137	WJ Cronje (70*) and SM Pollock (75)	v Zimbabwe at Johannesburg	1996-97
7th	114	MV Boucher (68) and L Klusener (75*)	v India at Nagpur	1999-2000
8th	138*	JM Kemp (100*) and AJ Hall (56*)	v India at Cape Town	2006-07
9th	61	SM Pollock (46) and J Botha (15*)	v Australia at Melbourne	2005-06
10th	67*	JA Morkel (23*) and M Ntini (42*)	v New Zealand at Napier	2003-04

Figures to 21.9.09. Updated records can be found at www.cricinfo.com/ci/engine/records

One-day International Records **SOUTH AFRICA**

Most catches

Fielders

106	HH Gibbs	
105	JH Kallis	
105	JN Rhodes	
104	SM Pollock	
73	WJ Cronje	

Most dismissals

Wicketkeepers		*Ct/St*
397	MV Boucher	377/20
165	DJ Richardson	148/17
18	AB de Villiers	18/0
9	SJ Palframan	9/0

Highest team totals

438-9	v Australia at Johannesburg	2005-06
418-5	v Zimbabwe at Potchefstroom	2006-07
392-6	v Pakistan at Centurion	2006-07
363-3	v Zimbabwe at Bulawayo	2001-02
358-4	v Bangladesh at Benoni	2008-09
356-4	v West Indies at St George's	2006-07
354-3	v Kenya at Cape Town	2001-02
353-3	v Netherland at Basseterre	2006-07
336-7	v Kenya at Bloemfontein	2008-09
329-6	v Zimbabwe at Durban	2004-05

438-9 was the highest total in all ODIs at the time, and came from 49.5 overs; all the others above were scored in 50 overs, apart from 353-3 (40)

Lowest team totals

Completed innings

69	v Australia at Sydney	1993-94
83	v England at Nottingham	2008
101*	v Pakistan at Sharjah	1999-2000
106	v Australia at Sydney	2001-02
107	v England at Lord's	2003
107	v England at Lord's	2003
108	v NZ at Mumbai	2006-07
123	v Aust at Wellington	1994-95
129	v Eng at East London	1995-96
145	v Australia at Durban	2008-09

* One batsman retired hurt. SA also had 50-overs totals of 140-9 (v WI ,1992-93) and 144-9 (v Aust, 1999-2000)

Most sixes

126	HH Gibbs	
120	JH Kallis	
94	WJ Cronje	
78	MV Boucher	
76	L Klusener	
55	SM Pollock	
52	JM Kemp	
47	JN Rhodes	
44	AB de Villiers	
33	DJ Cullinan	

Boucher (2), Pollock (3), Kemp (1) and de Villiers (4) also hit sixes for the Africa XI

Best strike rate

Runs per 100 balls		*Runs*
89.91	L Klusener	3576
89.29	N Boje	1410
85.79	HM Amla	574
85.55	SM Pollock	3193
85.55	AB de Villiers	2611
84.81	MV Boucher	4300
83.61	PL Symcox	694
83.32	HH Gibbs	8038
82.78	JM Kemp	1371
82.14	GC Smith	5251

Qualification: 500 runs

Most economical bowlers

Runs per over		*Wkts*
3.57	PS de Villiers	95
3.65	SM Pollock	387
3.94	CR Matthews	79
4.15	AA Donald	272
4.15	PL Symcox	72
4.28	BM McMillan	70
4.40	J Botha	41
4.44	WJ Cronje	114
4.50	RP Snell	44
4.51	N Boje	95
4.51	M Ntini	265
4.51	AJ Hall	95

Qualification: 2000 balls bowled

South Africa's one-day international results

	Played	*Won*	*Lost*	*Tied*	*No result*	*% win*
v Australia	77	35	39	3	0	47.40
v Bangladesh	13	12	1	0	0	92.30
v England	40	22	15	1	2	59.21
v India	57	35	20	0	2	63.63
v New Zealand	50	29	17	0	4	63.04
v Pakistan	52	35	16	0	1	68.62
v Sri Lanka	45	22	21	1	1	51.13
v West Indies	45	32	12	0	1	72.72
v Zimbabwe	27	24	2	0	1	92.30
v others (see below)	17	17	0	0	0	100.00
TOTAL	**423**	**263**	**143**	**5**	**12**	**64.59**

Other teams: Canada (P1, W1), Ireland (P2, W2), Kenya (P10, W10), Netherlands (P2, W2), Scotland (P1, W1), United Arab Emirates (P1, W1).

263

SRI LANKA
Test Match Records

Most appearances

128	M Muralitharan	
111	WPUJC Vaas	
110	ST Jayasuriya	
107	DPMD Jayawardene	
93	PA de Silva	
93	A Ranatunga	
90	MS Atapattu	
85	KC Sangakkara	
83	HP Tillakaratne	
57	TM Dilshan	

Ranatunga uniquely played in his country's first Test, and their 100th

Most runs

		Avge
8747	DPMD Jayawardene	53.33
7308	KC Sangakkara	55.36
6973	ST Jayasuriya	40.07
6361	PA de Silva	42.97
5502	MS Atapattu	39.02
5105	A Ranatunga	35.69
4545	HP Tillakaratne	42.87
3787	TT Samaraweera	51.89
3443	TM Dilshan	43.03
3089	WPUJC Vaas	24.32

RS Mahanama (2576) and AP Gurusinha (2452) also reached 2000 runs

Most wickets

		Avge
778	M Muralitharan	22.16
355	WPUJC Vaas	29.58
98	ST Jayasuriya	34.34
91	SL Malinga	33.80
88	CRD Fernando	34.90
85	GP Wickremasinghe	41.87
73	RJ Ratnayake	35.10
69	HDPK Dharmasena	42.31
64	DNT Zoysa	33.70
59	ALF de Mel	36.94
59	HMRKB Herath	34.42

Murali also took 5 wkts for the World XI

Highest scores

374	DPMD Jayawardene	v SA at Colombo	2006
340	ST Jayasuriya	v India at Colombo	1997-98
287	KC Sangakkara	v SA at Colombo	2006
270	KC Sangakkara	v Zim at Bulawayo	2003-04
267	PA de Silva	v NZ at Wellington	1990-91
253	ST Jayasuriya	v Pak at Faisalabad	2004-05
249	MS Atapattu	v Zim at Bulawayo	2003-04
242	DPMD Jayawardene	v India at Colombo	1998-99
240	DPMD Jayawardene	v Pak at Karachi	2008-09
237	DPMD Jayawardene	v SA at Galle	2004-05

Jayawardene made 26 Test centuries, de Silva and Sangakkara 20, Atapattu 16 and Jayasuriya 14

Best innings bowling

9-51	M Muralitharan	v Zimbabwe at Kandy	2001-02
9-65	M Muralitharan	v England at The Oval	1998
8-46	M Muralitharan	v West Indies at Kandy	2005
8-70	M Muralitharan	v England at Nottingham	2006
8-83	JR Ratnayeke	v Pakistan at Sialkot	1985-86
8-87	M Muralitharan	v India at Colombo	2001-02
7-46	M Muralitharan	v England at Galle	2003-04
7-71	WPUJC Vaas	v West Indies at Colombo	2001-02
7-84	M Muralitharan	v South Africa at Galle	2000-01
7-94	M Muralitharan	v Zimbabwe at Kandy	1997-98

Muralitharan has taken five or more wickets in an innings a record 66 times

Record wicket partnerships

1st	335	MS Atapattu (207*) and ST Jayasuriya (188)	v Pakistan at Kandy	2000
2nd	576	ST Jayasuriya (340) and RS Mahanama (225)	v India at Colombo	1997-98
3rd	624	KC Sangakkara (287) and DPMD Jayawardene (374)	v South Africa at Colombo	2006
4th	437	DPMD Jayawardene (240) and TT Samaraweera (231)	v Pakistan at Karachi	2008-09
5th	280	TT Samaraweera (138) and TM Dilshan (168)	v Bangladesh at Colombo	2005-06
6th	189*	PA de Silva (143*) and A Ranatunga (87*)	v Zimbabwe at Colombo	1997-98
7th	223*	HAPW Jayawardene (120*) and WPUJC Vaas (100*)	v Bangladesh at Colombo	2007
8th	170	DPMD Jayawardene (237) and WPUJC Vaas (69)	v South Africa at Galle	2004-05
9th	105	WPUJC Vaas (50*) and KMDN Kulasekera (64)	v England at Lord's	2006
10th	79	WPUJC Vaas (68*) and M Muralitharan (43)	v Australia at Kandy	2003-04

Figures to 21.9.09. Updated records can be found at **www.cricinfo.com/ci/engine/records**

Test Match Records
SRI LANKA

Most catches

Fielders

151	DPMD Jayawardene
89	HP Tillakaratne
78	ST Jayasuriya
68	M Muralitharan
58	MS Atapattu

Most dismissals

Wicketkeepers   Ct/St

151	KC Sangakkara	131/20
119	RS Kaluwitharana	93/26
78	HAPW Jayawardene	59/19
35	HP Tillakaratne	33/2
34	SAR Silva	33/1

Highest team totals

952-6d	v India at Colombo	1997-98
756-5d	v South Africa at Colombo	2006
713-3d	v Zimbabwe at Bulawayo	2003-04
644-7d	v Pakistan at Karachi	2008-09
628-8d	v England at Colombo	2003-04
627-9d	v West Indies at Colombo	2001-02
610-6d	v India at Colombo	2001-02
606	v Pakistan at Lahore	2008-09
600-6d	v India at Colombo	2008
591	v England at The Oval	1998

952-6d is the highest total in all Tests. In all Sri Lanka have reached 500 on 24 occasions

Lowest team totals

Completed innings

71	v Pakistan at Kandy	1994-95
73*	v Pakistan at Kandy	2005-06
81	v England at Colombo	2000-01
82	v India at Chandigarh	1990-91
93	v NZ at Wellington	1982-83
95	v S Africa at Cape Town	2000-01
97	v N Zealand at Kandy	1983-84
97	v Australia at Darwin	2004
101	v Pakistan at Kandy	1985-86
109	v Pakistan at Kandy	1985-86

* One batsman absent hurt

Best match bowling

16-220	M Muralitharan	v England at The Oval	1998
14-191	WPUJC Vaas	v West Indies at Colombo	2001-02
13-115	M Muralitharan	v Zimbabwe at Kandy	2001-02
13-171	M Muralitharan	v South Africa at Galle	2000
12-82	M Muralitharan	v Bangladesh at Kandy	2007
12-117	M Muralitharan	v Zimbabwe at Kandy	1997-98
12-225	M Muralitharan	v South Africa at Colombo	2006
11-93	M Muralitharan	v England at Galle	2003-04
11-110	M Muralitharan	v India at Colombo	2008
11-132	M Muralitharan	v England at Nottingham	2006

Muralitharan has taken ten or more wickets in a match a record 22 times; the only others to do it for Sri Lanka are Vaas (twice), UDU Chandana and BAW Mendis

Hat-tricks

DNT Zoysa	v Zimbabwe at Harare	1999-2000

He dismissed TR Gripper, MW Goodwin and NC Johnson with the first three balls of his first over, the second of the match.

Four hat-tricks have been taken against Sri Lanka in Tests, all of them for Pakistan: two by Wasim Akram (in successive Tests in the Asian Test Championship at Lahore and Dhaka in 1998-99), Abdul Razzaq (at Galle in 2000-01) and Mohammad Sami (at Lahore in 2001-02)

Sri Lanka's Test match results

	Played	Won	Lost	Drawn	Tied	% win
v Australia	20	1	13	6	0	5.00
v Bangladesh	12	12	0	0	0	100.00
v England	21	6	8	7	0	28.57
v India	29	5	11	13	0	17.24
v New Zealand	26	7	9	10	0	26.92
v Pakistan	37	9	15	13	0	24.32
v South Africa	17	4	8	5	0	23.52
v West Indies	12	6	3	3	0	50.00
v Zimbabwe	15	10	0	5	0	66.66
TOTAL	**189**	**60**	**67**	**62**	**0**	**31.74**

Figures to 21.9.09. Updated records can be found at www.cricinfo.com/ci/engine/records

SRI LANKA
One-day International Records

Most appearances

434	ST Jayasuriya	
325	M Muralitharan	
321	WPUJC Vaas	
308	PA de Silva	
302	DPMD Jayawardene	
269	A Ranatunga	
268	MS Atapattu	
247	KC Sangakkara	
213	RS Mahanama	
200	HP Tillakaratne	

*In all 18 Sri Lankans have played
more than 100 ODIs*

Most runs

		Avge
13277	ST Jayasuriya	32.86
9284	PA de Silva	34.90
8529	MS Atapattu	37.57
8009	DPMD Jayawardene	31.40
7456	A Ranatunga	35.84
7335	KC Sangakkara	35.78
5162	RS Mahanama	29.49
3950	RP Arnold	35.26
3902	AP Gurusinha	28.27
3789	HP Tillakaratne	29.60

*RS Kaluwitharana (3711) and TM
Dilshan (3492) also reached 3000 runs*

Most wickets

		Avge
500	M Muralitharan	22.75
399	WPUJC Vaas	27.45
316	ST Jayasuriya	36.50
163	CRD Fernando	30.53
151	UDU Chandana	31.72
138	HDPK Dharmasena	36.21
116	MF Maharoof	25.83
109	GP Wickremasinghe	39.64
108	DNT Zoysa	29.75
106	PA de Silva	39.40

*Muralitharan (11), Vaas (1), Jayasuriya
(3) and Fernando (4) all took wickets in
ODIs for composite teams*

Highest scores

189	ST Jayasuriya	v India at Sharjah	2000-01
157	ST Jayasuriya	v Netherlands at Amstelveen	2006
152	ST Jayasuriya	v England at Leeds	2006
151*	ST Jayasuriya	v India at Mumbai	1996-97
145	PA de Silva	v Kenya at Kandy	1995-96
140	ST Jayasuriya	v N Zealand at Bloemfontein	1994-95
138*	KC Sangakkara	v India at Jaipur	2005-06
137*	TM Dilshan	v Pakistan at Lahore	2008-09
134*	ST Jayasuriya	v Pakistan at Lahore	1997-98
134	PA de Silva	v Pakistan at Sharjah	1996-97
134	ST Jayasuriya	v Pakistan at Singapore	1995-96

*ST Jayasuriya has scored 28 ODI centuries, MS Atapattu and
PA de Silva 11, DPMD Jayawardene and KC Sangakkara 10*

Best bowling figures

8-19	WPUJC Vaas	v Zimbabwe at Colombo	2001-02
7-30	M Muralitharan	v India at Sharjah	2000-01
6-13	BAW Mendis	v India at Karachi	2008
6-14	MF Maharoof	v West Indies at Mumbai	2006-07
6-20	AD Mathews	v India at Colombo	2008-09
6-25	WPUJC Vaas	v B'desh at P'maritzburg	2002-03
6-27	CRD Fernando	v England at Colombo	2007-08
6-29	ST Jayasuriya	v England at Moratuwa	1992-93
6-29	BAW Mendis	v Zimbabwe at Harare	2008-09
5-9	M Muralitharan	v New Zealand at Sharjah	2001-02

*Vaas's 8-19 are the best bowling figures in all ODIs. In his
6-25 Vaas took a hat-trick with the first three balls of the
match, and four wickets in all in the first over*

Record wicket partnerships

1st	286	WU Tharanga (109) and ST Jayasuriya (152)	v England at Leeds	2006
2nd	170	S Wettimuny (74) and RL Dias (102)	v India at Delhi	1982-83
	170	ST Jayasuriya (120) and HP Tillakaratne (81*)	v New Zealand at Bloemfontein	2002-03
3rd	226	MS Atapattu (102*) and DPMD Jayawardene (128)	v India at Sharjah	2000-01
4th	171*	RS Mahanama (94*) and A Ranatunga (87*)	v West Indies at Lahore	1997-98
5th	166	ST Jayasuriya (189) and RP Arnold (52*)	v India at Sharjah	2000-01
6th	159	LPC Silva (67) and CK Kapugedera (95)	v West Indies at Port-of-Spain	2007-08
7th	126*	DPMD Jayawardene (94*) and UDU Chandana (44*)	v India at Dambulla	2005-06
8th	91	HDPK Dharmasena (51*) and DK Liyanage (43)	v West Indies at Port-of-Spain	1996-97
9th	76	RS Kalpage (44*) and WPUJC Vaas (33)	v Pakistan at Colombo	1994-95
10th	51	RP Arnold (103) and KSC de Silva (2*)	v Zimbabwe at Bulawayo	1999-2000

Figures to 21.9.09. Updated records can be found at **www.cricinfo.com/ci/engine/records**

One-day International Records

SRI LANKA

Most catches

Fielders

156	DPMD Jayawardene	
126	M Muralitharan	
122	ST Jayasuriya	
109	RS Mahanama	
95	PA de Silva	

Most dismissals

Wicketkeepers		*Ct/St*
278	KC Sangakkara	217/61
206	RS Kaluwitharana	131/75
45	HP Tillakaratne	39/6
34	DSBP Kuruppu	26/8
30	RG de Alwis	27/3

Highest team totals

443-9	v Netherlands at Amstelveen	2006
398-5	v Kenya at Kandy	1995-96
357-9	v Bangladesh at Lahore	2008
349-9	v Pakistan at Singapore	1995-96
343-5	v Australia at Sydney	2002-03
339-4	v Pakistan at Mohali	1996-97
332-8	v Bangladesh at Karachi	2008
329	v West Indies at Sharjah	1995-96
324-2	v England at Leeds	2006
321-6	v Bermuda at Port-of-Spain	2006-07

The 324-2 was scored in 37.3 overs

Lowest team totals

Completed innings

55	v W Indies at Sharjah	1986-87
78*	v Pakistan at Sharjah	2001-02
86	v W Indies at Manchester	1975
91	v Australia at Adelaide	1984-85
96	v India at Sharjah	1983-84
98	v S Africa at Colombo	1993-94
98	v India at Sharjah	1998-99
99	v England at Perth	1998-99
102	v W Indies at Brisbane	1995-96
105	v SA at Bloemfontein	1997-98

* One batsman absent hurt

Most sixes

268	ST Jayasuriya
102	PA de Silva
64	A Ranatunga
44	DPMD Jayawardene
42	AP Gurusinha
28	KC Sangakkara
23	CK Kapugedera
22	UDU Chandana
22	MF Maharoof
22	WPUJC Vaas

Jayasuriya also hit 2 for the Asia XI

Best strike rate

Runs per 100 balls		*Runs*
91.31	ST Jayasuriya	13277
86.80	RJ Ratnayake	612
85.50	MF Maharoof	973
82.14	TM Dilshan	3492
81.13	PA de Silva	9284
77.91	A Ranatunga	7456
77.70	RS Kaluwitharana	3711
75.97	M Muralitharan	642
75.96	DPMD Jayawardene	8009
75.07	LRD Mendis	1527

Qualification: 500 runs

Most economical bowlers

Runs per over		*Wkts*
3.89	M Muralitharan	500
4.18	WPUJC Vaas	399
4.18	SD Anurasiri	32
4.27	HDPK Dharmasena	138
4.29	CPH Ramanayake	68
4.29	VB John	34
4.42	KMDN Kulasekara	74
4.50	DS de Silva	32
4.50	RS Kalpage	73
4.52	DNT Zoysa	108

Qualification: 2000 balls bowled

Sri Lanka's one-day international results

	Played	Won	Lost	Tied	No result	% win
v Australia	68	20	46	0	2	30.30
v Bangladesh	26	24	2	0	0	92.30
v England	43	21	22	0	0	48.83
v India	113	43	60	0	10	41.74
v New Zealand	69	31	34	1	3	47.72
v Pakistan	119	45	70	1	3	39.22
v South Africa	45	21	22	1	1	48.86
v West Indies	46	18	26	0	2	40.90
v Zimbabwe	43	36	6	0	1	85.71
v others (see below)	13	12	1	0	0	92.30
TOTAL	585	271	289	3	22	48.40

Other teams: Bermuda (P1, W1), Canada (P1, W1), Ireland (P1, W1), Kenya (P5, W4, L1), Netherlands (P3, W3), United Arab Emirates (P2, W2).

WEST INDIES
Test Match Records

Most appearances

132	CA Walsh	
130	BC Lara	
121	S Chanderpaul	
121	IVA Richards	
116	DL Haynes	
110	CH Lloyd	
108	CG Greenidge	
102	CL Hooper	
98	CEL Ambrose	
93	GS Sobers	

Sobers played 85 successive Tests between 1954-55 and 1971-72

Most runs

		Avge
11912	BC Lara	53.17
8576	S Chanderpaul	49.28
8540	IVA Richards	50.23
8032	GS Sobers	57.78
7558	CG Greenidge	44.72
7515	CH Lloyd	46.67
7487	DL Haynes	42.29
6227	RB Kanhai	47.53
5949	RB Richardson	44.39
5762	CL Hooper	36.46

Greenidge and Haynes put on 6482 runs together, the Test record by any pair of batsmen

Most wickets

		Avge
519	CA Walsh	24.44
405	CEL Ambrose	20.99
376	MD Marshall	20.94
309	LR Gibbs	29.09
259	J Garner	20.97
249	MA Holding	23.68
235	GS Sobers	34.03
202	AME Roberts	25.61
192	WW Hall	26.38
161	IR Bishop	24.27

In all 18 West Indians have reached 100 Test wickets

Highest scores

400*	BC Lara	v England at St John's	2003-04
375	BC Lara	v England at St John's	1993-94
365*	GS Sobers	v Pakistan at Kingston	1957-58
317	CH Gayle	v South Africa at St John's	2004-05
302	LG Rowe	v England at Bridgetown	1973-74
291	IVA Richards	v England at The Oval	1976
291	RR Sarwan	v England at Bridgetown	2008-09
277	BC Lara	v Australia at Sydney	1992-93
270*	GA Headley	v England at Kingston	1934-35
261*	RR Sarwan	v Bangladesh at Kingston	2003-04
261	FMM Worrell	v England at Nottingham	1950

Lara scored 34 Test centuries, Sobers 26, Richards 24

Best innings bowling

9-95	JM Noreiga	v India at Port-of-Spain	1970-71
8-29	CEH Croft	v Pakistan at Port-of-Spain	1976-77
8-38	LR Gibbs	v India at Bridgetown	1961-62
8-45	CEL Ambrose	v England at Bridgetown	1989-90
8-92	MA Holding	v England at The Oval	1976
8-104	AL Valentine	v England at Manchester	1950
7-22	MD Marshall	v England at Manchester	1988
7-25	CEL Ambrose	v Australia at Perth	1992-93
7-37	CA Walsh	v New Zealand at Wellington	1994-95
7-49	S Ramadhin	v England at Birmingham	1957

Valentine was playing in his first Test, Croft and Noreiga in their second

Record wicket partnerships

1st	298	CG Greenidge (149) and DL Haynes (167)	v England at St John's	1989-90
2nd	446	CC Hunte (260) and GS Sobers (365*)	v Pakistan at Kingston	1957-58
3rd	338	ED Weekes (206) and FMM Worrell (167)	v England at Port-of-Spain	1953-54
4th	399	GS Sobers (226) and FMM Worrell (197*)	v England at Bridgetown	1959-60
5th	322	BC Lara (213) and JC Adams (94)	v Australia at Kingston	1998-99
6th	282*	BC Lara (400*) and RD Jacobs (107*)	v England at St John's	2003-04
7th	347	DS Atkinson (219) and CC Depeiaza (122)	v Australia at Bridgetown	1954-55
8th	148	JC Adams (101*) and FA Rose (69)	v Zimbabwe at Kingston	1999-2000
9th	161	CH Lloyd (161*) and AME Roberts (68)	v India at Calcutta	1983-84
10th	106	CL Hooper (178*) and CA Walsh (30)	v Pakistan at St John's	1992-93

Figures to 21.9.09. Updated records can be found at **www.cricinfo.com/ci/engine/records**

Test Match Records

WEST INDIES

Most catches

Fielders

164	BC Lara	
122	IVA Richards	
115	CL Hooper	
109	GS Sobers	
96	CG Greenidge	

Most dismissals

Wicketkeepers   *Ct/St*

270	PJL Dujon	265/5
219	RD Jacobs	207/12
189	DL Murray	181/8
105	D Ramdin	103/2
101	JR Murray	98/3

Highest team totals

790-3d	v Pakistan at Kingston	1957-58
751-5d	v England at St John's	2003-04
749-9d	v England at Bridgetown	2008-09
747	v South Africa at St John's	2004-05
692-8d	v England at The Oval	1995
687-8d	v England at The Oval	1976
681-8d	v England at Port-of-Spain	1953-54
660-5d	v New Zealand at Wellington	1994-95
652-8d	v England at Lord's	1973
644-8d	v India at Delhi	1958-59
631-8d	v India at Kingston	1961-62
631	v India at Delhi	1948-49

West Indies have passed 600 in Tests on seven further occasions

Lowest team totals

Completed innings

47	v England at Kingston	2003-04
51	v Aust at Port-of-Spain	1998-99
53	v Pakistan at Faisalabad	1986-87
54	v England at Lord's	2000
61	v England at Leeds	2000
76	v Pakistan at Dacca	1958-59
77	v NZ at Auckland	1955-56
78	v Australia at Sydney	1951-52
82	v Australia at Brisbane	2000-01
86*	v England at The Oval	1957

*One batsman absent hurt

Best match bowling

14-149	MA Holding	v England at The Oval	1976
13-55	CA Walsh	v N Zealand at Wellington	1994-95
12-121	AME Roberts	v India at Madras	1974-75
11-84	CEL Ambrose	v England at Port-of-Spain	1993-94
11-89	MD Marshall	v India at Port-of-Spain	1988-89
11-107	MA Holding	v Australia at Melbourne	1981-82
11-120	MD Marshall	v N Zealand at Bridgetown	1984-85
11-126	WW Hall	v India at Kanpur	1958-59
11-134	CD Collymore	v Pakistan at Kingston	2004-05
11-147	KD Boyce	v England at The Oval	1973

Marshall took ten or more wickets in a Test four times, Ambrose and Walsh three

Hat-tricks

WW Hall	v Pakistan at Lahore	1958-59

The first Test hat-trick not for England or Australia.

LR Gibbs	v Australia at Adelaide	1960-61

Gibbs had taken three wickets in four balls in the previous Test, at Sydney.

CA Walsh	v Australia at Brisbane	1988-89

The first Test hat-trick to be split over two innings.

JJC Lawson	v Australia at Bridgetown	2002-03

Also split over two innings

West Indies' Test match results

	Played	Won	Lost	Drawn	Tied	% win
v Australia	105	32	50	22	1	30.47
v Bangladesh	6	3	2	1	0	50.00
v England	145	53	43	49	0	36.55
v India	82	30	11	41	0	36.58
v New Zealand	37	10	9	18	0	27.02
v Pakistan	44	14	15	15	0	31.81
v South Africa	22	3	14	5	0	13.63
v Sri Lanka	12	3	6	3	0	25.00
v Zimbabwe	6	4	0	2	0	66.66
TOTAL	**459**	**152**	**150**	**156**	**1**	**33.11**

Figures to 21.9.09. Updated records can be found at **www.cricinfo.com/ci/engine/records**

WEST INDIES *One-day International Records*

Most appearances

295	BC Lara	
252	S Chanderpaul	
238	DL Haynes	
227	CL Hooper	
224	RB Richardson	
205	CA Walsh	
202	CH Gayle	
187	IVA Richards	
176	CEL Ambrose	
169	PJL Dujon	

In all 24 West Indians have played more than 100 ODIs

Most runs

		Avge
10348	BC Lara	40.90
8648	DL Haynes	41.37
8250	S Chanderpaul	41.66
7374	CH Gayle	40.29
6721	IVA Richards	47.00
6248	RB Richardson	33.41
5761	CL Hooper	35.34
5134	CG Greenidge	45.03
4907	RR Sarwan	43.04
3675	PV Simmons	28.93

Gayle and Lara scored 19 ODI centuries, Haynes 17, Greenidge and Richards 11

Most wickets

		Avge
227	CA Walsh	30.47
225	CEL Ambrose	24.12
193	CL Hooper	36.05
157	MD Marshall	26.96
151	CH Gayle	33.64
146	J Garner	18.84
142	MA Holding	21.36
130	M Dillon	32.44
118	IR Bishop	26.50
118	IVA Richards	35.83

DJ Bravo (114), WKM Benjamin (100) and RA Harper (100) also reached 100

Highest scores

189*	IVA Richards	v England at Manchester	1984
181	IVA Richards	v Sri Lanka at Karachi	1987-88
169	BC Lara	v Sri Lanka at Sharjah	1995-96
157*	XM Marshall	v Canada at King City	2008-09
156	BC Lara	v Pakistan at Adelaide	2004-05
153*	IVA Richards	v Australia at Melbourne	1979-80
153*	CH Gayle	v Zimbabwe at Bulawayo	2003-04
153	BC Lara	v Pakistan at Sharjah	1993-94
152*	DL Haynes	v India at Georgetown	1988-89
152*	CH Gayle	v S Africa at Johannesburg	2003-04
152	CH Gayle	v Kenya at Nairobi	2001-02

S Chanderpaul scored 150 v SA at East London in 1998-99

Best bowling figures

7-51	WW Davis	v Australia at Leeds	1983
6-15	CEH Croft	v England at Kingstown	1980-81
6-22	FH Edwards	v Zimbabwe at Harare	2003-04
6-29	BP Patterson	v India at Nagpur	1987-88
6-41	IVA Richards	v India at Delhi	1989-90
6-50	AH Gray	v Aust at Port-of-Spain	1990-91
5-1	CA Walsh	v Sri Lanka at Sharjah	1986-87
5-17	CEL Ambrose	v Australia at Melbourne	1988-89
5-22	AME Roberts	v England at Adelaide	1979-80
5-22	WKM Benjamin	v Sri Lanka at Bombay	1993-94

Edwards's feat was in his first ODI; he had earlier taken 5-36 on his Test debut

Record wicket partnerships

1st	200*	SC Williams (78*) and S Chanderpaul (109*)	v India at Bridgetown	1996-97
2nd	221	CG Greenidge (115) and IVA Richards (149)	v India at Jamshedpur	1983-84
3rd	195*	CG Greenidge (105*) and HA Gomes (75*)	v Zimbabwe at Worcester	1983
4th	226	S Chanderpaul (150) and CL Hooper (108)	v South Africa at East London	1998-99
5th	154	CL Hooper (112*) and S Chanderpaul (67)	v Pakistan at Sharjah	2001-02
6th	154	RB Richardson (122) and PJL Dujon (53)	v Pakistan at Sharjah	1991-92
7th	115	PJL Dujon (57*) and MD Marshall (66)	v Pakistan at Gujranwala	1986-87
8th	84	RL Powell (76) and CD Collymore (3)	v India at Toronto	1999-2000
9th	77	RR Sarwan (65) and IDR Bradshaw (37)	v New Zealand at Christchurch	2005-06
10th	106*	IVA Richards (189*) and MA Holding (12*)	v England at Manchester	1984

Figures to 21.9.09. Updated records can be found at **www.cricinfo.com/ci/engine/records**

One-day International Records — WEST INDIES

Most catches

Fielders

120	CL Hooper
117	BC Lara
100	IVA Richards
89	CH Gayle
75	RB Richardson

Most dismissals

	Wicketkeepers	Ct/St
204	PJL Dujon	183/21
189	RD Jacobs	160/29
96	D Ramdin	91/5
68	CO Browne	59/9
51	JR Murray	44/7

Highest team totals

360-4	v Sri Lanka at Karachi	1987-88
347-6	v Zimbabwe at Bulawayo	2003-04
339-4	v Pakistan at Adelaide	2004-05
333-6	v Zimbabwe at Georgetown	2005-06
333-7	v Sri Lanka at Sharjah	1995-96
333-8	v India at Jamshedpur	1983-84
324-4	v India at Ahmedabad	2002-03
324-8	v India at Nagpur	2006-07
315-4	v Pakistan at Port-of-Spain	1987-88
315-6	v India at Vijayawada	2002-03

All these totals came from 50 overs except 333-8 (45) and 315-4 (47)

Lowest team totals

Completed innings

54	v S Africa at Cape Town	2003-04
80	v Sri Lanka at Mumbai	2006-07
87	v Australia at Sydney	1992-93
91	v Zimbabwe at Sydney	2000-01
93	v Kenya at Pune	1995-96
103	v Pak at Melbourne	1996-97
110	v Australia at Manchester	1999
111	v Pak at Melbourne	1983-84
113	v Aust at Kuala Lumpur	2006-07
114	v Pak at Pt-of-Spain	1999-2000

The 87 was in a match reduced to 30 overs: Australia made 101-9

Most sixes

150	CH Gayle
133	BC Lara
126	IVA Richards
81	CG Greenidge
80	S Chanderpaul
75	RL Powell
65	CL Hooper
54	RB Richardson
53	DL Haynes
50	RR Sarwan

XM Marshall (12) holds the West Indian record for sixes in an innings

Best strike rate

Runs per 100 balls		Runs
101.54	DR Smith	791
96.66	RL Powell	2085
90.20	IVA Richards	6721
83.01	CH Gayle	7374
81.22	CH Lloyd	1977
81.40	D Ramdin	740
81.19	DJ Bravo	1511
79.62	BC Lara	10348
77.08	RR Sarwan	4907
76.64	MD Marshall	955

Qualification: 500 runs

Most economical bowlers

Runs per over		Wkts
3.09	J Garner	146
3.32	MA Holding	142
3.40	AME Roberts	87
3.48	CEL Ambrose	225
3.53	MD Marshall	157
3.83	CA Walsh	227
3.97	RA Harper	100
4.00	CE Cuffy	41
4.09	EAE Baptiste	36
4.15	WKM Benjamin	100

Qualification: 2000 balls bowled

West Indies' one-day international results

	Played	Won	Lost	Tied	No result	% win
v Australia	119	57	58	2	2	49.57
v Bangladesh	16	11	3	0	2	78.57
v England	82	41	37	0	4	52.56
v India	94	54	37	1	2	59.23
v New Zealand	51	24	20	0	7	54.54
v Pakistan	113	64	47	2	0	57.52
v South Africa	45	12	32	0	1	27.27
v Sri Lanka	46	26	18	0	2	59.09
v Zimbabwe	36	27	8	0	1	77.14
v others (see below)	15	13	1	0	1	86.66
TOTAL	**617**	**329**	**261**	**5**	**22**	**55.71**

Other teams: Bermuda (P1, W1), Canada (P3, W3), Ireland (P2, W1, NR1), Kenya (P6, W5, L1), Netherlands (P1, W1), Scotland (P2, W2).

INTERNATIONAL SCHEDULE 2009-10

	Tests	ODIs
October 2009		
Champions Trophy final in South Africa (Oct 5)		
India v Australia	–	7
Bangladesh v Zimbabwe	–	5
November 2009		
South Africa v England	4	5
Australia v West Indies	3	–
India v Sri Lanka	3	5
December 2009		
New Zealand v Pakistan	3	–
Australia v Pakistan	3	5
Bangladesh v India	2	–
January 2010		
Bangladesh v India v Sri Lanka	–	7*
New Zealand v Bangladesh	1	3
February 2010		
Australia v West Indies	–	5
Pakistan v England	3*	5*
New Zealand v Australia	2	5
India v South Africa	3	5
March 2010		
West Indies v Zimbabwe	–	3
April 2010		
Asia Cup in Bangladesh	–	7*
ICC World Twenty20 in West Indies	–	–

	Tests	ODIs
May 2010		
ICC World Twenty20 finals in Barbados (May 16)		
England v Bangladesh	2	3
West Indies v South Africa	4	5
Zimbabwe v India	–	3*
June 2010		
England v Australia	–	5
July 2010		
Pakistan v Australia in England	2	–
England v Pakistan	4	5
Sri Lanka v India v New Zealand	–	4*
September 2010		
Pakistan v Bangladesh	2	3
South Africa v Zimbabwe	–	3*
October 2010		
India v Australia	–	5
Bangladesh v New Zealand	2	3
Pakistan v South Africa	3*	5*
November 2010		
India v New Zealand	3	5
Sri Lanka v West Indies	3	5
December 2010		
Australia v England	5	5
Bangladesh v Zimbabwe	–	5*

Details subject to change. Home side shown first. Some tours may continue into the month after the one shown above. An asterisk signifies that the number of matches is unconfirmed